71-99

Inter-Act

Using Interpersonal

Communication Skills

From the Wadsworth Series in Speech Communication

Austin J. Freeley, *Argumentation and Debate:*
Critical Thinking for Reasoned Decision Making, 8/e

Cheryl Hamilton, with Cordell Parker, *Communicating for Results:*
A Guide for Business and the Professions, 4/e

Clella Jaffe, *Public Speaking: A Cultural Perspective*

James A. Jaksa and Michael S. Pritchard, *Communication Ethics:*
Methods of Analysis, 2/e

Charles U. Larson, *Persuasion: Reception and Responsibility, 7/e*

Stephen Littlejohn, *Theories of Human Communication, 4/e*

Gay Lumsden and Donald Lumsden, *Communicating in Groups and Teams:*
Sharing Leadership

Katherine Miller, *Organizational Communication: Approaches and Processes*

Rebecca Rubin, Alan Rubin, and Linda Piele, *Communication Research:*
Strategies and Sources, 3/e

Larry A. Samovar and Richard E. Porter, *Communication Between Cultures, 2/e*

Larry A. Samovar and Richard E. Porter, *Intercultural Communication: A Reader, 7/e*

Sarah Trenholm and Arthur Jensen, *Interpersonal Communication, 2/e*

Julia T. Wood, *Gendered Lives: Communication, Gender, and Culture*

Julia T. Wood, *Relational Communication: Continuity and Change in Personal*
Relationships

Rudolph Verderber, *The Challenge of Effective Speaking, 9/e*

Rudolph Verderber, *Communicate!, 7/e*

Fred Williams, *The New Communications, 3/e*

Inter-Act

Using Interpersonal

Communication Skills

SEVENTH EDITION

RUDOLPH F. VERDERBER

Distinguished Teaching Professor of Communication,
University of Cincinnati

KATHLEEN S. VERDERBER

Northern Kentucky University

Wadsworth Publishing Company

I⟨T⟩P™ An International Thomson Publishing Company

Belmont • Albany • Bonn • Boston • Cincinnati • Detroit • London • Madrid • Melbourne
Mexico City • New York • Paris • San Francisco • Singapore • Tokyo • Toronto • Washington

Communications Editor: Todd R. Armstrong
Editorial Assistants: Joshua King, Laura Murray
Production Services Coordinator: Debby Kramer
Production: Books By Design, Inc.
Design: Books By Design, Inc.
Print Buyer: Karen Hunt

Permissions Editor: Bob Kauser
Copy Editor: Nancy Bell Scott
Cover Design and Illustration: Joe Biafore/
   Books By Design, Inc.
Compositor: Thompson Type
Printer: R. R. Donnelley & Sons
Cover Printer: Phoenix Color Corporation

For more information, contact Wadsworth Publishing Company:

Wadsworth Publishing Company
10 Davis Drive
Belmont, California 94002, USA

International Thomson Publishing Europe
Berkshire House 168-173
High Holborn
London, WC1V 7AA, England

Thomas Nelson Australia
102 Dodds Street
South Melbourne 3205
Victoria, Australia

Nelson Canada
1120 Birchmount Road
Scarborough, Ontario
Canada M1K 5G4

International Thomson Editors
Campos Eliseos 385, Piso 7
Col. Polanco
11560 México D.F. México

International Thomson Publishing GmbH
Königswinterer Strasse 418
53227 Bonn, Germany

International Thomson Publishing Asia
221 Henderson Road
#05-10 Henderson Building
Singapore 0315

International Thomson Publishing Japan
Hirakawacho Kyowa Building, 3F
2-2-1 Hirakawacho
Chiyoda-ku, Tokyo 102, Japan

Photo credits appear on page 433, which constitutes an extension of the copyright page.

Library of Congress Cataloging-in-Publication Data

Verderber, Rudolph F.
    Inter-act : using interpersonal communication skills / Rudolph F.
Verderber, Kathleen S. Verderber. — 7th ed.
        p.   cm.
    Includes bibliographical references and index.
    ISBN 0-534-19560-1
    1. Interpersonal communication. 2. Interpersonal relations.
 I. Verderber, Kathleen S., 1949–   . II. Title. III. Title:
Inter-act.
BF637.C45V47   1994
158'.2—dc20   94-20884

Brief Contents

Preface xv

PART I **Understanding Interpersonal Communication**   **3**
   1. Interpersonal Communication: An Orientation   5
   2. Perceptions of Self and Others   37
   3. Verbal Communication   71
   4. Nonverbal Communication   101

PART II **Developing Interpersonal Skills**   **133**
   5. Communication in Relationships   135
   6. Communicating Ideas and Feelings   173
   7. Listening Skills   203
   8. Empathic Response Skills   231
   9. Interpersonal Influence   263
   10. Managing Conflict   295

PART III **Communication in Professional Relationships**   **321**
   11. Communication in Work Relationships   323
   12. Interpersonal Communication in Groups   351
   13. Leadership in Group Communication   375
   14. Job Interviewing   395

   Appendix A: Glossary of Basic Communication Skills   413
   Appendix B: Glossary of Communication Problems   421
   Index   423

Complete Contents

Preface   xv

PART I   Understanding Interpersonal Communication   3

   1   **Interpersonal Communication: An Orientation**   5

Interpersonal Communication Defined   7

The Complex Process of Interpersonal Communication   8

  Context   8

  Participants   11

  Messages   13

  Channels   14

  Noise   15

  Feedback   15

  A Model of the Communication Process   16

Functions of Interpersonal Communication   19

  The Psychological Function   19

  The Social Function   19

  The Decision-Making Function   20

Principles of Interpersonal Communication   21

  Interpersonal Communication Has Purpose   22

  Interpersonal Behavior Is Continuous   22

  Interpersonal Communication Messages Vary in Conscious Encoding   23

  Interpersonal Communication Is Relational   25

  Interpersonal Communication Is Learned   26

Achievement of Interpersonal Competence   27

Development of Communication Skills   28

  A Learning Model   29

  Communication Improvement Goal Statements   31

  Summary   *34*

  Featured Reading   *34*

  Notes   *34*

  2   **Perception of Self and Others**   37

Perception   39

  Selection   39

  Organization   41

  Interpretation   42

  Perception and Communication   42

Perception of Self   43

  The Self-Concept   43

Self-Image   44
Accuracy of Self-Image   47
Role of Self-Perceptions in Communication   48
Self-Esteem   49
Improving Perception of Self   51
Cultural Considerations   52
Perception of Others   53
Physical Characteristics and Social Behaviors   54
Stereotyping   55
Emotional States   58
Cultural and Gender Considerations   60
Improving Social Perception   62
Summary   66
Communication Improvement Goal Statements   67
Featured Reading   67
Notes   68

3   **Verbal Communication**   71
The Nature and Use of Language   73
Language and Meaning   75
Complications in Using Words: Denotation and Connotation   77
Denotation   77
Connotation   77
Speaking Clearly   79
Precision   80
Specificity and Concreteness   80
Improving Precision and Specificity/Concreteness   82
Dating Generalizations   85
Indexing Generalizations   86
Cultural Considerations   88
Gender Considerations   89
Speaking Appropriately   91
Formal Versus Informal Language   92
Freedom from Jargon and Unnecessary Technical Expressions   92
Sensitivity   92
Effect of Insensitive Language   96
Summary   97
Communication Improvement Goal Statement   98
Featured Reading   98
Notes   99

4   **Nonverbal Communication**   101
The Nature of Nonverbal Communication   103
Body Motions   105
Eye Contact   105
Facial Expression   106

Gesture   106
Posture   106
Poise   107
Improvement in the Use of Body Motions   107
The Use of Body Motions   108
Paralanguage   111
Vocal Characteristics   111
Vocal Interferences   112
Self-Presentation   114
Clothing   114
Touch   116
Chronemics   116
Communication Through Management of Your Environment   118
Space   118
Temperature, Lighting, and Color   122
Implementing Your Understanding of Nonverbal Communication   123
Encoding and Decoding   124

Cultural and Gender Considerations   124

Summary   127
Communication Improvement Goal Statement   128
Featured Reading   128
Notes   129

PART II   Developing Interpersonal Skills   133

   5   **Communication in Relationships   135**
Theoretical Perspectives on Relationships   137
Interpersonal Needs Theory   137
Exchange Theory   139
The Nature of Relationships   142
Acquaintances   143
Friends   143
Close Friends or Intimates   145
Communication in the Life Cycle of Relationships   151
Starting or Building Relationships   152
Stabilizing Relationships   156
Relationship Distintegration   163
Summary   168
Communication Improvement Goal Statement   168
Featured Reading   169
Notes   169

   6   **Communicating Ideas and Feelings   173**
Communicating Ideas: Conversation and Information Sharing   175
Characteristics of Effective Conversationalists   175
Guidelines for Maintaining Conversational Coherence   178
Self-Disclosure   183

Cultural and Gender Considerations   185
Guidelines for Appropriate Self-Disclosure   186
Disclosing Feelings   188
Withholding or Masking Feelings   189
Displaying Feelings   189
Describing Feelings   191
Owning Feelings and Opinions   197
Summary   199
Communication Improvement Goal Statement   199
Featured Reading   200
Notes   200

7 **Listening Skills**   203
Attending—Focusing Attention   206
Understanding—Listening Actively   210
Determine the Organization   211
Attend to Nonverbal Cues   211
Ask Questions   212
Silently Paraphrase   214
Remembering—Retaining Information   214
Rehearsal   215
Constructing Mnemonics   216
Note Taking   216
Evaluating—Listening Critically   220
Separating Facts from Inferences   221
Evaluating Inferences   222
Summary   226
Communication Improvement Goal Statement   227
Featured Reading   228
Notes   229

8 **Empathic Response Skills**   231
Empathizing   233
Detecting and Identifying Feelings   234
Responding Appropriately   234
İncreasing Empathy   235
Clarifying Meaning   237
Questioning   237
Paraphrasing   240
Helping Responses   244
Supporting   244
Interpreting   248
Praise   249
Constructive Criticism   251
Problem Responses   257
Irrelevant Responses   257

Tangential Responses   258
Incongruous Responses   258
Interrupting Responses   259
Summary   260
Communication Improvement Goal Statement   260
Featured Reading   260
Notes   261

9   Interpersonal Influence   263

Compliance Gaining Through Persuasion   265
Reasoning   267
Credibility   269
Kindling Emotions   273
Assertiveness   276
Contrasting Methods of Coping with Adversity   278
Examples of Passive, Aggressive, and Assertive Responses   279

Cultural Considerations   282

Assertiveness and Social Power   284
Types of Power   285
Summary   290
Communication Improvement Goal Statement   291
Featured Reading   291
Notes   292

10   Managing Conflict   295

The Nature of Conflict   297
Patterns of Managing Conflict   297
Withdrawal   297
Surrender   299
Aggression   300
Persuasion   300
Discussion   301
Guidelines for a Constructive Program of Managing Conflict   302
Use Mutual Desire for Successful Management   302
Recognize the Types of Conflict   303
Cooperate Rather Than Compete   307
Read the Nonverbal Signs   310
Use Humor   311
Communicate Directly   312
Negotiate the Conflict   312
Seek Outside Help   313
Learn from Conflict-Management Failures   315
Summary   316
Communication Improvement Goal Statement   317
Featured Reading   317
Notes   318

PART III Communication in Professional Relationships   **321**

   11 Communication in Work Relationships   **323**

Characteristics of Work Organizations   325

Supervisor-Subordinate Relationships   333

  Vertical Dyadic Linkages Theory   335

Co-Worker Relationships   339

Relationships with Customers and Clients   342

  Failure to Recognize the Dependence in the Relationship   343

  Formation of Adversarial Relationships   344

  Lack of Control   345

  Use of Technical Jargon   346

Summary   347

Featured Reading   348

Notes   349

  12 Interpersonal Communication in Groups   **351**

Characteristics of Effective Work Groups   353

  A Good Work Environment   354

  An Optimum Number of Members   354

  Cohesiveness   354

  Commitment to the Task   355

  Development of and Adherence to Group Norms   356

  Consensus   356

  Filling of Key Role Requirements   357

Roles of Group Members   357

  Task Roles   357

  Maintenance Roles   360

  Negative Roles   362

Problem Solving in Groups   364

  Defining the Problem   364

  Analyzing the Problem   366

  Determining Possible Solutions   367

  Selecting the Best Solution or Combination of Solutions   369

Summary   371

Featured Reading   371

Notes   372

  13 Leadership in Group Communication   **375**

What Is Leadership?   377

Leadership Traits   378

Leadership Styles   379

Preparing for Leadership   381

Functions of Group Leadership   383

  Preparing the Meeting Place   383

  Planning the Agenda   383

  Orienting Group Members   384

Giving Everyone an Equal Opportunity to Speak   385
Asking Appropriate Questions   386
Summarizing When Necessary   388
Summary   391
Featured Reading   391
Notes   392

14 Job Interviewing   395

Questions in Interviewing   397
    Open versus Closed Questions   397
    Neutral versus Leading Questions   397
    Primary versus Follow-up Questions   398
Responsibilities of the Interviewer   399
    Determining the Procedure   400
    Conducting the Interview   400
Responsibilities of the Job Applicant   404
    Preparing for the Interview   404
    The Interview   406
Summary   409
Featured Reading   410
Notes   411

Appendix A: Glossary of Basic Communication Skills   413
Appendix B: Glossary of Communication Problems   421
Index   423

Preface

Although we had hoped that over the last several years we would see progress in former President Bush's goal for a "kinder, gentler nation," we have seen just the opposite. Part of our failure to achieve this goal is the continued deterioration in effective interpersonal communication. Increased instances of prejudice, racism, sexism, spouse and child abuse, and the use of aggression and even firearms to solve conflict are all related in some ways to our general inability to relate to others in interpersonally appropriate ways. Unfortunately, television characters—primary role models for many children and teenagers—seem to glorify the behaviors of those who are often the worst role models of appropriate interpersonal interaction.

As a result, it is easy to despair. But despairing does nothing to solve the problem. As never before, our society needs to focus attention on our interpersonal communication, especially between men and women and across cultures. For those who don't have the necessary interpersonal skills, it is time to learn them; for those who know the kind of behavior that is appropriate, it is time to practice that behavior. In this new edition, we have tried to clear a path toward civility.

Philosophy of the Text

Instructors bring different approaches to teaching communication. Some tend to emphasize theory and research, while others focus on skills acquisition and practice. In this text we try to incorporate relevant theory and research, but we firmly believe that theory and research are only important if they help students become more competent interpersonal communicators. Further, achieving interpersonal competence is a goal that students of all ages and backgrounds can relate to and aspire to, something we try to acknowledge by treating readers with respect and using a diversity of examples.

We believe that with a combination of theory, skills practice, and competency evaluation, students (1) learn to *understand* the major concepts from communication theory and research, (2) become able to *recognize* those concepts in their own experience, and (3) have access to a range of choices concerning their communication behavior, thus *increasing their communication behavioral flexibility*. In addition, students can *export* what they learn in this class and begin a process of *lifelong development of communication competence.* These goals have guided the development of the learning model that is at the foundation of *Inter-Act.*

Goals of This Edition

This seventh edition of *Inter-Act* has been carefully revised with the following goals in mind: (1) preserve the strengths that have sustained it through six successful editions; (2) clarify and enhance the learning model, making the book even more pedagogically effective; (3) freshen and update the text in both content and style; and (4) emphasize cultural and gender diversity in the effective use of interpersonal skills.

Focusing on communication between men and women and across cultures is so important that throughout the first two parts of the book we have called special attention to gender and cross-cultural issues. The text focuses on skills that are applicable across most common communication situations in the United States. We are also aware, however, that how we use these skills and how well they will be received may be dependent on whether the communication is male to male, female to female, or male to female. Likewise, we are aware that much of the research that has been done to validate the effectiveness of the skills forming the core of this book have been conducted in Western European and white middle class North American contexts. Since we know that behaviors considered appropriate in one cultural context may be considered inappropriate in another, we have included examples of the ways other cultures may view interpersonally competent communication.

STRENGTHS

This edition preserves and enhances the strengths that have made *Inter-Act* successful. Among them are:

- *Competency-based orientation.* The text does not stop with theory, but shows students concretely how to translate theory and research into communications behaviors.
- *A clear, concise, down-to-earth writing style.* Writing style is a key part of the learning model, because it makes the material comprehensible and relevant.
- *Ample examples provided throughout.*
- *Numerous in-chapter practice exercises.*

- *Glossaries of communication skills and problems,* which conveniently survey and review a wealth of information for students.

THE LEARNING MODEL

The learning model employed in *Inter-Act* uses seven integrated steps. Students use these steps in the *communication improvement goal statement* exercises that are introduced in Chapter 1 and revisited in each subsequent chapter. The goal statement exercises invite students to analyze their specific communication strengths and weaknesses, and commit themselves to improving their interpersonal competence in self-selected, but well-defined, ways. The seven steps in the learning model are:

1. Theoretical base of research-supporting skills

2. Steps involved in skill performance

3. Examples of skill usage

4. Self-assessment leading to commitment to change

5. Practice in using skills

6. Reflection on experiences in real-life situations

7. Review of what you have learned

Several features of the model are unique or unusual. First, the model emphasizes explicit self-assessment. Second, it provides for concrete ways of extending learning outside the classroom. Third, it is the basis for communication improvement goal statements that are both specific and flexible. Finally, it is iterative and developmental because students repeat the process as they are exposed to new material.

CONTENT AND STYLISTIC CHANGES

Content Changes In this edition we have made numerous content changes that contribute to the pedagogical strength of the text.

1. Issues of gender and cross-cultural communication are introduced in Chapter 1 and subsequently integrated throughout the text. New emphasis has been given to how gender and cultural diversity relate to specific theories and skills.

2. Intimate and family communication issues have been integrated into the main body of the text, especially in Chapter 5 (on relationships) and Chapter 10 (on conflict).

3. The text draws on current research. As would be expected, the research has been updated throughout the text. In each chapter more attention is given to describing the theoretical basis for the skills.

For those who are familiar with or have used the last edition of *Inter-Act*, here is a brief chapter by chapter summary of the most significant changes:

Chapter 1: We have revised the introductory chapter to emphasize the role that cultural and gender diversity play in effective communication. The revised chapter also stresses writing communication goal statements rather than learning contracts.

Chapter 2: We have completely revised this chapter to sharpen understanding of the role of perception in defining self-concept and relating to others. The section on self-concept has been revised to differentiate among self-concept, self-image, and self-esteem. The section on perception of others has greater discussion of prejudice, racism, and sexism. The book now discusses how culture and gender affect both self-concept and perception of others.

Chapter 3: We have made minor revisions of the first parts of the chapter and have added a significant amount of material concerning gender and cultural issues in verbal communication.

Chapter 4: We have revised our discussion of nonverbal communication to reflect gender and cultural differences.

Chapter 5: We have completely revised this chapter to integrate information that was formerly in modules on intimate and family communication. In addition, we have included more information on friendship and a much stronger section on stabilizing relationships.

Chapter 6: We have revised the section on communicating feelings to include a section in self-disclosure that considers cultural differences.

Chapter 7: We have revised this chapter significantly to help unify the elements of effective listening. We have simplified analysis of reasoning in the section on critical listening.

Chapters 8 and 9: We have revised examples in both of these chapters.

Chapter 10: We have revised and reorganized this chapter to include material from former modules on intimate and family communication.

Chapter 11: We have expanded the module in the last edition to build a chapter that proved a firm foundation for Part III of the book: Communication in Professional Relationships.

Chapters 12 and 13: We have expanded these former modules to chapter length.

Chapter 14: We have combined former modules on interviewing for information and job interviewing to form a single, stronger chapter on interviewing.

● ● **Stylistic Changes** In this edition we have made stylistic changes that contribute to readability.

1. The organization has been streamlined wherever possible. The tendency is for textbooks to lengthen in each edition; we have made a special effort to not lengthen the book by eliminating duplication of ideas and integrating former modules on family and intimate communication.

2. New and more diverse examples are provided, with special attention given to the diverse student population.

3. Although much of the text is prescriptive in nature, special care has been taken to speak directly to the student without seeming to preach.

Pedagogical Features

The following features support the learning model described above, enabling readers to translate theory and research into communication behaviors, recognize and practice their communication skills, and extend their learning outside the classroom.

Chapter objectives: Each chapter begins with student objectives.

In-chapter practice sections: Each chapter contains numerous exercises designed to help students reinforce information they have learned. In addition, many practice sections now include journal entries, suggestions for analysis that allow students to reflect on some of their experiences with the material that has been covered in that section and to analyze whether and how they have used the skills they have learned.

Communication skills summary charts: Each skill presented in the text is summarized in a communication skills summary chart with a definition of the skill, a brief description of its use, steps for using the skill, and an example to illustrate the skill in practice. The communication skills glossary in

Appendix A collects the summaries of all thirty major skills discussed in the book.

Chapter summaries: Each chapter includes a summary of the key ideas in the chapter.

Communication improvement goals statements: At the end of each chapter in Parts I and II, students are encouraged to write communication improvement goals statements to help them with their mastery of a key skill within the chapter.

Featured readings: At the end of each chapter we feature a book that is related to the material in the chapter. In some cases these are popular books that have reached best-seller status, such as John Gray's *Men Are from Mars, Women Are from Venus* and Richard Nelson Bolles's *What Color Is Your Parachute? A Practical Manual for Job-Hunters and Career-Changers.* In other cases the recommended readings are particularly provocative books that encourage the student to think about one or more of the concepts presented in the chapter. Examples include Richard C. Huseman and John D. Hatfield's *Managing the Equity Factor: Or "After All I've Done for You . . ."* and Robert E. Alberti and Michael L. Emmons's *Your Perfect Right: A Guide to Assertive Living.* In all cases, the detailed annotations show how these books can help students extend their learning.

Skills and problems glossaries: Appendix A provides a complete glossary of the more than thirty skills covered in the text and Appendix B contains a glossary of sixteen communication problems that students are likely to encounter. The glossaries capture the spirit of *Inter-Act* in that they show concise definitions with concrete applications, guidelines, and examples.

In sum, we have tried to create a book instructors and students will see as not merely a textbook, but a set of resources for understanding and dealing effectively with real-life issues in interpersonal communication.

SUPPLEMENTARY MATERIALS

As a user of this text you also have access to supplementary materials developed at Wadsworth.

Voices: A Selection of Multicultural Readings: A booklet of readings that highlight gender and cultural diversity in communication. These have been chosen to stimulate student thinking and discussion. The readings are drawn from various resources and perspectives. All focus on how certain aspects of communication are experienced by members of particular cultural or gender groups or comment on how communication is used to define relationships within or between groups. Our hope is that the readings in the booklet might serve as a catalyst to further students' understanding of diversity.

Instructor's Manual: Includes pre- and post-test competency surveys, role-playing exercises, experiential learning exercises, discussion questions, written assignments, possible course schedules, suggested midterm and final exam questions (multiple choice and essay) with page references and answer keys, and transparency masters.

Computerized Testing: All test questions in the Instructor's Manual are available on disk for the IBM PC and compatibles, the Apple II series, and the Macintosh.

Videotapes: On adoption, the instructor may choose from Wadsworth's highly acclaimed Skills on Tape videoseries, including the Interpersonal Competence tapes developed at Golden West College by Sharon Ratliffe and Dave Hudson.

Acknowledgments

We would like to thank the following instructors for providing helpful reviews of our manuscript: Dale Bluman, Shippensburg University; Joseph Coppolino, Nassau Community College; Sharon Ratliffe, Golden West Community College; Georgia Swanson, Baldwin Wallace College; Mike Wallace, Indiana University–Purdue University at Indianapolis; and Dianna Wynn, Prince George's Community College.

Take this short walk through

Inter-Act

SEVENTH EDITION

... and see how active learning

will help you

communicate effectively —

step by step by step.

Interpersonal communication isn't a spectator sport. Right from the start, this action-oriented text guides you step by step in understanding and mastering communication skills.

Through **INTER-ACT**'s seven-step learning model — applied systematically throughout — you'll learn concepts and theories, then see them at work in realistic examples. You'll learn and practice the steps in each skill, perform self-assessment exercises, and then apply what you've learned in and out of the classroom.

Here's a walk-through of just what you'll find as you study **INTER-ACT**. You're just a step away from beginning to communicate successfully in your own relationships.

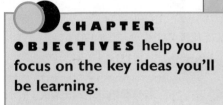

CHAPTER OBJECTIVES help you focus on the key ideas you'll be learning.

OBJECTIVES

After you have read this chapter, you should be able to define and/or explain:

Contrasts between verbal and nonverbal communication

Types of body motions

Five functions of nonverbal communication

Paralanguage and its major elements

How clothing, touching behavior, and use of time affect self-presentation

How the use of space communicates

Ways that temperature, lighting, and color affect communication

Ways of implementing your understanding of nonverbal communication

Cultural and gender considerations

PRACTICE SECTIONS throughout each chapter reinforce important information while giving you the chance to put communications concepts to work. By doing the exercises and practicing skills as you study, you'll be better prepared to use your new skills where they count the most — outside of the classroom.

PRACTICE IN

Empathizing

BY YOURSELF

Consider the following three comments you might hear from a friend:

1. Tyrell sent me flowers for no apparent reason.

2. I got a C on the test.

3. I banged my head on the door frame.

In each of these cases, the speaker could have any of at least three states of mind: The speaker could look at the event as positive or humorous, as negative or troublesome, or as neither. List the nonverbal cues that you would expect to see to explain each of the possible frames of mind; then phrase statements that would show your recognition of each perceived state.

IN GROUPS

Have each person in the group relate a recent experience to which they had an emotional response without labeling the response. The response need not be a dramatic one. After the speaker has related an episode, have the group discuss what emotional states they perceive the speaker to have experienced as well as describe the verbal and nonverbal cues that led them to their conclusions. Then group members should indicate whether they were

able to empathize based on experiences or based on fantasy. Finally, the group should solicit comments from the speaker concerning the accuracy of their perceptions.

JOURNAL ENTRY

Recall the last time you effectively empathized with another person. Write a short analysis of the episode. Be sure to cover the following: What type of relationship do you have with this person? How long have you known the person? What was the person's emotional state? How did you recognize it?

2. Suppose that you and a close friend (or fiancé or spouse) were involved in the conflicts above. Select two of them and prepare a procedure that you believe would be most likely to manage the conflicts.

WITH A GROUP

Discuss your conflict management plans to determine the likelihood of success of each.

JOURNAL ENTRY

Recount in your journal a recent conflict situation in which you believe you "won" or "lost." What contributed to the outcome? Did you have any control? What skills mentioned in this chapter might have improved the means of resolving the conflict? Reflect on a time when you won a battle but lost the war; that is, you appeared to come out ahead at the moment but the long-term quality of the relationship was damaged. What behaviors were responsible for the damage? What might you have done to salvage the relationship?

● ◆ ■ Summary

Conflict is often defined as interaction between persons expressing opposing interests, views, or opinions. We cope with conflicts in a variety of ways. Negative behaviors include withdrawal, surrender, and aggression. Positive behaviors include discussion and persuasion.

Conflict management begins with a mutual desire to manage conflict successfully. Those in conflict may begin by trying to identify the true subject of the conflict. Although pseudoconflicts are not really conflicts at all, there are many sources of genuine conflict. They may be content conflicts over facts, interpretations of facts, definitions, or choices; they may be value conflicts

JOURNAL ENTRIES are often included in the Practice Sections. They ask you to analyze *how* you have used the skills under discussion. By reflecting on your own experiences, you'll internalize the material — a key step in incorporating behavioral skills into your daily interactions.

● Basic Communication Skills

SKILL	USE	PROCEDURE	EXAMPLE
Paraphrasing Putting into words your understanding of the meaning you get from another's statement.	To increase listening efficiency; to avoid message confusion; to discover the speaker's motivation.	1. Listen carefully. 2. Determine what the message means to you. 3. Restate the message using your own words to show the meaning you received from the message.	Grace says, "At two minutes to five, the boss gave me three letters that had to be in the mail that evening!" Bonita replies, "If I understand you correctly, you were really resentful that the boss would dump important work on you right before closing time."
Supporting Saying something that soothes, reduces tension, or pacifies.	To help people feel better about themselves or what they have said or done.	1. Listen to what the person is saying. 2. Try to empathize with the person's feelings. 3. Phrase a reply that is in harmony with these feelings. 4. Supplement your verbal response with appropriate nonverbal responses. 5. Indicate your willingness to be of help if possible.	In response to Tony's statement, "I'm really frosted that I didn't get the promotion," Alex replies, "I can understand your disappointment; you've really worked hard for it."

(4) supplement your verbal response with appropriate nonverbal responses, and (5) if it seems appropriate, indicate your willingness to help.

INTERPRETING

When a person sees only one possible explanation for a given event, the most helpful response may provide an interpretation. *Interpreting* consists of attempting to point out an alternative or hidden view of

SKILLS SUMMARY CHARTS give you a quick overview of each skill presented in the text. They include a definition of the skill, a description of its use, steps involved, and an example of the skill in practice. They will be helpful in reviewing and reinforcing what you've learned.

Cultural and Gender Considerations

In this chapter we have tried to focus on nonverbal analysis that will provide you with the greatest chance of improving your communication competence in the use of nonverbal communication. Although the conclusions drawn are valid in general, specific cultural and gender differences need to be considered.

Cultural Differences Major cultural differences occur in eye contact, body motions, touch, and perceptions of time and space.

While a majority of people in the United States and other Western cultures expect those with whom they are communicating to "look them in the eye," Larry Samovar and Richard Porter conclude from their review of research that direct eye contact is not a custom throughout the world.[17] In Japan, for example, people are taught not to look another in the eye but to look at a position around the Adam's apple. Chinese, Indonesians, and rural Mexicans also lower their eyes as a sign of deference—to them, too much eye contact is a sign of bad manners. Arabs, in contrast, look directly into the eyes of the person with whom they are talking for long periods—to them direct eye contact shows interest. There are also differences in use of eye contact in the subcultures of the United States. For instance, African-Americans use more continuous eye contact than whites when they are speaking but less when they are listening.[18]

People of other cultures also show considerable differences in use of gestures, movements, and facial expression. Gestures in particular can assume completely different meanings. For instance, the forming of a circle with the thumb and forefinger—the OK sign in the United States—means zero or worthless in France, a symbol for money in Japan, a curse in some Arab countries, and an obscene gesture in Germany, Brazil, and Australia.[19] In addition, displays of emotion vary. For instance, in some Eastern cultures, people have been socialized to deintensify emotional behavior cues, whereas members of other cultures have been socialized to amplify their displays of

ness of B's perception checks. The exercise continues until each person in the group has a chance to be A, B, and C. After completing the exercise, the participants discuss how the skill of perception checking affected the accuracy of the communication.

Summary

Perception is the process of gathering sensory information and assigning meaning to it. Our perceptions are a result of our selection, organization, and interpretation of sensory information. Inaccurate perceptions cause us to see the world not as it is but as we would like it to be.

The self-concept is the total of a person's generalizations about self; it is presented publicly through the roles we enact. Our self-image, our perception of our self-concept, is formed through self-appraisal and is influenced by our reactions to our experiences and the reactions and responses of others. Our self-image affects communication by creating self-fulfilling prophecies and by filtering messages we receive. Our self-esteem is our evaluation of ourselves in either positive or negative ways. Our self-esteem and communication relate to influence communication style, to moderate competing internal messages, and to influence our perception of others.

Perception also plays an important role in forming impressions of others. Factors likely to influence our social perceptions are physical characteristics and social behaviors, stereotyping, and emotional states. Because research shows that the accuracy of people's perceptions and judgments varies considerably, your communication will be most successful if you do not rely entirely on your impressions to determine how another person feels or what that person is really like. You will improve (or at least better understand) your perceptions of others if you take into account physical characteristics and social behaviors, stereotyping, and emotional states.

You can learn to improve perception if you actively question the accuracy of your perceptions, seek more information to verify perceptions, talk with

---

CULTURAL CONSIDERATIONS and GENDER CONSIDERATIONS sections, marked throughout the text with icons, help you become more conscious of how diversity in gender and culture can affect interpersonal communication.

CHAPTER SUMMARIES provide you with yet another chance to reinforce what you've learned by summarizing key ideas presented in the chapter.

Summary

Responding appropriately is the final phase of listening. Responding well involves a complete set of skills.

Appropriate responses show a person's empathy. Empathy relates to determining the emotional state of another person and responding in an appropriate manner. Empathic responses recognize the person's right to his or her feelings and show that we can share in those feelings.

Clarifying responses help to ensure that people are sharing the same meanings. Questioning and paraphrasing are two skills that you can use to ensure understanding. Well-phrased questions are specific and sensitive. Paraphrases can check understanding of message content, feelings, or both.

Helping responses give people information about themselves or their behavior. These responses include supporting, interpreting, praising, and giving constructive criticism. Both praise and criticism should be specific and timely. In addition, several guidelines can ensure that criticism is beneficial: Make sure the person is interested in hearing criticism, describe the behavior on which the criticism is based, precede negative statements with positive ones if possible, be specific, criticize only recent behavior, direct criticism at behavior the person can do something about, and show what a person can do to correct a problem.

Problem responses hinder communication by planting the seeds of discontent within people about themselves or about the relationship. Furthermore, inappropriate responses can scuttle efforts at understanding meaning. Irrelevant, tangential, incongruous, and interrupting responses are some of the most common types of problem responses.

Communication Improvement Goal Statement

Select one of the response skills that you would most like to improve: empathy, questioning, paraphrasing, supporting, interpreting, praising, asking for criticism, or giving criticism. Write a communication improvement goal statement following the guidelines on page 33 of Chapter 1.

Featured Reading

"I Don't Know What to Say . . .": How to Help and Support Someone Who Is Dying
Robert Buckman
(Boston: Little, Brown and Company, 1989)

Undoubtedly one of the most difficult challenges for a person is learning how to respond to those who are seriously ill and who are dying. Dr. Robert

special way. Intimate relationships can be discussed in terms of family relationships, male relationships, female relationships, and male-female relationships.

Relationships go through a life cycle that includes starting or building, stabilizing, and ending. In the starting or building stage, people are attracted to each other, strike up a conversation, keep conversations going, and move to more intimate levels. People nurture good relationships through the skills of describing, equality, openness, and provisionalism. Many of our relationships end. We may terminate them in interpersonally sound ways or in ways that destroy any chance of continuing the relationship on any meaningful level.

Communication Improvement Goal Statement

Select a skill from among speaking descriptively, equally, openly, and provisionally and that you would most like to improve. Write a communication improvement goal statement following the guidelines on page 33 of Chapter 1.

COMMUNICA-TION IMPROVEMENT GOAL STATEMENTS (at the end of each chapter in Parts I and II) help you analyze your specific strengths and weaknesses and commit to improving your interpersonal skills in concrete ways. You'll use the steps in the Verderbers' seven-step learning model in these exercises.

A FEATURED READING at the end of each chapter offers a synopsis of a popular and/or provocative book that you might want to read to supplement the chapter material. For instance, *Men Are from Mars, Women Are from Venus* is a best-selling book that will tell you more about the differences in communication styles between men and women. It's just one example of the Verderbers' many suggestions.

A SKILLS GLOSSARY at the back of the book combines all the Skills Summary Charts presented throughout the text. **A PROBLEMS GLOSSARY** pinpoints 16 common communication obstacles and suggests how to overcome them. Together they provide a helpful reference for you to use whenever you want to brush up on your skills.

That's all there is to it. Now it's time to start your own step-by-step journey toward more effective interpersonal communication — with **INTER-ACT**!

Inter-Act

Using Interpersonal

Communication Skills

PART

I

Understanding Interpersonal Communication

In this four-chapter unit we present the concepts that are the foundation for understanding and improving your interpersonal communication. In Chapter 1 you will learn some basic definitions that are necessary for understanding interpersonal communication. In Chapter 2 you will see how your perceptions and your ability to understand yourself affect how you communicate with others. In Chapters 3 and 4 you will study how both verbal behavior and nonverbal behavior are used and interpreted during interpersonal communication episodes.

CHAPTER ONE

Interpersonal Communication: An Orientation

After you have read this chapter, you should be able to define and/or explain:

Transactional process of interpersonal communication ✓

Interrelationships among context, participants, messages, channels, noise, and feedback

Psychological, social, and decision-making functions of interpersonal communication ✓

Basic principles of interpersonal communication

Nature of communication competence ✓

Interpersonal communication learning model ✓

Communication improvement goal statements

"Brent, I was up until 12:30 and you still weren't home. What time did you get in?"

"A while after that."

"How much is 'a while'?"

"I said, a while!"

"Was it 1:00? 1:30? 2:00?"

"Dad, why are you always on my back about what time I get in? Don't you trust me?"

"It's not a matter of trust, it's just that . . ."

"Forget it. I don't want to talk about it."

"Well, if you can't tell me when you got in, I'll damn well tell you that you're not going to get the car again until you can act in a more responsible manner!"

"We'll see about that," Brent mutters to himself as he stomps off to his room.

"Marcia, I wanted to talk with you about your work. I've been very concerned. Your last two reports have been late, and both of them appear to have been hastily written. Is there anything wrong?"

"I know my work hasn't been good lately, Juanita. I've really had a bad couple of weeks."

"Is it anything you'd like to talk about?"

"Well, my brother's engagement is off, and I've been spending a lot of time helping him through it. On top of that, I've been fighting an infection that has kept my energy level at zero. But the medication the doctor gave me is finally having some effect, and I think I'm getting back on track."

"I'm glad you're feeling better. As I said, I was just worried. Your work has always been top-notch—I thought there must have been something else happening."

"Thanks for caring and for being so patient with me. I probably should have come in to talk with you about it, but I really thought I'd be OK sooner. As I said, though, I think I'm about back in shape. I've already got a draft of the sales report done, and I should have time to rework it and get it to you by tomorrow."

These examples of typical conversations each represent an interpersonal communication episode. The first one is obviously a conversational failure; the second seems more successful. Why did the first encounter end as it did? What factors combined to make the second conversation seem more successful? By the time you have finished reading this chapter, you should be able to identify some of the reasons that the conversations evolved as they did.

In this chapter we (1) define interpersonal communication, (2) explore how the complex process of interpersonal communication works, (3) explain the purposes of interpersonal communication, (4) identify several basic principles of interpersonal communication, (5) identify how one achieves interpersonal competence, and (6) discuss how to set goals for improving your own interpersonal communication skills.

Interpersonal Communication Defined

Interpersonal communication is defined as the transactional process of creating meaning. Three concepts are key in this definition. First, when we say interpersonal communication is a *process,* we are acknowledging that it is a systematic series of behaviors with a purpose that occur over a period of time. A twenty-minute phone conversation and a five-minute talk with the same friend between classes are both examples of the process of interpersonal communication. During any communication process, meaning is occurring.

Second, central to our definition of communication is the process of creating meaning. *Meaning* is the content and intention of communication behavior, and the significance that is assigned to it. *Content* is the specific information conveyed in the behavior—the "what" of communication. *Intention* is the speaker's reason for performing the behavior—the "why" of the communication. *Significance* is the value of the communication—"how important" the communication is.

Third, by *transactional* we mean that those involved in the process of interpersonal communication are *mutually* responsible for the meaning that each internalizes during and after the interaction. For example, suppose Joe says to his brother, "Go upstairs and get the thingamajig off my whatchamacallit." The shared meaning that has been created, or the extent to which this message is effective, depends on what happens next. If his brother says, "OK," runs upstairs, and returns with the object that Joe seeks, then one of many shared meanings will have been successfully created. If, however, Joe's brother responds, "Go get it yourself—I'm not your slave," a different shared meaning of Joe's request will have been created. Or if Joe's brother says, "I don't mind fetching for you, but I don't know what you want me to get," yet another kind of shared meaning has been created. The key point here is that Joe's original statement has no meaning in this process until his brother responds. Furthermore, his brother's response will be given meaning through Joe's subsequent activity.

The Complex Process of Interpersonal Communication

Because you have been communicating for as long as you can remember, the process may seem to be almost second nature. But in reality, competent interpersonal communication is difficult to achieve because communication is a complex process. Whether ideas and feelings are indeed shared effectively and appropriately by those communicating depends on the interrelationship of many elements in the process. Seven of the most important are context, participants, messages, channels, noise, and feedback.

CONTEXT

The context of interpersonal communication affects the expectations of the participants, the meaning these participants receive, and their subsequent behavior. A context is the (1) physical, (2) social, (3) historical, (4) psychological, and (5) cultural circumstances that surround a communication episode.

Physical Setting The physical setting of a communication episode includes factors such as the location of the episode; environmental factors such as heat, lighting, and noise; the physical distance between communicators; seating arrangements; and the time of day. Each of these factors can affect the communication. Physical context helps to define what behaviors or

● **The context of interpersonal communication affects the expectations of the participants, the meaning these participants receive, and their subsequent behavior.**

messages will be seen as socially appropriate and thus indicates to participants what type of conversation to expect. For example, the meaning shared in a conversation may be affected by whether it is held in a crowded company cafeteria or in an elegant candlelit restaurant. In Chapter 4 you will learn more about how the physical setting may affect the expectations of participants and the meanings they receive.

● ● **Social Setting** The social setting is determined by whether the communication episode takes place among family members, friends, acquaintances, work associates, or strangers. In some cases competent communication in a family setting differs from competent communication in a work or friendship setting. The meaning that is shared in an interaction may differ because of social setting. For example, Darren may understand that his father is showing affection when he calls him "Dunderhead" at home; but Darren may interpret the same behavior as a demeaning put-down when his father, who coaches Darren's basketball team, uses that term in front of Darren's teammates at practice. Why? Because the social setting is different.

Historical Setting The historical setting is derived from both the general historical events and from the meanings created during previous communication episodes between the particular participants. For instance, suppose one morning Carlos tells Shelby that he will retrieve the draft of the report they had left for their boss to read. As Shelby enters the office that afternoon, she sees Carlos and says, "Did you get it?" Another person listening to the conversation would have no idea what Shelby is talking about. Yet Carlos may well reply, "It's on my desk." What is *it*? The report, of course. Shelby and Carlos understand one another because the subject of their conversation was determined in an earlier exchange.

More subtly, we are aware of people's reactions to situations that on the surface seem inconsequential. For instance, as Joanne hangs up the phone she says, "My brother said he'll be stopping over this evening," to which Manuel might reply, "Oh, not this again—Joanne, you've got to quit caving in to your brother!" Manuel's reaction speaks to a historical context. If Manuel perceives that the only time Joanne's brother "stops by" is to hit Joanne up for a few dollars, the very fact that he is coming over provokes Manuel to react to the historical reality.

Much of the conflict between people in intimate relationships derives from such personal historical contexts. Yet in the broader scope, the history of a country or group can also affect communication. For example, in the United States, our historical treatment of women and minorities provides a context that can make communication between diverse people difficult. We will explore these issues throughout this book.

Psychological Setting Psychological setting refers to the moods and feelings each person brings to an episode. For instance, suppose Corinne is under a great deal of stress. The person she hired to type a report into her computer couldn't get it done, so the time Corinne must spend doing it herself cuts into the time she had planned to spend finishing the outline for a speech she is to give the next day. If her husband bounds into the apartment and jokingly suggests that she take a speed-typing course, Corinne may lose her normally good sense of humor and become angry. Why? Because her feelings of stress affect the meaning she infers from her husband's remarks.

Cultural Setting Cultural setting is the final aspect of context. A *culture* is composed of the shared beliefs, values, and norms that affect the behaviors of a relatively large group of people.[1] For example, we can speak of African-American[2] culture, British culture, Muslim culture, gay culture, middle-class culture, or corporate culture. Peter Andersen points out that culture is an inseparable part of the communication process.[3]

This system of shared beliefs, values, and norms can often be discerned through the symbols, rituals, and behaviors of members of the culture. Thus, for example, wearing hats and T-shirts with a capital X on them (in honor of Malcolm X) has come to symbolize important African-American values for many people. Similarly, celebrating Passover is a significant Jewish ritual that serves to remind participants of their culturally important belief in their special relationship to God.

Although shared beliefs and values are important characteristics of culture, it is the norms or communication rules of a culture that affect the context in which people interact. *Rules* are the unwritten underlying guidelines for what is viewed as acceptable communication behavior within a particular culture. Rules give us clues as to what kinds of messages and behavior are proper in a given physical or social context or with a particular person or group of people, and they provide us a framework in which to interpret the behavior of others. For instance, if Shamir, an international student, has been social-ized in his Middle Eastern culture to believe that it is unacceptable to talk with women who are not members of his family, this culturally based com-munication rule will constrain his behavior when he speaks with Janine, an outgoing single young American woman, on a class project. Because her cultural communication rules are different, she will not understand that she is violating a rule of his culture with her natural bubbly behavior, and she may misconstrue his discomfort as shyness, aloofness, or callousness. Usually we learn the communication rules of a culture different from ours through experience. Children whose native culture encourages spontaneous expres-sion and tolerates interrupting others may find it difficult to attend schools where the rule is to sit quietly and raise their hands to be recognized. When we communicate with people of a different race, sex, nationality, religion, political affiliation, class, organization, or group, effective communication is likely to be more difficult than when we communicate with people from our own culture.

In summary, the physical, social, historical, psychological, and cultural settings work together to comprise the context of a communication episode.

PARTICIPANTS

Central to any communication episode are the individuals involved in the process. Differences among individuals influence how well they are able to communicate. While people differ in an infinite number of ways, several especially influence their communication.

First, people's physical differences, including race, sex, age, and level of physical ability, are likely to have a significant effect on their communication. Because humans learn through the processes of association and generalization, we more easily identify with and understand those with whom we share similar physical characteristics.[4] The more two people are similar to one another, the better either person is able to predict the behavior of the other. When we first meet a stranger of the opposite sex, or of a different race, age group, or level of physical ability, these differences are likely to provide significant challenges to us in our communication encounter.

Second, people's psychological differences, including personality, self-confidence, attitudes, and values, are likely to affect their communication. For example, by personality some people are introverts who seem quiet and shy. They are likely to experience some difficulty with extroverts who appear to be noisy and outgoing. Similarly, some people with high self-esteem who assert their opinions as though they are facts may seem overbearing to less self-confident people who may phrase statements of fact as questions. If we are not sensitive others' values, we may unintentionally offend them.

Third, people's differences in social experiences are likely to affect their communication. Different family, friendship, and work experiences provide different "road maps" or scripts that guide people during current communication episodes.[5] In *There Are No Children Here: The Story of Two Boys Growing Up in the Other America*, a recent best-seller, Alex Kotlowitz describes how one young boy adapted to growing up in a neighborhood where he saw many young neighbors killed and where other boys his age became junior gang associates.[6] At the age of twelve he no longer allowed himself to have "friends"; instead he had "associates," reasoning that it wouldn't hurt so much if he lost an "associate." Early decisions about relationships based on one's social experiences, such as the decision made by this boy, become the road maps that guide communication in a variety of situations across one's life.

Fourth, people's differences in knowledge and skills are likely to affect their communication. Through educational experiences people have the opportunity to acquire language and communication skills that can enable them to express a wide variety of ideas and feelings. Thus more widely read and better-educated people are likely to express themselves far differently from less widely read and educated people.

Fifth, people's gender and cultural differences result in different perspectives and life experiences that affect their communication. When we are aware of such differences, we tend to see them as barriers to communication. The more one person differs from another, the less either person is able to predict the other's behavior. When people do not believe they know how another person will behave, fear often results. Some people respond to their fear by withdrawing or becoming compliant, whereas others mask their fear with aggressive behavior. Throughout this text we consider differences between males and females and between people from different cultures that affect skill usage.

MESSAGES

In interpersonal communication, meaning is created through the sending and receiving of messages. It is easy to think of messages as simply the words transmitted from one person to another. Actually, messages are far more complex. They include the elements of meaning and symbols, encoding and decoding, and form or organization.

● ● **Meaning and Symbols** The pure ideas and feelings that exist in a person's mind represent *meanings*. You may have ideas about how to study for your next exam, what your career goal is, and whether taxes should be raised or lowered; you also may have feelings such as jealousy, anger, and love. The meanings you have within you, however, cannot be transferred magically into another's mind. To share these ideas and feelings you form messages comprising both verbal symbols and nonverbal symbols. *Symbols* are words, sounds, and actions that represent specific content meaning. As you speak, you choose words to convey your meaning. At the same time, facial expressions, eye contact, gestures, and tone of voice—all nonverbal cues—accompany your words and also affect the meaning your listener receives from the symbols you use. As you listen, you use both the verbal symbols and the nonverbal cues and assign meanings to them.

● ● **Encoding and Decoding** The cognitive thinking process of transforming ideas and feelings into symbols and organizing them into a message is called *encoding* a message; the process of transforming messages of another person back into one's own ideas and feelings is called *decoding*. You have been communicating for so long that you probably don't consciously think about either the encoding or the decoding process. When your eyelids grow heavy and you say, "I'm beat," you aren't consciously thinking, "I wonder what symbols I can use to best express the sensation I am now experiencing." Conversely, when you hear the words "I'm beat" and see the red, heavy-lidded eyes of another person, you are not likely to think, "*Beat* means to hit, but it is also slang for tired, which means growing weary or feeling a need for sleep; therefore, the person's verbal utterance expresses a need for sleep and the nonverbal behavior of the eyes confirms the accuracy of the statement." Nevertheless, psychologists and linguists have established that these encoding and decoding processes do occur.

You probably become aware of the encoding process only when you must grope for words. Have you ever been able to visualize a simple object in your mind while blanking on the word used to symbolize it? Or have you ever sensed that the right word was on the tip of your tongue? Likewise, at times you become aware of the decoding process when you must figure out the meaning of an unfamiliar word by the way it is used in a sentence or when you try to figure out what a person really means by paying close attention to tone of voice, gesture, and other nonverbal cues.

Because meaning is created jointly between the participants, even when communicators select words carefully, one person may perceive a meaning different from what the other intended. For instance, suppose Noreen asks, "Would you like to hear what I found out about the marketing plan?" If Ramon says, "Yes, I'm very interested in your story," from the sound of Ramon's voice, Noreen may perceive the unintended meaning that Ramon believes what she is about to say may not be true; or Noreen may think that regardless of what Ramon said, from the look on his face he is really saying, "I'm bored stiff."

The processes that facilitate encoding and decoding messages are at the heart of interpersonal communication. Thus many skills presented in this book relate directly to improving your message formation and the accuracy of your interpretations of messages you receive so that your effectiveness and appropriateness are enhanced. In Chapters 3 and 4, we will study how language and nonverbal cues can increase the likelihood of being understood accurately. In Chapters 6, 7, and 8, we will consider how we can increase the likelihood that the meaning we receive from messages is accurate.

● ● **Forms or Organization** When meaning is complex, people need to communicate it in sections or in a certain order. In these situations, choices are made about how to organize the message. For instance, when Olga tells Connie about the apartment she looked at yesterday, her symbols take a certain form. If her description is organized spatially and thus moves logically from one room to the next, Connie is more likely to correctly understand the apartment layout than if Olga describes the apartment in order of the size of each room.

CHANNELS

Once formed, messages are transmitted through sensory channels. Oral messages are conveyed from one person to another through sound waves; written and nonverbal messages, including signed messages, facial expressions, gestures, and movement, are conveyed through light waves. Although interpersonal communication usually uses two basic channels—light and sound—

people can and do communicate via any of the five sensory channels. A fragrant scent and a firm handshake may be as important as what is seen or heard.

NOISE

Noise is any stimulus, external or internal to the participants, or caused by message symbols, that interferes with the sharing of meaning. Thus noise makes it less likely that meaning will be shared. Much effort is needed to overcome external, internal, and semantic noises.

● ● **External Noise** The sights, sounds, and other stimuli in the environment that draw people's attention away from what is being said or done are known as external noise. For instance, while a person is giving directions on how to work the new food processor, your attention may be drawn to the audio system that is softly playing an old favorite song of yours. The music is external noise. External noise does not have to be a sound, however. Perhaps, while the person gives the directions, your attention is drawn momentarily to an attractive man or woman. Such visual distraction also constitutes external noise.

● ● **Internal Noise** Thoughts and feelings that interfere with the communication process are known as internal noise. Have you ever found yourself daydreaming when someone was trying to tell you something? Perhaps your mind wanders to thoughts of a club you visited last night or to the argument you had with a friend this morning. If you have tuned out the words of the person with whom you are communicating and tuned in to a daydream or a past conversation, you have experienced internal noise.

● ● **Semantic Noise** The unintended meanings aroused by certain symbols that inhibit the accuracy of decoding are known as semantic noise. Suppose a friend describes a forty-year-old secretary as "the girl in the office." If you think of *girl* as a condescending term for a forty-year-old woman, you might not even hear the rest of what your friend has to say. Rather, you might focus on the chauvinistic message such symbol use has for you. Symbols that are derogatory to a person or group, such as ethnic slurs, often cause semantic noise; profanity can have the same effect.

FEEDBACK

Feedback is the response to a message. This response reflects what meaning has been created and shared through the original message. Feedback indicates to the person sending a message whether and how that message was heard,

● *Feedback* is the response to a message. It indicates to the sender whether and how that message was heard, seen, and understood.

seen, and understood. If the verbal or nonverbal response message indicates to the sender that the intended personal meaning was not shared, the originator may reencode the original personal meaning in order to align the shared meaning with the initiator's original personal meaning. This reencoded message also constitutes feedback because it gives meaning to the original receiver's response.

In several chapters in this textbook, especially Chapter 7, we emphasize the development of feedback skills, because failure to check understanding of the meaning of messages accounts for a great deal of communication failure.

A MODEL OF THE COMMUNICATION PROCESS

Let's look at a pictorial representation to see how these factors of interpersonal communication interrelate during a communication exchange. Figure 1.1 illustrates the interpersonal communication process. In the mind of

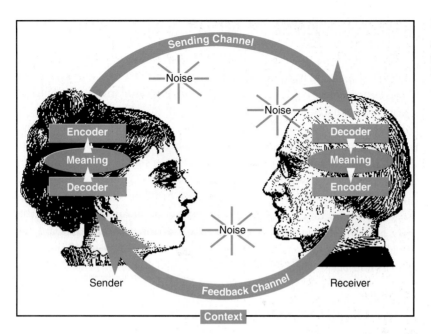

Figure 1.1

A model of communication between two individuals

the sender there is a personal meaning, a thought or a feeling that the person wants to share. That thought or feeling is created, shaped, and affected by the speaker's physical attributes, psychological make-up and state, social experiences, and knowledge and skills. To turn the meaning into a message, the speaker must encode it by way of channels, usually sound (speech) and light (nonverbal behavior).

Remember that the message consists of language and behavior. It is turned back into meaning by the receiver through the decoding process. This decoding process is affected by the receiver's total field of experience, that is, by the receiver's unique combination of the same factors that affected the sender's message construction. On decoding and interpreting the message, the original receiver encodes the verbal and nonverbal reactions to the original message and transmits it back to the sender through the selected channels. The sender who receives the feedback decodes it in order to interpret the response he or she is getting from the receiver. The process repeats.

In this illustration, the area around the sender and the receiver represents the context, including the physical, social, historical, psychological, and cultural factors that provide a backdrop for the interaction. During the entire transaction, external, internal, and semantic noise that can affect the ability of the sender and receiver to share meanings may be occurring at various points.

Let's review the process of an interpersonal transaction by looking at a specific example. At the breakfast table (physical context), Joel says to his wife, Debra, "Hey, babe, what do you say we go out to dinner tonight?" Debra (responding to the message she has received) frowns and says, "I don't know that going for a pizza excites me much." Joel perceives that Debra has not understood his meaning and seeks to remedy this. Nonverbally he puts a lilt in his voice, and verbally he says, "I meant, let's go to the Chalet." Debra may now gasp and say, "The Chalet? You have a deal!" Because the participants are now satisfied with the meaning that has been shared, they may end their interaction or change topics. The inaccurate meaning initially created may have resulted from Debra's perception of the type of restaurant Joel usually is willing to pay for (prior history) or from irritation with Joel's use of the word *babe*, which she finds annoying (semantic noise).

Identifying Communication Factors

BY YOURSELF

For the following episode identify the contextual factors, participant differences, messages, channels, noise, and feedback.

Jessica and her daughter Rita are shopping. As they walk through an elegant boutique, Rita, who is feeling especially happy, sees a blouse she wants. With a look of great anticipation and excitement, Rita says, "Look at this, Mom—it's beautiful. May I try it on?" Jessica, who is worried about the cost, frowns, shrugs her shoulders, and says hesitantly, "Well—yes—I guess so." Rita, noticing her mother's hesitation, continues, "And it's marked down to twenty-seven dollars!" Jessica relaxes, smiles, and says, "Yes, it is attractive. Try it on. If it fits, let's buy it."

JOURNAL ENTRY

Here and at appropriate places in the following chapters, we offer suggestions for journal entries. Journal entries are reflections—your thoughts about and your reactions to interpersonal communication events. You may think of these as a set of personal observations.

Think of two communication episodes that you participated in recently. One should be an episode that you thought went very well. The other should be one that you thought went poorly. Compare and contrast the episodes. Describe the context factors in the episode, the participant differences, the messages used to create the meaning, the channels used, any noise that interfered with the messages and meaning, and the shared feedback.

Functions of Interpersonal Communication

Interpersonal communication serves psychological, social, and decision-making functions that touch every aspect of our lives.

THE PSYCHOLOGICAL FUNCTION

Interpersonal communication serves two psychological functions: It is the process through which we meet our interpersonal needs for interaction with others, and it provides a mirror through which we can see ourselves.

We Communicate to Meet Our Social Needs. Psychologists tell us that we are by nature social animals; that is, people need other people just as they need food, water, shelter, and so on. Deprived of all contact with others, most people hallucinate, lose their motor coordination, and become generally maladjusted.[7] Although we have all heard of hermits who choose to live and function alone, they are the exception. Most of us need to talk with others. Often what we talk about is unimportant. We may converse happily for hours about relatively inconsequential matters, exchanging little real information. But we may carry away from the interaction the pleasant, satisfied feeling that comes from having met a need.

We Communicate to Enhance and Maintain Our Sense of Self. Through our communication we seek confirmation of who and what we are. How do you know what you are good at? In part you know this from what people tell you. Did you run a good meeting? Did you do the job as expected? Do you have the right to be happy? angry? guilty? You learn the answer to questions such as these in part from what others say. We will explore this important function of interpersonal communication in detail in Chapter 2.

THE SOCIAL FUNCTION

Interpersonal communication serves a social function: Through it we develop and maintain our relationships with others. We get to know others through our communication with them. Depending on the results of a first conversation with another person, you may decide to remain simple acquaintances or you may try to build a closer relationship. Regardless of the type of relationship—social, work, friendship, or intimate—few relationships stay the same. Because communication is the process through which we develop, change, and maintain relationships, we will explore both personal and professional relationships in Parts II and III.

THE DECISION-MAKING FUNCTION

As well as being social animals, we are also decision makers. Starting with whether or not you wanted to get up this morning, through what you ate for breakfast, to whether or not you decided to go to class, you have made countless decisions already today. Some of these decisions you made alone; others you made in consultation with one or more other people. Communication fulfills two functions in the decision-making process: Through it (1) we gain information relevant to the decision situation, and (2) we influence others and are influenced by them.

● Accurate and timely information is a key to understanding and to effective decision making.

● ● **Communication Enables Information Exchange.** Accurate and timely information is a key to effective decision making. While we obtain some information through observation, some through reading, and some through television, we receive a great deal of information during our conversations with others. For example, Jeff runs out to pick up the morning paper. As he hurries through the door, Tom asks, "What's it like out there this morning?" Jeff replies, "Wow, it's cold—it couldn't be more than twenty degrees." Tom says, "I was going to wear my jacket, but I guess I'd better break out the old winter coat." This brief conversation is typical of countless information exchanges. Because decisions of all kinds are improved with information, we will discuss skills for information exchange in Chapter 6.

● ● **Communication Can Serve to Influence.** The results of many decisions we make involve the agreement or cooperation of other people; consequently, a second function of decision-making communication is influence. Examples include convincing your friends to go to a play rather than to a movie, listening to the volunteer who is campaigning door to door to gather voter support for a political candidate, persuading your children to do their homework, and (an old favorite) trying to convince an instructor to change your course grade. Some theorists even argue that the primary purpose of all communication efforts is to influence the behavior of others. We will study skills associated with the decision-making function of communication in Chapters 9, 12, and 13.

Observing Communication

JOURNAL ENTRY

Keep a log of the various communication episodes you engage in today. Tonight, categorize each episode according to the psychological, social, and decision-making functions it served; each episode may serve more than one function. Were you surprised by the variety of communication you engaged in during such a relatively short period of time?

Principles of Interpersonal Communication

Based on our discussion of its process and functions, we can identify several underlying principles of interpersonal communication. These principles are important because they apply to all your communication efforts, regardless of setting.

INTERPERSONAL COMMUNICATION HAS PURPOSE

A person talking with another has a purpose for doing so, or—as Kathy Kellermann, a leading researcher on interpersonal contexts, puts it—all communication is goal-directed,[8] whether or not the purpose is conscious. Let's consider two examples of clearly purposeful communication. Maya goes to the library to do research for a paper. When she consults the card catalog, she discovers that an important source she needs is on microfilm. She knows neither where the microfilm room is nor how to use the equipment. Therefore she decides to ask the librarian where the microfilm room is and, when she finds the room, to ask the attendant how to use the equipment. When Maya speaks to the librarian, her purpose is to gain information. Her communication will be effective if, her meaning shared, she is directed to the correct room and if someone there explains the use of the equipment to her.

Suppose Maya wants to use her parents' new car this weekend to drive her friends to the beach. She knows her parents will be reluctant to let her drive the new car, so she will need to offer some good reasons for their allowing her to do so. Moreover, she knows that she must not lose her temper or in any way endanger the positive communication climate she hopes to establish. Maya's purpose in this case is to influence. She will have achieved her goal if her parents consent to let her use the car.

Now let's consider an example in which a person may not be aware of purpose. When Donnel passes Kyle on the street and says, "Kyle—what's happening?" it is not likely that Donnel consciously thinks, "I see Kyle coming. I haven't talked with Kyle for a while. I hope (1) that Kyle is aware that I recognize him, (2) that he realizes the lines of communication between us are still open, and (3) that he understands I don't have the time to talk with him right now, but that I might like to later. So I'll say, 'Kyle—what's happening?'" In this case the social obligation to recognize Kyle is met spontaneously with the first acceptable expression that comes to Donnel's mind. Regardless of whether Donnel consciously thinks about the purpose, it still motivates his behavior. In this case Donnel will have achieved his goal if Kyle responds with an equally casual greeting.

INTERPERSONAL BEHAVIOR IS CONTINUOUS

Because communication can be nonverbal as well as verbal, we are always sending behavioral messages from which others may draw inferences or meaning. Even if you are silent or absent, another person may infer meaning from your silence or absence. Why? Because your silence or absence repre-

● Because communication can be nonverbal as well as verbal, we are always sending behavioral "messages" from which others may draw inferences or meaning.

sents a reaction to your environment and to the people around you. If you are cold, you may shiver; if you are hot or nervous, you may perspire; if you are bored, happy, or confused, your face may show it. Whether you like or dislike what you are hearing, your body will reflect it. As a communicator you need to be aware of the kinds of messages, overt or implicit, you are sending that may carry meaning you do not intend.

INTERPERSONAL COMMUNICATION MESSAGES VARY IN CONSCIOUS ENCODING

Although we have already said that interpersonal communication is purposeful, the amount of conscious preparation time varies considerably. As we discussed earlier in this chapter, sharing meanings with another person involves encoding messages into verbal and nonverbal symbols. This encoding process may occur spontaneously, may be based on a "script" that you have learned or rehearsed, or may be carefully considered based on your understanding of the situation in which you find yourself.[9]

For each of us there are times when our interpersonal communication reflects a spontaneous expression of emotion. When this happens, our messages are encoded without much conscious thought. For example, when you burn your finger, you may blurt out "Ouch," or a similar expression. When something goes right, you may react with a broad smile. In this sense much of our communication is spontaneous and natural; however, not all spontaneous communication is appropriate. For instance, if someone accidentally stepped on your toe and you blurted out, "Watch what you're doing, butt-head," the receiver would likely become defensive. In Chapter 6 we will suggest more appropriate ways of communicating negative feelings.

At other times, however, our communication is "scripted." R. P. Abelson defines a *script* as a "highly stylized sequence of typical events in a well understood situation."[10] Thus in some communication episodes we use conversational phrases that we have learned from our past encounters and judge to be appropriate to the present situation. To use scripted reactions effectively, we learn or practice them until they become automatic. Many of these scripts are learned in childhood. For example, when you want the sugar bowl but cannot reach it, you may say, "Please pass the sugar," followed by "Thank you" when someone complies. This conversational sequence comes from the "table manners script" that you may have had drilled into you at home. Scripts enable us to use messages that are appropriate to the situation and are likely to increase our effectiveness of communication. Because scripts are based on past experiences, many are culturally bound. That is, they are appropriate for a particular relationship in a certain situation within a specific culture. One goal of this text is to acquaint you with general scripts (or skills) that can be adapted for use in your communication encounters across a variety of relationships, situations, and cultures. The text will provide you with opportunities to practice these scripts in a variety of contexts and will suggest when certain scripts may be useful.

Messages also may be carefully constructed to meet a particular situation. Constructed messages are those that we encode at the moment to respond to the situation for which our known scripts are inadequate. These messages help us communicate both effectively and appropriately.

Creatively constructed responses are perhaps the ideal communication vehicle. When you find yourself able both to envision what you want to say and to construct how you say it, you are likely to form messages that allow your intended meaning to be shared. Another goal of this text is to help you become so familiar with a variety of message-forming skills that you can use them to construct effective and appropriate messages.

INTERPERSONAL COMMUNICATION IS RELATIONAL

Saying that interpersonal communication is relational means that in any communication episode people not only share content meaning but also negotiate their relationship. For instance, when Laura says to Jennie, "I've remembered to bring the map," she not only is reporting information but, through the way she says it, may also be communicating, "You can always depend on me" or "I am superior to you—if it weren't for me we would be missing an important document for our trip."

Two aspects of relationships can be negotiated during an interaction. One aspect is the affect (love to hate) present in the relationship. For instance, when Jose says, "Hal, good to see you," the nonverbal behavior that accompanies the words may show Hal whether Jose is genuinely happy to see him (positive affect) or not. For instance, if Jose smiles, has a sincere sound to his voice, looks Hal in the eye, and perhaps pats him on the back or shakes his hand firmly, Hal will recognize the signs of affection. If, however, Jose speaks quickly with no vocal inflection and with a deadpan facial expression, Hal will perceive the comment as solely meeting some social expectation.

Another aspect of the relational nature of interpersonal communication seeks to define who is in control.[11] Thus, when Gary says to Sue, "I know you're concerned about the budget, but I'll see to it that we have money to cover everything," he can, through his words and the sound of his voice, be saying that he is "in charge" of finances, that he is in control. How Sue responds to Gary determines the true nature of the relationship. The control aspect of relationships can be viewed as complementary or symmetrical.

In a complementary relationship one person lets the other define who is to have greater power. Thus the communication messages of one person may assert dominance while the communication messages of the other person accepts the assertion. In some cases the relationship is clarified in part by the nature of the context. For instance, in traditional American businesses most boss-employee relationships are complementary, with the boss in the control position. Thus, when the boss assigns Kim a certain job to do, Kim is likely to accept the assignment and do it. Or, in the preceding example, if Sue's response to Gary's asserting control of the budget is, "OK, Gary, I agree, you should handle our finances," the relationship would be viewed as complementary.

In a symmetrical relationship people do not agree about who is in control. As one person shows a need to take control, the other challenges the person's right and asserts his or her own power. Or as one person abdicates power the other refuses to assume it. For example, when Gary says, "I think we need to cut back on credit card expenses for a couple of months," and Sue responds,

"No way! I need a new suit for work, the car needs new tires, and you promised we could replace the couch," both people are challenging each other's right to control. In contrast, when Gary asks, "Do you think we need to cut back on credit card expenses for a couple of months?" and Sue responds, "Gee, I'm not sure, what do you think?" both are seeking to give up control to the other.

Relational control is not negotiated in a single exchange but through many message exchanges over time. The interaction of communication messages, as shown through both language and nonverbal behavior, defines and clarifies the complementary or symmetrical nature of people's relationships. In complementary relationships open conflict is less prevalent than in symmetrical ones, but in symmetrical relationships power is more likely to be evenly shared.

INTERPERSONAL COMMUNICATION IS LEARNED

Because interpersonal communication appears to be a natural, inborn ability, most people pay little attention to the skills that make up their communication styles. Each of us tends to think, "I act naturally." Thus we often don't really try to improve our behavior. Moreover, some people make no conscious effort to improve their skill levels because they do not appreciate how improving their skills can benefit them and because they may not recognize their current inadequacies. Because of our background, each of us has some of the communication skills we need to be effective in our dealings with others. However, we all lack some of the skills we need. As a result, each of us can benefit from continuous learning and skill practice.

Observing Relationships

JOURNAL ENTRY

Think of a relationship you have that is primarily complementary in nature. How did it come to be this way? Has it changed over time? How satisfying do you find it to be? Now think of a relationship you have that is primarily symmetrical. How did this relationship come to be this way? Has it changed over time? Think of the last two conversations you have had in each of these relationships. Write down a portion of each conversation as best you can remember it. What do you notice about the messages you sent? Are they similar in tone and form in both encounters? If not, describe how they differed. Why do you think these differences occurred?

Achievement of Interpersonal Competence

Communication competence is "the ability to adapt messages appropriately to the interaction context."[12] To meet this definition, communication must be perceived as effective and appropriate. Communication is *effective* if it achieves its goal; it is *appropriate* if it fits the situation in which it is used.

Let's return for a moment to the dialogues you read at the opening of this chapter. The first dialogue was ineffective because neither Brent nor his father achieved their goals: Brent was unable to convince his father that he was mature enough to monitor his own curfew, and Brent's father did not find out what time Brent came in or why he was late. Communication is appropriate when each participant believes that the other person has abided by the social rules of behavior that apply to the type of relationship and conversation they have.[13] The conversation between Brent and his father failed also because neither person perceived the process as appropriate. Brent was angry over what he may have believed to be his father's lack of trust, and his father

● Communication must be perceived as effective and appropriate. Communication is effective if it achieves its goal; it is appropriate if it fits the situation in which it is used.

was upset by Brent's unwillingness to provide a direct answer to a question from his parent.

In contrast, the second dialogue was both more effective and more appropriate. Juanita was able to determine what had been affecting Marcia's work performance and was assured that it would improve; Marcia was able to share her recent problems with her boss. Marcia perceived Juanita's inquiry to be appropriate because Juanita is her boss and has a right to be concerned. Further, Marcia's explanation was acceptable in part because it was accompanied by an apology. Marcia acknowledged that she had not performed as well as she should have and that she had not informed Juanita of her problems. Thus their conversation appropriately followed the social expectations for boss-employee relationships.

The definition of competent communication acknowledges that competence is an inference or judgment that one person makes about another. We create the perception that we are competent communicators through the use of communication skills. The greater your skill repertoire, the more likely you are to be able to construct and interpret messages appropriately and effectively. Thus if you develop and use the interpersonal communication skills you will be studying in this course, you are likely to be perceived as a competent communicator. The skills repertoire you have enables you to initiate and manage your social interactions. Getting to know people, building and maintaining relationships, developing intimacy, dealing with your family, and learning to cope with people of different races, sexes, religions, and cultures all depend on your use of key interpersonal communication skills.

Throughout this book we will focus on the skills that can improve your communication effectiveness and aid you in behaving appropriately. To understand when certain skills are useful, you must also understand many important concepts about communication and relationships. The study of interpersonal communication theories and research lays a foundation for skill development because they provide insight into and evidence about how to communicate effectively and appropriately. Thus, while focusing on skill development in this book, we will also discuss the theories and some of the supporting research that will help you to understand why certain skills are useful and when these skills are appropriate.

Development of Communication Skills

In the remainder of this book you will be introduced to more than thirty specific communication skills that can be grouped into six broad categories:

1. *Nonverbal skills* relate to your intentional use of facial expression, sound of voice, and gestures.

2. *Verbal skills* relate to increasing the clarity of your messages through the wordings you use.

3. *Self-presentational skills* help you to help other people better understand who you are.

4. *Listening and responding skills* help you to interpret others' meanings and share the meanings you receive.

5. *Influence skills* help you to persuade others to change their attitude or behavior.

6. *Climate skills* create a positive climate in which effective communication is more likely to occur.

If you practice these skills and make them a part of your repertoire, they can help you to achieve your communication purposes and become a competent communicator. You already know and use some of these skills, although you may not be aware of why you use them or why they work. Other skills may not currently be part of your repertoire; however, you will enhance your competence if you work hard and learn new interpersonal skills during this course.

Some of the skills presented in this book are universal. Others are grounded in the cultural system of the United States white middle class, and they may seem odd to you if you are from another cultural background. Throughout the text you will notice that we try to point out how cultural differences may affect skill usage. We invite you to be active in this process and to think about and discuss in class any observations, insights, and concerns that you have about the appropriateness and effectiveness of these skills for communicating in other cultures.

A LEARNING MODEL

Learning to use a new skill is difficult because you must not only understand the skill but also become comfortable accomplishing the skill in real-life situations. It's one thing to recognize the music as *Clair de Lune* by Debussy, but quite another to be able to play it artistically on a piano. Because some of the communication skills may not be in your repertoire now, as you work on them you are likely to feel awkward and to see the skills as creating unrealistic or phony-sounding messages. Just as fingers need to practice music patterns to play smoothly, so too may you need to practice the skills so that they become part of you and sound natural to you. The material in this book is arranged specifically to help you learn and practice these skills and overcome that awkwardness.

To expect that you will master all of these skills during a single course would be unrealistic. Effective communication is a lifelong adventure of which this course is only a beginning. But to help you maximize what you can accomplish during the course, this book uses a systematic learning model that provides the theoretical base for the skills, breaks each skill into easy-to-understand steps, cites both good and poor examples of skill usage, assesses progress, offers opportunities to practice, reflects on performance, and reviews key ideas.

● ● **Theoretical Base** Skill learning begins when you understand how and why certain skills are effective and appropriate. Therefore, when we present a particular skill, we also discuss the theoretical material and research that support it.

● ● **Steps** The second step of the learning model involves breaking down complex actions into the specific behaviors necessary to perform the skill. Thus we specifically outline the steps involved in skill performance so that you can see how it works.

● ● **Examples** The third step of the learning model is to analyze examples of both effective and ineffective skill usage. By studying examples of effective skill usage, you will learn to identify the skills when you hear them being used. By examining ineffective examples, you will understand more clearly the consequences of poor skill usage.

● ● **Assessment** The fourth step of the learning model involves self-assessment and commitment to change. To improve your communication skills, you must actively evaluate how well you currently perform each skill. When your self-assessment uncovers a skill deficiency, you need to develop a plan for improvement and prepare learning goals. At the end of each chapter you will be encouraged to write a goal related to that chapter's material.

● ● **Practice** The fifth step of the learning model involves putting your knowledge of skills into practice. Throughout this book you will find exercises designed specifically to help you try out the skills in situations that should be familiar to you. Some exercises require you to practice alone; other exercises encourage you to practice with other members of the class. You may want to practice using these skills with a friend or family member as well.

● ● **Reflection** The sixth step of the learning model involves extending implementation of skills into real-life situations. You will be encouraged to write journal entries to help you reflect on your personal communication experiences and analyze whether and how you have used the skills you are learning. At the end of each chapter we also review a book you might wish to read. The books focus on one or more of the skills discussed in the chapter and will expand your theoretical perspective on applying the skills.

● ● **Review** The final step of the learning model is a review of what you have learned. In this book we supply three different kinds of opportunities for review: (1) periodic summaries of the skills covered so far in a chapter, (2) a summary of all the material covered at the end of each chapter, and (3) a complete glossary of the more than thirty skills covered in the text, as well as a glossary of typical communication problems, at the end of the book. Because for most of us learning involves repetition, we encourage you to review continuously what you have learned. Rereading the summaries and glossaries is a good way to begin each review session.

COMMUNICATION IMPROVEMENT GOAL STATEMENTS

To get the most from this course, we suggest that you set personal goals to improve specific skills in your own interpersonal communication repertoire. To do this, we recommend that you commit to specific goals by writing formal communication goal statements. Why write goal statements? A familiar saying goes, "The road to hell is paved with good intentions." Regardless of how serious you are about changing some aspect of your communication, bringing about changes in behavior takes time and effort. Writing specific goals makes it more likely that your good intentions to improve don't get lost in the busyness of your life.

Psychologists who study motivation have found that when people set specific challenging goals they achieve at a higher level than when they simply commit to "do their best." Research also shows that by writing down a description of the change you wish to make, formulating a plan for completing it, and having another person witness your pledge, you are more likely to honor the commitment you have made than if you simply make a mental resolution.

● ● **Assessing Your Skills** Before you can write a goal statement, you must first analyze your current communication skills repertoire. We recommend that at the end of each chapter, after you have studied and practiced using the skills, you choose the one or two you think may help you most, and write a goal statement about improving them.

● ● **Developing Written Goal Statements** The written goal statements we suggest have four parts.

1. *Describe the problem.* Goal setting begins by analyzing a problem situation and determining what skills might help you to be more effective in that
circumstance. In this first part, then, describe specific circumstances in which
you feel the skills of the chapter could help you. For example: "*Problem:*
Currently, my boss tends to give me all the routine and/or less interesting
tasks. When something really exciting comes along, he gives those tasks to
Jones or Marshall. Consequently, I feel angry because I find myself thinking
I'm being overlooked, but I don't say anything about it. So I want to improve
my ability to describe my feelings of anger to him"; or "*Problem:* When my
mother talks with me, I find myself daydreaming or rehearsing my replies.
Consequently, I miss important points or misinterpret what she is telling me.
Then she gets angry. I want to improve my ability to listen attentively to what
my mother is telling me."

2. *Describe the specific goal.* A goal is *specific* if it is measurable and you
know when you have achieved it. For example, after Chapter 4, "Nonverbal
Communication," you might write, "*Goal:* To make eye contact with my boss
when I talk to her on five of the next six occasions." Or after Chapter 6,
"Communicating Ideas and Feelings," you might write, "*Goal:* To feel comfortable in describing my feelings of anger to my boss when he gives me
routine tasks to accomplish."

3. *Outline a specific procedure for reaching the goal.* In each chapter you
will learn the steps necessary to acquire specific skills. In this section of your
goal statement, you will apply the skill(s) steps to the specific problem situation. This step is critical because successful behavioral change requires that
you state your objective in terms of specific behaviors you can adopt or
modify. For example: "*Procedure:* I will practice the steps of describing feelings in order to identify the specific feeling I am experiencing, to encode the
emotion I am feeling accurately, to indicate what has triggered the feeling,
and to make sure that I indicate that the feeling is mine. I will then put that
procedure into operation when I am talking with my boss"; or "*Procedure:*
I will practice the steps of paraphrasing. When my mother talks, I will focus on her and listen carefully to the message, I will pause to think about
what the message means to me, and I will develop a message that conveys
the intent or content meaning. I will send that message and repeat this process until I feel confident that Mom and I have shared meaning and I understand her."

4. *Devise a method of determining when the goal has been reached.* Because
a good goal is measurable, the fourth part of your goal-setting effort is to

determine your minimum requirements for knowing you have achieved a given goal. For example: "*Test of Achieving Goal:* This goal will be considered achieved when I have described my feelings to my boss on four consecutive occasions when his behavior has excluded me"; or "*Test of Achieving Goal:* This goal will be considered achieved when my parents no longer complain to me about ignoring them when they are speaking to me."

Once you have completed all four parts of this goal-setting process, you may want to ask someone to witness your commitment and serve as a consultant, coach, and support person. You might want to ask this of a classmate, who should be in a good position to understand and help (and perhaps you can be support for his or her goal statements in return). If one of your goals relates to a particular relationship, you also should consider telling that person about your goal; knowing that you are trying to improve, he or she may be willing to help. Periodically you can meet with your consultant to assess your progress, troubleshoot problems, and develop additional procedures for reaching your goal.

At the end of each chapter you will be challenged to develop a goal statement related to the material presented. The form in Figure 1.2 may be photocopied for each goal statement that you write.

Figure 1.2

Written goal statement

Description of the Problem:

Goal:

Procedure:

Test of Achieving Goal:

● ◆ ■ Summary

We have defined interpersonal communication as the transactional process of creating meaning. Interpersonal communication is transactional because the meaning that is created occurs between the two participants based on both the original message and the response to it.

The communication process occurs in a context between different people who send and receive messages (feedback) using sensory channels that become distorted by noise.

Interpersonal communication serves psychological, social, and decision-making functions. People communicate for psychological reasons to meet social needs and to maintain a sense of self; people also communicate to develop and maintain relationships. During decision making, people communicate to share information and to influence others.

Based on our understanding of interpersonal communication, several general principles have been developed. First, interpersonal communication is purposeful. Second, interpersonal communication is continuous. Third, interpersonal communication messages vary in degree of conscious encoding; they may be spontaneous, scripted, or contrived. Fourth, interpersonal communication is relational, defining the power and affection between people; relational definitions can be complementary or symmetrical. Fifth, and most important, interpersonal communication is learned.

Effective interpersonal communication transactions depend on the communication competence of the individuals who are conversing. Because the communication situations you face are complex and diverse, the key to communication competence is behavioral flexibility, which is based on having a wide variety of interpersonal skills available for use.

Skills can be learned, developed, and improved, so you can help to enhance your learning this term by writing goal statements to systematically improve your skill repertoire.

● ◆ ■ Featured Reading

In each subsequent chapter we will review a book that features one or more of the skills discussed in that chapter.

● ◆ ■ Notes

1. Myron W. Lustig and Jolene Koester, *Intercultural Competence: Interpersonal Communication Across Cultures* (New York: HarperCollins, 1993), p. 41.

2. Although people of this subculture may refer to themselves most frequently as African-American, Afro-American, or black American, for the sake of consistency in this text we use *African-American*.

3. Peter Andersen, "Explaining Intercultural Differences in Nonverbal Communication," in Larry A. Samovar and Richard E. Porter, eds., *Intercultural Communication: A Reader*, 7th ed. (Belmont, Calif.: Wadsworth, 1994), p. 229.

4. Kay Deaux, Francis C. Dane, and Lawrence S. Wrightsman, *Social Psychology*, 5th ed. (Belmont, Calif.: Wadsworth, 1993), p. 232.

5. R. P. Abelson, "Script in Attitude Formation and Decision Making," in J. Carroll and T. Payne, eds., *Cognition and Social Behavior* (Hillsdale, N.J.: Erlbaum, 1976), p. 33.

6. Alex Kotlowitz, *There Are No Children Here: The Story of Two Boys Growing up in the Other America* (New York: Doubleday, 1991).

7. John A. R. Wilson, Mildred C. Robick, and William B. Michael, *Psychological Foundations of Learning and Teaching*, 2nd ed. (New York: McGraw-Hill, 1974), p. 26.

8. Kathy Kellermann, "Communication: Inherently Strategic and Primarily Automatic," *Communication Monographs* 59 (September 1992): 288.

9. Kathleen K. Reardon, *Interpersonal Communication: Where Minds Meet* (Belmont, Calif.: Wadsworth, 1987), pp. 11–12.

10. Abelson, p. 33.

11. Paul Watzlawick, Janet H. Beavin, and Don D. Jackson, *Pragmatics of Human Communication* (New York: W. W. Norton, 1967), p. 51.

12. Brian H. Spitzberg and William R. Cupach, *Interpersonal Communication Competence* (Beverly Hills, Calif.: Sage, 1984), p. 63.

13. Ibid., p. 100.

CHAPTER TWO

Perception of Self and Others

OBJECTIVES

After you have read this chapter, you should be able to define and/or explain:

Perception ✓

Processes of selection, organization, and interpretation ✓

Self-concept ✓

Contrasts between self-image and self-esteem ✓

Role of self-perceptions in communications

Factors affecting the accuracy of perceptions of others ✓

Cultural and gender considerations ✓

Methods of improving social perception

As was traditional at Grafton, Inc., all new employees were invited to an orientation party in the Board of Directors' Room. This occasion was Pat's first chance to meet many of the new employees. As people were chatting before the formal orientation began, Pat's attention was drawn to a person on the opposite side of the room whose facial expression and sparkle in the eye impressed Pat tremendously. While pretending to make small talk with others, Pat slowly maneuvered across the room to talk with this person.

Stop right here and, without rereading the material, answer the following question: Is the person maneuvering across the room male or female? How do you know? Now reread the passage. Were you correct?

The questions in the preceding paragraph asked you to assess your perceptions. As a matter of fact, the passage does not identify the sex of the person. Still, you likely drew some conclusion about the sex of the person based on your perception of what was likely to be male or female behavior. Pat was drawn to the person because the facial expression and eye sparkle gave Pat information that led Pat to want to learn more about the person.

What makes perception so important to interpersonal communication study? As we look at the communication model presented in Chapter 1, we see that perception comes into play at every stage: Your perceptions of information affect your messages; your perceptions of environment affect how you send your message; your perceptions of your listeners affect how you will shape your message; and your perceptions of how your listeners react to you affect the outcome of your message.

In this chapter we consider how your perception of yourself and others affects your communication. We begin by examining some basic facts about perception—most significantly, that perception is more subjective than most of us realize. Finally, we consider methods of improving both self-perception and perception of others, and we consider these issues within the framework of the theory of uncertainty reduction.

Perception

Perception is the process of gathering sensory information and assigning meaning to it. Your eyes, ears, nose, skin, and taste buds gather information; your brain selects from among the items of information gathered, organizes the information, and finally interprets and evaluates it. The result is perception.

Notice that perception involves actively processing sensory data. For this reason, perception does not necessarily provide an accurate representation of the event being perceived. At times our perceptions of the world, other people, and ourselves are highly accurate, but at other times we may distort what comes to us through our senses to such an extent that our perceptions have little to do with reality. Because we base our behavioral responses on what we perceive, our communication is likely to be ineffective when our perceptions are flawed.

We can think of the perceptual process as occurring in three stages: selection, organization, and interpretation. Although the three stages of perception happen almost simultaneously, let's consider them one at a time.

SELECTION

You are subject to a constant barrage of sensory stimuli, yet you focus attention on relatively little of it. For instance, right now, as you read this book, you are focusing your attention on making sense out of the written material on this page rather than on the various sights and sounds around you. If your concentration lapses for a moment, the sound of a dog or a song in the background may capture your attention, making it difficult for you to refocus on the book. But if you can refocus, the noise again blends into the background. On what bases are these selections made?

Of course, selection is determined in part by the physiological limitations of our senses. Obviously, if you are nearsighted or hard of hearing, you won't perceive many stimuli in your environment. But even when the senses are keen, they convey information about only a portion of the physical world. Your eyes do not see light at infrared or ultraviolet wavelengths; you don't perceive the sound of dog whistles. More significant for our purposes, what we perceive is limited even further by three psychological factors: interest, need, and expectation.

Interest A key factor in determining what we perceive is interest. What do people hear when a person is talking to them about a basketball game? A rabid sports fan may hear all the statistics that are presented; a person familiar only with the star player may hear only the portion of the explanation that recounts the star player's contribution; a person not at all interested in basketball may hear only a jumble of meaningless facts.

Need A second factor in selecting what we perceive is need. If you drive to school, you focus on traffic lights; cars in front of, behind, and next to you; people darting across streets; and potholes in the road. Passengers in the car, however, may be oblivious to these sights because they have no need to notice them.

Expectation The expectations we form on the basis of experience are a third factor in the selection process. To illustrate, take a moment to read the phrases in the triangles in Figure 2.1.

Figure 2.1

A sensory test of expectation

If you are not familiar with this test, you probably read the three triangles as "Paris in the springtime," "Once in a lifetime," and "Bird in the hand." But if you look closely, you will see something different. We tend not to see the repeated words because we don't expect them to be there. We are so familiar with the phrases that our active perception stops once we recognize the phrase.

The combined effect of sensory capability, interest, need, and expectation is to sharply limit our perceptions to a relatively small selection of stimuli that actually impinge on our senses. Now let's consider how the way we process our perceptions adds another layer of subjectivity to perception.

O R G A N I Z A T I O N

Information is received from the senses by the brain. Once the brain selects the information, it organizes its selections. The meaning you obtain from a perception depends not only on what is selected but on how it is organized.

The organization of perceptions depends on many factors, including degree of ambiguity and your emotional state. The more ambiguous or complicated the information, the more difficult it is to organize. Most people have been startled by something they saw from the corner of their eye, only to discover that what they thought they saw was far different from what was actually there. Similarly, most people have mistakenly recognized a stranger as someone they know because they saw what seemed to them a familiar coat or hairstyle or gesture. The more ambiguous the information, the more time it takes to go through the organizational process and the greater the likelihood of error.

Apparently, the brain follows certain principles in making sense out of random external elements. Gestalt psychologists consider simplicity (perceiving complex stimuli in simple forms), pattern (perceiving even random stimuli along common lines), proximity (perceiving stimuli that are close together as related), and good form (perceiving complete forms even when parts are missing). To exemplify these principles, picture yourself attending your next class. When you enter, students may be seated throughout the room, but you are likely to perceive them in simplified terms: your class. In addition, instead of perceiving the class as individuals, you are likely to seek patterns; you may perceive them as males and females or as young, middle-aged, and elderly. As you notice three people set off from the rest of the people in class, you are likely to perceive them as having something in common. Finally, as you speak to a person sitting next to you, that person may perceive the meaning of your sentences correctly even if you leave out an occasional word or use the wrong word.

INTERPRETATION

Once the brain selects and organizes sensory information, it interprets the information to make sense of it. *Interpretation* is the process of explaining what has been selected and organized. Because people seldom select the same stimuli or organize stimuli in exactly the same way, they often arrive at different interpretations of events or people's behavior. These differences in interpretation directly affect our communication.

Whereas in the processes of selection and organization we identify, in the process of interpretation we evaluate. For instance, two women who are walking through a shopping mall pass a clothing store displaying a heavily sequined formal dress. Lorraine takes a long look and thinks to herself, "That's gorgeous," whereas Anita thinks, "That's trashy."

PERCEPTION AND COMMUNICATION

Although people believe strongly in the accuracy of their senses, their perceptions may well be inaccurate. The degree of inaccuracy varies from insignificant to profound, but communication based on inaccurate perceptions is likely to be misleading. If Lorraine and Anita recount their experiences later that day, their communication could create very misleading conclusions about apparel. For instance, Lorraine might say, "I wish I had the money to shop at Dawson's—I saw a formal that I'd die for." In contrast, Anita might say, "I don't know what's with the designers these days. Dawson's devoted their entire front window to an evening gown that was dreadfully trashy— and they wanted a fortune for it."

To this point, we have been discussing the process of perception—how we select, organize, and interpret stimuli. We have illustrated this process at the level of physical perception to show that subjectivity enters into even relatively simple perceptions. In the remainder of this chapter, we examine social perception, or social cognition, which consists of those processes by which people perceive themselves and others. As we will see, both our self-perception and our perception of others significantly affect communication transactions.

Analyzing Your Perceptions

BY YOURSELF

Take a minute to look at everything around you. Now close your eyes and describe what you "saw." Open your eyes and look again. What did you miss? How can you explain why you selected the items you were able to describe? What caused you to notice these and not other aspects of the scene?

Perception of Self

How we communicate depends a great deal on how we define and evaluate ourselves. Yet our definitions and evaluations are a result of our perceptions—and as we have already seen, perceptions are not necessarily accurate. In this section we consider the self by looking at the related concepts of self-concept, self-image, and self-esteem.

THE SELF-CONCEPT

The *self-concept* is what a person thinks he or she is. It is the total of a person's generalizations about self—it organizes and guides the processing information about self. Although the self-concept is well formed by the time we become adults, we continue to present it publicly through various roles we assume. A *role* is a pattern of learned behavior that people adopt to meet the perceived needs of a particular context. Based on how we appraise ourselves and how others respond to us, we may choose or be forced to take on various roles. For example, during the day you may enact the roles of student, brother or sister, and sales clerk.

Roles that we enact may result from relationships we form, cultural expectations, groups we choose to identify with, and our own decisions. Cultural expectations are easy to illustrate. Each of us learns that our culture has a prototype for the behaviors expected in meeting such roles as father, mother, lawyer, or doctor.

The expectations of a specific group may also influence our roles. Our family, our church group, our athletic team, our theater club—every group expects us to behave in role-appropriate ways. For instance, if you were the oldest child in a large family, your parents may have cast you in the role of oldest brother that involved such functions as disciplinarian, brothers' and sisters' keeper, or housekeeper, depending on how they see family relationships. Or if your peers look on you as a joker, you may go along by enacting your role, laughing and telling funny stories even though you really feel imposed on or hurt.

Other roles are products of our own expectations. You may present yourself as an organized person, with-it parent, or serious student to fit your perception of self based on your own wishes to reflect a role you have chosen to play.

Everyone, then, enacts numerous roles. Some roles that we enact in private may be different from those we use in public. For instance, Samantha, who is perceived as a warm, quiet, sensitive person in her family group, may choose to enact the role of a boisterous "party animal" in a friendship group.

44

● Everyone enacts numerous roles. Some roles that we enact in private may be different from those we use in public.

With each new situation, we may test a role we know how to enact or we may decide to try to enact a new role.

The term *working self-concept* has been used to denote the specific aspects of one's identity that are activated by the role one is enacting at a particular time.[1] The working self-concept changes as we change roles: "To some extent we become different people as we move from situation to situation."[2]

The diversity of the roles we enact helps us to withstand stressful situations. If a person enacted only the role of student, for example, he or she might be devastated by being forced to withdraw from school for a while. When that one role ends, a large part of the person's self-concept ends as well. In contrast, a person who is the product of many roles is more protected from negative events. Thus the student who sees himself or herself also as father, mother, friend, and sales clerk will have these roles (these parts of the self-concept) to identify with if he or she cannot be a student for a period of time.

SELF-IMAGE

Our *self-image*, our perception of our self-concept, is formed through self-appraisal and is influenced by our reactions to our experiences and the reactions and responses of others.

● ● **Self-Appraisal** We form impressions about ourselves partly from what we see. We look at ourselves in the mirror and make judgments about our weight and size, the clothes we wear, and our smile. If we like what we see, we may feel good about ourselves. If we don't like what we see, we may try to change. Perhaps we will go on a diet, buy some new clothes, get our hair styled differently, or begin jogging. If we don't like what we see, and cannot or are unwilling to change, we may begin to develop negative feelings about ourselves.

● We form impressions about ourselves partly from what we see. If we like what we see, we may feel good about ourselves.

Our self-appraisal may also result from our reactions to our experiences. Through experience we learn what we are good at and what we like. If you can strike up conversations with strangers and get them to talk with you without causing yourself undue anxiety, you will probably consider yourself friendly, engaging, or interesting to talk with. The first experience we have tends to play a greater part in shaping our self-image than do later ones.[3] For instance, teenagers who are rejected in their first effort to get a date may become more reluctant to risk asking people out in the future. Regardless of the outcome of a single experience, if additional experiences produce results similar to the first experience, the initial perception will be strengthened. Interestingly, we are more likely to draw conclusions based on what we choose to do rather than on what we choose not to do. For example, although people who sketch may see themselves as artistic, people who do not sketch do not necessarily see themselves as nonartistic.[4]

In general, then, the more positive our response to the experiences we have—whether as a cook, lover, decision maker, student, worker, or parent—the more positive our self-image around that role becomes. Likewise, the greater the number of negative interpretations we make, the more negatively we view our self-image in that role.

● ● **Reactions and Responses of Others** In addition to our self-perceptions, our self-image stems from how others react and respond to us. Suppose that after you've given your opinion on developing alternative means of marketing a product, one of your co-workers tells you, "You're a very creative thinker." Comments like this are apt to positively affect your perception of self, especially if you respect the person making the comment. In fact, research shows that immediate, positive feedback is a powerful modifier of one's self-image.[5] And, just as positive comments may have a great impact, so too may negative comments. We tend to use other persons' comments to validate, reinforce, or alter our perception of who and what we are. The more positive comments we hear about ourselves, the more positive our total self-image becomes.

Since development of self-image begins early in life, the first and perhaps most important responses from others come from parents and other family members.[6] One major responsibility that family members have to one another is to "talk" (family talk includes both verbal and nonverbal communication elements) in ways that will contribute to their development of strong self-images, especially for younger children. Family members' self-images are enhanced by statements of praise ("Roberto, you really did a nice job of cleaning your room" and "Mom, that was really nice of you to let Jasmine stay overnight at Beverly's house"); statements of acceptance and support ("If you have good reasons to drop out of the Glee Club, we accept your decision" and "Andy doesn't see eye to eye with us, but he's welcome in our home because he's your friend, and we respect that"); and statements of love ("Bart, I know it hurts to play poorly in front of your family, but we love you and we'll be here again next game" and "We both love you very much, Mario"). Of course, these verbal statements will be perceived as positive only when they are accompanied by appropriate nonverbal gestures and tones of voice.

Unfortunately, in many families communication is very damaging to self-image, especially to the developing self-images of children. Statements supplemented by nonverbal reinforcing gestures and tones of voice that tease, blame, and evaluate are particularly damaging. All too common are teasing questions ("How are you today, clumsy?" and "Are you still going to be sucking your thumb when you're twenty-one?"); blaming statements ("You know, if I didn't have to raise you, I could be back at college" and "No, you didn't drop the plate, but your constant whining made me so nervous that I dropped it"); and evaluations ("Terri, why are you trying to make breakfast when you know you can't even boil water?" and "Marty, didn't you learn how to add? If what you want to do in life involves numbers, you'd better think of a different profession"). Children and teenagers store remarks like these in their minds, where they may hear the comments over and over until they believe them.

But even adults in the family can be hurt by inappropriate verbal and nonverbal communication. Some husbands and wives are so browbeaten by their spouse that they lose all confidence in their abilities. For instance, a spouse who is constantly hounded about his or her "inability to add and subtract accurately" may refuse to have anything to do with family finances. An occasional negative statement like those quoted above may not have a lasting effect, but if the family's normal communication style is negative—teasing, blaming, and evaluating—damaged self-images and lowered self-esteem are likely to result.

ACCURACY OF SELF-IMAGE

The reality or accuracy of our self-image depends on the accuracy of our perceptions and how we process them. Everyone experiences some success and failure and hears some praise and blame. If we focus awareness on successful experiences and positive responses only, our self-image will probably be distorted, but positive. If, however, we perceive and dwell on negative experiences and remember only the criticism we receive, our self-image may be negatively distorted. In neither case does the self-image necessarily conform to reality. Yet our perception of self is more likely than our true abilities to affect our behavior. For example, Sean may objectively have the ability to be a good leader, but if he doesn't perceive himself as a good leader, he won't choose to lead.

The gap between our inaccurate self-perceptions and reality is called *incongruence*, "the degree of disparity that exists between one's self-image and one's actual experience."[7] What is ideal, of course, is for a person's self-image to be congruent, that is, reasonably accurate. In reality, however, everyone experiences some incongruence—and problems occur when the disparity is wide.

ROLE OF SELF-PERCEPTIONS IN COMMUNICATION

Our beliefs about ourselves affect what we think about and what we talk about. Research documents the conclusion that our self-conceptions regulate and direct our behavior.[8] Likewise, the way we think and talk can affect the self-concept and self-image. Two ways that interaction between self-image and communication relate are in creating self-fulfilling prophecies and in filtering messages received from others.

● ● **Creating Self-fulfilling Prophecies** Using your communication as a vehicle, your self-image begins to shape reality through self-fulfilling prophecies—predictions that come true because, consciously or not, you believed and said that they would.

Self-fulfilling prophecies can affect your interpersonal performance. For example, Stefan sees himself as quite social and able to get to know people easily; he says, "I'm going to have fun at the party tonight." As a result of his positive self-image, he looks forward to encountering strangers and, just as he predicted, makes several new acquaintanceships and enjoys himself. Austin, however, sees himself as uncomfortable in new situations; he says, "I doubt I'll know anyone—I'm going to have a miserable time!" Because he fears encountering strangers, he feels awkward about introducing himself and, just as he predicted, spends much of his time standing alone and thinking about when he can leave. Research does suggest a direct relationship between poor self-image and communication anxiety.[9]

In addition, people with a positive self-image view success positively, confident that they can repeat successes; people with a negative self-image fear that success is likely to be a mistake and thus do not believe that they can repeat successes.[10]

● ● **Filtering Messages** How we feel about ourselves can also affect our communication by filtering what others say to us. Even though we may receive all messages accurately (that is, our ears receive the messages and our brain records them), we do not listen equally to all of them. Moreover, the messages we choose to listen to will probably be those that reinforce our self-image. If someone says something that contradicts our perception, we are likely to act as if it had never been said. For example, you prepare an agenda for your study group and someone comments that you're a good organizer; you may ignore it, not really hear it, or perhaps reply, "Oh, it really wasn't that good" or "Anyone could have done that—it was nothing special." If you think you are a good organizer, however, you will seek out messages that reinforce this positive view and screen out those that don't.

Self-image, then, is both a result and a filter of others' comments. Certain comments help form a self-image; then that image begins to work as a filter, screening out selected messages. At times, however, comments will get past the filter and change the self-image, and then the newly changed self-image begins to filter other comments. Thus changes in self-concept do occur.

SELF-ESTEEM

Our _self-esteem_ is our evaluation of ourselves in either positive or negative ways. In effect, self-esteem is the evaluative aspect of self-concept. Three ways that interaction between self-esteem and communication relate are to influence communication style, to moderate competing internal messages, and to influence our perception of others.

● ● **Influencing Communication Style** Recent research demonstrates that because differences in self-esteem affect behavior in achievement and causal attribution, people with low self-esteem often disapprove of themselves and speak in ways that reflect this disapproval.[11] For instance, people may show an expectation of rejection by others by saying things such as "What I did probably wasn't that important to the company, so I probably won't get a merit raise." Or since they have difficulty defending their own views, they may discount them with statements such as "I have reasons for supporting Hanson, but I guess they're not that good—Parker's probably the better candidate." In contrast, people with higher self-esteem usually express positive views of themselves and make statements that show an expectation of acceptance. They are likely to state opinions such as "My suggestions helped the company diversify its sales campaign, so I think I'll probably get a good raise on that basis alone." Likewise, they are apt to be able to defend their views even in the face of opposing argument. For instance, if someone criticizes Amber for supporting Hanson, she might say, "You might criticize my support, but I think my reasons for supporting Hanson are good ones."

Why does self-esteem affect communication style? It makes sense that a person with low self-esteem is likely to be unsure of the value of his or her contributions and expect others to view them negatively. In contrast, a person with high self-esteem is likely to be more confident of the value of his or her contributions and expect others to see their value. Whether or not low self-esteem views are realistic, people who hold them accept others' real or imagined negative views as additional evidence that they are indeed unworthy.

Moderating Competing Internal Messages   A particularly interesting function of self-esteem is to moderate internal messages. When we are thinking, we are in fact talking to ourselves. (Some people even go so far as to do much of their thinking aloud.) When faced with a decision, we may be especially conscious of the different and often competing voices in our head. Perhaps after returning from a job interview you had a conversation much like Corey's: "I think I made a pretty good impression on the personnel director—I mean, she talked with me for a long time. Well, she talked with me, but maybe she was just trying to be nice. After all, it was her job. No, she didn't have to spend that much time with me. And she really lit up when I talked about the internship I had at Federated. So, she said she was interested in my internship. Talking about that is not exactly telling me that it would make a difference in her view of me as a prospective employee." Notice that several of the messages in this internal conversation are competing. What determines which voice Corey listens to? Self-esteem is a moderator in the choice. If Corey feels good about himself, he will probably conclude that the interviewer was sincere, and he'll feel good about the interview. If he feels down about his life and his behavior, however, he may well believe that he doesn't have a chance for the job.

Influencing Perception of Others   Self-image and self-esteem are important not only because they influence our communication behavior but also because they affect how we perceive others. First, the more accurate our self-image, the more accurately we can perceive others. Both self-perception and perception of others start with our ability to process data accurately. Second, the higher our self-esteem, the more likely we are to view others favorably. Studies have shown that people who accept themselves as they are tend to be more accepting of others; similarly, those with low self-esteem are more likely to find fault with others. Third, our own personal characteristics influence the type of characteristics we are likely to perceive in others. For example, people who are secure tend to see others positively rather than negatively. If you recall that we respond to the world as we perceive it (and not necessarily as it is), you can readily see how low self-esteem can account for misunderstandings and communication breakdowns.

IMPROVING PERCEPTION OF SELF

Overall, we can improve our self-perceptions. But even though we are constantly growing and developing, we are likely to resist changes in our self-image and self-esteem that may square better with reality. People with high self-esteem seem more resistant to change, perhaps because they are already processing information in a way that is consistent with their sense of self.

People with low self-esteem are more likely to change, because their self-impressions tend to be more malleable. Thus people with low self-esteem may be able to improve their self-image if they can be shown that data support such a change of view. Without help, many of us are bent on maintaining a negative view. For instance, suppose that in high school you didn't do very well in French. In fact, at some point, a parent or teacher may have said, "Face up to it, foreign language is not your thing." Then you arrive at college and find that you must take another year of foreign language. As the semester progresses, you find yourself completing homework in a reasonable amount of time and getting average or better grades. Nevertheless, when your professor, adviser, or friend says, "Are you going to continue with French?" you find yourself saying, "No, I've been lucky—I'm not very good at French." Again, stubbornly maintaining that "you can't do it" cements artificial limits that may be detrimental to your overall growth.

Change comes only through realistic assessment of strengths and weaknesses. In order to make any conscious change in self-esteem, we must be aware of our behavior to determine how self-esteem influences it. We have to recognize that some kinds of behavior are more likely to attract positive responses. And we need to engage in those kinds of behavior. In this book we consider many specific communication behaviors that are designed to increase your communication competence. As you start to perfect the use of these skills, you are likely to begin receiving positive responses to your behavior. If your self-esteem tends to be low, if you think that people just don't like you or don't have confidence in you, these positive responses will demonstrate that people acted negatively not toward you, but toward your behavior. For instance, imagine that someone does a favor for you. If, instead of ignoring the behavior, you praise the person and offer nonverbal signs of being pleased, that person is likely to begin to treat you as a more pleasant individual; this, in turn, may strengthen your perception of self as a good person.

Cultural Considerations

Culture influences perception and affects participants' views of self. Most U.S. citizens share what is called the Western view of self, which holds that the individual is an autonomous entity comprising distinct abilities, traits, motives, and values, and that these attributes cause behavior. Moreover, people with this Western view seek to maintain an independence from others to discover and express their uniqueness. Yet people from most of the rest of the world don't share this view. For instance, many Eastern cultures neither assume nor value independence—the goal of many cultures is to maintain *interdependence* among individuals.[12] To make this comparison more vivid, where the U.S. culture espouses the maxim "It's the squeaky wheel that gets the grease," Eastern cultures, including Japanese, Chinese, and Australian, espouse the maxim "The nail that sticks up shall be hammered down."

What are the implications for interpersonal communication? Interdependent selves will be more attentive and sensitive to others than will independent selves. Thus, in U.S. culture, it seems important to socialize children away from helplessness and dependence in order to help them be more self-sufficient and independent. In many other cultures the child is seen as needing to be acculturated toward greater dependency.[13]

Analyzing Self

BY YOURSELF

1. *How you see yourself:* On a blank sheet of paper, list characteristics that describe how you see yourself by completing the statement "I am" over and over again. List as many characteristics as you can think of. These statements will represent your "working self-concept." When you can think of no more, go back through the list. Label the positive statements with a *P*; label the negative statements with an *N*. How many statements are positive? How many are negative?

2. *How others see you:* On a second sheet of paper, list characteristics that describe how others see you by completing the statement "Other people believe that I am" over and over again. When you can think of no

no physical characteristics or things you can see [handwritten margin note]

more, go back through the list and label and tally positive and negative statements.

3. *How you wish you were:* On a third sheet of paper, list characteristics that describe how you wish you were by completing the statement "I wish I were" over and over again. When you can think of no more, go back through the list and label and tally positive and negative statements.

4. After you have compared the lists, noting similarities and differences, write a short statement that describes what you have learned about yourself and your self-concept. Can you think of ways your self-concept may have influenced your communication with others?

5. For three days, record the various situations you experience. Describe the images you chose to project in each. At the conclusion of this three-day observation period, write an analysis of your self-monitoring. To what extent does your communication behavior differ and remain the same across situations? What factors in a situation seem to trigger certain behaviors in you? How satisfied are you with the images or "selves" that you displayed in each situation? What pleased you most? What pleased you least?

Perception of Others

As we encounter strangers, we are faced with several questions: Do we have anything in common? Will they accept me? Will we be able to get along? We begin with some frustration in attempts to obtain the information to answer these questions, a process that Charles Berger and James Brada called "uncertainty reduction."[14] This theory states that we seek information about others, for if we are uncertain about what they are like, we will have a difficult time predicting their behavior. In this section we focus on our use of perception as a means of coping with uncertainty. In Chapter 5 of this text we will explore uncertainty reduction theory in greater detail as we see its relevance to developing relationships.

Our perceptions of others are the result of impressions formed on the basis of sensory data we take in, our organization and processing of those data, and the attributes we select to explain behavior. When two people meet, they form initial impressions to guide their behavior. As they continue to interact, these perceptions will be reinforced, intensified, or changed. As is true of our self-perceptions, our social perceptions aren't always accurate. The factors likely to influence our social perceptions are physical characteristics and social behaviors, stereotyping, and emotional states.

PHYSICAL CHARACTERISTICS AND SOCIAL BEHAVIORS

Social perceptions, especially the important first impressions, are often made on the basis of people's physical characteristics and social behaviors. Depending on a person's physical attractiveness (facial characteristics, height, weight, grooming, dress, and sound of voice), people are likely to categorize others as friendly, courageous, intelligent, cool, or their opposite.[15] For instance, in one study professional women dressed in jackets were assessed as more powerful than professional women dressed in other clothing.[16] In some cases a person does not even need a live encounter to attribute a trait to another person. Show a friend a picture of your child, uncle, or grandmother, and your friend may well form impressions of your relative's personality on the basis of the photo alone.

First impressions are also made on the basis of perceptions of a person's social behaviors—sometimes even of a single behavior. For instance, after a company orientation social, Caleb asks Sara what she thought of Gavin, a fellow working with Caleb on the Goodman account. Sara, who had observed Gavin interrupt Yolanda once to emphasize his view as she was recounting the events of last year's social, may say, "Gavin? He's really rude."

● **We attribute traits to people on the basis of their physical characteristics. What traits would you attribute to the woman and man shown in this photo? What might you say about the person of whom we see only the arm?**

Often the behaviors we use in making these impressions are based on gender. Leslie Zebrowitz states that males are more likely to describe others in terms of their abilities ("She writes well"), whereas females are more likely to describe others in terms of their self-concepts ("She thinks she's a good writer"). Likewise, she says that there are gender differences in categorizing the behaviors. Males' descriptions include more nonsocial activities ("He likes to fly model airplanes"), whereas females' observations include more interpersonal interactions ("He likes to get together with his friends").[17] Similarly, our cultural heritage strongly influences how we perceive members of another culture.

Research suggests that people may form highly complex perceptions of someone's personality based on very limited observation. Such judgments are the result of what is called "implicit personality theories," a set of assumptions people have developed about what physical characteristics and personality traits are associated with one another.[18]

Because your own implicit personality theory says that certain traits go together, you are likely to judge a person's other characteristics after observing a single trait without further verification. This tendency is known as the *halo effect*. For instance, Heather sees Martina as a warm person. Heather's implicit personality theory correlates warmth with goodness and goodness with honesty. As a result, she perceives Martina as being both good and honest as well as warm. In reality, Martina may be warm but dishonest. Thus, if a friend accuses Martina of lying about an important matter, Heather may leap to Martina's defense because the halo effect leads her to assume that Martina is honest.

A halo effect can also work to a person's disadvantage when it concerns a negative perception. In fact, T. D. Hollman has found that negative information more strongly influences our impressions of others than does positive information.[19]

Halo effects seem to occur most frequently under one or more of three conditions: (1) when the perceiver is judging traits with which he or she has limited experience, (2) when the traits have strong moral overtones, and (3) when the perception is of a person that the perceiver knows well.

Given limited amounts of information, then, we fill in details. This tendency to fill in details leads to a second biasing factor in social perception: stereotyping.

STEREOTYPING

Perhaps the most commonly known barrier to our accurate judgment of others is our tendency to stereotype. Stereotyping is the formation of an oversimplified opinion or uncritical judgment of others. It often involves assigning characteristics to individuals solely on the basis of their membership in a certain class or category. Stereotyping is a very common perceptual shortcut. We are likely to develop generalized opinions about any group we encounter. Subsequently, any number of perceptual cues—skin color, style of dress, a religious medal, gray hair, gender, and so on—can lead us to automatically project our generalized opinions onto a specific individual.

It is important to note that stereotypes engender three different types of perceptual inaccuracies. First is stereotypic inaccuracy—the tendency to view a group as more less stereotypic than it actually is (saying the Gammas really value or undervalue scholarship when their collective grade point average is only slightly above or below the average for the school). Second is valence inaccuracy—the tendency to view a group as more or less positive than it is (saying the Gammas are the most or least popular group on campus when they are not). Third is dispersion accuracy—the tendency to see a group as more or less variable than it actually is (saying that all Gammas are good students when the group represents a variety of grades).[20]

Stereotyping contributes to perceptual inaccuracies by ignoring individual differences. It causes us to assume certain characteristics simply because a person happens to be a member of the stereotyped group. For instance, if Dave held a stereotype that stockbrokers are unethical, that would not mean that Denise, a highly principled woman, is unethical even if we discover that a majority of stockbrokers are unethical. You may be able to think of instances when you have been the victim of a stereotype based on your gender, age, ethnic heritage, social class, physical characteristics, or other qualities. If so, you know how damaging and unfair stereotypes can be.

If stereotypes lead to inaccurate perceptions, why do they persist? There are at least two good reasons. First, we tend to believe that stereotypes are helpful.[21] Although people may learn to go beyond a stereotype in forming opinions of individuals, stereotypes provide a working hypothesis. That is, when encountering a person from a different race or culture, we are likely to attribute characteristics of our stereotype to the person and act as if that stereotype is accurate until we get sufficient information to judge the person as an individual.[22] In short, it is easier to base our perceptions of a person or group of people on a stereotype than to take the time to learn about each individual we encounter. Second, stereotyping provides some people with a certain amount of comfort. Believing generalizations—that whites are racist, blacks are lazy, old people are stubborn, Italians are naturally hotheaded, or women are too emotional to be capable of reasoning under stress—enables a person to "know" how to treat new acquaintances.

As these examples suggest, stereotyping and prejudice go hand in hand. Prejudice is an unjustified attitude toward a person or group. For instance, when Rosie discovers that Wasif, a man she has just met, is a Muslim, she is stereotyping him if she views him solely in terms of her perception of Muslims' beliefs about women rather than in terms of his individual behavior. Moreover, to the extent that Rosie permits her stereotype to govern her responses to Wasif, she will be guilty of prejudice. In this case Wasif may never get the chance to be known for who he really is.

Prejudice, like stereotypes, can be very resistant to change. People who are prejudiced are likely to continue maintaining their prejudices even in the face of evidence that disproves them. Suppose that Lou, an African-American man, stereotypes all whites as racist. When Lou meets Phil, a white man, Lou will believe that Phil is racist. If someone confronts Lou with evidence that Phil treats all people alike regardless of race, Lou may refuse to acknowledge the evidence, find some alternative explanation, or reject its source.

Racism and sexism are two enactments of prejudice that cause major problems in relationships in our society. Racism and sexism are defined as any behaviors, however insignificant, that limit people to rigid stereotypic roles based solely on race or gender. Because such attitudes can be both deeply ingrained and often subtle, it is easy to overlook behaviors we engage in that in some way meet this definition of racist or sexist behavior. Remember, the behavior may seem insignificant. For instance, leaving more space between you and another person on a bus, on a plane, in a lounge, or at a counter in a restaurant—a space wider than you would leave if the person sitting next to you were of your race—is racist behavior. Telling jokes, laughing at jokes, or encouraging repetition of jokes that demean people of other races or the opposite sex is racist/sexist behavior. Ignoring the presence or the worth of the comments of another person because that person is of another race or the opposite sex is racist/sexist behavior. We may say, "But I didn't mean anything by what I did"; however, our behavior will be perceived as racist/sexist, and it will seriously harm our attempts to communicate.

More recently, definitions of both racism and sexism have been reconsidered on the basis of the presence or absence of the variable of power. From this perspective, racism and sexism occur when the majority culture uses its various positions of power and control to explicitly or implicitly deny or inhibit the rights of minority cultures, including women. Notice that women have been defined as a minority even though women outnumber men. Classification of women as a minority is a function not of numbers, but of the subjection of women and other minorities to repressive acts by the major white/male culture.

This definition does not say that African-Americans, Asian-Americans, Hispanic-Americans, and women can't be prejudiced. But it does say that as a result of the lack of a significant power base, minorities are unable to enact their prejudice in ways that explicitly or implicitly deny or inhibit the rights of the majority white/male culture. Thus, under this definition, true racism or sexism is limited to behaviors against those in lower power positions.

Although we understand the thinking behind these definitions, from an interpersonal communication standpoint whether behavior is truly racist, sexist, or "only" prejudice differs only in degree. Thus we continue to hold the view that any prejudicial behavior should be identified and eliminated. Because racial and gender stereotypes are deeply ingrained in our culture, very few people manage to completely avoid behaving or thinking in a prejudiced manner. By becoming aware of our own prejudicial attitudes and behaviors, we can guard against automatically assuming that other people feel and act the same way we do and thus inhibiting communication. We can also guard against saying or doing things that offend other people and perpetuate racial and sex-role stereotypes. If people are confronted with enough information over a long enough period, their attitudes may change.

Of course, prejudicial behavior is not limited to race and sex. For instance, in a recent study by Theodore Grove and Doris Werkman, conversations with visibly disabled strangers produced relatively more negative predicted outcome values than conversations with able-bodied strangers.[23] Similarly, homosexuals have long experienced prejudice. In short, we must recognize the potential of prejudicial behavior with any group of people who are different from ourselves.

EMOTIONAL STATES

A final barrier to accurate judgments of others involves our emotional state. Various research studies completed by Joseph Forgas led him to conclude that "there is a broad and pervasive tendency for people to perceive and interpret others in terms of their feelings at the time."[24] If, for example, you are having a "down" day, your perception of a person you are meeting for the first time will probably be more negative than if you were having a good day. When you receive a low grade on a paper you thought was well written, your perceptions of people around you will surely be colored by your negative feeling. If, however, you receive an *A* on an important paper that you weren't sure was good, you're likely to perceive everything and everyone around you positively. Whether our perceptions of another person are positive or negative, we can ask ourselves before acting on them how our feelings may have affected our perceptions.

Our emotions also cause us to engage in selective perceptions. For instance, we are likely to think highly of someone we would like to be with. If

● People are likely to perceive and interpret events in terms of their feelings at the time. If you are having a "down" day, your perceptions may be more negative than if you are having a good day.

Anya sees Nick as a man with whom she would like to develop a strong relationship, she will tend to see the positive side of Nick's personality and overlook or ignore the negative side that is apparent to others. A person in love is often oblivious of the loved one's faults. Once two people have married, however, they may begin to see the negative traits of their partners, traits that perhaps were obvious to others all along.

Our emotions also may affect our attributions.[25] _Attributions_ are reasons we give for others' behavior. In addition to making judgments about people, we attempt to construct reasons for people's behavior. According to attribution theory, what we determine—rightly or wrongly—to be the causes of others' behavior has a direct impact on our perceptions of them.

For instance, suppose that you have made a luncheon appointment with a co-worker for noon at a restaurant a few blocks from work. You arrive at noon, but there is no sign of your co-worker. At 12:20, he is still a no-show. At this point, you are likely to construct causal attributions. If you like and respect your co-worker, you may attribute his lateness to a good reason: an important phone call at the last minute, the need to finish a job before lunch, or some accident that may have occurred; if you are not particularly fond of your co-worker, you are likely to attribute his lateness to forgetfulness, inconsiderateness, or malicious intent. In either case your causal attribution further affects your perception of the person. Like prejudices, causal attributions may be so strong that they resist contrary evidence. If you don't particularly care for the person, when he does arrive and explains that he had an emergency long-distance phone call, you are likely to disbelieve the reason or discount the urgency of the call. Being aware of the human tendency toward such cognitive biases can help you correct your perceptions and thus improve your communication.

Cultural and Gender Considerations

Members of the opposite sex or people from different cultures talking with each other are likely to experience difficulty sharing meaning because they approach the world with different perspectives. We sometimes think that we don't have to be so concerned with cultural differences because most of our communication will be with people similar to ourselves. But you don't have to cross national borders to encounter different cultures. The United States contains many, including African-American, Mexican-American, Hispanic-American, Asian-American, Native American, Appalachian, and others. And because differences are increasingly being experienced across generations, regions, social classes, and even neighborhoods, the need for awareness and sensitivity in our communications doesn't depend on someone's being from another country or otherwise so markedly "different" from ourselves. For instance, in the Los Angeles County School District, 108 different languages are spoken; in Hollywood High School alone, there are 85 different first languages for students.[26]

When confronted with strangers of the opposite sex or from different cultures, we tend to see differences as barriers to communication because they represent unknowns. The more one person differs from another, the less either person is able to predict the behavior of the other. When people are uncertain about how another person will behave, fear is a probable result. Some people express their fear by withdrawing or becoming compliant, and others mask their fear with aggressive behavior. Clearly, none of these behaviors improves communication; cultural and gender differences argue for a greater need for confronting our ignorance about what people are thinking, feeling, and valuing. In the final part of this chapter we focus on procedures that will enable us to improve our social perceptions of people regardless of their culture or gender.

Analyzing Perceptions of Others

BY YOURSELF

1. Think of a recent encounter you had with someone of a different race or ethnic background. Describe how you felt. To what extent were you comfortable with this person? How did the person's race or ethnic background influence how you acted or reacted?

2. Describe the last situation in which you found yourself where someone told a racist or sexist joke or made a racist or sexist remark. How did you react? How did others present react? If you are dissatisfied with how you reacted, write a script for how you wish you had reacted.

IN GROUPS

1. Your instructor will ask for three volunteers, who will leave the classroom. One at a time they will reenter the room and describe to the class a full-page magazine advertisement that the instructor has given them. On the basis of their descriptions, form a mental picture of the people in the ad. As each volunteer describes the ad, write five adjectives about the person or persons in the picture. When all three have finished, your instructor will show you the ad.

   a. What were the differences among the three descriptions?
   b. Which of the three descriptions helped you to form the most accurate picture? How did your image differ from the actual picture? How can you account for the differences?
   c. Now that you have seen the picture, again write five adjectives about the person or persons in the picture. Did your five adjectives change after you actually saw the picture? If so, how and why?

2. For the following situation, determine which of the factors discussed in this section contributed to the inaccuracy of the initial perception of the other person. Be able to defend your answers in class.

   Amanda was depressed. Her daughter was having problems in school, she had just been informed that her work hours were being cut back, and her mother was facing possible surgery. On her way home from campus, she stopped at the dry cleaner to pick up her laundry. A new man was working the counter. From looking at him, Amanda could tell he was quite old. She thought to herself that he could be a problem. When she requested her laundry, he asked to see her claim check. Because no one had ever asked her for this before, Amanda responded that she had thrown the receipt away. The man firmly replied, "Well, I'm not able to give you clothes without a claim check. It's policy." After demanding to see the manager and being informed that she had left for the day, Amanda stormed out of the building. "I'll fix him," she fumed to herself. "It's just like an old man to act so rigidly!"

IMPROVING SOCIAL PERCEPTION

Because inaccuracies in perception are common and influence how we communicate, improving perceptual accuracy is an important first step in becoming a competent communicator. The following guidelines can aid you in constructing a more realistic impression of others as well as in assessing the validity of your own perceptions.

1. *Seek more information to verify perceptions.* Once you have drawn a conclusion about others, you begin to behave in accordance with that conclusion. Has your perception been based on only one or two pieces of information? If so, try to collect further information before you allow yourself to form an impression so that you can increase the accuracy of your perceptions. It helps to note mentally that your perception is tentative, that is, subject to change. You can then make a conscious effort to collect more data in order to determine whether the original perception is accurate.

The best way to obtain information about people is to talk with them. If you have perceived someone as inconsiderate on the basis of one experience, hold that perception as tentative until you have a chance to talk further with the person. Only by talking with people can we get to know them; a sure way to maintain an inaccurate perception is to use it as a reason to avoid the person in question.

2. *Actively question the accuracy of your perceptions.* Too many people insist that "I was there—I know what I saw"; that is, they act on their perceptions as though the perceptions were reality. Questioning accuracy begins by saying, "I know what I think I saw, heard, tasted, smelled, or felt, but I could be wrong. What else could help me sort this out?" By accepting the possibility of error, you may be motivated to seek further verification. In situations where the accuracy of perception is important, take a few seconds to double-check. It will be worth the effort.

3. *Realize that perceptions of people may need to be changed over time.* Suppose that two years ago you heard a person denigrate the accomplishments of a friend of yours, and so you developed the perception that the person is mean spirited. The chances are that this one incident will lead you to expect mean-spirited behavior from this person. As demonstrated earlier in the chapter, we often perceive what we expect to perceive. As a result, you may perceive other behaviors as mean even though they are not. Willingness to change means making an effort to observe this person's behavior at other times without bias and being prepared to modify your perception if the person's behavior warrants it. People often saddle themselves with perceptions that are based on old or incomplete information, yet find it easier to stick with them, even if they are wrong, than to change them. It takes strength of character to say to yourself or others, "I was wrong." Your communication based on outdated, inaccurate perceptions can be more costly than revising your perceptions.

4. *Check perceptions verbally.* How can you be sure that the meanings you get from others' nonverbal cues are accurate? Before you act on any conclusion you draw from other people's behavior, make a perception check. A perception check is a verbal statement that reflects your own understanding of the meaning of another person's nonverbal cues. Perception checking calls for you to (1) watch the behavior of the other person, (2) ask yourself "What does that behavior mean to me?" and (3) put your interpretation of the behavior into words to learn whether your perception is accurate.

The following examples illustrate the use of perception checking.

Vera walks into the room with a completely blank expression. She neither speaks to Ann nor acknowledges that she is in the room. Vera sits on the edge of the bed and stares into space. Ann says, "Vera, I get the feeling that something has happened to put you in a state of shock. Am I right? Is there something I can do?"

Ted, the company messenger, delivers a memo to Erin. As Erin reads the note, her eyes brighten and she breaks into a smile. Ted says, "Hey, Erin, you seem really pleased. Am I right?"

Cesar, speaking in short, precise sentences with a sharp tone of voice, gives Bill his day's assignment. Bill says, "From the sound of your voice, Cesar, I can't help but get the impression that you're upset with me. Are you?"

In each of these examples, the final sentence is a perception check intended to test the receiver's perceptions of the sender's behavior. Notice that body language sometimes provides the clues, whereas at other times the tone of voice does. Also notice that the perception-checking statements do not express approval or disapproval of what is being received—they are purely descriptive statements of the perceptions.

The purpose of checking out any perception of behavior is to bring the meaning received through nonverbal cues into the verbal realm, where it can be verified or corrected. Let's carry through with Cesar and Bill's conversation. When Bill says, "I can't help but get the impression that you're upset with me. Are you?" Cesar may say either (1) "No, whatever gave you that impression?" in which case Bill can further describe the cues that he received; (2) "Yes, I am," in which case Bill can get Cesar to specify what has caused the feelings; or (3) "No, it's not you; it's just that three of my team members didn't show up for this shift." If Cesar is not upset with him, Bill can deal with what caused him to misinterpret Cesar's feelings; if Cesar is upset with him, Bill has the opportunity to change the behavior that caused Cesar to be upset.

To see what might happen when we respond without checking the accuracy of our perceptions, suppose that in place of the descriptive perception check Bill were to say, "Why are you so upset with me?" Bill would not be describing his perception—he would be making a judgment based on his perception. Replying as if his perception is obviously accurate amounts to mind reading. Unfortunately, few people can read minds that well, especially given all the subjective factors that influence perception. Bill's response could very well reflect his state of mind far more than it does Cesar's. When mind reading is substituted for perception checking, communication breakdowns are likely to occur.

Perhaps you are thinking, "Well, I know how to read other people's signals. I can tell perfectly well when another person is upset [or happy, angry, and so on] with me." And perhaps you are correct—most of the time. But if you do not check out your perception, you are still guessing what the other person is feeling and whether the person's anger or happiness is centered on you. If you reply judgmentally, the other person may well become defensive about the feelings you appear to be challenging. The response is then likely to be something like "Who said I'm upset?" or, more harshly, "What the hell are you talking about?" Such responses probably will trigger an escalating round of emotional outbursts and complete misunderstanding. Very little communication takes place when communicators lose their tempers.

When should you check your perceptions? Whenever the accuracy of your understanding is important (1) to your current communication, (2) to the relationship you have with the other person, or (3) to the conclusions you draw about that person. Most of us use this skill far too little, if at all. We assume that we have a perfectly accurate understanding of the meaning of another's behavioral cues; too often we are wrong. Especially in new relationships you will find perception checking an important skill to use.

Because a perception check is descriptive rather than judgmental, the other person is much less likely to react defensively. However, a perception

Basic Communication Skills

SKILL	USE	PROCEDURE	EXAMPLE
Perceptive Checking A verbal statement that reflects your understanding of the meaning of another person's nonverbal cues.	To clarify the meaning of nonverbal behavior.	1. Watch the behavior of another. Describe the behavior to yourself or aloud. 2. Ask yourself: What does that behavior mean to me? 3. Put your interpretation of the nonverbal behavior into words to verify your perception.	As Dale frowns while reading Paul's first draft of a memo, Paul says, "From the way you're frowning, I take it that you're not too pleased with the way I phrased the memo."

check may not always eliminate defensive behavior. There are times when a person's emotional stress is so great that calm, logical communication is nearly impossible. Through the selective use of perception checking, however, you can reduce the likelihood of misinterpreting another's nonverbal cues and thus the likelihood of defensiveness. As with most skills, to become competent, you must practice.

PRACTICE IN

Perception Checking

BY YOURSELF

1. Write down your responses to the following situations with well-phrased perception checks:

Franco comes home from the doctor's office with a pale face and slumped shoulders. Glancing at you with a forlorn look, he shrugs. You say:

As you return the tennis racket you borrowed from Liam, you smile and say, "Here's your racket." Liam stiffens, grabs the racket, and starts to walk away. You say:

Natalie comes dancing into her room with a huge grin on her face. You say:

In the past, your adviser has told you that almost any time would be all right for working out your next term's schedule. When you tell her you'll come by on Wednesday at 4 P.M., she pauses, frowns, sighs, and says "Uh" and nods. You say:

2. Compare your written responses to the guidelines for effective perception checking discussed earlier. Edit your responses where necessary in order to improve them. Now say them aloud. Do they sound natural? If not, revise them until they do.

IN GROUPS

Working with others in groups of three, A and B role-play a situation while C observes. During the conversation, A intentionally gives off various nonverbal cues to his or her feelings. B uses perception checking to determine if his or her perception of A's behavior is accurate. When they have finished, C discusses the behaviors observed and provides an analysis of the effectiveness of B's perception checks. The exercise continues until each person in the group has a chance to be A, B, and C. After completing the exercise, the participants discuss how the skill of perception checking affected the accuracy of the communication.

● ◆ ■ **Summary**

Perception is the process of gathering sensory information and assigning meaning to it. Our perceptions are a result of our selection, organization, and interpretation of sensory information. Inaccurate perceptions cause us to see the world not as it is but as we would like it to be.

The self-concept is the total of a person's generalizations about self; it is presented publicly through the roles we enact. Our self-image, our perception of our self-concept, is formed through self-appraisal and is influenced by our reactions to our experiences and the reactions and responses of others. Our self-image affects communication by creating self-fulfilling prophecies and by filtering messages we receive. Our self-esteem is our evaluation of ourselves in either positive or negative ways. Our self-esteem and communication relate to influence communication style, to moderate competing internal messages, and to influence our perception of others.

Perception also plays an important role in forming impressions of others. Factors likely to influence our social perceptions are physical characteristics and social behaviors, stereotyping, and emotional states. Because research shows that the accuracy of people's perceptions and judgments varies considerably, your communication will be most successful if you do not rely entirely on your impressions to determine how another person feels or what that person is really like. You will improve (or at least better understand) your perceptions of others if you take into account physical characteristics and social behaviors, stereotyping, and emotional states.

You can learn to improve perception if you actively question the accuracy of your perceptions, seek more information to verify perceptions, talk with the people about whom you are forming perceptions, realize that perceptions of people need to change over time, and check perceptions verbally before you react.

● ◆ ■ Communication Improvement Goal Statements

If you believe you need to improve your perception checking, write a communication improvement goal statement following the guidelines on pages 31–33 of Chapter 1.

● ◆ ■ Featured Reading

Men Are from Mars, Women Are from Venus
John Gray
(New York: HarperCollins, 1992)

John Gray's book, a best seller through much of 1993 and into 1994, is an excellent example of the importance of perception in male-female relationships. Using a metaphor of men as Martians and women as Venusians, Gray writes that once upon a time Martians and Venusians met, fell in love, and had happy relationships together because they respected and accepted their differences. Then they came to Earth and selective amnesia set in: They forgot they were from different planets.

Through this metaphor, Gray vivifies the common conflicts between men and women that result from basic perceptual differences. For instance, he points out that Martians go into their caves alone to sort out their problems; Venusians get together and openly talk about their problems. By being confronted with such differences in behavior, both Martians and Venusians gain a better understanding of how they can live together. In addition, these metaphorical references allow us to look at our behavior with a sense of humor.

At no time does Gray deride either Martian or Venusian behavior. Instead of arguing that Martians must be more Venusian or vice versa, he emphasizes only the need to understand the nature of the contrasting behaviors. For instance in his discussion of problem-solving behaviors he says, "A woman should not be judged for needing reassurance, just as a man should not be judged for needing to withdraw."

Since we as human beings are not going to change our basic nature, what can we do? Gray says that we learn how to adapt. Both men and women can engage in behaviors that show sensitivity to the needs of the other. For instance, men are counseled to give a woman a hug before doing anything else, to resist the temptation to solve her problems by empathizing instead, and to practice listening and asking questions. Likewise, when he forgets to pick up something, women are counseled to say, "It's OK. Would you do it next time you are out?"; to apologize and give him love when she has hurt him and she understands his hurt; and on special occasions to overlook his mistakes that might normally upset her.

Although the book seems to overemphasize stereotypes at times, it presents interesting observations about male-female relationships and the role of perception in developing them. You may also enjoy the light-hearted presentation of these significant differences and the conflicts they can present.

●◆■ Notes

1. H. Markus and P. Nurius, "Possible Selves," *American Psychologist* 41 (1986): 954–969.

2. Kay Deaux, Francis C. Dane, and Lawrence S. Wrightsman, *Social Psychology*, 5th ed. (Belmont, Calif.: Wadsworth, 1993), p. 56.

3. Paul J. Centi, *Up with the Positive: Out with the Negative* (Englewood Cliffs, N.J.: Prentice Hall, 1981).

4. Russell H. Fazio, Steven J. Sherman, and Paul M. Herr, "The Feature-Positive Effect in the Self-Perception Process: Does Not Doing Matter as Much as Doing?" *Journal of Personality and Social Psychology* 42 (1982): 411.

5. John Hattie, *Self-Concept* (Hillsdale, N.J.: Erlbaum, 1992), p. 251.

6. D. H. Demo, "Family Relations and the Self-Esteem of Adolescents and Their Parents," *Journal of Marriage and the Family* 49 (1987): 705–715.

7. Wayne Weiten, *Psychology: Themes and Variations* (Pacific Grove, Calif.: Brooks/Cole, 1989), p. 449.

8. Jonathon D. Brown and S. April Smart, "The Self and Social Conduct: Linking Self-Representations to Prosocial Behavior," *Journal of Personality and Social Psychology* 60 (1991): 368.

9. Lynne Kelly, "A Rose by Any Other Name Is Still a Rose: A Comparative Analysis of Reticence, Communication Apprehension, Unwillingness to Communicate, and Shyness," *Human Communication Research* 8 (1982): 102.

10. Hattie, p. 253.

11. Jennifer D. Campbell, "Self-Esteem and Clarity of the Self-Concept," *Journal of Personality and Social Psychology* 59 (1990): 538.

12. Hazel R. Markus and Shinobu Kitayama, "Cultural Variation in the Self-Concept," in Jaine Strauss and George R. Goethals, eds., *The Self: Interdisciplinary Approaches* (New York: Springer-Verlag, 1991), p. 19.

13. Judith V. Jordan, "The Relational Self: A New Perspective for Understanding Women's Development," in Jaine Strauss and George R. Goethals, eds., *The Self: Interdisciplinary Approaches* (New York: Springer-Verlag, 1991), p. 137.

14. See Charles R. Berger and James J. Brada, *Language and Social Knowledge: Uncertainty in Interpersonal Relations* (London: Arnold, 1982).

15. Leslie A. Zebrowitz, *Social Perception* (Pacific Grove, Calif.: Brooks/Cole, 1990), p. 44ff. In this section the author cites numerous recent specific studies to support claims of effects of demographic factors and personal characteristics on impression formation.

16. Linda E. Temple and Karen R. Loewen, "Perceptions of Power: First Impressions of a Woman Wearing a Jacket," *Perceptual and Motor Skills* 76 (February 1993): 345.

17. Zebrowitz, p. 24.

18. Deaux, Dane, and Wrightsman, pp. 88–89.

19. T. D. Hollman, "Employment Interviewer's Errors in Processing Positive and Negative Information," *Journal of Psychology* 56 (1972): 130–134.

20. Carles M. Judd and Bernadette Park, "Definition and Assessment of Accuracy in Social Stereotypes," *Psychological Review* 100 (January 1993): 111.

21. Deaux, Dane, and Wrightsman, p. 94.

22. Edward E. Jones, *Interpersonal Perception* (New York: W. H. Freeman, 1990), p. 110.

23. Theodore G. Grove and Doris L. Werkman, "Conversations with Able-Bodied and Visibly Disabled Strangers: An Adversarial Test of Predicted Outcome Value and Uncertainty Reduction Theories," *Human Communication Research* 17 (June 1991): 507.

24. Joseph P. Forgas, "Affect and Person Perception," in Joseph P. Forgas, ed., *Emotion and Social Judgments* (New York: Pergamon Press, 1991), p. 288.

25. Joseph P. Forgas, Gordon H. Bower, and Stephanie J. Moylan, "Praise or Blame? Affective Influences on Attributions for Achievement," *Journal of Personality and Social Psychology* 59 (1990): 809.

26. Myron W. Lustig and Jolene Koester, *Intercultural Competence: Interpersonal Communication Across Cultures* (New York: HarperCollins, 1993), p. 10.

CHAPTER THREE

Verbal Communication

OBJECTIVES

After you have read this chapter, you should be able to define and/or explain:

Uses of language in human communication ✓

Relationship between language and meaning

Contrasts between word denotation and word connotation ✓

Precise words and specific and concrete words

Ways to date and index generalizations ✓

Cultural and gender considerations ✓

Nature of appropriate and inappropriate language

p. 92-96

As Jeff was leaning over the ladder and tapping the wall lightly he asked Lavonne, "Would you bring me that thing I put on the whatdoyacallit over there?"

"Sure," Lavonne replied. As she handed him a small, plastic object she asked, "Is this the thing you find the hickies with?"

"Right—those little fellows are hard to find without one. Now you want this thingamabob centered, right?"

"Looks good to me."

"You know," Jeff said, "I was wondering about something Morrison said at work today."

"What was that?"

"Well, we were working on the Whatshisface account when Morrison says, 'I just can't understand what you're trying to say sometimes.' You could have knocked me over with a feather."

"Hm, I never have any trouble figuring out what you mean."

"Well, I'm not going to lose any sleep over it. By the way, we need a couple of gizmos to hang the thing on."

"There's some in the doodad—I'll get them for you."

Do Jeff and Lavonne have a problem? Jeff is hanging a picture on the living room wall and he needs a stud finder to locate the metal nails that will indicate where the two-by-fours are as well as a couple of metal hangers.

Many serious students of our culture are concerned by modern Americans' apparent lack of sophistication in their use of the English language. Although many close friends and family members like Jeff and Lavonne often seem to understand one another regardless of word selection or grammar, other people can't always afford the luxury of such intuitive communication. In important contexts such as meeting with your professor, talking with your boss, coping with conflict, interviewing for a job, or discussing issues in a work group, a premium is placed on effective use of language. In the marketplace, failure to communicate clearly verbally can be a major problem.

We begin this chapter by discussing how people use language, including culture and gender considerations. Next we examine the relationship between language and meaning, with emphasis on denotation and connotation. Finally, we consider skills that focus on speaking clearly and speaking appropriately.

The Nature and Use of Language

Language is the systematic means of communicating ideas or feelings by the use of sounds and symbols that have commonly understood meanings. Some scholars believe that the human capability to think and communicate symbolically best distinguishes us from other species. Language is used in a variety of ways in human communication.

1. *We use language to designate, label, and define.* Language symbols (that is, words) serve to designate, label, and define thoughts, feelings, objects, people, and experiences so that they may be shared with other people. Certain limitations, however, are built into our use of language symbols. For instance, in referring to a classmate as a "mature adult," you are defining him or her differently from referring to that same classmate as a "student," "singer," or "basketball player." Whichever label you choose, you are calling attention to some particular aspect of that person; in addition, you are suggesting how others should define and thus act toward that person. In short, when we designate and define, we also limit. How might your perceptions and behaviors toward a person labeled a "singer" be different from those toward a person labeled an "athlete"?

When we experience a phenomenon that is unlabeled—that is, for which there is no word—we find it difficult to discuss. The end result is that either the phenomenon is not discussed or we create words to designate or label it so that we can engage in discussion. For instance, over the years women felt uncomfortable when they were subjects of unwanted comments directed to them and to other behaviors. But for a long time discussion of these behaviors was difficult because they were unnamed. Only in the last fifteen or twenty years have we designated such behavior as "sexual harassment." As Julia T. Wood, a leading scholar in gender research, points out, "Because it wasn't named, sexual harassment was not visible or salient, making it difficult

● **Words designate, label, and define thoughts, feelings, objects, people, and experiences. For instance, people will have a different meaning depending on whether you identify an object as a "flask," a "decorative object," an "artifact," or a "hand made snapping turtle rattle."**

to recognize, think about, or stop."[1] Once we began to use the term, we could discuss its nature and determine what kinds of behavior fell within and outside of the term. This labeling has given people, especially women, the opportunity to combat those behaviors that were inappropriate but rampant.

2. *We use language to evaluate.* Language scholars emphasize the value-laden characteristics of language: We give the things we talk about a positive or negative slant simply by the words we use to refer to them.[2] Consider the seemingly simple statement "The chairs in the den are pea green." Even this description may be perceived as a judgment about the chairs, depending on the associations "pea green" has for the listener. Other word choices convey evaluations more implicitly. For instance, if you observe Kirk taking his time to make a decision, you could speak of him as either "thoughtful and deliberate" or "wishy-washy." Likewise, you can call what your friend is cooking on the grill either "prime steak" or "animal flesh." Clearly, the meaning you transmit varies greatly with your choice of words. The value-laden nature of language requires us to select our words with great care or run the risk of creating reactions we don't intend.

3. *We use language to discuss things outside our immediate experience.* Language enables us to speak hypothetically, to talk about past and future events, and to communicate about people and things that are not present. Through language we can discuss where we hope to be in five years, analyze a conversation two acquaintances had last week, or learn about the history that shapes the world we live in. Language enables us to learn from others' experiences, to share a common heritage, and to develop a shared vision for the future.

We rely so much on what we learn through language that we sometimes react to the words rather than to the reality. For instance, if Greer says that a certain attorney is a "vulture," your perception of the attorney's behavior is not based on direct experience but on your perception of Greer's assessment. Yet that verbal assessment may influence you as much as a direct experience of the person in question.

4. *We use language to talk about language.* As a result of this self-reflexive aspect of language, we can discuss how we phrased a question and consider whether better phrasing would have resulted in a more precise question and thus a more informative answer. For instance, another person listening to Greer's analysis might say, "Greer, the term *vulture* doesn't really describe that person accurately."

Collectively, we use language to create, maintain, and alter our environments. Yet language can be thought of as a two-edged sword: The functions it performs carry a price in the rich possibilities for misunderstanding. To see how misunderstandings arise, we need to consider how language communicates meaning.

LANGUAGE AND MEANING

On the surface, the relationship between language and meaning seems perfectly clear: We select the correct word, and people will interpret our meanings correctly. In fact, the relationship between language and meaning is not nearly so simple. Why? For two reasons: The use of language is creative, and language must be learned. When we speak, we use language to create new sentences that represent our meaning. Although on occasion we repeat other people's constructions to represent what we are thinking or feeling, most of our speech differs significantly from everyone else's. Language creativity is especially noticeable in children. When children don't know the common designation for a thought, they create one out of the context. For instance, children may refer to restaurants as "meal stores" or to sirens as "scary whistles." But all of us create different ways of expressing shared experiences. To illustrate this idea, have three people who witnessed the same event describe what they saw. Although there will be many similarities, each description will reflect unique, creative approaches to the details.

Moreover, each generation within a culture must learn its language anew. But members of each generation may learn only a portion of the meanings of the previous generation. In addition, they are likely to create new or different meanings for the words they learn. For instance, the third edition of the *American Heritage Dictionary* contains 10,000 new words and usages such as *mediagenic* (attractive and appealing to viewers and readers of the news media) and *hip hop* (street subculture language including rap).[3] And as examples of our constantly giving new meanings to old words, in some parts of the country *stupid* means "cool," as in "That's a really stupid shirt"; *played* means "no longer relevant or rewarding," as in "This party is played, let's split"; and *dap* means "compliment," as in "We got lots of daps at the office today."[4]

Why do these changes occur? Language is arbitrary. We give meaning to the sounds that represent words and change the uses of words. Of course, meanings don't become a part of our "dictionary" until enough people in a language community accept the meaning. Thus, for every one of the last ten years, some one hundred thousand new words and changes in meanings have been noted, but the compilers of the *American Heritage Dictionary* believed that only 10,000 of them had gained enough support to become a recognized part of the language.

Changes also occur because of the need to reflect and create perceptions. If we encounter a situation that no word in our vocabulary can describe, we are likely either to form a new word or to use an old word in a new way to describe it. Likewise, if we see an object that is different from any object we have a word for, we choose a new word to label it. Speakers of English in the 1940s would have no idea what the term *couch potato* means. Only recently has the perception of people who are chronic television viewers been rendered into language with this addition to modern dictionaries.

Complications in Using Words: Denotation and Connotation

What is the meaning of a given word that a person used in his or her conversation? You may think that's a straightforward question—the meaning is the dictionary definition. In fact, words have at least two kinds of meaning that communicators need to know about: words not only have a "naming" function (denotation) but also convey emotional overtones (connotation). Often these overtones play a significant role in communication. Let's consider both the denotation and connotation of words.

DENOTATION

Denotation is the direct, explicit meaning people give to a word; in short, denotation is the meaning given in a dictionary. But even denotation is a more complex concept than we may think. Many words are defined differently in various dictionaries, have multiple meanings, and can change meaning; furthermore, the meaning of a word can be influenced by its context.

For example, no two dictionaries are going to give exactly the same meaning for an abstract word like *justice;* moreover, most words, and especially the words we use most often, have more than one distinct meaning. In addition, words change in meaning over time. Take the word *gay.* In the 1950s, *gay* meant joyous, merry, happy, or bright. Today, of course, *gay* generally refers to a homosexual person. If you describe another person as gay and you mean happy or joyous, you are likely to be misunderstood.

Context has perhaps the most important effect on the denotation of a word. The position of a word in a sentence and the other words around it are likely to change the denotation. Think of the difference communicated between "Bryce plays a really mean drum" and "The way Bryce talked to Rhoda was downright mean." Or suppose a man says to a woman, "Let's get together." The context of their relationship will affect what "get together" means. If the context isn't properly understood, the wording may lead to a real misunderstanding.

CONNOTATION

Whereas denotation refers to the standard dictionary meaning given to a word, connotation refers to the feelings or evaluations associated with a word. And although word denotation affects meaning and may create misunderstanding, sensitivity to word connotation may be even more important.

● Connotation refers to the feelings or evaluations associated with a word. What connotation would this child appear to have for *dog?*

C. K. Ogden and I. A. Richards were among the first scholars to consider the misunderstandings resulting from the failure of communicators to realize that their subjective reactions to words will be a product of their life experiences.[5] For instance, the meaning of Carla's simple statement to her husband, Esteban, "Uncle Alonzo wants to give our son a dog for a birthday present," depends far more on the sender's and receiver's experiences with dogs than it does on the dictionary definition of a dog as "a highly variable carnivorous domesticated mammal, probably descended from the common wolf." If Carla defines *dog* as a warm cuddly creature that's fun to have around and Esteban defines *dog* as a nasty animal that leaves messes to be cleaned up and presents danger to anyone crossing its path, they will have conflicting reactions to this potential gift. Similarly, when Melissa whispers to Trisha, "Jane had an abortion last week," Trisha's reaction to the news depends far more on her connotation of the word *abortion* than on its denotation.

What is the value to you of this kind of knowledge in your verbal communication? Suppose you are talking with people about problems such as crime, teenage pregnancies, drugs, AIDS, and welfare. You will need to be very careful how you use words such as *liberal, conservative, police officer, taxes, homeless, gay rights,* and *obscenity,* to name but a few. You may recall that in the 1992 presidential campaign, Bill Clinton had to work very hard to defuse George Bush's accusation that he was a typical "liberal." There is nothing inherently wrong with being either liberal or conservative—both words denote credible political positions. But by making an issue of the "L" word, Bush sought to capitalize on negative connotations such as "free spending" and "soft on crime" that had worked so well in his campaign against Michael Dukakis four years earlier.

PRACTICE IN

Denotation and Connotation

BY YOURSELF

1. Compile a list of current slang or "in" words. Discuss how the meanings you assign to these words differ from the meanings your parents or grandparents assign to them (for example, "He's bad!").

2. Write your own definition of each of the following words; then consult a dictionary and check how closely your definition matches the dictionary's.

building	justice	love	ring	success
band	glass	peace	freedom	honor

IN GROUPS

1. Working in groups, select several common nouns, such as *college* and *industry*. Each person should list at least five adjectives that he or she associates with the word. When you have finished, compare the results. In what ways are your meanings (the connotations the words have for you) different?

2. Stage an event for the class, such as a person coming into class during the professor's lecture to check whether the window shades are working correctly. At the end of the event, send three people into the hall. Then call in each individually to describe the event. Afterward, discuss the creativity in language shown by the three observers.

Speaking Clearly

Clarity is basic to effective communication. We want to choose our language with care to improve the chances that the messages we intend to send are the messages that our listeners receive. Unclear language gives a listener such a range of possible meaning to choose from that shared meaning may be impossible. Furthermore, unclear language runs the risk of frustrating the listener and arousing unintended emotional reactions.

You can clarify your language by selecting precise, specific, and concrete words and by dating and indexing generalizations.

PRECISION

Selecting the most precise word means selecting the word that most accurately expresses your meaning. Too often—especially in our interpersonal communication—we tend to get sloppy. We use a word that isn't quite right, hoping our listeners will understand the point anyway. Suppose that in a discussion with co-workers on budgetary problems in your organization you say, "The problem lies with our inventory." *Inventory* is a very precise word that means "any idle resource that is waiting to be used." If the problem in fact is a matter of product marketing or sales strategies, *inventory* fails to convey the meaning intended.

Precision is especially important when you are trying to communicate a specific shade of meaning. Suppose you want to make a point about a politician defending her principal adviser, who was accused of mishandling campaign funds. Notice the changes in the meaning of the sentence "What she's trying to get is a complete acquittal" if, instead of *acquittal,* you use *vindication* or *whitewashing.* Or notice the changes in the meaning of the sentence "Quentin said that we need a new approach to the problem" if, instead of *said,* you use *hinted, indicated, suggested, insisted,* or *shouted.* Notice, too, the subtle shifts in meaning if you substitute a more precise word for *new,* such as *revised, fresh,* or *innovative.*

SPECIFICITY AND CONCRETENESS

Whereas speaking precisely means selecting words that give the most accurate image, speaking specifically and concretely means selecting words that put that image in sharp focus. Specific words indicate a single item within a category; concrete words give a single representation of an abstract concept or value. Often the first words that come to mind when we speak are general and abstract, thereby forcing the listener to choose from many possible images rather than picturing a single focused image. The more listeners are called on to provide their own images, the more they will see meanings different from what we intend. For instance, if Nevah says that Ruben is a "blue-collar worker," you may picture an unlimited number of occupations that fall within this broad category. If, instead, she says he is a "construction worker," the number of possible images you can picture is reduced. And if she says "a bulldozer operator," your image snaps into focus.

The terms *general* and *specific* refer to categories, and the terms *abstract* and *concrete* refer to ideas or values. Concrete language turns an abstract idea or value into one that appeals to our senses—it not only conveys information but also helps us to form mental pictures. Sometimes you can make the image more concrete with a better word. Thus, whereas the word *talk* is abstract, *rant* is concrete, for it brings to mind a type of talk that we can visualize. At other times you can make the image more concrete by adding an example. When Linda says, "Rashad is very loyal," the meaning of *loyal* (faithful to an idea, person, company, and so on) may be fuzzy to the listener; to avoid ambiguity and confusion, Linda might add, "He never criticizes a friend behind her back." By expressing the concept of loyalty with a concrete example, her listeners would be more apt to understand what she meant.

Semanticists speak of levels of abstraction. In many instances, you can take an idea from a general, abstract level and move it to a specific, concrete level through a series of words. For example, in talking about workers, we could write down a sequence that moved from the general term *worker* to *blue-collar worker* to *construction worker* to *construction vehicle operator* to *bulldozer operator* (see also Figure 3.1 for another example).

Clarifying our language often requires using both more precise and more specific and concrete words. Suppose you were reporting the graduation rate of athletes to a community group. You might say, "At our school, some athletes are graduating about on time, but a whole lot of them aren't." In this context, "some athletes," "about on time," and "a whole lot" are neither precise nor specific. The range of what people might understand by "some," "about," and "a whole lot" is too wide. See how much clearer the sentence would be if you said, "At State University, roughly 60 percent of athletes on scholarship graduate within five years of the time they started. The problem is that in such 'revenue' sports as football and men's basketball, the number

Art
Painting
Oil painting
Impressionist oil painting
Renoir's *La Promenade*

Figure 3.1

Levels of abstraction

Basic Communication Skills

SKILL	USE	PROCEDURE	EXAMPLE
Precision Choosing words that are recognized by others in our culture as symbolizing those thoughts and feelings.	To increase the probability of the receiver's decoding the message accurately.	1. Assess whether the word or phrase used is less precise than it should be. 2. Pause to mentally brainstorm alternatives. 3. Select a more precise word.	"Bill, would you go get my watch off the [thinks hutch, mentally corrects] buffet?"
Specific, Concrete Words Using words that indicate a single item within a category or a single representation of an abstract concept or value.	To help the listener picture thoughts analogous to the speaker's.	1. Assess whether the word or phrase used is less specific than it should be. 2. Pause to mentally brainstorm alternative choices. 3. Select a more specific word.	Instead of saying, "Bring the stuff for the audit," say, "Bring the records and receipts from the last year for the audit."

drops to under 30 percent." As this example shows, being precise and specific can involve doing research to nail down exact facts and figures.

Are precision and specificity/concreteness a necessity in every conversation? Perhaps not. When you and a friend engage in informal, "for the fun of it" interaction, the need for high degrees of clarity may be less. But when you are in, say, a conflict situation where the other person may be looking for anything to fight about, or in an encounter with your supervisor on the job, the need for precise, specific, concrete language is great. Because you are likely to need to speak more clearly in many contexts, why not use clear language in all situations so that you are more likely to be clear when it really matters?

IMPROVING PRECISION AND SPECIFICITY/CONCRETENESS

Two ways to learn to speak more precisely and specifically are (1) building your working vocabulary and (2) practicing a structured brainstorming model.

● ● **Vocabulary Building** How clearly we speak, and therefore how well we will be understood, depends on our vocabulary. In general, the smaller our vocabulary, the greater the potential difficulty in communicating effectively. As a speaker, a meager vocabulary gives you fewer choices from which to select the word you want; as a listener, you are limited in your ability to understand the words used. Thus, the richer your vocabulary, the more accurate your communication is likely to be. Although precise, specific wording does not ensure effective communication (the person to whom you are speaking may not have mastery of a particular word, or other contextual factors may interfere), you are more likely to communicate effectively if your choice is precise and specific.

One way to increase your vocabulary is to use a basic vocabulary book such as *Word Smart,* by Adam Robinson and the staff of the *Princeton Review,* which was designed for SAT and GRE preparation.[6] Or you could complete the "Word Power" feature in the *Reader's Digest* magazine, a monthly quiz that could increase your vocabulary by as many as twenty words per month.

A second way to increase your vocabulary is to take a more active role in working with the words you read and hear every day. You can begin by noting words that people use in their conversations with you that you cannot define precisely. For instance, suppose Jack says, "I was inundated with phone calls today." If you can't define *inundated,* you could ask Jack what he meant. Or you could make a note of the word, look up its meaning at the first opportunity, and review what Jack said to see whether the dictionary meaning matched Jack's statement. Most dictionaries define *inundated* with synonyms like *overwhelmed* or *flooded.* If you then say to yourself, "Jack was inundated—overwhelmed or flooded—with phone calls today," you will tend to remember that meaning and apply it the next time you hear the word. You can follow the same procedure in your reading. As you read today's assignment in one of your courses, circle any words whose meanings you are unsure of. After you have finished the assignment, look them up. If you follow this practice faithfully, you will soon increase your vocabulary noticeably.

Although a person with a relatively small vocabulary can communicate most ideas clearly (of the 150,000 words in *Webster's Ninth New Collegiate Dictionary,* some 5,000 of them make up 98 percent of the words in most books we read),[7] a person with a 50,000- to 60,000-word vocabulary has many more choices of words with which to frame complex ideas and communicate shades of meaning more sharply.

Structured Brainstorming A second way to develop clarity in speaking is to consciously use structured brainstorming during practice sessions. Brainstorming is an uncritical, nonevaluative process of generating ideas, much like the old word-association process. Thus when you are trying to think of more precise or more specific and concrete words for music, you might brainstorm *classical, nostalgic, big band, rock, heavy metal,* and *new age.*

You can increase your precision, specificity, and concreteness in the following ways: (1) As you talk, quickly assess whether a word or phrase you used is less precise or less specific and concrete than it should be. (2) Pause to mentally brainstorm alternative choices. (3) Select the most precise or most specific and concrete word.

For example, if you are talking about preregistration, you might think, "Preregistration is bad." At this point stop and ask yourself, What words would be more precise than *bad*? Perhaps *painful, frustrating,* and *demeaning.* Then restate the sentence: "Preregistration is frustrating." Or suppose you are talking about a game. You might consider saying, "The game was really sloppy." Stop. What words would be more specific than *game*? *Offense? Defense? Passing*? Then restate the sentence: "The passing was really sloppy."

Improvement of language skills requires hard work, and the brainstorming process should only be done consciously in practice, at least initially. As you gain skill with the process, you may find that you can make such adjustments in everyday conversation. For instance, in your conversation, you might state ideas in the following ways:

"I think that many of the boss's statements are very [split-second pause while thinking: I want the word that means 'know-it-all'] dogmatic."

"To move these things, we'll need a van—I'm sorry, I don't mean van, I mean one of those extra-large station wagons."

"Mike was a jerk yesterday—well, I guess I mean he was inconsiderate."

"I agree that Pauline is a tough manager, but I think she's a good one because she is fair—she treats everyone exactly alike."

When we are relaxed and confident, our word choice usually flows smoothly and is likely to be most effective. When we are under pressure, however, our ability to select the best symbols to convey our thoughts is likely to deteriorate. For example, in a large family, you may have heard harried parents verbally list all of their children's names before finally calling the child they want by the right name.

The human brain, like a computer, is a marvelous storage and retrieval system, but like a computer, it functions better under certain conditions. More often than not, our brains fail when we are under pressure or when we speak before we think. People sometimes think one thing and say something entirely different. For example, a math professor might say, "We all remember that the numerator is on the bottom and the denominator is on the top of the fraction, so when we divide fractions. . . ." "Professor," a voice from the third row interrupts, "You said the numerator is on the bottom and. . . ." "Is that what I said?" the professor replies. "Well, you know what I meant." Did everyone in the class know? Maybe not.

You will know that you have made strides in improving precision, specificity, and concreteness when you find that your language is precise and specific even under pressure.

DATING GENERALIZATIONS

To *date generalizations* means to specify a time referent that indicates when a given fact was true or known to be true. We draw conclusions based on information. If the information is inaccurate, the conclusions drawn from that information are likely to be inaccurate as well. A common source of inaccuracy is the presentation of information as if it were current when in fact it may be outdated. For instance, Parker says, "I'm going to be transferred to Henderson City." Yoshi replies, "Good luck—they've had some real trouble with their schools." On the basis of Yoshi's statement, Parker may worry about the effect that his move will have on his children. What he doesn't know is that Yoshi's information about the problem in Henderson City is five years old; Henderson City still may have problems, but it may not. Had Yoshi replied, "I know they had some real trouble with their schools five years ago. I'm not sure what the situation is now, but you may want to check," Parker would look at the information differently.

Nearly everything changes with time. Some changes are imperceptible; others are so extensive as to make old information inaccurate, obsolete, and even dangerous. To date your generalizations, (1) consider when you knew the information about an object, a person, or a place to be true, and (2) if your statement is not based on current information, be sure to include a reference to when you knew the information was valid.

Consider each of the following examples. Those on the left contain undated generalizations, and those on the right contain dated generalizations.

Palm Springs is really popular with the college crowd.	When we were in Palm Springs *two years ago*, it was really popular with the college crowd.
Professor Powell brings great enthusiasm to her teaching.	Professor Powell brings great enthusiasm to her teaching—at least she did *last quarter* in communication theory.
The Beast is considered the most exciting roller coaster in the country.	*Five years ago*, the Beast was considered the most exciting roller coaster in the country.

You think Mary's depressed? I'm
surprised. She seemed her regular
high-spirited self when I talked
with her.

You think Mary's depressed? I'm
surprised. She seemed her regular
high-spirited self when I talked
with her *the day before yesterday.*

We have no power to prevent change. Yet we can increase the effectiveness of our messages through verbally acknowledging the reality of change if we date the statements we make.

INDEXING GENERALIZATIONS

Indexing is a companion skill to dating. Through dating, we acknowledge differences caused by the passing of time; indexing generalizations allows us to acknowledge the innate differences among groups of people, objects, or places. *Indexing* is the mental or verbal practice of accounting for individual differences that guards against the tendency to make unwarranted generalizations.

Generalizing allows people to use what they have learned from one experience and apply it to another. So, when Tiesha learns that tomatoes and squash grow better if the ground is fertilized, she reasons that fertilizing will help all of her vegetables grow better. Likewise, when Miguel notices that his girlfriend seems to enjoy the fragrance of the new aftershave he is wearing, he is likely to wear it again when they are together. Tiesha and Miguel have used what they learned from one experience and applied it to another—they have generalized.

You will recall from Chapter 2 that misuse of generalization—stereotyping—contributes to perceptual inaccuracies because it ignores individual differences. Thus, just because men have greater physical strength in general than do women does not mean that Max (one man) is stronger than Barbara (one woman). Likewise, just because Otto, a German, is industrious does not mean that all Germans are industrious or that Peter, who also is German, is industrious.

Now that we have considered the need to account for individual differences, let's see how the skill of indexing is used. Technically, indexing calls for acknowledging differences by mentally assigning numbers to each member of a class. So in the class of men, we have man_1, man_2, man_3, and so forth; in the class of Chevrolets, we have $Chevrolet_1$, $Chevrolet_2$, $Chevrolet_3$, and so forth. Of course, in real life, people don't index by number.

The process of indexing actual statements goes as follows: (1) Consider whether what you want to say is about a specific object, person, or place or whether it is a generalization about a class to which the object, person, or place belongs. (2) If what you want to say is a generalization, qualify it

Basic Communication Skills

SKILL	USE	PROCEDURE	EXAMPLE
Dating Generalizations			
Including a specific time referent that indicates when a fact was true.	To avoid the pitfalls of language that allow you to speak of a dynamic world in static terms.	1. Before you make a statement, consider when the observation was true. 2. If not based on present information, include when it was true.	When Jake says, "How good a hitter is Steve?" Mark replies by dating his evaluation: "When I worked with him two years ago, he couldn't hit the curve."
Indexing Generalizations			
Mentally or verbally accounting for individual differences.	To avoid "allness" in speaking.	1. Before you make a statement, consider whether it pertains to a specific object, person, or place. 2. If you use a generalization, inform the listener that it is not necessarily accurate.	"He's a politician and I don't trust him, although he may be different from most politicians I know."

appropriately so that your assertion does not go beyond the evidence that supports it.

Here are several statements that illustrate the process of indexing. Those on the left are generalizations, and those on the right are indexed examples.

Because men are stronger than women, Max is stronger than Barbara.	*In general,* men are stronger than women, so Max is probably stronger than Barbara.
State's got to have a good economics department; the university is ranked among the top twenty in the nation.	Because State's among the top twenty schools in the nation, the economics department should be a good one, *although it may be an exception.*
Claude is sure to be outgoing; Matthew is, and they're both Joneses.	Claude is likely to be outgoing because his brother Matthew is (they're both Joneses), *but Claude could be different.*
Your Chevrolet should go fifty thousand miles before you need a brake job; Jerry's did.	Your Chevrolet may well go fifty thousand miles before you need a brake job; Jerry's did, *but of course, all Chevrolets aren't the same.*

All people generalize at one time or another, but by indexing statements, we can avoid the problems that hasty generalization sometimes creates.

 ## Cultural Considerations

From a cultural standpoint, differences in verbal communication may be explained by what E. T. Hall described as low- and high-context communication.[8] According to Hall, a high-context communication message is one in which "most of the information is either in the physical context or internalized in the person, while very little is in the coded, explicit, transmitted part of the message." In contrast, a low-context communication message is one in which "the mass of information is vested in the explicit code."[9] Cultures of nations can be placed on a continuum between the two extremes. The culture of the United States is classified near the lower end, with cultures of the countries of Western Europe. Most Asian cultures fall toward the high-context end.[10]

What does this mean to students of communication? On a verbal communication dimension, members of low-context cultures tend to communicate in a direct fashion, whereas members of high-context cultures tend to communicate in an indirect fashion. Thus, people from Western, or low-context, cultures tend to favor precision in language, whereas people from Eastern, or high-context, cultures tend to favor ambiguities.[11] Typically, Asians are comfortable talking for hours without clearly expressing an opinion; they can be suspicious of direct verbal expressions of love and respect. Instead of expecting direct verbal expressions, those in high context cultures understand from context cues that love or respect is meant. In contrast, people from low-context cultures prize clear and direct communication. Their approach may be characterized by expressions such as "Say what you mean" and "Don't beat around the bush."[12]

Problems with clarity across cultures are at times humorous, for words that have one precise or specific meaning in one language or subculture may have an entirely different precise or specific meaning in another. For instance, Chevrolet created cross-cultural misunderstanding on a large scale when it marketed its Nova model in Latin America. Sales were terrible because Chevrolet didn't realize that Nova (*no va*) means "no go" in Spanish. Likewise, a student reported to his professor that he suffered some embarrassment in South Africa when, in response to his host's asking whether he would like more food, he replied, "I'm stuffed." He didn't know why his host thought the response humorous until his host told him that in his culture the expression "I'm stuffed" means "I'm pregnant."

People who speak different languages expect to have some problem communicating and thus seem to take extra care to keep that barrier from becoming insurmountable. Surprisingly, language becomes a greater barrier for two people from different cultures who are speaking the same language because they tend to believe they mean the same things when they use the same words. For example, if a person says that the government wants what is "best for the people," it would seem that others should have no difficulty understanding what is meant. Yet "best for the people" can and does mean many different things depending on one's politics, priorities, and so on. When someone from another culture uses a word and you perceive that word as particularly important to understanding, you might ask for concrete examples so that you can be sure of what the person means.

 ## Gender Considerations

Gender differences in language usage may also be explained by a basic difference in orientation. Edwin and Shirley Ardener argue that the language of the culture of the United States has an inherent male bias, meaning that men have created the meanings for the group. As a result, the feminine voice has been "muted."[13] This means that women tend to be less expressive in public situations than men and, more important, tend to monitor their own communications more intensely than men. In *Gender and Communication*, Pearson, Turner, and Todd-Mancillas summarize differences in language usage between men and women that seem consistent with the "muted group" theory.[14] Among those that seem to have the greatest support are the following:

Women tend to use both more intensifiers and more hedges than men. Intensifiers are words that intensify, or give strength to, the words being described. Thus women are likely to make far greater use of words such as *awfully, quite,* and *so.* Hedges soften or weaken meaning. Thus women are more likely to use words such as *somewhat, perhaps,* or *maybe.* Women tend to add tag questions to their sentences more than men. Tag questions are questions relating to the same statement that a person has just made, for instance, saying "That was a really powerful speech, wasn't it?" or "They all had the same tutor, didn't they?" Even though we all use tag questions at times when we are not certain or when we are trying to get more information, women tend to use far more than men, perhaps to appear less dogmatic in their communication.

Julia Wood sees these differences in language as representing contrasting views of the role of communication for women and men. For women, she

● A high-context communication message is one in which "most of the information is either in the physical context or internalized in the person, while very little is in the coded, explicit, transmitted part of the message."

says, "communication is a primary way to establish and maintain relationships with others"; for men, communication is used as a means of "exerting control, preserving independence, and enhancing status."[15] Yet specific language differences between men and women are not actually as different as the stereotypes of their language. For instance, men are perceived as using more sexual or profane language than women, when in reality few descriptive studies support this conclusion.[16] To the extent that men and women do differ in their use of language, both may profit by learning from the other's example.

Clarity

BY YOURSELF

1. For each word listed, try to find three words or phrases that are more specific or more concrete.

implements	building	nice	education
clothes	colors	chair	bad
happy	stuff	things	car

2. Make the following statements clearer by editing words that are not precise or not specific and concrete:

"You know I love basketball. Well, I'm practicing a lot because I want to get better."

"Paula, I'm really bummed out. Everything is going down the tubes. You know what I mean?"

"Well, she just does these things to tick me off. Like, just a whole lot of stuff—and she knows it!"

"I just bought a beautiful outfit—I mean, it is really in style. You'll love it."

"I've got to remember to bring my things the next time I visit."

IN GROUPS

Have two members of the group discuss one of the topics listed below. The rest of the group should observe when dating and indexing are used, how well they are being used, and when they should have been used. Each person in the group should have an opportunity to practice.

equal opportunity laws	politicians
food preferences	wedding rituals
job interviewers	minority groups in college
cars	college course requirements

Speaking Appropriately

The last few years have seen a growing controversy over "political correctness," especially on college campuses. Although several issues germane to the debate on political correctness go beyond the scope of this chapter, at the heart of this controversy is the question of what language behaviors are appropriate—and what language behaviors are inappropriate. *Speaking appropriately* means using language that adapts to the needs, interests, knowledge, and attitudes of the listener and avoiding language that alienates. Appropriate language has the positive value of cementing the bond of trust between the parties in a communication transaction. When people like and trust you, they are apt to believe you. The more hostile people are to you and your ideas, the more care you need to take to use language that is sensitive to their needs. Yet, under strain, or in your eagerness to make a point, you may sometimes say things you do not really mean or express feelings that are unlikely to be accepted by strangers. If you do that, you may lose all that you have gained. In this section we look specifically at appropriate and inappropriate language.

FORMAL VERSUS INFORMAL LANGUAGE

Language is appropriate when it is neither too formal nor too informal for the situation. In Chapter 1 we discussed the communication rules that guide our communication behavior. One of those rules is to adapt language to the specific person or group to which we are speaking. Thus, in an interpersonal setting, we are likely to use more informal language when we are talking with our best friend and more formal language when we are talking with our parents. In a group setting, we are likely to use more informal language when we are talking with a group of our peers and more formal language when we are talking with a group of managers. In each of these situations, the differences in our language are appropriate.

FREEDOM FROM JARGON AND UNNECESSARY TECHNICAL EXPRESSIONS

Language is appropriate when it is free of jargon and unnecessary technical expressions. Many of us become so immersed in our work or hobbies that we forget that people not in our line of work or not interested in our hobbies cannot understand language that seems a natural part of our own daily communication. For instance, when a computer whiz converses with a computer-illiterate friend about computers, the whiz wants to carry on about RAM, bits, bytes, and other technical jargon. But unless the whiz can learn to express ideas in language that his friend understands, little communication will take place. In short, anytime you talk with people outside your specific work or hobby area, you need to carefully explain, if not abandon, the technical jargon and speak in language recognizable to the person with whom you are talking.

SENSITIVITY

Language is appropriate when it is sensitive to usages that others perceive as offensive. Some of our mistakes in language result from using expressions that are perceived as sexist, racist, or otherwise biased—that is, any language that is perceived as belittling any person or group of people by virtue of their sex, race, age, handicap, or other identifying characteristic. Two of the most prevalent linguistic uses that communicate an insensitivity are generic language and nonparallel language.

● Marking means adding sex, race, age, or other designations unnecessarily to a general word. If we described Julie Krone as a female jockey, we would be marking.

● ● **Generic Language** Generic language is a problem because it excludes a group of people, grammatically or connotatively, on the basis of sex, race, or other characteristics. Let's consider some examples.

1. Generic *he*. Traditionally, English grammar called for the use of the masculine pronoun *he* to stand for the entire class of humans regardless of sex. So, in the past, standard English called for usage such as "When a person shops, he should have a clear idea of what he wants to buy." Even though such a statement is grammatically correct, it is now considered sexist because it inherently excludes females. Despite traditional usage, it would be hard to maintain that we picture people of both sexes when we hear the word *he*.

Guideline: Do not construct sentences that use only male pronouns when no sexual reference is intended. You can often avoid this in one of two ways: (1) Use plurals. For instance, instead of saying, "Since a doctor has high status, his views may be believed regardless of the topic," you could say, "Since doctors have high status, their views may be believed regardless of the topic." (2) Use both the male and female pronouns. For instance, "Since a doctor has high status, his or her views may be believed regardless of the topic." These changes may seem small, but they may make the difference between alienating or not alienating the people with whom you are speaking.

2. Generic *man.* A second problem results from the traditional reliance on the use of the generic *man.* Many words that have become a common part of our language are inherently sexist because they seem to apply to only one gender. Consider the term *man-made.* It means that a product was produced by human beings, but its underlying connotation is that a male human being made the item. Using such terms when speaking about all human beings is troubling, but using them to describe the behavior or accomplishments of women (as in the sentence "Sally is particularly proud of her pies because they are totally man-made") is ludicrous.

Guideline: Avoid using words that carry built-in sexism, such as *policeman, postman, chairman, man-made,* and *mankind.* For most expressions of this kind, you can use or create suitable alternatives. For instance, for the first three examples, you can use *police officer, mail carrier,* and *chairperson.* For *man-made* and *mankind,* you can change the constructions. Instead of "All of mankind benefits," you might say "All the people in the world benefit." Instead of "The products are man-made," you might say "The products are made entirely by hand" (or by people or by human beings).

Nonparallel Language Because it treats groups of people differently, nonparallel language is also belittling. Marking and unnecessary association are two common forms of nonparallelism.

1. *Marking.* Marking means adding sex, race, age, or other designations unnecessarily to a general word. For instance, the word *doctors* represents all people with medical degrees. To describe Jones as a doctor is to treat Jones linguistically as a member of the class of doctors. For example, you might say, "Jones, a doctor, contributed a great deal to the campaign." If, however, you said, "Jones, a woman doctor" (or an African-American doctor, or an old doctor, or a handicapped doctor), you would be marking. By marking, you may be perceived as trivializing the person's role by emphasizing an irrelevant characteristic. If you say, "Jones is a really good female doctor" (or African-American doctor, or old doctor, or handicapped doctor), you may be intending to praise Jones. In reality, your listeners can interpret the sentence as saying that Jones is a good doctor for a woman (or an African-American, or an old person, or a handicapped person) but not necessarily as good as a male doctor (or a white, young, or unhandicapped doctor).

Guideline: Avoid markers. If it is relevant to identify a person by sex, race, age, and so on, do so, but leave such markers out of your labeling when they are irrelevant. One test of whether a characteristic is relevant and appropriate is whether you would mention the person's sex, race, or age (and so on) regardless of what sex, race, or age the person happens to be. It is relevant to specify "female doctor," for example, only if in that context it would be

Basic Communication Skills

SKILL	USE	PROCEDURE	EXAMPLE
Appropriateness Using language that adapts to a specific person or persons and the context of the conversation.	To increase interaction effectiveness.	1. Assess whether the word or phrase used is less appropriate than it should be. 2. Pause to mentally brainstorm alternatives. 3. Select a more appropriate word.	When talking to a minister, Jamie thinks, "I just feel so bummed out," but says, "I just feel so depressed lately."

equally relevant to specify "male doctor." In general, leave sex, race, age, and other markers out of your labeling.

2. *Unnecessary association.* Another form of nonparallelism is to emphasize one person's association with another when you are not talking about the other person. Often you will hear a speaker say something like "Gladys Thompson, whose husband is CEO of Acme Inc., is the chairperson for this year's United Way campaign." In response to this sentence, you might say that the association of Gladys Thompson with her husband gives further credentials to Gladys Thompson. But using the association may be seen to imply that Gladys Thompson is important not because of her own accomplishment but because of her husband's. The following illustrates a more flagrant example of unnecessary association: "Dorothy Jones, the award-winning principal at Central High School, and wife of Bill Jones, a local contractor, is chairperson for this year's Minority Scholarship campaign." Here Bill Jones's occupation and relationship to Dorothy Jones are clearly irrelevant. In either case the pairing takes away from the person who is supposed to be the focus.

Guideline: Avoid associating a person irrelevantly with others. If the person has done or said something noteworthy, you should recognize it without making unnecessary associations.

Very few people can escape all unfair language. By monitoring your usage, however, you can guard against frustrating your attempts to communicate by assuming that others will react to your language the same way you do, and you can guard against saying or doing things that offend others and perpetuate outdated sex roles, racial stereotypes, and other biased language.

How can you speak more appropriately? (1) Assess whether the word or phrase used is less appropriate than it should be, (2) pause to mentally brainstorm alternatives, and (3) select a more appropriate word.

EFFECT OF INSENSITIVE LANGUAGE

You have heard children shout, "Sticks and stones may break my bones, but words will never hurt me." This saying may be popular among children because they know it is a lie, but it gives them a defense against cruel name-calling. Whether or not we admit it, words do hurt—sometimes permanently. Think of the great personal damage done to individuals throughout history as a result of being called "hillbilly," "nigger," "fag," or "yid." Think of the fights started by one person calling another's sister or girlfriend a "whore." Of course, we all know that it is not the words alone that are so powerful; it is the context of the words—the situation, the feelings of the participants, the time, the place, or the tone of voice. You may recall circumstances in which a friend called you a name or used a four-letter word to describe you and you did not even flinch; you may also recall other circumstances in which someone else made you furious by calling you something far less offensive.

We should always be aware that our language has repercussions. When we do not understand or are not sensitive to our listeners' frame of reference, we may state our ideas in language that distorts the intended communication. Many times a single inappropriate sentence may be enough to ruin an entire interaction. For example, if you say, "And we all know the problem originates downtown," you may be alluding to the city government. However, if the listeners associate downtown not with the seat of government but with the residential area of an ethnic or social group, the sentence will have an entirely different meaning to them. Being specific will help you to avoid such problems; recognizing that some words communicate far more than their dictionary meanings will help even more.

PRACTICE IN

Appropriateness

BY YOURSELF
Develop nonsexist alternatives to the following:

firemen	foreman	serviceman	brakeman
airman	stewardess	craftsman	repairman
councilman	doorman	night watchman	anchorman
coed	waitress	bellman	

IN GROUPS
Have group members share incidents in which the bias in another person's language was offensive. How might that language have been amended to prevent the offense?

JOURNAL ENTRY

Tape-record at least ten minutes of a conversation you have with a friend or a family member. Talk about a subject that you hold strong views about: affirmative action, welfare, school levies, candidates for office. Be sure to get the permission of the other person before you tape. At first you may feel self-conscious about having a recorder going. But as your discussion progresses, you will probably be able to converse normally.

Play back the tape and take notes of sections where your language might have been clearer. Using these notes, write better expressions of your ideas for each section you noted by using more precise and specific/concrete language and by dating and indexing generalizations.

Replay the tape. This time take notes on any racist, sexist, or biased expressions that you used. Using these notes, write more appropriate expressions to replace the ones you used.

Write a paragraph or two that describes what you have learned about your use of language from this experience.

●◆■ Summary

Language is a system of symbols used for communicating. Through language we designate, label, and define; evaluate; talk about things outside our immediate experience; and talk about language itself.

You will be a more effective communicator if you recognize that language symbols are arbitrary, that language is learned and is creative, and that language and perception are interrelated.

The denotation of a word is its dictionary meaning. Despite the ease with which we can check a dictionary meaning, word denotation can still present problems because most words have more than one dictionary meaning, changes in meanings occur faster than dictionaries are revised, words take on different meanings as they are used in different contexts, and meanings can become obscured as words become more abstract.

The connotation of a word is the emotional and value significance the word has for the listener. Regardless of how a dictionary defines a word, we carry with us meanings that stem from our experience with the object, thought, or action the word represents.

You can improve your clarity of language by selecting the most precise and the most specific and concrete word possible and by dating and indexing generalizations.

Speaking appropriately means using language that adapts to the needs, interests, knowledge, and attitudes of the listener and avoiding language that alienates. Inappropriate language can be minimized by avoiding exclusionary usages such as the generic *he* and the generic *man* and by eliminating non-parallel usages such as marking and unnecessary association.

● ◆ ■ Communication Improvement Goal Statement

If you believe you need to improve your use of dating generalization, indexing generalizations, precision, specificity, or appropriateness, write a communication improvement goal statement following the guidelines on pages 31–33 of Chapter 1.

● ◆ ■ Featured Reading

Strictly Speaking: Will America Be the Death of English?
Edwin Newman
(New York: Warner Books, 1974)

Nearly twenty years ago, Edwin Newman, the noted author and NBC commentator, wrote his book analyzing what he perceived as the decline of language in the United States. He argued not only that eloquence has departed but that simple direct speech has given way to pomposity and banality. Implied in his analysis was that unclear language is often a sign of unclear thinking. Although these criticisms are twenty years old, they are still relevant today.

Newman argues that language sets the tone for a society. He says that since we must speak and read, we should be able to get some pleasure and inspiration from these activities. The colorful phrase, the flight of fancy, as well as the accurate description of a place or an event and the precise formulation of an idea, all brighten the world. Moreover, he argues that since nothing is more important to a society than the language it uses, society would be better off if we spoke and wrote with exactness and grace.

Although his message is an important one, the real joy of the book is in the countless true-to-life examples of unclear, deceitful, and much of the time ridiculous phrasings that have become part and parcel of language usage in government, education, and business. Some of the situations he refers to are no longer topical, but countless language examples he cites, such as "Back to square one," "That's the name of the game," "Back to the drawing board," are still heard in today's commercials, government briefings, business explanations, and academic announcements. In short, this is an extremely humorous book about a serious topic.

●◆■ **Notes**

1. Julia T. Wood, *Gendered Lives: Communication, Gender, and Culture* (Belmont, Calif.: Wadsworth, 1994), p. 129.

2. I. A. Richards, *The Philosophy of Rhetoric* (New York: Oxford University Press, 1965), p. 3.

3. *The American Heritage Dictionary*, 3rd ed. (Boston: Houghton Mifflin, 1992).

4. "Buzzwords," *Newsweek*, August 26, 1991, p. 6.

5. C. K. Ogden and I. A. Richards, *The Meaning of Meaning* (London: Kegan, Paul, Trench, Trubner, 1923).

6. Adam Robinson and the staff of the *Princeton Review, Word Smart* (New York: Villard Books, 1993).

7. I. S. P. Nation, *Teaching and Learning Vocabulary* (New York: Newbury House, 1990), p. 16.

8. E. T. Hall, *Beyond Culture* (New York: Doubleday, 1976).

9. Ibid., p. 91.

10. William B. Gudykunst and Young Yun Kim, *Communicating with Strangers: An Approach to Intercultural Communication*, 2nd ed. (New York: McGraw-Hill, 1992), pp. 44–45.

11. Ibid., p. 158.

12. Donald Levine, *The Flight from Ambiguity* (Chicago: University of Chicago Press, 1985), p. 28.

13. For a more complete explanation of muted group theory, see Stephen Littlejohn, *Theories of Human Communication*, 4th ed. (Belmont, Calif.: Wadsworth, 1992), pp. 241–243.

14. Judy Cornelia Pearson, Lynn H. Turner, and William Todd-Mancillas, *Gender and Communication*, 2nd ed. (Dubuque, Iowa: Wm. C. Brown, 1991), pp. 106–121.

15. Wood, pp. 141, 143.

16. Pearson, Turner, and Todd-Mancillas, p. 108.

CHAPTER FOUR

Nonverbal Communication

Nonverbal Communication

O B J E C T I V E S

After you have read this chapter, you should be able to define and/or explain:

Contrasts between verbal and nonverbal communication

Types of body motions

Five functions of nonverbal communication

Paralanguage and its major elements

How clothing, touching behavior, and use of time affect self-presentation

How the use of space communicates

Ways that temperature, lighting, and color affect communication

Ways of implementing your understanding of nonverbal communication

Cultural and gender considerations

Elisa moves forward smoothly on the tennis court to take the high, easy bounce and put the ball away. Instead of the super shot she anticipates, she hits the ball into the net. She groans and throws her racket on the ground in disgust.

As he picks up his fifth card in the hand of draw poker, Devon breaks into a wide smile. Quickly, he looks around the table to see whether anyone caught the smile,

and then he resumes his "poker face."

"No doubt about it, Maggie, you were terrific," Hillary says with a sarcastic sneer in her voice.

"Allison, listen," Jack said in a soft but firm tone of voice. Riveting his eyes on hers, he continued, "I need your support on this proposal. If you will stay with me, I know you'll see some things happening that you're really going to like."

In each of the four preceding examples you may have noticed how people used nonverbal communication in their messages. Although nonverbal communication usually accompanies verbal communication, we discuss it separately in order to stress the unique features of the nonverbal code.

In communication, as in so many matters, actions speak louder than words. Actions in the form of nonverbal communication elements are critical to the communication process and provide as much as 65 percent of the social meaning in interpersonal communication.[1] Moreover, how we are perceived as communicators is based in part on our ability to use nonverbal skills appropriately.

In this chapter we provide a framework for analyzing and improving nonverbal communication. We begin by studying the nature of nonverbal communication and the way verbal and nonverbal communication interrelate. We then look at the major elements of nonverbal communication: body motions, paralanguage, self-presentation, and management of the environment. We conclude with a section on implementing nonverbal communication.

The Nature of Nonverbal Communication

Nonverbal communication includes both bodily motions and sounds of voice that are used intentionally with regularity by a social community.[2] It also includes how clothing, furniture, lighting, temperature, and color may affect the meaning of communication that takes place.

Before considering these, let's see how nonverbal communication differs from verbal communication. Nonverbal communication is more ambiguous, is continuous, is multichanneled, offers more insight into emotional states, and is culturally determined.

Nonverbal Communication Is More Ambiguous. Nonverbal communication is ambiguous in part because nonverbal cues may be sent either intentionally or unintentionally and in part because the same behaviors can represent many different messages. For example, a person who smiles may intend to communicate a sense of friendliness. When a receiver interprets the smile as friendly, communication has taken place. But a smile can mean many other things; it can serve as a cover-up for nervousness, for example. At other times a smile may have no communication intent—it may be a response to a random thought about something pleasant that happened earlier in the day. Nevertheless, other people will try to decode the smile and assign meaning to it.

Nonverbal Communication Is Continuous. Verbal symbols begin when sound comes from the mouth and end when that sound stops. In contrast, nonverbal communication continues for as long as people are in one another's presence. For instance, suppose Rodriguez steps into Baker's office and asks, "Have you received the new bid from our paper supplier yet?" From the moment he enters the office, Rodriguez is communicating. He may rush in or stroll in casually, he may relax in a chair or loom over Baker's desk, he may have a soft or a cutting tone to his voice. When he hears

● Whereas words do not necessarily communicate the depth of a person's feelings, nonverbal reactions do. When something strikes you as funny, you may smile slightly or laugh loudly depending on how amused you feel.

the response, he may smile or frown. All these nonverbal behaviors affect the meaning conveyed by the words of his question.

Nonverbal Communication Is Multichanneled. Words come to us one at a time, in a single channel; we hear spoken words, we see printed or written words. Nonverbal cues, however, may be seen, heard, felt, smelled, or tasted, and several of these cues may occur simultaneously. For instance, if you tell a friend, "I'll go to bat for you," the meaning your friend receives depends on the language and your tone of voice, your facial expressions, and your gestures.

Nonverbal Communication Offers More Insight into Emotional States. Whereas words do not necessarily communicate the depth of a person's feelings, nonverbal reactions do. For instance, when you hear that a close friend has disclosed damaging personal information about you that you discussed in confidence, your body will show some nonverbal sign of pain even if you say, "It's nothing." When something strikes you as funny, you may smile slightly or laugh loudly, depending on how amused you feel. When you are sad, the corner of your mouth may twitch or your eyes might fill with tears even though your words do not convey sadness. As a result, when verbal and nonverbal reactions seem to be in conflict, people are likely to place more stock in nonverbal cues.

● ● **Meanings of Nonverbal Communication Are Culturally Determined.** Although people from around the world employ many of the same nonverbal cues, they use them differently. For instance, a smile may mean positive experience, it may mean enjoyment with contact, it may mean saving of face. At the same time, even though languages differ so much that people are unable to understand the words of a person speaking a foreign language, they may well be able to understand some of what the person is thinking or feeling through nonverbal cues. Although not all nonverbal signs carry the same meanings in every culture, there are many commonalities. For example, people from different cultures often share the same facial expressions for communicating emotions such as happiness, anger, fear, and surprise. In fact, in their review of research, Paul Ekman and H. Oster found "remarkable cross-cultural similarity in facial expressions and their interpretations."[3]

Now let us consider the nonverbal elements that comprise nonverbal communication. Later in the chapter we focus on specific ways that cultures may differ in their uses of these nonverbal elements.

Body Motions

Of all nonverbal behavior, you are probably most familiar with *kinesics,* the technical name for body motions. The major types of body motions are eye contact, facial expression, gesture, posture, and poise.

EYE CONTACT

Eye contact, also referred to as *gaze,* involves looking directly at the person or people with whom we are communicating. In addition to meeting psychological needs, we monitor the effect of our communication through eye contact. For instance, by maintaining eye contact with a person, you can tell when the person is paying attention to your words, when the person is involved in what you are saying, whether what you are saying is causing anxiety, and whether the person you are talking with has something to hide.

The amount of eye contact differs from person to person and from situation to situation. Studies show that people are likely to look at each other 50 to 60 percent of the time as they converse. For the talker, the average amount of eye contact is about 40 percent; for the listener, the average is nearer 70 percent.[4] We generally maintain better eye contact when we are discussing topics with which we are comfortable, when we are genuinely interested in a person's comments or reactions, or when we are trying to influence the other person. Conversely, we tend to avoid eye contact when we are discussing topics that make us uncomfortable; when we lack interest in the topic or person; or when we are embarrassed, ashamed, or trying to hide something. Of course, these are only tendencies; some individuals are skilled in using eye contact and other cues deceptively.

Because people often judge others by the degree of eye contact, you want to ensure that your eye contact behavior is perceived as appropriate. You may need to alter your behavior if you find that you maintain a less-than-normal amount of eye contact either when you are concerned about the person or topic of conversation, when you feel confident, or when you have no cause to feel shame or embarrassment.

FACIAL EXPRESSION

Facial expression involves the arrangement of facial muscles to communicate emotional states or reactions to messages. The three sets of muscles that we manipulate to form facial expressions are the brow and forehead; the eyes, eyelids, and root of the nose; and the cheeks, mouth, remainder of the nose, and chin.[5] Normally, our facial expressions mirror our thoughts or feelings. Paul Ekman and W. V. Friesen have discovered that across cultures people recognize those expressions conveying six basic emotions: happiness, sadness, surprise, fear, anger, and disgust.

GESTURE

Gestures are the movements of hands, arms, and fingers that we use to describe or to emphasize. Thus, when a person says, "about this high" or "nearly this round," we expect to see a gesture accompany the verbal description. Likewise, when a person says, "Put that down" or "Listen to me," a pointing finger, pounding fist, or some other gesture often reinforces the point. People do vary, however, in the amount of gesturing that accompanies their speech—some people "talk with their hands" far more than others.

POSTURE

Posture involves the positioning and movement of the body. Changes in posture can also communicate. For instance, suddenly sitting upright and leaning forward show intensity of attention, standing up may signal "I'm done now," and turning one's back shows a cutting off of attention.

SKILL	USE	PROCEDURE	EXAMPLE
Eye Contact Looking directly at people while you are talking with them.	To strengthen the sense of interaction.	1. Consciously look at the face of another while you are talking. 2. If your eyes drift away, try to bring them back.	[Not applicable]

POISE

Poise refers to assurance of manner. As much as 20 percent of the population experience high degrees of nervousness in encountering strangers, speaking in a group, and in public speaking settings.[6] Others may feel extremely comfortable when encountering strangers but get quite tense in another setting, such as speaking in a group or speaking in public. For most people, nervousness decreases as they gain confidence in their ability to function well in the particular setting. Mastery of the skills discussed in this text, for instance, should help you to cope with the nervousness you might face in different interpersonal communication situations.

IMPROVEMENT IN USE OF BODY MOTIONS

You can improve your use of body motions if you are willing to practice. Let's consider eye contact as an example. To begin your program of improvement, create a situation in which you are the speaker. As you talk, concentrate on looking at the source of your attention. You can even practice by holding "conversations" with objects in your room. For a minute, talk to your book, then shift your attention to your lamp, and, finally, talk to the window. Once you become conscious of maintaining eye contact with objects, you can continue to practice by having a close friend help you monitor the amount of your eye contact. For example, you might say to your friend, "As I'm telling you about the movie I saw, I'd like you to keep track of how much I look at you while I talk. When I'm done, tell me if you thought I looked at you 25 percent, 50 percent, 75 percent, or nearly all the time." The friend can also raise a hand when you are (or are not) maintaining eye contact, to make you aware of your gazing behavior. If you need to practice eye contact in the role of listener or receiver, have your friend tell you about something that happened; then ask how much you maintained eye contact while you were listening. Whether you are practicing improvement in eye contact, facial expression, gesture, posture, or poise, you can follow the same procedure.

THE USE OF BODY MOTIONS

An awareness of *how* we use body motions is crucial to your understanding of nonverbal communication. To the unobservant, all body motion may appear to be random movement; however, body movements serve important communication functions.[7]

1. *Nonverbal communication may be used to take the place of a word or phrase.* Just as we learn what words mean, so we learn what various signs and gestures mean. As coded by Ekman and Friesen, when nonverbal symbols take the place of a word or phrase, they are called *emblems*.[8] A contemporary North American dictionary of nonverbal emblems would include definitions such as "everything is go" for thumbs up; "peace" for the extension of the first and second finger in a V shape; "no" for shaking the head from side to side and "yes" for nodding; and "maybe," "I don't care," or "I don't know" for shrugging the shoulders.

In many contexts, emblems are used as a complete language. *Sign language* refers to systems of gestures that include sign languages of the deaf and

● **Complementary uses of nonverbal communication are called illustrators. One of the ways we use gestures is to emphasize.**

alternate sign languages used by Trappist monks in Europe and the women of Australia.[9]

2. *Nonverbal communication may be used to complement what a speaker is saying.* These complementary uses of nonverbal communication are called *illustrators.* We use gestures to illustrate in at least five ways: (1) to *emphasize* speech: A man may pound the table in front of him as he says, "Don't bug me"; (2) to show the *path* or *direction* of thought: A professor may move her hands on an imaginary continuum when she says, "The papers ranged from very good to very bad"; (3) to show *position:* A waiter may point when he says, "Take that table"; (4) to *describe*: People may use their hands to indicate size as they say, "The ball is about three inches in diameter"; and (5) to *mimic*: People may nod their heads as they say, "Did you see the way he nodded?"

At the same time, nonverbal communication can detract from a speaker's message if its use is inappropriate or calls attention to itself rather than adding to the speaker's meaning (think of a speaker who fidgets or paces unnecessarily while giving a speech).

3. *Nonverbal communication can augment the verbal expression of feelings.* Nonverbal behaviors that augment the verbal expression of feelings are called *affect displays.* If you drag yourself out of bed in the morning and stub your toe as you stumble to the bathroom, a grimace expressing pain is likely to accompany your verbal comment. (Do you have a favorite word for these occasions?) More often than not, these spur-of-the-moment displays are not intended as conscious communication. One reason for labeling such reactions as "displays" is that the reaction will take place automatically whether you are alone or whether someone else is present, and it will probably be quite noticeable.

People generally react through their body motions in one of four ways: (1) Sometimes people show less emotion with their body than they are really feeling. Dan, a baseball player, may refuse to rub the spot where he has been struck by a pitch, and Natasha may deliberately control her facial expression to play down the pain she feels when she learns that her niece is chemically dependent. (2) Sometimes people show more emotion with their bodies than they are really feeling. Thus nine-year-old Ken may howl and jump up and down when his brother happens to bump into him in the hall. (3) Sometimes people act as if nothing has happened regardless of how they are feeling. Eli may go about his business even though he just received news that his mother is in the hospital. (4) Sometimes people react in a manner totally different from what we would expect in the situation. For instance, Maria may smile when someone makes a cutting remark about her appearance. Because people differ in the way they display feelings, we need to be very careful about the conclusions we draw from nonverbal cues. It is very easy to be fooled.

4. *Nonverbal communication may be used to control or regulate the flow of a conversation or other communication transaction.* Nonverbal cues such as shifting eye contact, slight head movements, shifts in posture, raising of the eyebrows, and nodding of the head tell a person when to continue, to repeat, to elaborate, to hurry up, or to finish, and are called *regulators* because they control the flow of conversation. Good public speakers learn to adjust what they are saying and how they are saying it on the basis of such audience cues.

5. *Nonverbal communication may be used to relieve tension.* As we listen to people and watch them while they speak, they may scratch their head, tap their foot, or wring their hands. These unplanned releases of energy, called *adaptors,* serve to reduce the stress a speaker may be feeling.

Analyzing Body Motions

BY YOURSELF

1. What use of gestures do you make when you speak? Write an example of times when you use body motions as emblems, illustrators, affect displays, regulators, or adaptors.

2. Observe others' use of nonverbal behavior when they are giving instructions, criticizing, apologizing, or supporting a statement. Do their nonverbal cues help or hurt the effectiveness of their communication? How?

WITH ANOTHER

1. Working with a partner, try to communicate for a full minute or two entirely through nonverbal communication on a subject such as how to clean a piece of machinery, knit a sweater, or play a card game. At the end of the minute or two, analyze your efforts. What kinds of information did you find easiest to communicate nonverbally? What kinds of information did you feel the greatest frustration in communicating?

2. Prepare a short personal experience to communicate to another person. Before you begin, give the person clear directions about what he or she should be looking for in your use of eye contact, facial expression, gesture, or posture. When you have finished, have the person share his or her findings with you. Use what you learned from one practice session to serve as a foundation for the next session.

JOURNAL ENTRIES

1. Watch a television situation comedy with which you are familiar. Turn the volume off. At the end of five minutes, try to summarize the plot and the

emotional state of the characters. In your journal, discuss the aspects of nonverbal communication that enabled you to feel confident of your summary. Also discuss what frustrations, if any, resulted from not being able to hear the dialogue.

2. From a position far enough away so that you cannot hear the conversation, observe a group of at least three people talking in a restaurant. On the basis of eye contact, facial expression, gesture, and so on, write in your journal the conclusions about each person's reaction to or involvement in the conversation. Use as your theme the statement that as much as 65 percent of social meaning in interpersonal communication comes from nonverbal cues.

Paralanguage

In contrast to kinesic behavior, which refers to the bodily movements we see, *paralanguage*, or *vocalics*, refers to the nonverbal sounds we hear. Paralanguage concerns how something is said rather than what is said. We have all developed some sensitivity to the cues people give through their voices. Let's consider two major categories of paralanguage: vocal characteristics and vocal interferences.

VOCAL CHARACTERISTICS

The four major characteristics of voice are pitch (highness or lowness of tone), volume (loudness), rate (speed), and quality (the sound of the voice). Each of these characteristics, by itself or in concert with one or more of the others, either complements, supplements, or contradicts the meaning conveyed by the words themselves. For example, people talk loudly when they wish to be heard at great distances or in noisy settings, but some people also talk loudly when they are angry and softly when they are being loving. People tend to raise and lower vocal pitch to accompany changes in volume. They may also raise the pitch when they are nervous or lower the pitch when they are trying to be forceful. People may talk more rapidly when they are happy, frightened, or nervous and more slowly when they are unsure or are trying to emphasize a point.

In addition to combined changes in volume, pitch, and rate, each of us uses a slightly different quality of voice to communicate a particular state of mind. We may associate complaints with a whiny, nasal quality; seductive invitation with a soft, breathy quality; and anger with a strident, harsh quality. To each of these different qualities we assign some kind of a value judgment about how people are feeling or what they are thinking.

Note, however, that none of these particular differences in voice quality necessarily has the meaning we assign. Some people have high-pitched or breathy or nasal or strident voices all the time. Perhaps some people use these different qualities for reasons other than what we perceive. Nevertheless, how people say what they say does convey meaning, whether intended or not. Our purpose here is to make you more aware of the meanings received through paralanguage, not to suggest the need for changes in your own paralanguage. If you have concerns about your vocal characteristics, talk them over with your professor.

VOCAL INTERFERENCES

Vocal interferences are sounds that interrupt or intrude into fluent speech. Some interferences cause distraction and, occasionally, total communication breakdown. Excessive vocal interferences are bad speech habits that we develop over time. The most common interferences that creep into our speech include the "uh's," "er's," "well's," and "OK's" and those nearly universal interrupters of Americans' conversation, "you know" and "like."

Vocal interferences are difficult to eliminate from our speech, but they can be reduced through a program of awareness and practice. Vocal interferences are often caused by a fear of momentary silence. We have been taught that it is impolite to interrupt another person until the flow of sound stops. A problem occurs for people when they pause for the right word or idea because they fear that the second or two it takes for them to come up with the word may be perceived by listeners as "dead air time." Therefore, they fill the dead air time with sound that, more often than not, has no meaning. For some speakers the customary filler sounds are "uh" or "er"; for others they are "well" or "um." Although the chance of being interrupted may be real (some people will seek to interrupt at any pause), the intrusion of an excessive number of fillers is a high price to pay to prevent an occasional interruption.

Equally prevalent, and perhaps even more disruptive than "uh" and "um," is the incessant use of "you know" and "like." The "you know" habit may begin as a way to find out whether what they are saying is already known by others. For some, "you know" may be a source of identification; some people seek to show that they and those to whom they are talking have common knowledge as a binding element. For most people, however, the flooding of sentences with "you know" is simply a bad habit resulting in incoherent statements such as "you know, Maxwell is, you know, a good, you know, lecturer."

Similarly, the use of "like" may start from making comparisons such as "He's hot, he looks like Tom Cruise." Soon the comparisons become shortcuts, as in "He's like really hot!" Finally, the use of "like" becomes pure filler: "Like, he's really cool, like I can't really explain it, but I'll tell you he's like wow!"

Curiously, no matter how irritating the use of "you know" or "like" may be to listeners, they are unlikely to acknowledge their irritation. Although you may feel uncomfortable pointing out this irritant in others' speech, you should request others to tell you whether you are an offender. Keep in mind that even if such interferences are accepted between peers in everyday speech, they can be quite inappropriate to more formal settings such as a job interview or a problem-solving group. But the habits tend to persist across settings.

In the normal give-and-take of conversation, even the most fluent speakers may use an occasional "uh," "like," or "you know." Interferences become a problem when they are perceived by others as excessive and when they begin to call attention to themselves and so prevent listeners from concentrating on meaning. With some practice, you can limit the occurrence of vocal interferences in your speech. Here are some steps you can take.

1. *Train yourself to hear your interferences.* Even people with a major problem seem to be unaware of the interferences they use. You can train your ear in at least two ways.

   a. Tape-record yourself talking for several minutes about any subject— the game you saw yesterday, the course you plan to take next term, or anything else that comes to mind. Before you play it back, estimate the number of times you think you peppered your speech with "uh's," "you know's," and "like's." Then compare the actual number with your estimate. As your ear becomes trained, your estimates will be closer to the actual number.

   b. Have a close friend listen to you and raise a hand every time you use a filler such as "uh" or "you know." You may find the experience traumatic or nerve-wracking, but your ear will soon start to pick up the vocal interferences as fast as the listener.

2. *Practice to see how long you can go without using a vocal interference.* Start out by trying to talk for fifteen seconds. Continue to increase the time until you can talk for two minutes without a single interference. Meaning may suffer; you may spend a disproportionate amount of time avoiding interferences. Still, it is good practice.

3. *Mentally note your use of interferences in conversation.* You will be making real headway when you can recognize your own interferences in normal conversation without affecting the flow. When you reach this stage, you will find yourself beginning to avoid or limit the use of interferences.

Ridding yourself of these habits is hard work—you will have to train your ear to catch your usage. But the work is worth it.

Paralanguage

BY YOURSELF

1. What happens to your voice in stressful situations? When does your pitch go up? down? When do you talk loudly? softly? When are you likely to talk fast? slowly? Are you aware of these changes, or do you need feedback on how you use paralanguage?

2. Are there any vocal interferences that you use frequently? Are you always aware of their use? How might you try to reduce or eliminate their use?

IN GROUPS

1. Have two persons of the group role-play various situations. For instance, a student has received a low grade on her theme that she worked on for hours and she wishes to confront her instructor, a person who does not have much patience when talking with students. The rest of the group should listen for paralanguage and discuss it.

2. Each person in the group should try to talk continuously for two minutes. When it is your turn, you can select your own topic—a movie you saw recently, the success of your school team, difficulties you are having at work, and so forth. Whenever the speaker uses an interference, one member of the group should raise a hand. At the end of two minutes, count the number of times hands were raised. Give everyone two chances. See who can use the fewest interferences.

Self-Presentation

People learn a great deal about us from the way we choose to present ourselves nonverbally. Elements over which we have some control include choice of clothing, amount of touch, and the way we treat time.

CLOTHING

Although our reactions to other people's appearance vary in intensity, we do draw conclusions about others based on the way they dress. Because choice of clothing communicates a message, you need to determine what you are trying to say and then dress accordingly.

● **Although our reactions to other people's appearance vary in intensity, we do draw conclusions about others based on the way they dress.**

Defense attorneys understand this principle very well. They know that a defendant charged with assault and battery would be foolish to show up in the courtroom wearing a black leather jacket, jeans, and boots. Similarly, business managers generally have a clear idea of the images they want their businesses to project. To succeed with those businesses, you must dress in a way that is in line with those images.[10] Thus the woman who goes into an interview with a major oil company in sweatpants and a tanktop had better have a lot going for her if she expects even to be heard, let alone considered for the job.

People have a right to their individuality. Nevertheless, clothes are perceived by others as clues to our attitudes and behaviors. Part of being a skilled communicator is realizing that clothes do communicate, and the message they send depends as much on the receiver's perceptions as it does on your own intentions.

TOUCH

Touch, known as *haptics,* is often considered to be the most basic form of communication; as such it is a fundamental aspect of nonverbal communication in general and of self-presentation in particular. We use our hands to pat, slap, pinch, stroke, hold, embrace, and tickle. We employ such touching behaviors for a variety of reasons ranging from random and impersonal to purposeful and intimate. We shake hands to be sociable and polite, we pat a person on the back for encouragement, we hug a person to show love.

But whether people touch and like to be touched is a matter of individual preference and cultural background. Although America as a culture is relatively noncontact oriented, the kinds and amounts of touching behavior within our society vary widely. Behavior that seems impersonal to one person may be very intimate or threatening to another. Moreover, the perceived appropriateness of touch differs with the context, so that a normally touch-oriented person may act differently in public or with a large group of people. Once again, remember that what you communicate by touching (or by not touching) depends not only on your intentions but on the expectations of those with whom you interact.

The complexities of touch lead Judee Burgoon, a major researcher in nonverbal behavior, and her associates to conclude that touch is one of the most provocative but least understood nonverbal behaviors. And although touching can often be perceived positively, at the end of a recent article examining reactions to touch they conclude that many more investigations must be done before we can prescribe when and what kinds of touch are advisable in interpersonal contexts.[11]

CHRONEMICS

Chronemics is the study of how we use and structure time. Its significance to our nonverbal behavior is that people perceive actions and reactions on the basis of when they occur.[12] Thus, how we manage time and how we react to others' use and management of time are important aspects of self-presentation.

The aspect of time that is probably most important to self-presentation is what Edward T. Hall, a leading researcher in nonverbal communication, refers to as informal time,[13] time usages that are learned through observation and imitation. We focus here on three aspects of informal time: duration, activity, and punctuality.

Duration refers to the amount of time that we regard as appropriate for certain events. For instance, people expect a sermon to last twenty to thirty minutes, a typical class to run fifty minutes, and a movie to be roughly two hours long. When the length of an event differs significantly from our expectations, the time involved becomes an obstacle to communication. We grow impatient with the professor who holds us beyond normal class time; we become frustrated if someone seems to cut short an interview or an intimate exchange. Our sensitivity to duration is an important aspect of our self-presentation.

Activity refers to what people perceive should be done in a given period, including the time of day that is considered appropriate for certain activities to take place. Most of us work during the day, sleep at night, eat lunch around midday, and so on. When someone engages in behavior at a time that we deem inappropriate, we are likely to react negatively. For instance, Kirsten, who is normally quite willing to discuss interpersonal problems with her employees, is likely to show irritation if an employee calls during her dinner hour to discuss a problem she had with a client.

Punctuality, which refers to meeting a time expectation, may be the most important of these three aspects because so many of us draw conclusions about people based on it. If your professor asks you to stop by her office at 10:00 A.M., her opinion of you may be affected if you knock on her door at 9:45, at 10:00, at 10:10, or at 10:30. Likewise, your perceptions of your professor might alter depending on whether or not she is in her office when you get there.

Keep in mind, however, that any discussion of time is culturally based. Later in the chapter we look at several specific cultural views that must be considered in our analysis of nonverbal communication.

Analyzing Self-Presentation

JOURNAL ENTRIES

1. Take a clothing inventory. Divide your clothes into three groups: those you wear for special occasions, those you wear for everyday activities, and those you wear for "grubbing around." Over the next week, note how your interactions with others are affected by your clothing. Do you act differently when wearing one type of clothing rather than another? Do others treat you differently? Write the results in your journal.

2. Next time you go to class, dress completely differently from how you normally do. Notice what effect, if any, this has on your communication with those around you. Write the results in your journal.

3. Analyze your reaction to people's time behavior. In your journal describe an incident where someone's violation of your time behavior caused communication problems with you.

4. Observe the conversations of men and women and people of different cultures. In your journal discuss what conclusions can you draw about their touching behavior based on these observations.

Communication Through Management of Your Environment

In addition to the way we use body motions, paralanguage, and self-presentation, we communicate nonverbally through management of the physical environment. The principal elements of the environment over which we can exercise control are space, temperature, lighting, and color.

SPACE

How much control we have over space depends on whether we are dealing with permanent structures, movable objects within space, or informal space.

Management of Permanent Structures The buildings in which we live and work and the parts of those buildings that cannot be moved fall into the category of permanent structures. Although we may not have much control over the creation of such elements, we do exercise control in our selection of them. For instance, when you rent an apartment or buy a condominium or home, you consider whether the structures are in tune with your life-style. People who select a fourth-floor loft may view themselves differently from those who select one-room efficiencies. Business people, doctors, and lawyers usually search with care to find surroundings that fit the image they want to communicate. In addition, specific features of that choice affect our communication within that environment. For instance, people who live in apartment buildings are likely to become better acquainted with neighbors who live across the hall and next door than with those who live on other floors.

Management of Movable Objects Within Space We have the opportunity to manage objects in space by arranging and rearranging them

● **Whether the space is a dormitory room, a living room, a seminar room, or a classroom, you can move the furnishings around until you achieve the effect you want.**

to create the desired atmosphere. Whether the space is a dormitory room, a living room, a seminar room, or a classroom, you can move the furnishings around until you achieve the effect you want. For example, in a living room, you can arrange furniture in a way that contributes to conversation or that focuses attention on a television set. A room with Victorian furniture and hard-backed chairs arranged formally will produce an entirely different kind of conversation from a room with a thick carpet, pillows, beanbag chairs, and a low sectional sofa. In general, the more formal the arrangement, the more formal the communication setting.

A supervisor's office will give you clues about the kind of climate that he or she is trying to establish just by the arrangement of the office and where visitors are expected to sit. A supervisor who shows you to a chair across the desk may be saying, "Let's talk business—I'm the boss and you're the employee." Such an arrangement, with the desk between you and the supervisor, lends itself to formal conversation. However, the supervisor who shows you to a chair at the side of her desk may be saying, "Don't be nervous—let's just chat." In this case the lack of any formal barrier between you and the supervisor, as well as the relatively small space, is designed to lead to much more informal conversation. Although such conclusions about the management of objects within space should not be regarded as absolute, the use of space nevertheless is one index of how people are going to treat you and how they expect you to treat them.

The effect of the arrangement of objects on communication can be illustrated by examining your various classrooms. The communication atmosphere of a classroom in which several rows of chairs face the lectern differs from that of a classroom in which chairs are grouped into one large circle or one in which there are four or five smaller circles. In the first environment, most students anticipate a lecture format. In the second setting, they might expect a give-and-take discussion between the instructor and members of the class. In the third one, they might expect the class to work on group projects.

Management of Informal Space The space around the place we are occupying at the moment is known as informal space. The study of informal space is called *proxemics*. Managing informal space requires some understanding of attitudes toward both space around us and our territory.

You are probably aware that communication is influenced by the distances between people. Edward T. Hall has studied the four distinct, generally accepted distances for different types of conversations in our dominant culture.[14] Intimate distance, up to eighteen inches, is appropriate for private conversations between close friends. Personal distance, from eighteen inches to four feet, is the space in which casual conversation occurs. Social distance, from four to twelve feet, is conducive to impersonal business such as job interviews. Public distance is anything more than twelve feet. Note that these four distances were not determined arbitrarily; they represent descriptions of what many people consider appropriate in various situations. Individuals do, of course, vary.

Of greatest concern to us is the intimate distance, that which we regard as appropriate for intimate conversation with close friends, parents, and younger children. People usually become uncomfortable when "outsiders" violate this intimate distance. For instance, in a movie theater that is less than one-quarter full, couples will tend to leave a seat or more between them and another couple. If a stranger sits right next to you in such a setting, you are likely to feel uncomfortable and may even move away.

Intrusions into our intimate space are acceptable only when all involved follow the unwritten rules. When packed into a crowded elevator and possibly touching others, for example, people often try to stand rigidly, look at the floor or the indicator above the door, and pretend they are not touching. Sometimes they exchange sheepish smiles or otherwise acknowledge the mutual invasion of intimate distance.

Interpersonal problems occur when one person violates the behavioral expectations of another. For instance, Jaron may come from a family that conducts informal conversations with others at a range closer than the eighteen-inch limit that most Americans place on intimate space. Thus, when he talks to a colleague at work and moves in closer than eighteen inches, the co-worker may back away from him during the conversation. Another example of violation of expectations occurs when people engage in nonverbal behaviors that may be defined as sexual harassment. Dominic, in an apparently playful mood, may use posture, movements, or gestures that Daniela interprets as somewhat threatening to her. In keeping with current sentiments toward harassment, people need to be especially sensitive to others' definition of intimate space.

Normally, our intimate or personal space moves when we move because we tend to define these spaces in terms of our current location. Yet in many situations we seek to claim a given space whether or not we are occupying it currently. That is, we are likely to look at certain space as our territory, as space over which we may claim ownership. If Cheyenne decides to eat lunch at the company commissary, the space at the table she selects becomes her territory. Suppose that during lunch Cheyenne leaves her territory to get butter for her roll. The chair she left, the food on the table, and the space around that food are "hers," and she will expect others to stay away. If, when she returns, Cheyenne finds that someone at the table has moved a glass or a dish into the area that she regards as her territory, she is likely to feel resentful.

Many people stake out their territory with markers. For example, Ramon, who is planning to eat in the commissary, finds an empty table and puts his newspaper on the table and his coat on a chair before he gets his food. If someone comes along while Ramon is gone, moves his newspaper and coat to the floor, and occupies his space, that person is violating what Ramon perceives as his territory.

As a student of nonverbal communication, you must understand, however, that other people may not look at either the space around you or your territory in quite the same way as you do. That the majority of Americans have learned the same basic rules governing the management of space does not mean that everyone shares the same respect for the rules or treats the consequences of breaking the rules in the same way. Thus it is important to be observant so that you can be sensitive to how others react to your behaviors.

TEMPERATURE, LIGHTING, AND COLOR

Three other elements of the environment that people seem sensitive to and over which they generally have considerable control are temperature, lighting, and color.

Temperature acts as a stimulant or deterrent to communication. To illustrate the negative effect of temperature on communication, recall when the June or September heat made listening to the teacher in a stuffy classroom especially difficult. Or, if you live in the northern part of the country, think of how a sudden cold snap that rendered buildings much colder than normal made concentration that much more difficult.

Lighting can also act as a stimulant or deterrent to communication. In lecture halls and reading rooms, bright light is expected—it encourages good listening and comfortable reading. By contrast, in a chic restaurant, a music listening room, or a television lounge, you expect the lighting to be soft and rather dim, which makes for a cozy atmosphere and leads to intimate conversation.[15]

Differences in *color* seem to have a particularly significant effect on how people behave: We react to color both emotionally and physically. For instance, many people see red as exciting and stimulating, blue as comfortable and soothing, yellow as cheerful and jovial. Interior designers thus will decorate in blues when they are trying to create a peaceful, serene atmosphere for a living room, whereas they will decorate in reds and yellows when they are trying to create a stimulating atmosphere for a playroom.

Color has other associations as well. We describe a cowardly person as yellow, a jealous person as green with envy, an angry person as seeing red; Mondays, of course, are often seen as blue. The effect of color is most noticeable when the color violates our expectations. Mashed potatoes tinted green in honor of Saint Patrick's Day may nauseate diners who are not color blind, even before they attempt to eat.

Analyzing Effects of Environment

BY YOURSELF

1. How territorial are you? Make a list of territories that you "own." What do you do when those territories are invaded?

2. Analyze your use of personal space. What are your expectations about space when you are talking with an instructor? When you are talking with a good friend? When you are talking with a stranger? How do they differ?

WITH ANOTHER

1. Visit six different restaurants in your city. Choose several that specialize in fast food and several that specialize in more leisurely dining. Make notes on the management of objects within space as well as on the color and lighting. What conclusions can you draw?

2. Enlist the aid of a friend. Start on the opposite sides of the room (at least twenty feet apart) and begin to walk toward each other. (1) Stop when twelve feet apart and hold a conversation; (2) stop when seven feet apart and hold a conversation; (3) stop when one or two feet apart and hold a conversation; (4) continue moving closer and conversing until you feel uncomfortable. Step back until the distance seems comfortable. Notice how far apart you are. Compare your reactions to your friend's.

JOURNAL ENTRIES

1. Change the arrangement of furniture in your dorm room or a room of your home. Observe people's reactions. In your journal comment on whether these changes seem to affect the conversations of the people who are usually in these spaces.

2. Think of where you live (dorm, apartment, house). How well do you know your neighbors? Which of your neighbors do you know best? In your journal discuss how you can account for interactions with neighbors by where you live in relation to them.

Implementing Your Understanding of Nonverbal Communication

Ultimately, the question is whether increasing your understanding of the nature of nonverbal communication has any effect on the success of your interactions with others. From a theoretical position, Robert Feldman, Pierre Philippot, and Robert Custrini conclude that with relatively unskilled communicators, improving their use of nonverbal behavior should improve their social competence.[16] Yet their analysis of research suggests that nonverbal performance is so complex that causal relationships are still unclear. Can we gain competence in the nonverbal domain? Let's consider how encoding and decoding can affect our understanding of nonverbal communication.

ENCODING AND DECODING

From an encoding standpoint, since much of our nonverbal behavior is spontaneous, altering nonverbal behaviors is very difficult. For instance, simply knowing that you are a person who engages in strong nonverbal reactions to verbal messages will not enable you to alter your reactions. However, knowing your typical nonverbal reactions will allow you to explain them to people who don't know you well. When you overreact nonverbally to a person's negative feedback, you can say something like "You're likely to think that my negative reaction means that I don't want to hear your comments. The fact is that I tend to grimace in the face of criticism, but really, I need to hear it."

From a decoding standpoint, you have already studied the skill that allows you to test your interpretation of nonverbal response—perception checking. To be sure that you have understood a person's nonverbal reactions, state your interpretation. For instance, suppose a person gives a negative nonverbal reaction to constructive criticism. Before you conclude that the person can't handle such comments, you might say, "From the look on your face and the sound of your voice, I get the impression either that you don't want to hear negative comments or that you think the comments are off base—am I right?" And perception checking may be even more important in interpreting nonverbal behaviors of people of the opposite sex or of a different culture or subculture.

Cultural and Gender Considerations

In this chapter we have tried to focus on nonverbal analysis that will provide you with the greatest chance of improving your communication competence in the use of nonverbal communication. Although the conclusions drawn are valid in general, specific cultural and gender differences need to be considered.

Cultural Differences Major cultural differences occur in eye contact, body motions, touch, and perceptions of time and space.

While a majority of people in the United States and other Western cultures expect those with whom they are communicating to "look them in the eye," Larry Samovar and Richard Porter conclude from their review of research that direct eye contact is not a custom throughout the world.[17] In Japan, for example, people are taught not to look another in the eye but to look at a position around the Adam's apple. Chinese, Indonesians, and rural Mexicans also lower their eyes as a sign of deference—to them, too much eye contact is a sign of bad manners. Arabs, in contrast, look directly into the eyes of the person with whom they are talking for long periods—to them direct eye contact shows interest. There are also differences in use of eye contact in the subcultures of the United States. For instance, African-Americans use more continuous eye contact than whites when they are speaking but less when they are listening.[18]

People of other cultures also show considerable differences in use of gestures, movements, and facial expression. Gestures in particular can assume completely different meanings. For instance, the forming of a circle with the thumb and forefinger—the OK sign in the United States—means zero or worthless in France, a symbol for money in Japan, a curse in some Arab countries, and an obscene gesture in Germany, Brazil, and Australia.[19] In addition, displays of emotion vary. For instance, in some Eastern cultures, people have been socialized to deintensify emotional behavior cues, whereas members of other cultures have been socialized to amplify their displays of emotions. The cultural differences that are related to emotional displays are often reflected in the interpretation that can be given to facial expressions.[20]

Differences in touching behavior are, according to William Gudykunst and Young Yun Kim, highly correlated with culture: "People in high contact cultures evaluate 'close' as positive and good, and evaluate 'far' as negative and bad. People in low contact cultures evaluate 'close' as negative and bad, and 'far' as positive and good."[21] Specifically, Latin America and the Mediterranean countries are high contact, the United States is moderate contact, and the Far East is low contact.

A particularly important area of differences concerns perceptions of time. In general, people in Western Europe, the United States, and Canada are likely to view time monochronically; that is, we compartmentalize our time and schedule one event at a time, exemplified by our tendency to emphasize schedules and value promptness. As a result, in the United States, being even a few minutes late may require you to acknowledge your lateness. Being ten to fifteen minutes late usually requires an apology, and being more than thirty minutes late is likely to be perceived as an insult requiring a great deal of explanation to earn forgiveness.[22]

People from other cultural backgrounds, such as those from the Middle East, tend to view time polychronically, a view that resists compartmentalization and involves engaging in several activities at the same time. To those following a polychronic view of time, lateness is common and is not considered unusual, and the concept of a schedule that is supposed to be adhered to may be meaningless. In Latin American or in Arab cultures, for instance, it is not unusual for a person to be more than thirty minutes "late," behavior that is likely to occasion only a few words of apology.[23]

Although we have been focusing on differences among people from other countries, these differences may be seen in different cultures within the United States as well. For instance people from Latin-American or African-American cultures may also show a more polychronic view of time in their behavior.

There is, then, no universally held "right" way of viewing time designations. A white North American with a business appointment in Latin America might be very frustrated with what he or she regards as a cavalier attitude toward time; likewise, a Latin American with a business appointment with a white North American might be frustrated by the perceived rigidity of time schedules.

Finally, people from non-European or North American backgrounds have different attitudes about what constitutes appropriate distances for various interactions. Recall that white people in the United States typically consider the space of up to a foot or eighteen inches from their bodies as personal or intimate space, and they expect people not to violate that space. Middle Eastern men, however, seek to move much closer to other men when they are talking. Thus, when an Arab man talks with a white man from the United States, one of the two is likely to be uncomfortable. Either the white American will experience a sense of territorial invasion or the Arab will feel himself too far removed for serious conversation.

Problems in communicating with strangers occur at times because we are uncertain and anxious about the meanings of nonverbal cues. And when strangers violate our expectations of nonverbal usage, we tend to behave negatively.[24]

● ● **Gender Differences** Although researchers have tried to identify specific problems that result from gender differences in nonverbal communication, these differences may be more apparent than real. Few real differences have been documented, but people tend to believe that more differences exist.

One definite difference appears to be in eye contact or gaze. Women tend to engage in more frequent eye contact during conversations than do men.[25] And women tend to hold eye contact more than men regardless of the sex of the person with whom they are interacting.[26]

Likewise, some differences appear in use of facial expression and gesture. Women tend to smile more than men, but their smiles are harder to interpret. Men's smiles generally mean positive feelings, whereas women's smiles tend to be suggestions of responding to affiliation and friendliness.[27] Concerning gesture, Judy Pearson, Lynn Turner, and William Todd-Mancillas assert that the style of use of gestures by women and men is so different that people can distinguish masculinity and femininity on the basis of gesture alone.[28] For instance, women are more likely to keep their arms close to their body, less likely to lean forward with their body, play more often with their hair or clothing, and tap their hands more often than men.

Finally, women tend more than men to initiate and respond to touch. The conclusion drawn is that touch may be perceived as "feminine-appropriate behavior" and "masculine-inappropriate behavior."[29]

The major difference between men and women appears to be more in the interpretation than in the use of nonverbals. Major male-female relationship difficulties are often characterized by the failure to encode and decode non-verbal messages accurately. Patricia Noller recommends that men particularly need to be involved in communication skills training, because they generally seem less sensitive to the meaning of women's nonverbal behaviors than women are to men's.[30] This interpretive ability seems to have long-range implications. For instance, Noller found that couples with a high degree of marital satisfaction were likely to be accurate in decoding each other's non-verbal messages and in predicting whether or not their spouse would correctly decode their messages.

Recognizing Cultural Differences

BY YOURSELF

For the next few days, record instances of your communication with people from different cultures in which their nonverbal behavior was different from what you expected in that situation. Indicate the results of the times you used perception checking to clarify the meaning.

Summary

Nonverbal communication refers to how people communicate by nonverbal means, that is, through the use of body motions, paralanguage, self-presentation, and environment. The nature of nonverbal communication is revealed through its contrasts with verbal communication. Nonverbal communication is more ambiguous, is continuous, is multichanneled, and gives more insight into emotional states. In addition, meanings of nonverbal communication are culturally determined.

Perhaps the most obvious aspect of nonverbal communication is what and how a person communicates through body motions and paralanguage. Eye contact, facial expression, gesture, posture, and poise are five major types of body motions. Eye contact is especially important because people will form judgments about you and your message based on the amount of eye contact you make. Body motions act as emblems, illustrators, affect displays, regulators, and adaptors. Likewise, a person's vocal characteristics and vocal interferences affect the meaning communicated.

Although verbal and nonverbal communication work together best when they are complementary, nonverbal cues may replace or even contradict verbal symbols. Generally, nonverbal communication is more to be trusted when verbal and nonverbal cues are in conflict.

Self-presentation, manifested in factors such as clothing, touching behavior, and use of time, further affects communication. The environment is an often overlooked aspect of nonverbal communication. Yet the way people arrange and react to space and the way they control or react to temperature, lighting, and color contribute to the nature of the communication that will occur.

Your understanding of nonverbal communication often translates into changes in both encoding (greater use of describing feelings) and decoding (greater use of perception checking). Both of these skills are especially important in coping with cultural and gender differences. Cultural differences occur with eye contact or gaze, gesture, touching behavior, and perceptions of time and space. These differences are real, and effective communicators must be sensitive to them. Some gender differences are found in gaze, facial expression, gesture, and touch. The major difference between men and women is not so much their use of nonverbals as it is their interpretation of them.

●◆■ Communication Improvement Goal Statement

If you would like to improve your eye contact, write a communication improvement goal statement following the guidelines on page 33 in Chapter 1.

●◆■ Featured Reading

The Power of the Eyes
Patricia Webbink
(New York: Springer Publishing, 1986)

More than two thousand years ago, Cicero, the great Roman orator and writer, observed that the eyes are the mirror of the mind. In recent years numerous scholars have focused on the importance of facial features and the special importance of the eyes for understanding messages and relationships. Patricia Webbink, a psychologist who began her research on the power of the eyes more than twenty years ago, draws from hundreds of studies to put this most important element of nonverbal communication into focus for us. The result is a book that is more than just a review of eye behavior research. Rather, Webbink has penned a series of essays on human relations, drawing examples from the social and behavioral sciences, the arts, politics, the news media, and even comic strips. She points out that our gaze not only is a major aspect of communication but has a syntax of its own.

She begins by explaining how eye contact fits within the overall system of verbal and nonverbal communication. In subsequent chapters she examines eye contact in relation to the distribution of power within a society. The kind of gaze that occurs between people reflects their social roles. A separate essay explores eye contact and intimacy. Nonverbal communication, and especially eye contact, is a significant channel for showing intimacy between people. In a chapter on eye contact and symbolism, Webbink provides a unique examination of the sociocultural heritage of the eyes through history. After examining the evidence of mythology, religion, visual and dramatic arts, language, literature, folklore, and custom, one is convinced of the author's thesis that the eyes have provided "a rich poetry of images and meaning in human consciousness through the ages."

The book provides an excellent summary of research findings from a variety of disciplines. Yet, because of the excellent choice of examples and the diversity of references, it is relatively easy to understand. Both the novice and the student of eye contact should benefit from reading *The Power of the Eyes*.

● ◆ ■ Notes

1. Judee K. Burgoon, David B. Buller, and W. Gill Woodall, *Nonverbal Communication: The Unspoken Dialogue* (New York: Harper & Row, 1989), p. 155.

2. Ibid., p. 33.

3. Paul Ekman and H. Oster, "Facial Expression of Emotion," *Annual Review of Psychology* 30 (1979): 527–554.

4. Mark L. Knapp and Judith A. Hall, *Nonverbal Communication in Human Interaction*, 3rd ed. (New York: Holt, Rinehart & Winston, 1992), p. 298.

5. Paul Ekman and W. V. Friesen, *Unmasking the Face* (Englewood Cliffs, N.J.: Prentice-Hall, 1975), pp. 137–138.

6. Virginia P. Richmond and James C. McCroskey, *Communication: Apprehension,*

Avoidance, and Effectiveness, 2nd ed. (Scottsdale, Ariz.: Gorsuch Scarisbrick, 1989), pp. 94–101.

7. Paul Ekman and W. V. Friesen, "The Repertoire of Nonverbal Behavior: Categories, Origins, Usage, and Coding," *Semiotica* I (1969): 49–98.

8. Ibid.

9. Dale Leathers, *Successful Nonverbal Communication: Principles and Applications* (New York: Macmillan, 1992), p. 75.

10. Two of the influential books that report the power of clothing are John T. Molloy's *New Dress for Success* (New York: Warner Books, 1988) and Pamela Satran's *Dress Smart: The Thinking Women's Guide to Style* (New York: Doubleday, 1989).

11. Judee K. Burgoon, Joseph B. Walther, and E. James Baesler, "Interpretations, Evaluations, and Consequences of Interpersonal Touch," *Human Communication Research* 19 (December 1992): 259.

12. Knapp and Hall, p. 59.

13. Edward T. Hall, *The Silent Language* (Greenwich, Conn.: Fawcett, 1959), p. 135.

14. Edward T. Hall, *The Hidden Dimension* (Garden City, N.Y.: Doubleday, 1969), pp. 116–125.

15. Knapp and Hall, p. 72.

16. Robert S. Feldman, Pierre Philippot, and Robert J. Custrini, "Social Competence and Nonverbal Behavior," in Robert S. Feldman and Bernard Rime, eds., *Fundamentals of Nonverbal Behavior* (New York: Cambridge University Press, 1991), p. 346.

17. Larry A. Samovar and Richard E. Porter, *Communication Between Cultures* (Belmont, Calif.: Wadsworth, 1991), p. 198.

18. Ibid., p. 199.

19. Roger E. Axtell, *Gestures: The Do's and Taboos of Body Language Around the World* (New York: Wiley, 1991), p. 47.

20. J. R. Davitz, *The Communication of Emotional Meaning* (New York: McGraw-Hill, 1964), p. 14.

21. William B. Gudykunst and Young Yun Kim, *Communicating with Strangers: An Approach to Intercultural Communication*, 2nd ed. (New York: McGraw-Hill, 1992), p. 178.

22. Samovar and Porter, p. 220.

23. Gudykunst and Kim, p. 129.

24. Ibid., p. 186.

25. Donald J. Cegala and Alan L. Sillars, "Further Examination of Nonverbal Manifestations of Interaction Involvement," *Communication Reports* 2 (1989): 45.

26. Julia T. Wood, *Gendered Lives: Communication, Gender, and Culture* (Belmont, Calif.: Wadsworth, 1994), p. 164.

27. Judy Cornelia Pearson, Lynn H. Turner, and William Todd-Mancillas, *Gender and Communication*, 2nd ed. (Dubuque, Iowa: Wm. C. Brown, 1991), p. 137.

28. Ibid., p. 139.

29. Ibid., p. 142.

30. Patricia Noller, "Nonverbal Communication in Marriage," in Daniel Perlman and Steve Duck, eds., *Intimate Relationships: Development, Dynamics, and Deterioration* (Newbury Park, Calif.: Sage, 1987), p. 173.

PART

II

Developing Interpersonal Skills

Most of our interpersonal communication occurs within the context of our ongoing relationships. In this part we begin with an analysis of relationships. We continue with chapters that explore the communication skills necessary to the development of good relationships: communicating ideas and feelings, listening, responding, influencing, and managing conflict. With an increased repertoire of interpersonal communication skills, you can select the ones that are most appropriate for a particular communication situation.

CHAPTER FIVE

Communication in Relationships

OBJECTIVES

After you have read this chapter, you should be able to define and/or explain:

Interpersonal needs theory

Exchange theory

Types of relationships

Ways of starting a relationship

Maintaining relationships through descriptiveness, openness, provisionalism, and equality

Methods of ending a relationship

"Yvonne, wasn't that Pauli that I saw you with again? I thought Lonnie was your man."

"He is. Pauli and I are just friends—we've got a really solid relationship."

"Just friends! Come on, girl, I see you with him a lot. Are you sure he doesn't see it differently?"

"Yeah, I see him a lot because I am really able to talk with him. We're just comfortable with each other. But before you get too worried about his feelings, he and Leona have been an item for months."

"And she doesn't mind you spending time with her man? Are you sure you're not just fooling yourself?"

"Hey, I don't know whether she minds, but Pauli and I just aren't romantically involved. Actually, he's more like a brother to me. I tell him my fears and anxieties as well what's going right with me. And he talks with me about his problems, too. If something happened between us, I'd really miss him."

Yvonne is lucky because she has someone she can really talk with—she has a good relationship. Because so many of the interpersonal skills we use are for the purpose of starting, building, and maintaining relationships with others, we begin Part Two with an analysis of interpersonal relationships. An *interpersonal relationship* may be defined as "a series of interactions between two individuals known to each other."[1] A *good relationship* is one in which the interactions are satisfying to those involved.

Good relationships do not just happen, nor do they grow and maintain themselves automatically. In this chapter we lay the foundation for our discussion by considering two theories of why relationships develop. Then we explain the nature of relationships and the stages that typically comprise the life cycle of a relationship, including the skills necessary to create a nurturing climate.

Theoretical Perspectives on Relationships

What determines whether or not we will try to build a relationship with another person? Why do some relationships never move beyond a certain level or begin to deteriorate? Two helpful theories—interpersonal needs theory and exchange theory—offer insights into these questions.

INTERPERSONAL NEEDS THEORY

Relationships, like communication itself, exist in part because they satisfy basic human needs. Interpersonal needs theory proposes that whether or not a relationship is started, built, or maintained depends on how well each person meets the interpersonal needs of the other. William Schutz, a psychologist, identifies three interpersonal needs that all of us have: affection, inclusion, and control.[2]

The need for *affection* reflects a desire to express and to receive love. The people you know probably run the gamut of showing and expressing affection both verbally and nonverbally. At one end of the spectrum are the "underpersonal" individuals—those who avoid close ties, seldom show strong feelings toward others, and shy away from people who show or want to show affection. At the other end of the spectrum are the "overpersonal" individuals—those who thrive on establishing "close" relationships with everyone. They think of all others as intimates, immediately confide in persons they have just met, and want everyone to consider them close friends. Somewhere in between these two extremes are "personal" people—those who can express and receive affection easily and who derive pleasure from many kinds of relationships with others.

The need for *inclusion* reflects a desire to be in the company of other people. According to Schutz, everyone has a need to be social. Yet people differ in the amount of interaction with others that will satisfy this need. At one extreme are "undersocial" individuals—those who usually want to be left alone. Occasionally, they seek company or enjoy being included with others if specifically invited, but they do not require a great deal of social interaction to feel satisfied. At the other extreme are "oversocial" people—those who need constant companionship and feel tense when they must be alone. If a party is happening, they must be there; if there is no party, they start one. Their doors are always open—everyone is welcome, and they expect others to welcome them. Of course, most of us do not belong to either of these extreme types. Rather, we are sometimes comfortable being alone and at other times need and enjoy interacting with others.

The need for *control* reflects a desire to successfully influence the events and people around us. As with the other two interpersonal needs, people vary in how much control they require. At one extreme are people who need no control, who seem to shun responsibility and do not want to be in charge of anything. The "abdicrats," as they are called by Schutz, are extremely submissive and are unlikely to make decisions or accept responsibility. At the other extreme are individuals who like to be—indeed, who feel they must be—in charge. Such "autocrats" need to dominate others at all times, and they become anxious if they cannot. They usurp responsibility from those who may have the authority to control a situation, and they try to determine every decision. Again, most people fall somewhere between these two extremes. These "democrats" need to lead at certain times, but at other times they are

● **Through verbal and nonverbal communication behavior, we display cues that reveal the level of our immediate interpersonal needs. Enduring relationships then are those in which both partners believe that their interpersonal needs are being fulfilled.**

content to follow the lead of others. Democrats can stand behind their ideas, but they also can be comfortable submitting to others, at least some of the time.

How can this analysis help us understand communication in relationships? Relationships develop and deteriorate in part because of the compatibility or incompatibility of individuals' interpersonal needs. Through verbal and non-verbal communication behavior, we display cues that reveal the level of our immediate interpersonal needs. As you interact with others, you can detect whether their needs for affection, inclusion, and control seem compatible with yours. Suppose that Emily and Isaac have been seeing each other regularly and see their relationship as close. If, in response to Isaac's attempt to put his arm around Emily while they watch television, Emily slightly stiffens, it might suggest that Emily doesn't have quite the same need for affection as Isaac. It should be emphasized that people's needs do differ; moreover, people's needs change over time. When other people's needs at any given time differ significantly from ours and we fail to understand that, we can misunderstand what's going wrong in our communication.

Schutz's theory of interpersonal needs is useful because it helps explain a great deal of interpersonal behavior.[3] In addition, research on this model has been generally supportive of its major themes.[4] Interpersonal needs theory does not, however, explain *how* people adjust to one another in their ongoing relationships. The next theory we discuss will help us to develop this understanding.

EXCHANGE THEORY

Another way of analyzing our relationships is on the basis of exchange ratios. John W. Thibaut and Harold H. Kelley, who originated exchange theory, believe that relationships can be understood in terms of the exchange of rewards and costs that takes place during the individuals' interaction.[5] *Rewards* are outcomes that are valued by the receiver. Some common rewards are good feelings, prestige, economic gain, and fulfillment of emotional needs. *Costs* are outcomes that the receiver does not wish to incur and include time, energy, and anxiety. For instance, Sharon may be eager to spend time talking with Jan if she anticipates feeling good as a result; she may be reluctant to spend that time if she expects to be depressed at the end of the conversation.

According to Thibaut and Kelley, people seek interaction situations in which their behaviors will yield an outcome of high reward and low cost. For example, if Jill runs into Keisha on campus, several communication options are available to Jill: She can ignore Keisha, she can smile, she can say "Hi" in

140

● People seek inter-
action situations in
which their behaviors
will yield an outcome
of high reward and
low cost. Enduring re-
lationships are those
in which both part-
ners believe that the
rewards of the rela-
tionship outweigh the
costs involved.

passing, or she can try to start a conversation. What Jill does will depend in part on her *cost-reward analysis* of the outcome of the interaction. For instance, if Jill had been thinking about calling Keisha to arrange a game of tennis, she will probably take the time now to attempt to seek that outcome—she will be willing to pay the cost of taking time and using energy in hopes of receiving a suitable reward, a tennis date. If Jill and Keisha do talk, the interchange will continue until one or both realize that the cost-reward ratio is falling below the satisfactory level. For Jill, this point might be reached once a tennis game is set. For Keisha, it might be reached when she perceives Jill's lack of interest at that moment in other topics of conversation.

This analysis can be extended from single interactions to relationships. If, over an extended period, a person's net rewards (reward minus cost) in a relationship fall below a certain level, that person will come to view the relationship itself as unsatisfactory or unpleasant. But if the net reward is higher than the level viewed as satisfactory, the person will regard the relationship or interaction as pleasant and satisfying.

Thibaut and Kelley suggest that the most desirable ratio between cost and reward varies from person to person and within one person from time to time. One reason people differ in their assessments of costs and rewards is that they have different definitions of what is satisfying. If people have a number of relationships they perceive as giving them a good cost-reward ratio, they will set a high satisfaction level and will probably not be satisfied with low-outcome relationships. By contrast, people who have few positive interactions will be satisfied with relationships and interactions that people who enjoy high-outcome relationships would find unattractive. For instance, Calvin may continue to see Erica even if she treats him very poorly because based on experiences he has in his other relationships, the rewards he gets from the relationship are on par.

The ratio of costs and rewards determines how attractive or unattractive a relationship or an interaction is to the individuals involved, but it does not indicate how long the relationship or interaction will last. Although it seems logical that people would terminate a relationship or an interaction in which costs exceed rewards, circumstances sometimes dictate that people will stay in a relationship that is plainly unsatisfactory.

Thibaut and Kelley's explanation for such a situation involves what they call the *comparison level of alternatives.* They suggest that the decision to continue in a relationship may depend on what alternatives or other choices a person perceives as available. Someone who feels dissatisfied will tend to leave a relationship or interaction if there is a realistic alternative that seems to promise a higher level of satisfaction. But if there are no such alternatives, the person may choose to stay in the situation because, unsatisfactory though it is, it is the best the person believes can be attained at that time. Thus, if Golda has four or five men she gets along well with, she is less likely to put up with Charley, who irritates her. If, however, Golda believes that Charley is the only man who can provide the companionship she is seeking, she will be more inclined to tolerate his irritating habits.

Like Schutz's interpersonal needs theory, Thibaut and Kelley's exchange theory helps to illuminate important aspects of relationship development. Yet critics of this theory point out an important limitation. Exchange theory suggests that people consciously and deliberately weigh the costs and rewards associated with any relationship or interaction—that is, that people rationally choose to continue or terminate relationships. Thus the theory assumes that people behave rationally from an economic standpoint: They seek out relationships that benefit them and avoid those that are costly.[6] In fact, although people may behave rationally in most situations, rational models such as Thibaut and Kelley's cannot always explain complex human behavior. Nevertheless, it can be useful to examine your relationships from a cost-reward perspective. Especially if the relationship is stagnating, you may recognize areas where costs are greater than rewards either for you or for the other person. If so, you may be able to change some aspects of the relationship before it deteriorates completely.

You may discover that it is fruitful to use both of these theories. What you (or your partner) count as "costs" and "rewards" may depend significantly on what your particular *needs* are. If your needs differ, you may misunderstand the other person's perceptions of rewards and costs. Looking at relationships in this way might help resolve misunderstandings and make us less defensive. That is, if you understand the other person's needs and can take his or her perceived costs and rewards into account, you may understand the situation better and in a way that is less destructive to your own self-esteem. How helpful this kind of analysis is in your relationships is likely to depend on your use of listening, sharing feelings, and empathic understanding skills.

PRACTICE IN Applying Needs and Exchange Theory

JOURNAL ENTRY

Think of one specific intimate relationship you have. Explain the development and maintenance of this relationship in terms of needs theory. Choose and use one specific interactional episode as evidence to support your explanation. Then explain the development and maintenance of this relationship using exchange theory. Again, focus on a single interactional episode. What insights into the relationship have you gained from these analyses? How might these insights affect your future interactions?

The Nature of Relationships

Relationships vary in their intensity as a function of the amount of information that each person shares with the other and the kinds of interactions between them. We generally classify the people with whom we have relationships as acquaintances, friends, and close friends or intimates.

ACQUAINTANCES

Acquaintances are people we know by name and talk with when the opportunity arises, but with whom our interactions are limited in quality and quantity. We become acquainted with those who live in our apartment building or dorm or in the house next door, who sit next to us in class, who go to our church or belong to our club. Many acquaintance relationships grow out of a particular context. Thus Melinda and Paige, who meet in biology class, may strike up an acquaintanceship, but they may make no effort to see each other outside of class; if they do meet in some other context, it is by chance.

FRIENDS

Over time we develop closer relationships with many of our acquaintances. *Friends* are people with whom we have negotiated more personal relationships voluntarily.[7] In early stages of friendship, people move toward interactions that are less role bound. That is, Melinda and Paige, who are acquaintances in biology class, may, as a result of in-class conversation, voluntarily decide to get together after school one afternoon just to talk. As they continue such voluntary meetings, they begin to speak of each other as friends. People move toward friendships because they like being with each other; they actively seek each other out because they enjoy each other's company.

Some of our friendships may develop in and remain in a specific context. Thus people often refer to their *tennis* friends, *office* friends, or *neighborhood* friends. However friendships may begin, they become more than acquaintanceships if the people involved find satisfaction with each other on many levels. Nevertheless, most of their interactions remain in the contexts of tennis, office, or neighborhood.

Good friendships are marked by high degrees of warmth and affection, trust, self-disclosure, commitment, and expectation that the relationship will grow and endure.[8]

One characteristic of friendship is warmth and affection. Friends often express this liking through time spent with each other. Friends look forward to being with each other because they experience a joy in each other's company, they enjoy talking with each other, and they enjoy sharing experiences.

A second characteristic of friendship is trust. *Trust* is placing confidence in another. Trust almost always involves some risk. In effect, trust is a prediction that if you put yourself in the hands of a friend, the result will be to your advantage rather than to your disadvantage. Friends earn trust by doing what is expected of them. If a person can be relied on to deliver on a promise,

● **Good friendships are marked by high degrees of warmth and affection.**

to keep a secret, or to provide some emotional support when needed, the strength of the friendship grows.

Third, friendship is likely to include relatively high levels of self-disclosure. As we will see in our discussion of self-disclosure in Chapter 6, through the disclosure and sharing of feelings people come to know and to understand each other better. Even with intimate relationships, there are limits to the amount of self-disclosure that is appropriate.

A fourth characteristic of friendship is a level of commitment. Friends are likely to sacrifice their time and energy to help when a friend is in need. Good friends will go out of their way to help each other when necessary. It may mean taking a friend to work when his or her car breaks down, or taking care of a child when a friend is sick or away on business, or helping with house repairs in times of emergencies.

Finally, friends believe that a relationship is enduring. For this reason, a change of job, a divorce, or a move to another city may not break that friendship. Some friends see each other only once or twice a year yet still consider themselves friends because when they are together, they share ideas and feelings freely and rely on each other's counsel.

CLOSE FRIENDS OR INTIMATES

Close friends or *intimates* are those with whom we share our deepest feelings. People may have countless acquaintances and many friends, but they are likely to have only a few truly intimate friends.

Close friends or intimates differ from "regular" friends mostly in degree of intimacy. For instance, although friends engage in levels of self-disclosure, they are not likely to share every aspect of their lives; intimate friends, however, often gain knowledge of the innermost being of their partner. Many same-sex friends feel more comfortable sharing their deepest secrets with their close friend than with their lover or spouse. As a result of this increasing amount of disclosure, close friends or intimates increase their investment in the relationship and develop a sense of "we-ness."

Likewise, the degree of intimacy between friends is often characterized by the extent to which one person gives up other relationships in order to devote more time and energy to the primary relationship. Especially when two people are testing the suitability of an enduring relationship—going together, engagement, or marriage—they spend long periods of time together.

Both the amount of intimacy and the nature of intimacy differ among family relationships, male relationships, female relationships, and male-female relationships.

Family Relationships Typically, a family may be defined as "a group of intimates who generate a sense of home and group identity, complete with strong ties of loyalty and emotion, and experience a history and a future."[9] Membership in a family may result from biological relationships, marital relationships, or voluntary psychological relationships with other members.

A person's first intimate friendships are likely to be with family members. For instance, small children first rely on their parents, then perhaps on a brother or sister. Family relationships may remain intimate ones; in many families sisters or brothers continue to see each other as their closest friends throughout their lives. During teen years and beyond, many other people develop closer friendships with people outside of the family.

Intimacy in family life is shown through family cohesion, adaptability, and communication.[10] Cohesion and adaptability are distinct processes with communication mediating between them.

Cohesion, of course, means "sticking together" and refers to the closeness and bonding of family members. What families do to help themselves stick together is an important function. However diverse individual family members may be, a cohesive force usually unites the family and differentiates family members from outsiders. For instance, if you have brothers or sisters, you may recall "knock-down drag-out" conflicts with them over any number of issues. Tension between siblings can be tremendous. As soon as someone from outside the family made a crack about your brother or sister, however, you suddenly found yourself joining together to repel the attack from the outsider. Family cohesion is developed and expressed through communication. A great deal of family energy and communication time are spent developing and maintaining family cohesion.

Regardless of how cohesive a family may be, the family unit as well as individual members change constantly over time. A second important function of the family is *adaptability*—how the family responds to change. Families are called on to change role relationships, power structures, and decision rules from year to year and sometimes from week to week. A family may appear remarkably stable for a long period of time but suddenly find that stability threatened by change in schools for one or more of the children, a new job for one of the parents, a death in the family, or a mother returning to the work force.

Changes in families may bring them closer together or drive them farther apart. For instance, a death in the family may lead to a greater level of cohesiveness than the family has had in years, or it may create such chaos that the family takes months or even years to return to its former level of cohesiveness. If the family is unable to adapt to such changes, its cohesiveness (and level of intimacy) may be irreparably damaged.

Male Relationships Throughout history, male relationships have been seen as the epitome of camaraderie. Large numbers of popular books, movies, and television shows have portrayed male comradeship and romanticized the male-bonding experience. Yet, using male behavior as a standard for defining intimacy has been questioned. For instance, sex-role expert Joseph Pleck has written that male bonding "may indicate sociability, but does not necessarily indicate intimacy."[11] During the last several years research has shown that male-male intimate behavior is qualitatively different from the standard definition that calls for "high levels of self-disclosure." As Julia Wood and Christopher Inman have pointed out in their summary of recent scholarship, men "appear to regard practical help, mutual assistance, and companionship as bench marks of caring."[12]

A great deal about relationships is revealed by what people talk about. The majority of conversation can be classified as topical (politics, work, events), relational (the friendship itself), and personal (one's thoughts and feelings).

Of the three, most men generally restrict their exchanges to the topical.[13] Likewise, men's friendships tend to focus on activities such as drinking, football, card playing, and hobbies. The topic about which men talk most frequently and in great depth is sports. The next most common topic among young men is sex.[14] Very few men discuss relational and personal issues with each other. After a decade-long study of five thousand men and women, Michael McGill found that only one man in ten has a friend with whom he discusses work, money, and marriage, and only one man in twenty has a friendship in which he discloses his feelings about himself or his sexual feelings.[15] The conclusion drawn from these data is that in their relationships with each other men have fun and loyalty but rarely the kind of intimacy that has been considered ideal.

What, then, is the primary nature of male friendships? Men see other men as filling roles.[16] Thus male friendship relates to specific aspects of their relationship rather than the relationship as a whole. Why are the traditional levels of intimacy between men low? Barriers to keeping males from achieving

● **Much of men's friendships focus on activities like drinking, football, card playing, and fishing.**

higher levels of intimacy have been attributed to male competition, aversion to emotional vulnerability and openness, homophobia, and a lack of role models.[17]

Female Relationships Female relationships seem to be the opposite of male friendships. Whereas male friendships lack intimacy and male conversation is largely topical, J. W. Hodgson and J. L. Fischer report that women have a greater capacity than men for experiencing the highest levels of intimacy.[18] Moreover, when women talk the great majority of their conversation tends to be on all three levels: topical (politics, work, events), relational (the friendship itself), and personal (one's thoughts and feelings), with the focus on relational and personal. Moreover, women's friendships develop more quickly than men's and tend to be more intense.

Despite the fact that female relationships are rich when measured by many of the criteria of effective interpersonal communication, females are not always satisfied with their female relationships. Because women care so much about others, they tend to experience the troubles of those close to them as their own.[19] This heavy emotional involvement can take its toll over time, leading to health costs and overdependence on the relationships.

Male-Female Relationships Male-female relationships may be characterized both as close, nonsexual friendships and as loving relationships that result in marriage. Intimacy is an important part of each.

Both friendship and loving male-female relationships are often frustrated by the fact that men and women seek intimacy in different ways. Male-female relationships are likely to run more smoothly when participants recognize and value the differing approaches. Men need to understand that for a woman, intimacy is defined as the sharing of information, feelings, secrets, and insights. Thus self-disclosing statements such as, "I really need your presence—I feel so warmly toward you" represent a female standard of showing intimacy. Women need to understand that for a man, intimacy is defined as practical help, mutual assistance, and companionship. Thus statements about what the man has done for an intimate friend, such as "While you were at the meeting, I washed your car and cleaned up the kitchen," represent a male standard of showing intimacy. So, whereas female intimacy is expressive, male intimacy is instrumental. In the past our society has valued a feminine preference for verbal disclosures as the measure of intimacy; recently more emphasis has been placed on the male tendency toward instrumental activity as equally important in determining intimacy.[20]

Both men and women have difficulty distinguishing between satisfying, intimate friendship relationships and romantic, sexual relationships. For many people it seems natural to assume that a close relationship between a man and a woman must become a romantic one that includes sex. In reality, romance and sex get in the way of good male-female relationships, for although romance and sex are enlarged and enlightened by friendship, friendship is often diminished by romance and sex. Sex is an intimate act that people often perform in the absence of intimacy—or as a substitute for it. That is, romance and sex may be a kind of an adventure pursued not for the mutual benefit of both parties but for the pleasure of the individual. The fact is that the intimacy of close friendship is harder to achieve and more solid than the capriciousness of romance and sex—we need to know we can count on it, like an anchor in those other stormy seas.[21]

At the same time, both men and women seek loving male-female relationships. Although we may have an intuitive sense of "being in love," the concept of love is difficult to define.

R. J. Sternberg offers a concrete definition of a loving relationship that includes three dimensions: intimacy (talking with and confiding in a partner), commitment (the desire to remain in the relationship), and passion (the feeling of sexual attraction and love for another).[22] Sternberg's descriptive definition recognizes that a loving relationship may contain high degrees of one, two, or all three components.

Ellen Berscheid and Elaine Walster offer a provocative analysis of loving relationships that focuses on the differences between what they call passionate and companionate love.[23] They say that passionate love is highly romantic and very intense—passionate lovers experience high levels of joy and sorrow. To passionate lovers, their love becomes all consuming: They experience frequent sexual contact, and the other person becomes the primary interest in life—all thoughts and energies go toward the person. While it lasts, passionate love is very exciting, but, Berscheid and Walster point out, passionate love seldom lasts. The partners may continue to love, but the love usually takes a different form—a form much more like companionate love.

Berscheid and Walster describe companionate love as much less intense, calmer, and more relaxed than passionate love. Companionate love leaves room for other people, other relationships, and pleasures other than romantic ones. Companionate lovers are quite content with less frequent and less intense sexual contact than passionate lovers. Trust is often the foundation of companionate love, and companionate lovers are more careful to honor their promises. From this analysis, we can see that Berscheid and Walster believe that, ultimately, companionate love is more stable, resting on a less fragile attachment.

To conclude our brief analysis of the nature of love, we look at the work of sociologist J. A. Lee, who considers six "styles" of love.[24] Lee says that *Eros,* the passionate love style, focuses on physical attraction and sensual satisfaction. _Storge_, the friendship love style, is characterized by caring and is based on similar interests and pursuits—a long-term relationship founded on mutual trust. _Mania_, the possessive and obsessive love style, is characterized by insecurity and dependence—possessive lovers become jealous easily. _Agape_, the selfless love style, sacrifices personal interests for the partner—selfless lovers give without expectation of return. They will share all they have and strive to keep their partner happy. _Pragma_, the practical love style, is characterized by a relationship based on satisfactory rewards. Finally, _Ludus_, the game-playing love style, is characterized by seeing love as fun, as a game that is not to be taken too seriously. Game-playing lovers like to flirt, keep partners guessing, and move in and out of relationships, allowing for no real commitment.

Underlying all three analyses is the theme that although passionate love provides the strongest motivation for a relationship, companionate forms are likely to sustain it in the long term.

In fact, most analysts seem to agree that an important caution for "young lovers" is not to let sex get in the way of allowing a loving relationship to develop. For some people—especially early in a passionate relationship—the sexual act defines the relationship as a loving one. What often happens then is that people confuse sex with an enduring relationship. And although good sex may in fact eventually be an important part of an enduring relationship, many bad relationships become apparent when the passion wears off.

A good marriage is the ultimate intimate relationship. In a good marriage, partners are likely to find great satisfaction in being with each other. J. D. Bloch, a psychologist who surveyed more than two thousand Americans, says 40 percent of all married people consider their spouse to be their best friend.[25] In a sample, 88 percent of married men and 78 percent of married women named their spouses as the person "closest" to them.[26]

Good marriages are those that survive the life cycle of honeymoon bliss, reality, and accommodation. Honeymoon bliss includes all the excitement of getting married and then that glorious week to several months when "everything is perfect." But soon "reality" sets in. Nearly all marital relationships become less intense and positive during the first year.[27] During this reality period, varying amounts of disillusionment set in. People discover that their partners are not perfect. Small things like snoring, biting fingernails, and leaving dirty clothes in a heap, and larger things like unwillingness to compromise, excessively permissive or strict views on issues, and the like, cause people to wonder how they can possibly live with this person for the rest of their life. Good marriages eventuate in accommodation. People not only learn to live with the faults of their spouse, but even learn to value many of the differences that for a while seemed so threatening. And during this time conjugal love replaces, or accompanies, romantic love.

Yet, even in many of the most accommodating of marriages, what husbands and wives get from each other is somewhat out of balance. Male and female intimacy needs continue to be different. Despite the fact that married women named their spouses as their closest friend, women still need close female friendships to satisfy all their needs. Men, however, report that their wives offer them the most satisfaction and emotional support of all the relationships in their lives—more than neighbor, co-worker, boss, parent, sibling, or same-sex and opposite-sex friends.[28]

Analyzing Relationships

BY YOURSELF

Make a list of the people you have spoken with in the last day or two. Now categorize each. Which are strangers? acquaintances? friends? intimates? Which began as role-based relationships and which as self-initiated?

IN GROUPS

1. Discuss how you determine whether a person is an acquaintance, a friend, or an intimate. What characteristics seem to signal that an acquaintance has become a friend and that a friend has become an intimate?

2. Contrast the nature of your communication with acquaintances and friends. What kinds of differences do you notice in the role of small talk and sharing feelings in each context?

Communication in the Life Cycle of Relationships

Even though no two relationships develop in exactly the same manner, scholars who have studied a variety of relationships have noted that they do seem to move through stages following a "life cycle." Mark Knapp, Steve Duck, Dalman A. Taylor, Irwin Altman, and Leslie Baxter are prominent scholars who have studied various aspects of the life cycle of relationships. Despite differences in terminology, their work suggests that relationships progress through starting or building, stability, and disintegration stages.[29]

STARTING OR BUILDING RELATIONSHIPS

Fundamental to starting or building a relationship is the need for information. We give information about ourselves to others so that they will have more accurate perceptions of who we are, and we seek information about others so that we can determine whether we wish to develop a relationship with them. Charles Berger and James Brada called this theory of the need for sharing information *uncertainty reduction.*[30]

All prospective relationships begin with uncertainty. If we don't know anything about another person, we don't know how to treat that person because we don't know how to predict his or her behavior. As we gather information we can make decisions about others on a rational basis. The strategies we use are passive, active, and interactive. Observing how a person relates to another person and drawing conclusions based on that observation is a passive strategy. Asking other people about the person you are interested in is an active strategy. Conversing with the person in question and sharing information about self is an interactive strategy.

Reduction of uncertainty seems to be important in all cultures in early stages of relationship development. People from some cultures may rely on passive methods of obtaining the information; people from other cultures may rely on more active or interactive strategies.[31]

Keep in mind that most people seek this information to predict the potential outcome of any communication. We are interested in whether continued communication is likely to produce positive or negative outcomes. It isn't only how much a person knows about another person, then, but how much that person wants to know, that is significant.[32]

In keeping with the spirit of categories suggested by Knapp and Taylor and Altman,[33] we will examine the communication activity in the starting or building part of the life cycle of relationships in terms of attraction, striking up a conversation, keeping conversation going, and moving toward intimacy.

● ● **Attraction** Attending college, working with a company, worshipping at a church or synagogue, and belonging to a club put you in contexts that help you to meet people. Yet, whether you are in a course with twenty-five other students, an aerobics class of fifteen, a prayer group at your place of worship, or a large business with hundreds of people, you may be attracted to only a small number of people out of that total. People are often first attracted to each other on the basis of physical characteristics.

But physical attractiveness appears to be only one door through which people pass to enter into a relationship. People also are attracted to those who are perceived as having similar social interests, work interests, back-

ground commonalities, attitudes and values, and personalities. The more interests people have in common, the more they are attracted to each other. Yet what people believe to be commonalities (based on initial perceptions) may not prove to be so. Moreover, even when the initial perceptions about common interests are correct over time, other factors may affect the relationship. And when the basis of attraction fades or proves invalid, the relationship suffers.

Relationships are also built on dissimilarities in personality. The saying "Opposites attract" is as accurate as "Birds of a feather flock together." Stated theoretically, relationships depend on mutual need fulfillment, so people can be attracted to those who are different from them as well as to those who are similar to them in order to fulfill their needs. Thus opposites attract when the differences between the people are seen as *complementary*. If each person's set of personality characteristics differs from the other's but each is able to satisfy the needs of the other, then the two people complement each other. In this sense a very outgoing person and a very shy person, although opposite in personality, may be attracted to each other because they "fit" together—

●People are attracted to those who are perceived as having similar social interests, work interests, background commonalities, attitudes and values, and personalities.

each provides something the other needs. Nevertheless, in addition to these complementary needs, or dissimilarities, some basis of similarity on which the relationship can grow must exist.

Striking Up a Conversation No matter how attractive you find someone, no relationship can begin until you talk with that person. Yet one of the most difficult situations for many people is the initial interaction with someone who, although attractive, is a complete stranger. Many people are so shy that, although they may be right next to the person whom they find attractive, they are unwilling or afraid to say a word. The first step to establishing a relationship, then, is building the courage to say something.

In most encounters, what happens in the first few minutes of an initial conversation will have a profound effect on the nature of the relationship that develops. As the old saying goes, you seldom get a second chance to create a first impression. How do you go about striking up a conversation with strangers in a way that will make a positive first impression? Although thinking up "getting to know you" lines is easy for some, many people become nearly tongue-tied when they want to meet someone and, as a result, make a bad first impression. For those of us who find starting conversations with strangers difficult, the following four strategies may be useful. Notice that each is developed in question form designed to invite the other person to respond. A cheerful answer to your question suggests interest in continuing. Refusal to answer or a curt reply may mean that the person isn't really interested in talking at this time.

1. *Formally or informally introduce yourself.* The simplest way to start a conversation with a person is to introduce yourself. For example, "Hi, my name is Gordon. What's yours?" may sound trite, but it works. Or if you feel uncomfortable with self-introduction, you might get a friend to introduce you.

2. *Refer to the physical context.* A common way to start a conversation is to refer to some aspect of the physical context. One of the oldest and most effective strategies is a comment on the weather, such as "This is awful weather for a game, isn't it?" Other contextual references include "They've really decorated this place beautifully, haven't they?" "I wonder how they are able to keep such a beautiful garden in this climate." and "Darlene and Verne have sure done a lovely job of remodeling this home. Did you ever see it before the renovation?"

3. *Refer to your thoughts or feelings.* A direct way to make contact is to comment on your thoughts and feelings, such as "I really like parties, don't you?" "I live on this floor too—do these steps bother you as much as they do me?" and "Doesn't it seem stuffy in here?"

4. *Refer to the other person.* "Pia seems to be an excellent hostess; have you known her long?" "I don't believe I've had the pleasure of seeing you before—do you work in marketing?"

Keeping Conversation Going Once two people have begun an interaction, they are likely to engage in relatively unthreatening conversations, that is, "small talk." Small talk typifies early stages of relationships and serves to meet many social needs with relatively low amounts of risk and disclosure of self and personal feelings. Moreover, small talk provides a basis on which to decide whether to move a relationship to the next level.

An effective type of small talk is simple idea-exchange. In *idea-exchange communication,* people share information that contains facts, opinions, and beliefs and that occasionally reflects values. Idea-exchange is a common type of communication between both new acquaintances and friends. At the office Pete may ask Walt about last night's sports scores, Gabrielle may talk with Louise about new cars, and Jamal may discuss the upcoming elections with Teresa. Or, on a more serious level, Pierre may talk with Gloria about the U.S. role in the Middle East, or Dave may seek Bill's views on abortion. Although the discussions of foreign policy and abortion are "deeper" than those conversations about sports or cars, both sets of conversations represent idea-exchanges. This type of communication is important to early stages of relationships because through it you learn what the other person is thinking, reassess your attraction level, and decide whether or not you want the relationship to grow.

A second type of small talk is gossip—relating information about people you both know, the accuracy of which may be unknown. Statements such as "Do you know Joel? I hear he has a really great job," "Would you believe that Mary Simmons and Tom Leavitt are going together? They never seemed to hit it off too well in the past," and "My sister Eileen is really working hard at losing weight. I saw her the other day and all she talked about was the diet she's on" are all examples of small talk. This kind of small talk occurs during all phases of a relationship but is most common in the early phase because it is considered safe. You can gossip for a long time with another person without really saying anything about yourself or without learning anything about the other person. Gossip may be a pleasant way to pass time with people you know but with whom you have no desire or need for a deeper relationship. It also provides a safe way to explore the potential for the relationship to grow, because it allows each person to see whether the other reacts similarly to the views expressed about the object of the gossip.

Gossip can, of course, be malicious. If the information exchanged is found to be inaccurate, the gossip may damage both the relationship in which it was exchanged and other relationships as well. More often than not, however, gossip represents a means of interacting amicably with others without becoming personally involved. This is why conversations at parties consist largely of gossip.

Moving to More Intimate Levels   In addition to engaging in small talk, people who are exploring moving to more intimate levels will begin to talk about more serious ideas and to share their feelings about important matters. Through the sharing of feelings and the process of self-disclosure you really come to know and understand another person. Although it is unrealistic, and perhaps undesirable, to expect to share feelings with a great many others, the achievement of a feelings-sharing level of communication with a few people is a highly beneficial communication goal. And when people find that they obtain satisfaction out of being together and are able to share ideas and feelings, their friendship grows.

People who are increasing the intimacy of their relationship begin to share feelings and disclose highly personal information. At this stage people are likely to seek out the other person for help with a problem. They may talk for hours, sharing both the joys and the sorrows of their lives. In Chapter 6, "Communicating Ideas and Feelings," we will discuss self-disclosure, description of feelings, and assertiveness in some detail.

As you may have noticed, the different kinds of communication that occur during the development of a relationship follow a continuum from impersonal-superficial to personal-deep. Because intimate relationships are time consuming and require a level of mutual trust that is difficult to attain, people generally have only one or two truly intimate friends at any one time.

STABILIZING RELATIONSHIPS

When two people have a satisfactory relationship, whether as acquaintances, as friends, or as intimates, they look for *stabilization:* a means of maintaining the relationship at that level for some time. Stabilization occurs when two people agree on what they want from each other and are satisfied that they are achieving it. For instance, you may have an acquaintance at work whom you can always count on when you need help on a project, and that person feels that he or she can count on you as well. Although you may have lunch together at work occasionally or may talk to each other at a business gathering, you have no other ties.

Because people become comfortable with others, they sometimes forget the behaviors that helped to make the relationship work in the first place.

Time after time we hear couples say something like "When we were going together he [or she] used to give frequent token gifts—he [or she] doesn't do that anymore." To be sure, in the heat of a growing relationship people engage in sharing behaviors that are unrealistic. But when these end completely, the relationship may suffer, especially if some other loving sign does not take its place. How often do we hear, "He [or she] never says 'I love you' anymore."

Once relationships are established, an important way to make ongoing communication within the relationship successful is to pay attention to maintaining a positive climate for communication, especially when the communication involves serious or sensitive issues. By "a positive climate for communication," we mean one that encourages the mutually satisfying discussion of ideas. Daniel Canary and Laura Stafford's research supports the idea that maintenance strategies seem to operate in conjunction with equity.[34] A positive climate is facilitated with communication that is perceived as descriptive, open, provisional, and equal.

● Through the sharing of feelings and the process of self-disclosure you really come to know and to understand another person.

● ● **Speaking Descriptively** Relationships thrive in a climate in which communication is descriptive rather than evaluative.[35] *Speaking descriptively* simply means stating what you see or hear in objective language, but it is deceptively difficult to do. Why? Because what you think is describing may be perceived to be evaluating or judging. For instance, if Hayley, as she walks out of a marketing strategy meeting with Juan, says, "Juan, that was a stupid idea, and everyone knew it," she would be making an evaluative statement. Labeling Juan's statement as "stupid" does not describe the problem with the statement. What, then, is descriptive language? If Hayley had said, "Juan, your idea was one that we had talked about just a few weeks ago, and everyone agreed that it didn't take into account the reality of the economy—that's why Doreen and Ivan treated the idea so summarily," she would be describing what Juan had done and why he had received such negative reaction.

How does evaluation affect the relationship climate? First, evaluation does not inform; it places a judgment on what has been said or done. Misunderstandings often result from a shortage of information. Before an evaluation can be understood, a person must have the data on which it was based. In conversation, however, people are inclined to skip over the information (the description). For instance, in a heated moment, the coach may pull Arnold from the game and say to him, "Keep up show-off play like that and you'll be on the bench permanently." Arnold may recognize that he made some offensive or defensive mistakes, but the term "show-off play" gives him no clear picture of the specific behaviors the coach resented. Arnold would have better understood the coach's evaluation of his behavior had the coach said, "Arnold, you're not following the plans. The last two times you had the ball, you had a chance to pass to an open man—in both cases, you took off-balance shots. Selfish show-off play is going to put you on the bench permanently."

Second, evaluations are likely to make other people defensive, especially if the evaluation is personal, negative, or contrary to the other person's perception. *Defensiveness* is a negative feeling or behavior that results when a person feels threatened. For instance, as Henry and Susan leave a musical comedy, Henry says, "That was a really enjoyable show." In a cutting tone, Susan replies, "Enjoyable? That shows your level of taste—it was the most miserable excuse for a professional production I've seen in a long time." Because Henry enjoyed the songs, her hostile evaluative statement is almost sure to draw a defensive reaction from him because it is both negative and an attack on his taste. Henry may sharply contradict Susan, or he may withdraw in anger from further communication with her. In either case, the climate for effective communication between them is likely to be spoiled, at least for the moment.

Basic Communication Skills

SKILL	USE	PROCEDURE	EXAMPLE
Descriptive Speaking			
Stating what you see or hear in objective language.	To create or promote a supportive climate.	1. Consider what you are about to say. 2. Consider whether it contains words or phrases that indicate or imply evaluation. 3. Recast the sentence to eliminate evaluation.	Instead of saying "That was a dumb thing you said to Marge," say "You told Marge that she could move in with us. Had you thought of how we would set up sleeping arrangements if she agreed to do it?"
Equality			
Seeing others as worthwhile as oneself.	To create or promote a supportive climate.	1. Consider what you are about to say. 2. Consider whether it contains words or phrases that indicate or imply that you are in some way superior to the receiver. 3. If so, recast the sentence to alter the tone.	Instead of saying, "As you gain maturity, you'll learn to cope with these situations," say, "That was a difficult one. But handling difficult ones helps you gain experience—and we all need experience to help us with special cases."

The descriptions you will want to use are of two types: (1) descriptions of behavior ("Did you know your eyes sparkle when you're happy?" or "Are you aware how much you increase the volume of your voice when you show me the mistakes that I made?") and (2) descriptions of feelings ("When you look at me like that, I feel warm inside" or "When you use that tone of voice, I get very defensive"). More detailed discussion of describing feelings will be presented on pages 191–196, and of describing behavior on page 253.

Speaking to Others as Equals Relationships grow in climates where the people treat each other as equals rather than in climates where one person is perceived as superior to another. In many circumstances people feel a need to be in control. To do so, they often create situations that force a complementary relationship. For instance, some people believe that their positions make them superior to those around them. Heads of departments or oldest members of the family may think that these designations give them a right to treat the people they talk with as subordinates. Whatever the basis for the assumption of superiority, however, projecting it often results in a negative rather than a positive communication climate, particularly when others involved are not convinced that the claim of superiority is justified. In contrast, choosing language that conveys an attitude of equality respects the humanity of the other person.

Equality in communication is usually shown by the exclusion of any words or nonverbal signs that might indicate the opposite. One way to alter statements that project personal superiority is to give the rationale for any statement that is designed to gain compliance from the other person. In a work setting, for example, a boss is a superior to a secretary. But line superiority does not mean that the boss is a better person, nor does it mean that the position alone gives the boss the right to treat the subordinate as an inferior whose feelings and needs are less important. So, instead of saying, "Bethany, get on this letter right away—I want it on my desk in twenty minutes," the boss could say, "Bethany, I got behind on framing this letter, and it really should be in the 3:00 mail. Do you think you could get it typed by 2:30 for me?" Even though the speaker is the boss, the second phrasing provides a reason for the request and shows sensitivity to the fact that the boss is responsible for the lateness.

In addition to choosing language carefully, we can be conscious of the effects of our tone of voice, facial expressions, dress, and manners. Through both words and actions showing that we are human beings—no better and no worse than others—we can create a positive climate for communication. By listening to others' ideas, by pitching in and working, and by respecting what others say, you can demonstrate an attitude of equality.

Speaking Openly *Speaking openly* means sharing true thoughts and feelings without resorting to manipulation and hidden agendas. Relationships grow best in a climate where the *agenda*—the subject or the purpose of the communication—is readily apparent. Suppose Rosa is having a conversation with her friend Brent, and she is thanking him for the information he gave her that helped her to write her report. The apparent reason for talking with him—the agenda—is to thank him. Sometimes in our interpersonal communication, we have an agenda that we have determined before the conversation, and sometimes agendas are made up as conversations develop.

Occasionally, however, participants in a conversation may have a secret underlying motive, known as a *hidden agenda*. For instance, if Rosa has been looking for Brent to find out what, if anything, he has been doing to schedule a band for the company's holiday party, Rosa's real reason for talking with Brent is her hidden agenda.

Communication between people who are trying to build a good relationship works best when the people involved understand what is going on in their conversations. When people aren't open about their reasons for talking, they risk erecting communication barriers. In some cases people use hidden agendas as a matter of tact, propriety, or lack of nerve. For example, Rosa may be too embarrassed to come right out and ask Brent whether he has done any calling yet, so she hopes that by thanking him for helping her, she can manipulate him into revealing whether he is meeting his responsibility for the party. In this case the hidden agenda may appear beneficial to Rosa. But when the real subject is revealed, her deviousness in trying to find out about his progress without his really knowing it may harm their relationship. He will be angry not only about her failure to be direct but also about her lack of trust.

When hidden agendas are discovered, the fragile bond of trust may be frayed or even broken, and with it the chance for a good relationship. Thus approaching a difficult problem directly is usually the best tactic. If Rosa really needs to know whether Brent has done anything about music for the party, she can have two agendas, but both should be open. For instance, after thanking him for helping her, Rosa could say, "Brent, I haven't heard from you yet about how you were coming in getting music for the party. Are you making any progress?" Dealing with the issue may prove difficult, but at least the difficulty will be the issue itself and not something else.

Hidden agendas also can turn into psychological games that can be destructive. A game is one person's attempt to manipulate another person's behavior until the manipulator gets some payoff, usually a predictable behavior. Notice the hidden agendas in the following two examples:

> Glen knows that Judy gets angry when he smokes in the bedroom, so he lights up in the bedroom and acts amazed when Judy loses her temper.

> Urie knows that Ming is likely to become very uncomfortable when his former girlfriend, Kyoka, is mentioned. So in her presence, Urie "innocently" asks, "Say, has anyone seen Kyoka lately?"

In both cases, the person's hidden agenda is to create a painful experience for the other person. If the behavior elicits the desired response, that person "wins." It is this win-lose element that makes such statements games.

Speaking Provisionally Relationships grow best in a climate where people are willing to state their beliefs, but there is a difference between stating a belief provisionally and stating it dogmatically. *Speaking provisionally* suggests that the ideas expressed are thought to be correct but may not be; dogmatic wordings leave no room for discussion. Whereas provisional language helps create or maintain a good climate for communication, dogmatic statements stop discussion and tend to create defensiveness.

Basic Communication Skills

SKILL	USE	PROCEDURE	EXAMPLE
Openness Feeling comfortable sharing true thoughts and feelings without resorting to manipulation and hidden agendas.	Helps create or maintain a positive communication climate.	1. Consider what you are about to say. 2. Determine whether the phrasing will cloud the issue or give misinformation about the goal of the conversation. 3. If it does, formulate a message that is clearer and more honest.	Instead of saying "Tom, I'm thinking of moving you to marketing for a while to give you broader experience" (a statement that is not open), say "Tom, you're not doing as well in the finance department as I had hoped, so I'm going to move you to marketing where you will be able to use your talents more directly."
Provisional Statements Wordings that suggest that an idea is an opinion or may not be entirely true.	Allows you to express your opinion but recognizes that others may have different ideas; helps create or maintain a positive communication climate.	1. Consider what you are about to say. 2. Determine whether it contains a wording that shows an attitude of finality or certainty. 3. If it does, add a qualifying statement that recognizes: (a) that the statement is your opinion, or (b) that the statement may not be entirely true or is true only under these circumstances.	Instead of saying, "That was the wrong way to sell the consumer on the product," say "I don't think that was the best way to sell the consumer the product" or "It seems to me that in this situation there were better ways of focusing on the strengths of the product."

Consider the differences between the two sentences in each of the following pairs:

"*If I remember correctly,* Dalton was the sales leader last month."
"*I'm telling you,* Dalton had the most sales last month."

"*I think you should consider* talking with Glenna before doing anything on your own."
"*You'd be an idiot* not to talk with Glenna before doing anything on this."

What differences did you notice? The first sentence of each pair is stated provisionally; the second is stated dogmatically. Why are the first sentences more likely to result in better interpersonal communication? First, the tentativeness of the phrasings is likely to be less antagonizing. Second, they acknowledge that the words come from the speaker—who may have it wrong. "I'm telling you" leaves no room for possible error; "If I remember correctly" not only leaves room for error but also shows that it is the speaker's recollection and not a statement of universal certainty.

Speaking provisionally may seem unassertive and wishy-washy, and if carried to extremes, it can be. But there is a world of difference between stating what you think to be true and phrasing your views in a way that is likely to arouse hostility. Speaking provisionally allows for conflicting opinions and the possibility that even a strongly held opinion may not be correct.

Now that we have considered four related skills—speaking descriptively, speaking to others as equals, speaking openly, and speaking provisionally, let's review the steps of ensuring that our statements meet these goals: (1) consider what you are about to say; (2) determine whether it contains a wording that shows an attitude of evaluation, superiority, or certainty; and (3) if it does, recast the sentence to change the tone. Many times we say things that hurt the climate because we are just not thinking. It's a good idea to follow the old advice of "engaging your brain before putting your mouth in action." Take a second to remind yourself that a single thoughtless sentence can take minutes, hours, or days to repair—if it is repairable.

RELATIONSHIP DISINTEGRATION

Regardless of how much one party would like a relationship to remain stable or become more intense, some relationships come to an end. Sometimes when a relationship ends we are sad; at other times it is a relief. Regardless of our feelings, it is helpful to know how to end a relationship in an interpersonally competent manner. Even the effects of a wrenching breakup can be somewhat improved with the conscious effort to use good interpersonal communication skills.

Just as researchers identify different stages in developing relationships, so too they identify different stages in deteriorating relationships.[36] In the spirit of the findings of these analyses, we will look at disintegrating relationships under the three headings of beginnings of dissatisfaction, drifting apart, and ending.

Beginnings of Dissatisfaction The first signs that a relationship is weakening are sometimes subtle indications of dissatisfaction. People begin to lose interest in the opinions and feelings of the other and their orientation changes from *we* to *I*. Subjects that once yielded free and open discussion become sources of conflict. The relationship begins to be characterized by an increase in "touchy" subjects, and people begin to experience more unresolved conflicts.

Why does this happen? Sometimes it happens because people rushed into a more advanced relationship than they could sustain. It is common for young people who are constantly testing relationships for long-term intimacy to misread the signs. For instance, Giselle and Leroy meet and find that they both enjoy rap music and dancing. As they pursue the relationship, they believe they have discovered other similarities that "make them just right" for each other. Soon they're going together, and they're sure that they will spend the rest of their lives together.

Before long, however, each notices things about the other that they hadn't seemed to notice before. For instance, Giselle really likes to be around many people—she constantly arranges situations where the two of them go out with two or more other people, and she enjoys parties. Leroy, however, likes to be alone with Giselle. Even when they go where others congregate, he likes to sit with Giselle alone. Suddenly they discover that they don't really like each other's idea of enjoyment. As two, three, four, or more of these differences occur, they learn that they really aren't as compatible as they had thought. When they discover that they can't work out these differences, they begin to become dissatisfied.

Often differentiation happens because people just change. For instance, Leroy says, "Giselle, you always used to enjoy going to games with me—early on, most of our social life was spent attending football and basketball games." Giselle replies, "That's right. I used to really enjoy that, but I don't anymore. I wasn't fooling you—I've changed." Or Giselle says, "Leroy, you always used to enjoy going on vacations with my family." Leroy replies, "That's right. I used to really enjoy that, but I don't anymore."

● ● **Drifting Apart** As deterioration progresses, people begin to drift apart. Their communication changes from deep sharing of ideas and feelings to small talk and other "safe" communication to no significant communication at all. It may seem strange that people who had so much to share can find themselves with nothing to talk about. But, in this stage, people don't see the need for an effort to build or maintain the relationship. Not only are they no longer interested in exchanging significant ideas, they may begin to avoid each other altogether, seeking out other people with whom to share interests and activities. Hostility need not be present; rather, this stage is likely to be marked by *indifference.*

Some married couples maintain this kind of relationship for years. Why would anyone want to be a part of such a relationship? Some people do it "for the children." Others stay in such a relationship because it is economically advantageous, and still others because of deeply held religious convictions. In other words, the relationship continues to serve some needs of the individuals even though it does not appear to meet their interpersonal needs for intimacy.

Ending The ultimate outcome of a deteriorating relationship is an ending. A relationship has ended when the people no longer interact with each other. As C. R. Cupach and S. Metts show, people give many reasons for termination, including poor communication, lack of fulfillment, differing life-styles and interests, rejection, outside interference, absence of rewards, and boredom.[37]

Unfortunately, when people decide to end a relationship, they sometimes look for reasons to blame each other rather than find equitable ways of bringing the relationship to an acceptable conclusion. When this happens, other relationships are usually affected. According to Leslie Baxter, in the termination stage people are likely to use strategies of manipulation, withdrawal/avoidance, positive tone, and open confrontation when trying to end relationships.[38]

Manipulative strategies of termination (put the blame on Mame) involve intentionally presenting evidence of a serious breech of faith, while leaving it to the other party to take direct action about the situation. These strategies are manipulative because the person is afraid to take responsibility for his or her actions. As a result, the person feels a need to make himself or herself the "hurt" party. Suppose that Paul wants to terminate his marriage, but does not want to take responsibility for suggesting the break. Over a period of months he sees to it that his wife will hear of his affair with another woman and he purposely sees to it that his shirts show lipstick stains and perfume scents that are not his wife's. At some point, his wife may then "kick him out of the house." This is an interpersonally ineffective strategy because it is dishonest.

Withdrawal/avoidance strategies of termination (what you don't know can't hurt you) involve indirect methods of achieving the goal of termination. Suppose that Judy is having tremendous difficulty with her parents, especially her mother, who continues to try to direct Judy's life even though Judy is twenty-five years old and a college graduate. To end this troublesome relationship (you can't very well divorce your parents), Judy takes a job in a different state where she can avoid seeing her parents (mother) except perhaps once a year. Although withdrawal/avoidance appears to provide a solution to interpersonal problems, it doesn't really deal with the issues that caused the interpersonal difficulty.

Positive tone strategies of termination (I/we have benefited, but it is time to move on) involve intentional use of positive communication strategies. Notice how the person in the following example terminates a relationship, but does it in an open, honest way that is likely to preserve respect for both parties: "Geoff, we've been going out together for a long time. And I think we've both enjoyed our relationship. But as much as I treasure our friendship, I've come to realize that I no longer have romantic feelings for you. Although this is hard, I respect you, and I wanted to be up front about my feelings. I hope that we'll be able to continue our friendship."

Open confrontation strategies of termination (honest appraisal) involve intentional methods that are direct and assertive. Like the positive tone strategy, open confrontation is also an open, honest method. It often takes courage to be honest, but it is interpersonally sound because it lets people know where they stand. Suppose that Jennifer wants to terminate her "going steady" relationship with Marshall, but she wants them to continue on good terms. One evening she says to Marshall, "I want you to know that I've really enjoyed our relationship, but during the last couple of weeks I've realized that although I like you very much, I don't believe that we have enough in common to ensure a successful marriage. I think we should begin to explore other relationships."

PRACTICE IN

Analyzing Stages of Relationships

BY YOURSELF

1. Label the following statements as E (evaluative), D (dogmatic), S (superior), or M (manipulative or portraying a hidden agenda). In each case rephrase the statement so that it is descriptive, equal, open, or provisional. The first one is completed for you. When you are done, share your revisions with other members of the class.

   __D__ a. "Shana, turn that off! No one can study with the radio on!"
   Suggested rephrasing: "Shana, I'd suggest turning the radio down or off. You may find that you can study better without the distraction."

   __E__ b. "Did you ever hear of such a tacky idea as having a formal wedding and using paper plates?"

   __D__ c. "That advertising program will never sell."

   __SD__ d. "Oh, Jack—you're so funny wearing plaids with stripes. Well, I guess that's a man for you!"

   __E__ e. "Malcolm, you're acting like a baby. You've got to learn to use your head."

   __M__ f. Noticing that she has only a short time before she intends to meet Gavin, Tori says, "Lydia, I don't see anything that looks right for you here. Let's plan to try Northgate Mall sometime next week."

___S___ g. "You may think you know how to handle the situation, but you are just not mature enough. I know when something's right for you."

Answers: b. E; c. D; d. S; e. E; f. M; g. S

2. Think of the last time you had a long discussion with another person. Which aspects of climate helped or hindered the effectiveness of that discussion?

3. Identify five people you consider to be your friends. In what kind of context did you first meet? What attracted you to them? What aspects of attraction have proved to be most important as the relationships developed?

4. Identify five people you consider to be acquaintances. List the ways in which communication with your acquaintances differs from communication with your friends.

5. Consider a recent relationship that has deteriorated. When did you notice that deterioration was taking place? What kinds of communication behavior marked the stages of deterioration?

JOURNAL ENTRIES

1. Think of two recent interactions you have had. Choose one that was characterized by a positive communication climate and one that was characterized by a negative climate. Recall as best you can some of the specific conversation from each interaction, and write it down like a script. Now analyze each script. Count specific instances of being descriptive and giving evaluation. Recall whether hidden agendas were evidenced. Count instances of provisional wordings and of dogmatic wordings. Look for instances where equality of interactants was present and instances where one person spoke in a way that conveyed an attitude of superiority. Discuss your results. How much did using or failing to use the four skills presented in this section contribute to the climate you experienced?

2. Consider a relationship that you have ended. Which of the four strategies discussed above best describes the way you ended the relationship? Was the termination conducted in a way that allowed for mutual respect? Or was it a messy situation that left you feeling uncomfortable? In your journal write how you feel about the way you terminated the relationship. If you believe your methods were positive discuss what contributed to that

feeling. If you believe your methods were negative, discuss what you might have done differently. Perhaps you can even write dialogue that exemplifies a more satisfactory interpersonal communication method.

●◆■ Summary

One of the main purposes of interpersonal communication is to develop and maintain relationships. A good relationship is any mutually satisfying interaction, on any level, with another person.

Relationships may build, stabilize, and disintegrate, often depending on the nature of the communication involved. Two theories about how relationships work are especially useful for explaining the dynamics of relationships. Schutz sees relationships in terms of the ability to meet the interpersonal needs of affection, inclusion, and control. Thibaut and Kelley see relationships as exchanges: People evaluate relationships through a cost-reward analysis, weighing the energy, time, and money invested against the satisfaction gained.

People engage in three types of relationships. Acquaintances are people we know by name and talk with, but with whom our interactions are limited in quality and quantity. Friends are people we spend time with voluntarily. Friendships are marked by degrees of warmth and affection, trust, self-disclosure, commitment, and expectation that the relationship will endure. Close or intimate friends are those with whom we share our deepest feelings, spend great amounts of time together, and mark the relationship in some special way. Intimate relationships can be discussed in terms of family relationships, male relationships, female relationships, and male-female relationships.

Relationships go through a life cycle that includes starting or building, stabilizing, and ending. In the starting or building stage, people are attracted to each other, strike up a conversation, keep conversations going, and move to more intimate levels. People nurture good relationships through the skills of describing, equality, openness, and provisionalism. Many of our relationships end. We may terminate them in interpersonally sound ways or in ways that destroy any chance of continuing the relationship on any meaningful level.

●◆■ Communication Improvement Goal Statement

Select a skill from among speaking descriptively, equally, openly, and provisionally and that you would most like to improve. Write a communication improvement goal statement following the guidelines on page 33 of Chapter 1.

● ◆ ■ Featured Reading

Managing the Equity Factor: Or "After All I've Done for You . . ."
Richard C. Huseman and John D. Hatfield
(Boston: Houghton Mifflin Company, 1989)

Huseman and Hatfield's book *Managing the Equity Factor* discusses how to apply the cost-reward theory, which we studied in this chapter. Moreover, their easily read discussion includes numerous insightfully written examples and illustrations to help us visualize the points they make.

The authors begin with the premise that many of us are frustrated when we believe that we have contributed more to a relationship than we have received. They argue that each of us has an internal system of checks and balances that influences the way we act in our relationships. They call this system the Equity Factor.

When we believe that equity in a relationship is out of balance, we act in some way to bring the relationship back into balance. In this book, Huseman and Hatfield expose the methods of gaining balance that are detrimental to relationships. For instance, when employees perceive inequitable treatment on the job, they may actively sabotage work until the Equity Factor rebalances. When people perceive inequitable treatment in a friendship, they may become highly irritable and/or behave so irrationally that the friendship is destroyed.

Huseman and Hatfield believe that by understanding the nature of the Equity Factor, we are better able to manage our relationships by achieving balance in constructive rather than destructive ways. They call the process of constructive balancing the Equity Power Paradigm. It includes developing perspective, positive expectations, goal setting, performance feedback, and engaging in novel, rewarding behavior. The authors provide behavioral guidelines and excellent examples of each of the factors in this paradigm.

● ◆ ■ Notes

1. Steve Duck and Robin Gilmour, eds., *Personal Relationships* (London: Academic Press, 1981), p. 2.

2. William Schutz, *The Interpersonal Underworld* (Palo Alto, Calif.: Science and Behavior Books, 1966), pp. 18–20.

3. Sarah Trenholm, *Human Communication Theory*, 2nd ed. (Englewood Cliffs, N.J.: Prentice Hall, 1991), p. 191.

4. Marvin Shaw, *Group Dynamics: The Psychology of Small Group Behavior*, 3rd ed. (New York: McGraw-Hill, 1981), pp. 228–231.

5. John W. Thibaut and Harold H. Kelley, *The Social Psychology of Groups*, 2nd ed. (New Brunswick, N.J.: Transaction Books, 1986), pp. 9–30.

6. Trenholm, p. 72.

7. Brian R. Patterson, Lorraine Bettini, and Jon F. Nussbaum, "The Meaning of Friendship Across the Life-span: Two Studies," *Communication Quarterly* 41 (Spring 1993): 145.

8. See M. Prisbell and J. F. Andersen, "The Importance of Perceived Homophily, Level of Uncertainty, Feeling Good, Safety, and Self-Disclosure in Interpersonal Relationships," *Communication Quarterly* 28 (Summer 1980): 22–33. They reinforce the importance of many of the characteristics we have listed.

9. Patricia Noller and Mary Anne Fitzpatrick, *Communication in Family Relationships* (Englewood Cliffs, N. J.: Prentice Hall, 1993), p. 19.

10. This "circumplex model" of family life, developed by David Olson and colleagues, explains specific aspects of the family functioning process. D. H. Olson, D. Sprenkle, and C. Russell, "Circumplex Model of Marital and Family Systems, I," *Family Process* 18 (1979): 3–28. Update: D. H. Olson, C. Russell, and D. Sprenkle, "Circumplex Model of Marital and Family Systems, VI," *Family Process* 22 (1983): 69–83.

11. J. H. Pleck, "Man to Man: Is Brotherhood Possible?" in N. Glazer-Malbin, ed., *Old Family/New Family: Interpersonal Relationships* (New York: Van Nostrand, 1975).

12. Julia T. Wood and Christopher C. Inman, "In a Different Mode: Masculine Styles of Communicating Closeness," *Journal of Applied Communication Research* 21 (August 1993): 291.

13. L. R. Davidson and L. Duberman, "Friendship: Communication and Interactional Patterns in Same-Sex Dyads," *Sex Roles* (August 1982): 820.

14. E. J. Aries and F. L. Johnson, "Close Friendship in Adulthood: Conversational Content Between Same-Sex Friends," *Sex Roles* (December 1983): 1189.

15. Michael E. McGill, *The McGill Report on Male Intimacy* (New York: Holt, Rinehart and Winston, 1985).

16. R. R. Bell, "Friendships of Women and Men," *Psychology of Women Quarterly* (Spring 1981): 404.

17. R. A. Lewis, "Emotional Intimacy Among Men," *Journal of Social Issues* 34 (1978): 108–121.

18. J. W. Hodgson and J. L. Fischer, "Sex Differences in Identity and Intimacy Development," *Journal of Youth and Adolescence* 8 (1979): 47.

19. "Psychology Revising Its View of Women," *New York Times,* March 20, 1984.

20. Wood and Inman, p. 280.

21. Letty Cotin Pogrebin, *Among Friends: Who We Like, Why We Like Them, and What We Do With Them* (New York: McGraw-Hill, 1987), p. 17.

22. R. J. Sternberg, "A Triangular Theory of Love," *Psychological Review* 93 (1986): 119–135.

23. Ellen Berscheid and Elaine Walster, *Interpersonal Attraction,* 2nd ed. (Reading, Mass.: Addison-Wesley, 1985).

24. J. A. Lee, *The Colors of Love: An Exploration of the Ways of Loving* (Don Mills, Ont.: New Press, 1973).

25. J. D. Bloch, *Friendship* (New York: Macmillan, 1980).

26. J. L. Fischer and L. R. Narus, Jr., "Sex Roles and Intimacy in Same Sex and Other Sex Relationships," *Psychology of Women Quarterly* (Spring 1981): 449.

27. Noller and Fitzpatrick, p. 178.

28. M. Argyle and A. Furnham, "Sources of Satisfaction and Conflict in Long-Term Relationships," *Journal of Marriage and the Family* 45 (August 1983): 490.

29. See Mark L. Knapp, *Interpersonal Communication and Human Relationships* (Boston: Allyn & Bacon, 1984); Dalman A. Taylor and Irwin Altman, "Communication in Interpersonal Relationships," in Michael E. Roloff and Gerald R. Miller, eds., *Interpersonal Processes: New Directions in Communication Research* (Beverly Hills, Calif.: Sage, 1987), p. 259; and Steve Duck, "How to Lose Friends Without Influencing People," in Roloff and Miller, eds., *Interpersonal Processes: New Directions in Communication Research*, pp. 290–291.

30. See Charles R. Berger and James J. Brada, *Language and Social Knowledge: Uncertainty in Interpersonal Relations* (London: Arnold, 1982).

31. William B. Gudykunst and Young Yun Kim, *Communicating with Strangers: An Approach to Intercultural Communication*, 2nd ed. (New York: McGraw-Hill, 1992), p. 194.

32. Kathy Kellermann and Rodney Reynolds, "When Ignorance Is Bliss: The Role of Motivation to Reduce Uncertainty in Uncertain Reduction Theory," *Human Communication Research* 17 (Fall 1990): 67.

33. For instance, whereas Mark Knapp, one of the first communication researchers to study building and deteriorating relationships, describes the development of a relationship as having five stages (which he labels initiating, experimenting, intensifying, integrating, and bonding), Dalman A. Taylor and Irwin Altman describe the development of a relationship as having four stages—orientation, exploratory, effective exchange, and stable exchange.

34. Daniel J. Canary and Laura Stafford, "Relational Maintenance Strategies and Equity in Marriage," *Communication Monographs* 59 (September 1992): 259.

35. A good background of descriptive versus evaluative, provisional versus dogmatic, and equal versus superior is laid in Jack R. Gibb, "Defensive Communication," *Journal of Communication* 11 (September 1961): 141–148.

36. Although both Knapp and Duck describe deteriorating relationships in four or five steps, they use different labels. Knapp calls them circumscribing, stagnating, avoiding, and terminating; Duck calls them breakdown phase, intrapsychic phase, diadic phase, social phase, and grave-dressing phase. See Mark L. Knapp, *Interpersonal Communication and Human Relationships* (Boston: Allyn & Bacon, 1984), and Steve Duck, "A Topography of Relationship Disengagement and Dissolution," in Steve Duck, ed., *Personal Relationships 4: Dissolving Personal Relationships* (London: Academic Press, 1982), pp. 1–30.

37. C. R. Cupach and S. Metts, "Accounts of Relational Dissolution: A comparison of Marital and Non-marital Relationships," *Communication Monographs* 53 (1986): 319–321.

38. Leslie Baxter, "Strategies for Ending Relationships: Two Studies," *Western Journal of Speech Communication* 46 (1982): 223–241.

CHAPTER SIX

Communicating Ideas and Feelings

OBJECTIVES

After you have read this chapter, you should be able to define and/or explain:

Characteristics of effective conversation

Conversational coherence

Turn taking

Self-disclosure

Cultural and gender considerations

Guidelines for disclosing

Describing feelings

Differences between displaying feelings and describing feelings

Owning feelings

Iris has just read the account of the change in requirements for her degree program. She is wondering how the changes will affect people like her and other underclassmen. During lunch with several fellow majors she begins a conversation on the subject. She says . . .

Luther has just been dumped by a woman he has been seeing for several months. The ending of the relationship is particularly painful to him because he was committed to it. That evening he gets together with his friend Phil to talk about how devastated he feels.

Iris and Luther are about to begin conversations. But the nature of their messages will be qualitatively different. Why? Iris will be sharing her ideas on the consequences of the change in requirements, so the effectiveness of her communication will depend on the quality of information that she presents. Luther will be sharing his feelings about breaking up, so the effectiveness of his communication will depend on his ability to disclose sensitive information about himself and describe his feelings.

Although communication is a dynamic, transactional process between people in relationships, one of the persons involved in the process must introduce topics of conversation. Moreover, even in the midst of a give-and-take interaction, one person may be focusing on presenting ideas and feelings rather than on responding to the other person's messages. Thus it is convenient to think in terms of both sender skills and receiver skills. In this chapter we consider the sender skills of communicating ideas, self-disclosure, and describing feelings.

Communicating Ideas: Conversation and Information Sharing

We tend to look up to people who are effective conversationalists. Yet we may not fully understand how to improve our own conversational abilities. In this section we examine skills for initiating and maintaining conversations. First, we consider broad characteristics of effective conversationalists, and then we turn to specific guidelines for maintaining conversational coherence.

CHARACTERISTICS OF EFFECTIVE CONVERSATIONALISTS

Being an effective conversationalist doesn't just occur. Although some people have what appears to be a natural gift for effective conversation, almost all of us can learn to be more effective participants. Effective conversationalists are likely to share many, if not all, of the following characteristics.

● ● **Effective Conversationalists Have Quality Information.** Although we sometimes think of conversation only as time passing, for many of us it is a primary source of information. John F. Kennedy is remembered by many as a Harvard graduate, but he often remarked that he learned much of what he knew through conversation. The key to solid, stimulating conversation is to have information that others value. Have you ever noticed how conversations come to life when one or more people have knowledge or expertise to share? Recently, a group of people were talking about the plight of the homeless and those who were stuck in almost uninhabitable housing owned by slumlords. The conversation picked up considerably when someone shared the specific information that she had gained over time. She spoke in detail about what she had learned from city officials who were studying problems of the homeless, and she talked about initiatives that had been taken by concerned individuals in the city. As a result of that one person's knowledge, the entire conversation was significantly more meaningful than it would have been.

You don't have to be an expert on a subject to have rewarding conversations. In general, though, the more you know about a range of subjects, the greater the chance that you will be an interesting conversationalist. Do you read a newspaper every day (not just the comics or the sports)? Do you read at least one news or special-interest magazine regularly? Do you sometimes watch television documentaries and news specials as well as entertainment

● **Effective conversationalists enjoy the give-and-take of informal discussion.**

and sports programs? (Of course, sports and entertainment are favorite topics of conversation, too—but not for everyone.) Do you make a point of going to the theater, to concerts, to museums or historical sites, and so on? If you answered "yes" to most of these questions, you are likely to have a fund of information you can call on in conversations. If you answered "no" to most of these questions, you may find yourself at a loss when you are trying to join social conversations. Exposing yourself to a broad array of information and experiences allows you to develop ideas that others will find interesting and provides grist for the conversation mill.

● ● **Effective Conversationalists Enjoy the Give-and-Take of Informal Discussion.** The best conversations usually occur when people enjoy interacting. Are you stimulated by listening to others present ideas?

Although some people regard a conversation as successful when they do all the talking, the other participants are likely to feel frustrated. A true conversation is not a one-way broadcast but an interaction that develops a shared meaning. In an effective conversation, you can expect to be the listener at least half the time. Are you likely to comment on, discuss, and even disagree with what someone else says? If you are, you probably enjoy the conversations you have. In addition, those you converse with can sense your enjoyment through the nonverbal messages you send. Listening and responding also involve specific skills, which we will consider in Chapters 7 and 8.

Effective Conversationalists Ask Good Questions. Many times the quality of your conversation depends on how well you can draw out the other person. Even when you are the major source of information in a conversation, the interaction will be satisfying to all only if the other people react to the issue being discussed. To encourage this kind of exchange, you need to develop your skill as a questioner. In Chapters 8 and 14 we will discuss types of and methods of phrasing questions.

Effective Conversationalists Have a Plan of Operation. Although many topics of conversation just "come up," more of our conversation than we may realize has a definable purpose that was known beforehand. For instance, you may be talking with your family to determine travel plans for the holidays, with your professor about how to study for his tests, or with a friend to get her support for a plan you want to bring to a church committee. Such purposeful conversations benefit from a conversational plan, a "consciously constructed conceptualization of one or more sequences of action aimed at achieving a goal."[1] Because conversation is a dynamic process for which you cannot plan for every possible response, the plan usually involves an opening approach and some idea of how to proceed given the most likely listener reactions. If your goal is to gain a friend's support for a proposal you want to bring to a church committee, you should anticipate possible reactions and have clear reasons and supporting data to offer for your plan.

Effective Conversationalists Are Willing to Try. No one becomes interesting, witty, provocative, and stimulating overnight. Becoming a good conversationalist requires practice and a bit of risk taking. Don't overlook opportunities to develop your conversational skills—scores of them occur every day.

GUIDELINES FOR MAINTAINING CONVERSATIONAL COHERENCE

The mark of effective conversation is conversational coherence, the extent to which conversational contributions of the people involved show relatedness[2] or, as Stephen Littlejohn puts it, the "connectedness and meaningfulness in conversation" that keeps a conversation well organized.[3] In this section we consider the topics of following the cooperative principle, crediting others, and turn taking.

Following the Cooperative Principle To achieve conversational coherence, H. Paul Grice has offered four conversational maxims that are organized around what he calls *the cooperative principle*—the need for contributions to be in line with the purpose of the conversation.[4] Grice's maxims are as follows:

1. *Try to provide an amount of information that is sufficient or necessary but not too much* (the quantity maxim). We can err by being either too brief or too wordy. Thus, if a person asked why you think the advertisement is ineffective, you would neither mumble some toss-off comment nor give a seven-minute lecture.

2. *Try to provide information that is truthful* (the quality maxim). Being truthful means not only avoiding deliberate lies or distortions but also taking care to avoid any kind of misrepresentation. Thus, if someone asked whether you know why the company is in a financial crisis, you wouldn't make up an explanation just to have something to say.

3. *Try to provide information that is relevant to what is being discussed* (the relevancy maxim). Including unrelated information disrupts conversational coherence. Thus, if you were asked about your boss's plans for the department, you wouldn't go into a recital of your problems getting along with the boss.

4. *Try to be specific and organized with your contributions* (the manner maxim). Coherence suffers when we give information that listeners find obscure, ambiguous, or disorganized. Thus, if someone asked you to explain how to use the new photocopier, you would walk the person through the steps of using it rather than ramble on about the machine's features in a confusing order.

When we sense that people are not conversing in the spirit of these maxims, we enact a set of interpretive procedures designed to help us figure out what is going on. For instance, suppose that Rob and Julia are standing by the watercooler, chatting about how employees are treated, when Rob says, "You know, we've all been a bit peeved at having to kick in twenty-five dollars to brighten up our conference room." If Julia then says, "The water just doesn't seem as cold as it should be," Rob will infer something about her response, such as "She must not want to talk about it, and she is telling me in a nice way that it's none of my business." Such an inference would be based on a conscious or unconscious analysis of her response, something like this: "Julia's comment isn't relevant, but there must be some point to it. I'm sure that she heard me, but rather than say what she thinks, she has chosen to say something irrelevant so I'll drop the topic."

K. Bach and R. M. Harnish have proposed two additional maxims they call the politeness maxim and the morality maxim.⁵ To comply with the politeness maxim, a speaker must not be obnoxious or rude; to comply with the morality maxim, a speaker avoids repeating information that is confidential, asking for privileged information, requiring the hearer to say or do something that she ought not to, or doing things for the hearer that the hearer has no interest in having done.

● ● **Crediting Others** A communication skill in keeping with this set of maxims is that of crediting others. *Crediting others* means verbally footnoting the source from which you have drawn your ideas. In a term paper you give credit to authors you have quoted or paraphrased by footnoting the sources. Similarly, when you use other people's words or ideas in your oral communication, you can credit the source. People get along better with others when they believe that their ideas and feelings have been properly recognized. Yet at times we may, through neglect or thoughtlessness, chip away at the very relationships we are trying to build or maintain.

Consider the following situation: Jorge suggests to Tina that their organization might make money by selling raffle tickets on a product they have bought at discount. Tina tells him that she thinks the idea is a good one. The next day, at a meeting of the group's fund-raising committee, Tina says, "What about buying a television at discount and selling raffle tickets? We could probably make a couple of hundred dollars!" The group responds immediately with comments such as "Great idea, Tina!" and "Tina, you always come up with good ideas." At this point, Jorge, the originator of the idea, will probably feel hurt or resentful that Tina is accepting credit for his idea. But if he says, "That was my idea," the group may think less of him for quibbling over whose idea it was.

In this instance it was Tina's responsibility to give credit to Jorge for originating the idea. Had Tina said, "Jorge had a great idea—what about buying a television at discount and selling raffle tickets?" the group probably would have reacted with the same enthusiasm, and Jorge would have felt gratified because he received credit for his idea. You can understand the importance of crediting if you think of the times you were hurt because an idea of yours was not credited.

Turn Taking A third aspect of conversational coherence involves mastering the skill of turn taking—engaging in appropriate conversational sequencing. Robert Nofsinger defines turn taking as "the various practices that participants use to change from one speaker to another."[6] Let's consider several guidelines that will help you with the turn-taking process.

Avoid speaking too often. People who consider themselves knowledgeable often feel a need to speak frequently. Yet it is usually inappropriate for any one person to dominate the conversation. If there are four people in a conversation, the ideal is for all four to have approximately the same number of turns. If you discover that you are speaking two or three times for every other person's one time, you are talking too often. To restrain yourself, you need to mentally check whether everyone else has had a chance to talk once before you talk a second time. If you find others violating this rule, you can help those who haven't been able to talk by saying something like, "Donna, I get the sense that you've been wanting to comment on this point."

Avoid turns that are too long. This guideline is in keeping with Grice's quantity maxim. People are likely to react negatively to those who appear to be making speeches rather than engaging in the ordinary give-and-take of conversation. You are likely to be engaging in turns that are too long when your statements are out of proportion to the maximum length of statements by others in the conversation.

Listen and watch for turn-taking and turn-exchanging cues. S. Duncan and D. W. Fiske have identified several cues that are associated with smooth turn taking. They focus on recognizing patterns of vocal tone, such as a decrease of loudness or a lowering of pitch, and use of gestures that seem to show obvious completion of a point.[7] When you observe people talk, look for those cues. Then, as you enter into the conversation, see whether you can still identify them.

Be careful of giving inadvertent turn-taking cues. For instance, suppose that you tend to lower your voice when you are not really done speaking or that you tend to take long pauses for emphasis when you expect to continue. In each of these cases you are likely to be interrupted, because lowering your voice and pausing are turn-taking cues that others are likely to act on. If you find yourself getting interrupted frequently, you might ask people whether you tend to give false cues. By the same token, you may come to recognize

that another person has a habit of giving these kinds of cues inadvertently, and learn not to interrupt when speaking with that person.

Listen for conversation-directing behavior. Although conversational rules are often broken, in general a person who relinquishes his or her turn may define who speaks next. For instance, when Leo concludes his turn by saying, "April, did you understand what he meant?" April has the right to the floor. Of course, if a person does not direct speaking behavior, the turn goes to the first person to speak.

Restrict interruptions to appropriate situations. Interruptions occur rather frequently in conversation. You may wonder why some people can interrupt without causing difficulty, whereas others cannot. The reason is often associated with the method of interruption. In general, interrupting for "clarification" and "agreement" (confirming) is interpersonally acceptable.[8] Interruptions likely to be accepted include relevant questions or paraphrases intended to clarify, such as "What do you mean by 'presumptuous'?" or "I get the

● **Effective communicators focus on recognizing patterns of vocal tone such as a decrease in volume or a lowering of pitch and use of gestures that seem to show obvious completion of a point.**

Basic Communication Skills

SKILL	USE	PROCEDURE	EXAMPLE
Turn Taking			
Engaging in appropriate conversational sequencing.	Determining when a speaker is at a place where a person could talk if he or she wanted to.	1. Avoid speaking too often. 2. Avoid turns that are too long. 3. Listen and watch for turn-taking and turn-exchanging cues. 4. Be careful of giving inadvertent turn-taking cues. 5. Listen for conversation-directing behavior. 6. Keep interruptions to situations that are appropriate. 7. Be sensitive to people's nonverbal reactions to your conversational method.	When John lowers his voice at the end of the statement "I really thought they were going to go ahead during those last few seconds," Melissa says, "I did, too."
Crediting Others			
Verbally identifying the source of ideas you are using.	To give credit to others in order to confirm them, avoid possible hard feelings, and clarify the source.	Include the names of sources of ideas.	"We've got to make some changes in our course offerings. Laura suggested that we offer a course in attitude change, and I agree."

sense that you think that presumptuous behavior is especially bad" and reinforcing statements such as "Good point, Max" or "I see what you mean, Rachel." Interruptions likely to be viewed as disruptive or incomplete include those that change the subject or that seem to minimize the contribution of the interrupted person.

Be sensitive to people's nonverbal reactions to your conversational method. If you notice people glaring or groaning when you interrupt, you need to apologize for the offense.

Conversation and Information Sharing

BY YOURSELF

1. List the five subject areas you believe you know the most about. Is there some variety in your repertoire of knowledge? To what extent does your repertoire help or hinder you in conversations?

2. Try deliberately to introduce greater variety in conversations with others. How well are you able to develop and maintain such conversations? Are they more or less satisfying than conversations on weather, sports, and daily happenings? Why?

JOURNAL ENTRY

For the next few days, keep a log of your conversations with others. At the end of each day, make a note of the people you talked with and the topics you talked about. Consider the following issues:

1. Was your turn-taking behavior appropriate? How do you know?

2. Did your contributions comply with the six maxims discussed in this chapter?

3. Were you sensitive to communicating directly and crediting sources of information?

Self-Disclosure

Effective interpersonal communication requires some degree of self-disclosure. In the broadest sense, *self-disclosure* means sharing biographical data, personal ideas, and feelings. Statements such as "I was five and a half feet tall in seventh grade" reveal biographical information—facts about you as an individual. Biographical disclosures are the easiest to make, for they are, in a manner of speaking, a matter of public record. By contrast, statements such as "I don't think prisons ever really rehabilitate criminals" disclose personal ideas and reveal what and how you think. And statements such as "I get scared whenever I have to make a speech" disclose feelings. In terms of accuracy in understanding of self and others, it is this last sense in which most people think of self-disclosure, that is, revealing personal, unknown information about self.

Self-disclosure is at the heart of what is called "social penetration theory." This theory says that the more people know each other as persons, the more *interpersonal* their communication becomes—likewise, the less they know, the more impersonal the communication becomes. G. R. Miller, a leading researcher in interpersonal relations, believes that through communication people move their knowledge of others from a cultural information level (information revealed in general social conversation), through a sociological level (communicating in relation to a person's group roles), to a psychological information level (knowing a person's individual traits, feelings, attitudes,

● **Through self-disclosure, people move their relationship from nonintimate levels to deeper, more personal ones.**

and so on).[9] Thus the role of communication is to move people from non-intimate levels to deeper, more personal ones.[10]

Usually, the more people know about a person, the better the chance that they will like that person. Yet self-disclosure does carry a degree of risk, for just as knowing a person better is likely to result in closer interpersonal relations, learning too much about a person may result in alienation. The statement "Familiarity breeds contempt" means that over time people may learn something that detracts from the relationship. Because some people fear that their disclosures could have negative rather than positive consequences, they prefer not to disclose.

Self-disclosure helps people to become more comfortable with each other, but unlimited self-disclosure may have negative effects. As Arthur Bochner has said, "There is no firm empirical basis for endorsing unconditional openness. A critical evaluation of the evidence suggests at most a restrained attitude toward the efficacy of self-disclosure."[11] By far the most consistent finding is that self-disclosure has the greatest positive effect on relationships when it is reciprocated.[12]

Cultural and Gender Considerations

As we might expect, levels of self-disclosure and appropriateness of disclosure differ from culture to culture. For instance, people from the United States tend to engage in higher rates of disclosure than people from Western Europe and the Far East.

Particularly in the beginning stages of a friendship, such cultural differences can easily lead to misperceptions and discomfort if the people involved are unaware of them. For instance, a person from the United States may perceive an acquaintance from an Eastern culture as reserved or less interested in pursuing a "genuine" friendship, whereas the acquaintance may see the person from the United States as discourteously assertive or excessively open about personal feelings and other private matters. Awareness of cultural differences can help us to recognize when we need to check out our perceptions instead of assume that everyone shares the standards of appropriateness and the verbal and nonverbal cues we are used to in our own culture.

Allowing for such differences, the question becomes whether advice about disclosure—that, when appropriate, it helps strengthen a relationship—holds across cultures. William Gudykunst and Young Yun Kim have discovered that across cultures social penetration—self-disclosure—increases when relationships become more intimate. In addition, they found that the more partners self-disclosed to each other, the more they were attracted to each other and the more uncertainty about each other was reduced.[13]

Moreover, consistent with conventional wisdom, women tend to disclose more than men, are disclosed to more than men, and are more aware than men of cues that affect their self-disclosure.[14] Of course, this generalization is not true in all cases.[15] In their discussion of differences in disclosure, Judy Pearson, Lynn Turner, and William Todd-Mancillas suggest several reasons that women tend to disclose more. For example, they say that women may disclose more because they are expected to (a kind of self-fulfilling prophecy), because self-disclosing is more important to women, and because of developmental differences.[16]

Differences in learned patterns of self-disclosure can create misunderstandings between men and women, especially in intimate relationships. In *You Just Don't Understand*, Deborah Tannen argues that one way to capture the differences between men's and women's verbal styles is to use the terms *report-talk* and *rapport-talk*. Her point is that men in our society are more likely to view conversation as report-talk—a way to share information, display knowledge, negotiate, and preserve independence. In contrast, women are more likely to use rapport-talk—a way to share experiences and establish bonds with others. When men and women fail to recognize these differences in the way they have learned to use conversation, the stage is set for misunderstandings about whether they are being truly open and intimate with one another. "Learning about style differences won't make them go away," Tannen remarks, "but it can banish mutual mystification and blame."[17]

GUIDELINES FOR APPROPRIATE SELF-DISCLOSURE

Although a risk-free life (probably impossible to attain) might be safe, some risk is vital to achieving satisfying interpersonal relationships. At the same time, too much risk can be more costly than we wish. The following are guidelines for determining an appropriate amount of self-disclosure in interpersonal encounters.

Self-disclose the kind of information you want others to disclose to you. When people are getting to know others, they look for information that is generally shared freely among people, such as information about hobbies, sports, school, and views of current events. These are the kinds of disclosures that you should make early in a relationship.

Self-disclose more intimate information only when you believe the disclosure represents an acceptable risk. There is always some risk involved in disclosing, but as you gain trust in another person, you perceive that the disclosure of more revealing information is less likely to have negative consequences. Incidentally, this guideline explains why people sometimes engage in intimate self-disclosure with bartenders or with people they meet in travel. They perceive the disclosures as safe (representing reasonable risk) because the person either does not know them or is in no position to use the information against them. Unfortunately, some people apparently lack the kinds of relationships with family and friends that would enable them to make these kinds of disclosures to them.

Move self-disclosure to deeper levels gradually. Because receiving self-disclosure can be as threatening as giving it, most people become uncomfortable when the level of disclosure exceeds their expectations. As a relationship develops, the depth of disclosure increases as well.

Reserve intimate or very personal self-disclosure for ongoing relationships. Disclosures about fears, loves, and other deep or intimate matters are most appropriate in close, well-established relationships. When people disclose deep secrets to acquaintances, they are engaging in potentially threatening behavior. Making such disclosures before a bond of trust is established risks alienating the other person. Moreover, people are often embarrassed by and

Basic Communication Skills

SKILL	USE	PROCEDURE	EXAMPLE
Self-Disclosure Sharing biographical data, personal ideas, and feelings that are unknown to another person.	Necessary to the initiation and development of a relationship.	1. Begin with information you want others to disclose. 2. Determine risk. Remember that people's attitudes about disclosure vary. 3. Move gradually to deeper levels. 4. Restrict intimate disclosures to long-term relationships. 5. Continue disclosure only if it is reciprocated.	May tells her current boyfriend, "I've been engaged three times before."

hostile toward others who try to saddle them with personal information in an effort to establish a relationship where none exists.

Continue intimate self-disclosure only if it is reciprocated. People expect a kind of equity in self-disclosure. When it is apparent that self-disclosure will not be returned, you should limit the amount of disclosure you make. Lack of reciprocation generally suggests that the person does not feel the relationship is one in which extensive self-disclosure is truly appropriate. When the response to your self-disclosure tells you that the disclosure was inappropriate, ask yourself what led to this effect. You can learn from a mistake and avoid making the same kind of mistake in the future.

PRACTICE IN

Determining Self-Disclosure Guidelines

BY YOURSELF

The following exercise will help you to recognize the variations in what people see as appropriate self-disclosure and provide you with a useful base of information from which to work. Label each of the following statements L (low risk), meaning you believe it is appropriate to disclose this information to almost any person; M (moderate risk), meaning you believe it is appropriate to disclose this information to persons you know fairly well and with whom you have already established a friendship; H (high risk), meaning you would disclose such information only to the few friends you have great trust in or to your most intimate friends; or X (unacceptable risk), meaning you would disclose it to no one.

_____ a. Your hobbies, how you like best to spend your spare time

_____ b. Your preferences and dislikes in music

_____ c. Your educational background and your feelings about it

_____ d. Your personal views on politics, the presidency, and foreign and domestic policy

_____ e. Your personal religious views and the nature of your religious participation

_____ f. Habits and reactions of yours that bother you at the moment

_____ g. Characteristics of yours that give you pride and satisfaction

_____ h. The unhappiest moments in your life—in detail

_____ i. The occasions in your life when you were happiest—in detail

_____ j. The actions you have most regretted taking in your life and why

_____ k. The main unfulfilled wishes and dreams in your life

_____ l. Your guiltiest secrets

_____ m. Your views on the way a husband and wife should live their marriage

_____ n. What to do, if anything, to stay fit

_____ o. The aspects of your body you are most pleased with

_____ p. The features of your appearance you are most displeased with and wish to change

_____ q. The person in your life whom you most resent and why

_____ r. Your use or abuse of alcohol and illegal drugs

_____ s. The people with whom you have been sexually intimate and the circumstances of your relationship with each

IN GROUPS (OPTIONAL)

Working in a group, discuss your labeling of the statements. The goal of the discussion is not to make any of the disclosures, only to discuss why you would make them and under what circumstances, or why not. The purpose of the discussion is to see how people differ in what they view as acceptable disclosure.

Disclosing Feelings

An extremely important aspect of self-disclosure is the sharing of feelings. We all experience feelings such as happiness at receiving an unexpected gift, sadness about the breakup of a relationship, or anger when we believe we have been taken advantage of. The question is whether to disclose such feelings, and if so, how. In general, the most effective way of dealing with feelings is neither to withhold them nor to display them indiscriminately but to describe them. Let's consider each of these forms of dealing with feelings.

WITHHOLDING OR MASKING FEELINGS

In most Western cultures, withholding feelings—that is, keeping them inside and not giving any verbal or nonverbal cues to their existence—is generally regarded as an inappropriate means of dealing with feelings. Withholding feelings is best exemplified by the good poker player who develops a "poker face," a neutral look that is impossible to decipher. The look is the same whether the player's cards are good or bad. Unfortunately, many people use poker faces in their relationships so that no one knows whether they are hurt, excited, or saddened. For instance, Doris feels very nervous when Anitra stands over her while Doris is working on her report. When Anitra says, "That first paragraph isn't very well written," Doris begins to seethe, yet she says nothing—she withholds her feelings.

Psychologists believe that habitually withholding feelings can lead to physical problems such as ulcers and heart disease, as well as psychological problems such as stress and depression. Moreover, people who withhold feelings are often perceived as cold, undemonstrative, and not much fun to be around.

Is withholding ever appropriate? When a situation is inconsequential, you may well choose to withhold your feelings. For instance, a stranger's inconsiderate behavior at a party may bother you, but there is often little to be gained by disclosing your feelings about it. You don't have an ongoing relationship with the person, and you can deal with the situation simply by moving to another part of the room. In the example of Doris seething at Anitra's behavior, however, withholding could be costly to both parties because Doris's feelings of irritation and tension are likely to affect their working relationship as well as Doris's well-being.

DISPLAYING FEELINGS

Displaying feelings means expressing those feelings through facial reactions, body responses, or paralinguistic reactions. Cheering over a great play at a sporting event, howling when you bang your head against the car doorjamb, and patting a co-worker on the back for doing something well are all displays of feelings.

Displays are usually appropriate when the feelings you are experiencing are positive. For instance, when your friend Simone does something nice for

● **When your friend does something nice for you, and you experience a feeling of joy, giving her a big hug is appropriate.**

you, and you experience a feeling of joy, giving her a big hug is appropriate; when your supervisor gives you an assignment you've wanted, a big smile and a "Thank you" is an appropriate display of your feeling of appreciation. In fact, many people need to be more demonstrative of good feelings than they typically are. The bumper sticker "Have you hugged your kid today?" reinforces the point that people we care about need open displays of love and affection.

Displays become detrimental to communication when the feelings you are experiencing are negative—especially when the display of a negative feeling appears to be an overreaction. For instance, when Anitra says to Doris, "That first paragraph isn't very well written," Doris displays her feelings of resentment by shouting, "Who the hell asked you for your opinion?" Such a display no doubt will embarrass and offend Anitra and short-circuit their communication. Although displays of negative feelings may make you feel better temporarily, they are likely to be bad for you interpersonally.

If neither withholding nor displaying negative feelings is effective, what is the most appropriate way to handle them? Describe them.

DESCRIBING FEELINGS

Describing feelings—stating the nature of your feelings in a calm, nonjudg-mental way—tends to be the most productive method of disclosing feelings. Describing feelings increases the chances of positive interaction and decreases the chances of short-circuiting lines of communication. Moreover, describing feelings teaches others how to treat us by explaining the effect of their behavior. This knowledge gives them the information they need to determine the appropriateness of that behavior. Thus, if you tell Ira that you feel flattered when he visits you, your description of how you feel should encourage him to visit you again. Likewise, if you tell Tony that you feel very angry when he borrows your jacket without asking, he is more likely to ask the next time. Describing your feelings allows you to exercise a measure of control over others' behavior simply by making them aware of the effects their actions have on you.

Many times people think they are describing when in fact they are displaying feelings or evaluating the other person's behavior. For instance, when questioned, Doris may believe her outburst, "Who the hell asked you for your opinion?" is a description of feelings. The first part of the communication practice at the end of this section focuses on your awareness of the difference between describing feelings and either displaying feelings or expressing evaluations.

If describing feelings is so important to effective communication, why don't more people do it regularly? There seem to be at least five reasons.

1. *Many people don't have a very good vocabulary of words for describing the various feelings they experience.* People can sense that they are angry; however, they may not be able to distinguish between feeling annoyed, betrayed, cheated, crushed, disturbed, envious, furious, infuriated, outraged, or shocked. Each of these terms describes a slightly different aspect of what many people lump together as anger. A surprising number of shades of meaning can be used to describe feelings, as shown in Figure 6.1. In the communication practice at the end of this section, we use this list to focus on developing your vocabulary so that you can describe your feelings more precisely.

2. *Many people believe that describing their true feelings reveals too much about them.* If you tell people what hurts you, you risk their using the information against you when they want to hurt you on purpose. Nevertheless, the potential benefits of revealing your true feelings far outweigh the risks. For instance, if Pete has a nickname for you that you don't like, and you tell Pete that calling you by that nickname upsets you, Pete does have the option

of calling you by that name when he wants to hurt you, but he is more likely to stop calling you by that name. If you don't describe your feelings to Pete, he probably will continue to call you by that name simply because he doesn't know any better. By saying nothing, you reinforce his behavior. The level of risk varies with each situation, but you will more often improve a relationship by describing feelings than be hurt by doing so.

   3. *Many people believe that if they describe feelings, others will make them feel guilty about having such feelings.* At a tender age we all learned about "tactful" behavior. Under the premise that "the truth sometimes hurts," we learn to avoid the truth by not saying anything or by telling little lies. Perhaps when you were young, your mother said, "Don't forget to give Grandma a great big kiss." At that time you may have blurted out, "Ugh—it makes me feel yucky to kiss Grandma. She's got a mustache." If your mother then responded, "That's terrible—Grandma loves you. Now you give her a kiss and never let me hear you talk like that again!" you probably felt guilty for having this "wrong" feeling. Yet the thought of kissing your grandmother did make you feel "yucky," whether or not it should have. In this case the issue was not your having the feelings but the way you talked about them. Chapter 8 will introduce skills for responding appropriately to others' feelings.

   4. *Many people believe that describing feelings causes harm to others or to a relationship.* If it really bothers Fyodor when his girlfriend, Heather, bites her fingernails, Fyodor may believe that describing his feelings may hurt her feelings so much that it will drive a wedge into their relationship. So it's better if Fyodor says nothing, right? Wrong! If Fyodor says nothing, he will still be irritated by Heather's behavior. In fact, as time goes on, Fyodor's irritation probably will cause him to lash out at Heather for other things because he can't bring himself to talk about the behavior that really bothers him. Heather will be hurt by Fyodor's behavior, but she won't understand why. By not describing his true feelings, Fyodor may well drive a wedge into their relationship anyway. But if Fyodor describes his feelings to Heather in a nonjudgmental way, she might try to quit biting her nails; they might get into a discussion in which he finds out she doesn't want to but that she just can't seem to stop, and he can help her in her efforts to stop; or Fyodor might come to see that it really is a small thing and it may not bother him as much. In short, describing feelings yields a better chance of a successful outcome than does not describing them.

   5. *Many people come from cultures that teach them to hide their feelings and emotions from others.* In some cultures, for example, harmony among the group or in the relationship is felt to be more important than individuals'

● **Describing feelings allows you to teach people how to treat you.**

personal feelings. People from such cultures may not describe their feelings out of concern for the health of the group.

To describe a feeling, proceed as follows: (1) Clearly identify your feeling. This sounds easier than it sometimes is. When people experience a feeling, they sometimes display it without thinking about it. To describe a feeling, you must be aware of exactly what you are feeling. (2) Put the emotion you are feeling into words—and be specific. Figure 6.1 provides a vocabulary of emotions to help you develop your ability to select the specific words that describe them. (3) Indicate what has triggered the feeling. The feeling results from some behavior, so identify the behavior. (4) Make sure that you acknowledge that the feeling is yours.

Figure 6.1

A list of more than 200 words that can describe feelings.

Words Related to *Angry*

agitated	annoyed	bitter	cranky
enraged	exasperated	furious	hostile
incensed	indignant	infuriated	irked
irritated	mad	offended	outraged
peeved	resentful	riled	steamed

Words Related to *Helpful*

agreeable	amiable	beneficial	caring
collegial	compassionate	constructive	cooperative
cordial	gentle	kindly	neighborly
obliging	supportive	useful	warm

Words Related to *Loving*

adoring	affectionate	amorous	aroused
caring	charming	fervent	gentle
heavenly	passionate	sensitive	tender

Words Related to *Embarrassed*

abashed	anxious	chagrined	confused
conspicuous	disconcerted	disgraced	distressed
flustered	humbled	humiliated	jittery
overwhelmed	rattled	ridiculous	shame-faced
sheepish	silly	troubled	uncomfortable

Words Related to *Surprised*

astonished	astounded	baffled	bewildered
confused	distracted	flustered	jarred
jolted	mystified	perplexed	puzzled
rattled	shocked	startled	stunned

Words Related to *Fearful*

afraid	agitated	alarmed	anxious
apprehensive	bullied	cornered	frightened
horrified	jittery	jumpy	nervous
petrified	scared	shaken	terrified
threatened	troubled	uneasy	worried

Words Related to *Disgusted*

afflicted	annoyed	nauseated	outraged
repelled	repulsed	revolted	sickened

Here are two examples of describing feelings: (1) "Thank you for your compliment [trigger]; I [the person having the feeling] feel gratified [the specific feeling] that you noticed the effort I made." (2) "When you criticize my cooking on days that I've worked as many hours as you have [trigger], I [the person having the feeling] feel very resentful" [the specific feeling].

Figure 6.1 (*continued*)

A list of more than 200 words that can describe feelings.

Words Related to *Hurt*

abused	awful	cheated	deprived
deserted	desperate	dismal	dreadful
forsaken	hassled	ignored	isolated
mistreated	offended	oppressed	pained
piqued	rejected	resentful	rotten
scorned	slighted	snubbed	wounded

Words Related to *Belittled*

betrayed	defeated	deflated	demeaned
diminished	disparaged	downgraded	foolish
helpless	inadequate	incapable	inferior
insulted	persecuted	powerless	underestimated
undervalued	unfit	unworthy	useless

Words Related to *Happy*

blissful	charmed	cheerful	contented
delighted	ecstatic	elated	exultant
fantastic	giddy	glad	gratified
high	joyous	jubilant	merry
pleased	satisfied	thrilled	tickled

Words Related to *Lonely*

abandoned	alone	bored	deserted
desolate	discarded	empty	excluded
forlorn	forsaken	ignored	isolated
jilted	lonesome	lost	rejected
renounced	scorned	slighted	snubbed

Words Related to *Sad*

blue	crestfallen	dejected	depressed
dismal	dour	downcast	gloomy
heavyhearted	joyless	low	melancholy
mirthless	miserable	moody	morose
pained	sorrowful	troubled	weary

Words Related to *Energetic*

animated	bold	brisk	dynamic
eager	forceful	frisky	hardy
inspired	kinetic	lively	peppy
potent	robust	spirited	sprightly
spry	vibrant	vigorous	vivacious

At first you may find it easier to describe positive feelings: "You know, your taking me to that movie really cheered me up" or "I really feel delighted when you offer to help me with the housework." As you gain success with positive descriptions, you can try describing negative feelings attributable to environmental factors: "It's so cloudy; I feel gloomy" or "When the wind howls through the crack, I really get jumpy." ~~Finally, you can move to negative descriptions resulting from what people have said or done:~~ "When you step in front of me like that, I'm really annoyed" or "I feel confused because of the tone of your voice."

Describing Feelings

BY YOURSELF

1. In each of the following sets of statements, place a D next to the statement or statements that describe feelings:

1. _____ a. That was a great movie!
   D _____ b. I was really cheered up by the story.
   _____ c. I feel this is worth an Oscar.
   _____ d. Terrific!

2. _____ a. I feel you're a good writer.
   D _____ b. Your writing brings me to tears.
   _____ c. [You pat the writer on the back] Good job.
   _____ d. Everyone likes your work.

3. _____ a. Yuck!
   _____ b. If things don't get better, I'm going to move.
   _____ c. Did you ever see such a hole!
   D _____ d. I feel depressed by the dark halls.

4. _____ a. I'm not adequate as a leader of this group.
   _____ b. Damn—I goofed!
   _____ c. I feel inadequate in my efforts to lead the group.
   D _____ d. I'm depressed by the effects of my leadership.

5. _____ a. I'm a winner.
   _____ b. I feel I won because I'm most qualified.
   _____ c. I did it! I won!
   D _____ d. I'm ecstatic about winning that award.

Answers: 1. b. (a) is expressive/evaluative; (c) is an evaluation dressed in descriptive clothing—that the word *feel* is in a statement does not mean the person is truly describing feelings. "This is worth an Oscar" is an evaluation, not a feeling; (d) is expressive/evaluative 2. b. (a) is expressive/evaluative (there's that word "feel" again); (c) is expressive; (d) is expressive/evaluative. 3. d. (a) is expressive but not a description of feelings; (c) is an evaluation in question form. 4. c and d. (a) is expressive/evaluative; (b) is expressive; (c) is similar to (a) except that here the is evaluative; (c) is expressive.

feeling is described, not stated as an evaluation. 5. d. (a) is evaluative; (b)

2. Look at each word in Figure 6.1 and say "I feel . . ." and try to identify the feeling this word would describe. Which words are meaningful enough to you that you could use them to help make your communication of feelings more precise?

IN GROUPS

Working with at least one other person, role-play typical situations (for example, Cody's roommate borrows his car without asking permission; the roommate comes into the room later and, giving Cody the keys, says, "Thanks for the car"), and then describe your feelings. After you finish, have the other person or people describe their feelings in response to the same situation. Continue the exercise until each member of the group has had two or three chances to practice describing feelings.

JOURNAL ENTRY

Think back over the events of the day. At any time during the day did you feel particularly happy, angry, disappointed, excited, or sad? How did you communicate your feelings to others? Under what circumstances, if any, did you describe your feelings? What appear to be your most common ways of displaying (expressing) your feelings? Discuss what you might do to make your sharing of feelings more interpersonally effective.

Owning Feelings and Opinions

Owning your feelings is a related self-disclosure skill. Instead of owning their feelings and opinions, people often tend to wrap them in impersonal or generalized language or attribute them to unknown or universal sources. Owning feelings or opinions (or crediting yourself) means making "I" statements to identify yourself as the source of a particular idea or feeling.

An "I" statement can be any statement that uses a first-person pronoun such as *I, my, me,* or *mine.* "I" statements help the listener understand fully and accurately the nature of the message. Consider the following paired statements:

"Advertising is the weakest department in the corporation."

"I believe advertising is the weakest department in the corporation."

"Everybody thinks Collins is unfair in his criticism."

"It seems to me that Collins is unfair in his criticism."

Basic Communication Skills

SKILL	USE	PROCEDURE	EXAMPLE
Describing Feelings Putting emotional state into words.	For self-disclosure; to teach people how to treat you.	1. Identify the feeling you are having specifically, for example, hate, anger, joy. 2. Put the feeling into words. 3. Indicate what has triggered the feeling. 4. Own your feeling.	"I'm depressed and discouraged because I didn't get the job" or "I'm feeling very warm and loving toward you right now because of the way you stood up for me when I was being put down by Leah."
Owning Feelings Making an "I" statement to identify yourself as the source of an idea or feeling.	To help the listener understand that the thought or feeling is yours.	When an idea, opinion, or feeling is yours, say so.	Instead of saying, "Maury's is the best restaurant in town," say, "I believe Maury's is the best restaurant in town."

"It's common knowledge that the boss favors anything that Bernardo does."

"In my opinion, the boss favors anything that Bernardo does."

"Nobody likes to be laughed at."

"Being laughed at embarrasses me."

Each of these examples contrasts a generalized or impersonal account with an "I" statement. Why do people use vague referents to others rather than owning their ideas and feelings? There are two basic reasons.

1. *To strengthen the power of their statements.* Saying "Everybody thinks Collins is unfair in his criticism" means that if listeners doubt the statement, they are bucking the collective evaluation of countless people. Of course, not everybody knows that Collins is unfair. In this instance the statement really means that one person holds the belief. People who think that their feelings or beliefs will not carry much power may feel the need to cite unknown or universal sources for those feelings or beliefs.

2. *To escape responsibility.* Similarly, people use collective statements such as "everybody agrees" and "anyone with any sense" to escape responsibility for their own feelings and thoughts. It seems far more difficult for a person to say, "I don't like Herb," than it is to say, "No one likes Herb."

The problem with generalized statements is that at best they are exaggerations and at worst they are deceitful. Being both accurate and honest with others requires taking responsibility for our own feelings and opinions. We all have a right to our reactions. If what you are saying is truly your opinion or an expression of how you really feel, let others know, and be willing to take responsibility for it. Otherwise, you may alienate people who would have respected your opinions or feelings even if they didn't agree with them.

PRACTICE IN

Owning Feelings and Opinions

BY YOURSELF

1. Are you likely to credit statements of your own? Under what circumstances?

2. Write down five opinions, beliefs, or feelings you have. Check to make sure each is phrased as an "I" statement. If not, correct each one. For example, "Nobody likes a sore loser" becomes "I don't like a sore loser."

● ◆ ■ Summary

In this chapter we discussed communicating ideas and feelings. Communicating ideas begins with initiating a conversation. People gravitate toward individuals who are knowledgeable, who enjoy interaction, who ask good questions, who have a plan, and who are willing to converse.

Good conversationalists know what is appropriate and what is inappropriate for keeping a conversation well organized. They maintain the cooperative principle by following maxims of quantity, quality, relevance, manner, politeness, and morality. They credit ideas of others; and they master turn taking by being sensitive to how often, how long, and when to speak, conversation-directing behavior, inappropriate interruptions, and nonverbal reactions.

Sharing feelings begins with self-disclosure statements, which reveal information about yourself that is unknown to others. Describing feelings is the skill that helps teach people how to treat you. Although displaying feelings may psychologically benefit the person doing the displaying, describing feelings represents a sounder way of handling feelings, especially negative ones. Owning feelings clarifies that you are the source of ideas and opinions.

● ◆ ■ Communication Improvement Goal Statement

Select one of the skills of crediting others, turn taking, describing feelings, or owning feelings that you would most like to improve. Write a communication improvement goal statement following the guidelines on page 33 of Chapter 1.

● ◆ ■ **Featured Reading**

Everyday Conversation

Robert E. Nofsinger

(Newbury Park, Calif.: Sage, 1991)

Although we all engage in conversation, many of us experience problems in talking with certain people or about particular subjects. As Nofsinger points out, at times we seem unable to get a word in edgewise or to get others to talk about the things we're interested in. Moreover, there are times when we feel that others have not really understood what we were saying. Nofsinger believes that by understanding some of the technical details of how conversation works and by taking advantage of its dynamics, we may become more skillful.

Nofsinger's book focuses on pragmatics—that is, the study of actual language use in specific situations. He suggests that everyday conversation is a collection of language games. It involves a defined set of behaviors, often called "moves." Moves are designed to contribute to the attainment of goals. The choice of which moves to make is a matter of tactics (what to do and what not to do) and strategy (the overall "game plan").

The book examines in detail how people actually conduct conversations. Chapters are devoted to in-depth discussions of conversational action (what people "do" in conversation, their "moves"), conversational sequences (how people order what they say), turn-taking practices and conventions, and methods for repairing conversational mistakes and misunderstandings. Throughout the book Nofsinger emphasizes how people conduct their conversations, rather than why they conduct them as they do. Thus the book has its foundations squarely in the study of communication, not psychological theory.

People who are adept at the art of conversation, as well as those who are mystified by it, will find this book valuable. Those adept at conversation will enhance their abilities by gaining additional insight into the conversational process. Those who have been mystified as to how to be an effective conversationalist will come to understand the conversational "game" more clearly. Because Nofsinger uses examples from real conversations to illustrate technical points, his book is as interesting as it is informative.

● ◆ ■ **Notes**

1. J. R. Hobbs and D. A. Evans, "Conversation as Planned Behavior," *Cognitive Science* 4 (1980): 349–377.

2. Mary L. McLaughlin, *Conversation: How Talk Is Organized* (Newbury Park, Calif.: Sage, 1984), pp. 88–89.

3. Stephen W. Littlejohn, *Theories of Human Communication*, 4th ed. (Belmont, Calif.: Wadsworth, 1992), p. 91.

4. H. P. Grice, "Logic and Conversation," in Peter Cole and Jerry L. Morgan, eds., *Syntax and Semantics*, Vol. 3: *Speech Acts* (New York: Academic Press, 1975), pp. 44–46.

5. K. Bach and R. M. Harnish, *Linguistic Communication and Speech Acts* (Cambridge, Mass.: MIT Press, 1979), p. 64.

6. Robert E. Nofsinger, *Everyday Conversation* (Newbury Park, Calif.: Sage, 1991), p. 81.

7. S. Duncan, Jr., and D. W. Fiske, *Face-to-Face Interaction: Research, Methods, and Theory* (Hillsdale, N.J.: Erlbaum, 1977), pp. 184–196.

8. C. W. Kennedy and C. T. Camden, "A New Look at Interruptions," *Western Journal of Speech Communication* 47 (1983): 55.

9. Littlejohn, pp. 274–275.

10. See Irwin Altman and Donald Taylor, *Social Penetration: The Development of Interpersonal Relationships* (New York: Holt, Rinehart and Winston, 1973). Altman and Taylor coined the phrase *social penetration.*

11. Arthur P. Bochner, "The Functions of Human Communicating in Interpersonal Bonding," in Carroll C. Arnold and John Waite Bowers, eds., *Handbook of Rhetorical and Communication Theory* (Needham Heights, Mass.: Allyn & Bacon, 1984), p. 608.

12. John H. Berg and Valerian J. Derlega, "Themes in the Study of Self-Disclosure," in John H. Berg and Valerian J. Derlega, eds., *Self-Disclosure: Theory, Research, and Therapy* (New York: Plenum Press, 1987), p. 4.

13. William B. Gudykunst and Young Yun Kim, *Communicating with Strangers: An Approach to Intercultural Communication*, 2nd ed. (New York: McGraw-Hill, 1992), p. 202.

14. Judy Cornelia Pearson, Lynn H. Turner, and William Todd-Mancillas, *Gender and Communication*, 2nd ed. (Dubuque, Iowa: Wm. C. Brown, 1991), p. 177.

15. Charles T. Hill and Donald E. Stull, "Gender and Self-Disclosure: Strategies for Exploring the Issues," in John H. Berg and Valerian J. Derlega, eds., *Self-Disclosure: Theory, Research, and Therapy* (New York: Plenum Press, 1987), p. 95.

16. Pearson, Turner, and Todd-Mancillas, p. 177.

17. Deborah Tannen, *You Just Don't Understand* (New York: Morrow, 1990), p. 48.

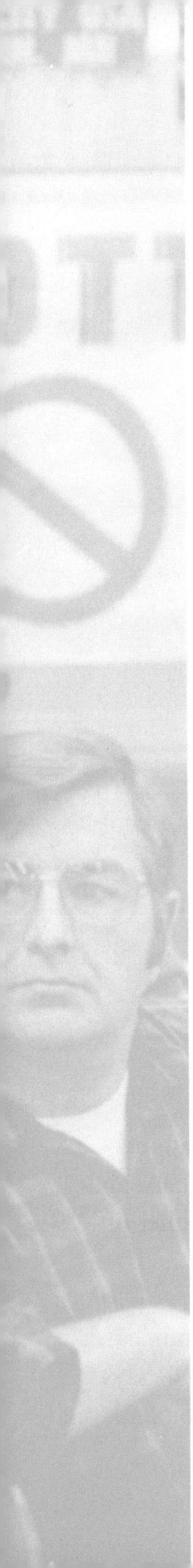

CHAPTER SEVEN

Listening Skills

OBJECTIVES

After you have read this chapter, you should be able to define and/or explain:

Focusing your attention

Listening actively

Three different devices for remembering information

Evaluating inferences

"Ah, Stella—it's so good to have someone to talk with, someone who really can understand what I'm saying."

"I know what you mean, Carl."

"I'm not sure just what I should do. Sally came home last night and just looked so tired."

"Tired—I know exactly what you mean. I've been exhausted lately myself."

"You see, Sally's been doing Yoshi's work while Yoshi has been out sick the last couple of weeks. Now, a couple of days were all right, but a couple of weeks are just too much for Sally to handle. Why, her own job takes as much energy as one woman has to spend."

"But then it's no wonder I've been exhausted, what with walking Kim to kindergarten every morning and getting her at noon, taking Jill to the doctor on the bus after school Monday, Jill and Ian both to crafts class at the Community Center on Tuesday . . ."

"I think Sally's just going to have to put her foot down. I said to her this morning, 'Sally, talk to Schulman—tell him you can't take it,' but she just says, 'I can handle it—and Yoshi would do the same for me.'"

"Now to top it off, Grandma Schmidt's staying with us for a few weeks while she recovers from her operation. Geez, my whole life is spent waiting on others."

"I know she wants to help Yoshi out, but she can only do so much before she's going to go under."

"Exhausted or not, I have to keep going. Well, have to run, Carl, the merry-go-round is about to start."

Stella thought, "Thank God I have a friend like Carl—someone who really listens to me."

Do you listen carefully to others? Or are your conversations more like the one between Stella and Carl? Although Stella and Carl may have a good relationship, in this example neither of them was listening very well. What are the consequences of poor listening to interpersonal communication?

First, poor listening accounts for many of the communication breakdowns between people. For instance, Chantelle says to Don, "I'm going to be with the film crew on location and won't be able to pick up LeKendra at 3:30, so you will have to pick her up." Don, catching a reference to the film crew, nods and says, "OK." Don realizes what he missed when at 4:15 he answers the phone only to hear LeKendra say, "Dad, aren't you picking me up?" Mistakes like these strain family relationships and leave a person open to questions about priorities.

Second, poor listening accounts for wasted time, energy, and money. For instance, Margot tells Jack, "I need you to run twenty-five on regular-size paper with a blue cover page and seventy-five on legal-size paper with a yellow cover page." Later in the day when Jack brings the forms Margot notices that the twenty-five with a blue cover are on legal-size paper and the rest with a yellow cover are on regular-size paper. When Margot says, "Jack, I said twenty-five on regular size and seventy-five on legal size," Jack replies, "Oh, I'm sorry, I mixed it up." Mistakes like these happen all too frequently.

Perhaps these problems wouldn't be so significant if listening played a smaller role in communication. But the fact is that in your daily communication you may spend more of your time listening than you do speaking, reading, and writing combined. One study found that college students spend 16 percent of their time speaking, 17 percent reading, 14 percent writing, and 53 percent listening.[1] Yet, after forty-eight hours, most listeners can remember only about 25 percent of what they heard.[2] Considering its importance and how little attention most of us pay to it, listening may be the most underrated of all communication skills.

What is listening? When Andrew Wolvin and Carolyn Coakley studied various definitions, they found more than twenty-five overlapping words and phrases that were used.[3] In this book we define *listening* as an active five-step process that includes attending, understanding, remembering, evaluating, and responding. Because each phase of listening requires distinct, specific skills, we discuss each separately—the first four in this chapter and the fifth, responding, in the next chapter.

Attending—Focusing Attention

The first phase of the listening process is to attend to—to focus our attention in such a way that we hear what people are saying and disregard extraneous sounds.

Attending is the perceptual process of selecting specific stimuli from the countless stimuli reaching the senses. Stop reading for a minute, and try to be conscious of all the sounds occurring around you. Perhaps you notice the humming of an electrical appliance, the rhythm of street traffic, the singing of birds, the footsteps in the hall, a cough from an adjoining room. Yet, while you were reading, you may have been unaware of these sounds and perceived your environment as quiet. In fact, our environment is seldom totally silent. But whereas some sounds intrude sharply on our consciousness, others go entirely unnoticed. Why is it that we "hear" or attend to some sounds and not others?

Although we hear any sounds emitted within our hearing range, we exercise a certain amount of psychological control over the sounds we attend to. For instance, as you and a friend chat while you walk to class, you both receive and attend to each other's words. At the same time you may physically "hear" footsteps behind you, the chiming of school bells, and birds singing, but you are able to block them out. In fact, you may be so unconscious of background noise that you would deny that certain sounds occurred.

Poor listeners are likely to exercise insufficient control over which sounds they attend to. Improving your listening skills begins with learning to bring some sounds to the foreground while keeping others in the background. People who have developed this skill are able to focus their attention so well that only sounds such as a fire alarm, a car crashing into a post, or the cry of their child can intrude on their attention.

Let's consider five techniques for consciously focusing attention.

1. *Try to eliminate physical impediments to listening.* First, we need to be assertive about seeing to it that conditions for listening are well maintained. If, for instance, the radio is playing so loudly that you are having difficulty hearing your roommate, you can turn down the radio while she is talking.

Second, we need to be aware of our own physical limitations. Nearly 15 million Americans suffer from some hearing impairment that may be significant enough to affect their ability to listen.[4] If you are among this number, you may wear a hearing aid or you may have learned to adapt to the problem. If you often miss spoken words and have to ask that they be repeated, however, you may have a hearing impairment you are unaware of that limits your listening effectiveness. If you suspect you have a hearing problem, undergo a

complete hearing examination. Most colleges have facilities for testing hearing acuity. The test is painless and is usually provided at small, if any, cost to the student.

2. *Get physically and mentally ready to listen.* Poor listening often results from our failure to get ready to listen. Many of us have developed a set of behaviors we associate with attentive listening. Suppose that a few minutes after class begins your professor says, "In the next two minutes, I'm going to cover some material that is especially important—in fact, I can guarantee that it will be on the test." How would you behave? Although we do not all behave the same way, we are likely to sit upright in our chairs, lean slightly forward, and cease any extraneous physical movement. Each of these are physical signs of being ready to listen. We may also look directly at the professor—when eye contact is not maintained, at least some information is lost.[5]

Mentally we are likely to direct all our attention to what the professor is saying, which includes attempting to block out the miscellaneous thoughts constantly passing through our minds. Recall that when people are talking

● **When we are ready to listen, we are likely to sit upright in our chairs, lean slightly forward, and cease any extraneous physical movement.**

with you, their ideas and feelings compete with the internal noise created by whatever is on your mind at the moment—a basketball game, a calculus test, a date you're excited about, a movie you've just seen. And what you're thinking about may be more pleasant to attend to than what someone is saying to you. Attending to these competing thoughts and feelings is one of the leading causes of poor listening.

3. *Make the shift from speaker to listener a complete one.* In the classroom where you listen continuously for long stretches, it is relatively easy to develop a "listening attitude." In conversation, however, you are called on to switch back and forth from speaker to listener so frequently that you may find it difficult at times to make these shifts completely. If, instead of listening, you spend your time rehearsing what you're going to say as soon as you have a chance, your listening effectiveness will take a nosedive. We have all experienced situations in which two persons talked right past each other—both participants in a conversation broadcasting and neither receiving! Especially when you are in a heated conversation, take a second to check yourself: Are you preparing speeches instead of listening? Shifting from the role of speaker to that of listener requires constant and continuous effort.

4. *Hear a person out before you react.* Far too often we stop listening before a person has finished speaking because we "know what the person is going to say." Yet until the person has finished, we don't have all the data necessary to form an appropriate response—our "knowing" what a person is going to say really is only a guess. Moreover, even if we guess right, the person may still feel that we weren't really listening, and the communication will suffer as a result. Accordingly, cultivate the habit of always letting a person complete his or her thought before you stop listening or try to respond. At times your attentive listening may be the best response you can make. Most of us need to learn the value of silence in freeing the speaker to think, feel, and express himself or herself. As the old Hebrew adage goes, "The beginning of wisdom is silence."

In addition to prematurely ceasing to listen, we often let certain mannerisms and words interfere with hearing a person out, perhaps to the extent of "tuning out." For instance, we may become annoyed when a speaker mutters, stammers, or talks in a monotone. But in these situations, we should work even harder at concentrating on what the person is saying.

Likewise, we may tune out when the speaker uses language or presents ideas that are irritating to us. Are there any words or ideas that create bursts of semantic noise for you, causing you to stop listening attentively? For instance, do you have a tendency to react negatively or tune out when people speak of *gay rights, skinheads, welfare frauds, political correctness,* or *rednecks*? To counteract this effect, try to let a warning light go on when a speaker trips the switch to your emotional reaction. Instead of tuning out or getting ready to fight, be aware of this "noise" and work that much harder to listen objectively. If you can do it, you will be more likely to receive the whole message accurately before you respond.

5. *Adjust to the listening goals of the situation.* Listening is similar to reading in that you need to adjust *how* you listen to the particular goal you wish to achieve and to the degree of difficulty of the material you will be receiving. The intensity with which you attend to a message should depend on whether your purpose or goal consists primarily of enjoyment, learning or understanding, evaluating or critiquing, or responding helpfully to the needs of another.

When your goal is primarily "pleasure listening," you can afford to listen without much intensity. People often speak of "vegging out in front of the tube." In most cases, they mean "listening" to comedy or light drama as a means of passing time pleasurably. Unfortunately, many people approach all situations as if they were listening to pass time. Yet how we listen should change qualitatively with the level of difficulty of the information.

Suppose that instead of watching a situation comedy, you turn to an information program on PBS—perhaps "Nova." Now you will likely decide that instead of just passing time, your goal is learning or understanding. In listening situations like attending to directions (how to get to a restaurant), to instructions (how to shift into reverse in a foreign car), and to explanations (a recounting of the new office procedures), the intensity of your listening is likely to increase, for the goal of understanding requires more careful attending. Moreover, you are likely to engage in a more active listening mode. In the next two sections of this chapter, we consider several skills for adjusting our listening when the goal is understanding and remembering.

At other times, you may determine that your goal is to listen critically. Every day we are flooded with countless messages—from friends and family members, co-workers, advertisers, political candidates—designed to influence our behavior. To choose wisely in these situations, we must not only listen more actively but also be able to recognize the facts, weigh them, separate emotional appeals, and determine the soundness of the conclusions presented. In the final section of this chapter, we consider several skills for adjusting to critical listening.

Listening to enable us to give helpful responses is a special challenge. Almost every day, people come to us to share their problems and concerns. Sometimes they simply want someone to talk with; other times they come to us for help. Many of the skills we will cover in Chapter 8 are response skills that will work for you in helping situations.

Attending

BY YOURSELF

Select an information-oriented program on your public television station (such as "Nova," "The MacNeil-Lehrer News Hour," or "Wall Street Week"). Watch at least twenty minutes of the show while lounging in a comfortable chair or while stretched out on the floor with music playing on a radio in the background. After about twenty minutes, quickly outline what you have learned. Now make a conscious decision to be attentive to the next twenty minutes of the show. Turn off the music and sit in a straight-back chair as you watch the program. Your goal is to increase your listening intensity in order to learn, so block out other distractions. After this twenty-minute segment, you should again outline what you remember.

Compare your notes. Is there any difference between the amount or quality of the information you retained? Discuss your results with your classmates. Are their results similar or different? Why?

Understanding—Listening Actively

The second phase of the listening process is understanding what we have heard. *Understanding* refers to the ability to decode a message by correctly assigning a meaning to it. Sometimes failure to understand is a result of people using words that are not in our vocabulary. Suppose someone asks, "Quelle heure est-il?" and you do not know French. You hear the sounds, but you are unable to understand that the person is asking "What time is it?" Even when people speak in your native language, they may use words that are not in your vocabulary; moreover, they may talk quickly, run together sounds, and mispronounce words so that you may have trouble decoding the message.

Understanding requires active listening. *Active listening* means using specific techniques to ensure your understanding. Because we can think faster than a speaker can talk, we can learn to process information while it is being given. Active listening techniques include determining the organization of the message, paying attention to nonverbal cues, asking questions to get necessary information, and silently paraphrasing the meanings we have understood. Let's consider these four procedures.

DETERMINE THE ORGANIZATION

Effective speakers are likely to have an overall organization for their information that includes purpose or goal, key ideas (or main points) to develop the purpose, and details to explain or support the main points. Active listeners pay attention to and seek out organizational patterns. Suppose that during a parents' meeting, Helen brings up the subject of teenage crime. As Helen talks, she may focus on the effects of poverty and broken homes. For each topic she may provide information she has read or heard. When Helen finishes speaking, her listeners will understand the message if they distinguish Helen's view of the causes of teenage crime (her purpose), the two specific factors she sees as causes (her key points), and the evidence she has provided to support each factor (details).

Sometimes people organize their messages in such a way that it is relatively easy to understand the purpose, key points, and details. At other times, however, we must supply the structure for ourselves. You can sort out the purpose, key points, and details of a complex message, and thus increase your understanding of the message, by mentally outlining the message. Asking "What am I supposed to know/do because I listened to this?" will allow you to determine purpose. Asking "What are the categories of information?" and "Why should I do/think this?" will enable you to identify key points. Asking "What's the support?" will enable you to identify the details.

ATTEND TO NONVERBAL CUES

Active listeners interpret messages more accurately when they observe the nonverbal behaviors that accompany the words, for meaning may be shown as much by the nonverbals as by the words that are spoken. In the chapter on nonverbal communication, we noted that up to 65 percent of the meaning of a social message may be carried nonverbally. Thus, when Franco says, "You really got through to Professor Grant on that one," whether you take his statement as a compliment or a jibe will depend on your perception of the sound of Franco's voice. Likewise, when Deborah says, "Go on, I can walk home from here," we must interpret cues such as tone of voice, body actions, and facial expression to tell whether she is sincerely interested in walking or whether she would really like a ride.

Whether you are listening to a co-worker explain her stance on an issue, a friend explain the process for hanging wallpaper, or a loved one explain why he or she is upset with you, you must listen to how something is said as well as to what is said. We will return to the interpretation of nonverbal cues when we discuss the important concept of empathy at the beginning of Chapter 8.

212

● Active listeners in-
terpret messages
more accurately when
they observe the non-
verbal behaviors that
accompany the words,
because meaning may
be shown as much by
the nonverbals as by
the words that are
spoken.

ASK QUESTIONS

Active listeners are willing to ask questions to help them obtain the information they need to understand. Yet many of us seem unwilling to question—we don't understand, but we say nothing. Sometimes people are too
shy or hesitant to admit that they do not know what the speaker meant. But
isn't it equally foolish to respond as if we understand when we really do not?
If your professor tells you that your term paper reached the "nadir," and you
smile and say "Thank you" even though you don't know what she is talking
about, that behavior is foolish. *Nadir* means the low point—the "pits." Although we may feel embarrassed that the word is not a part of our active

Basic Communication Skills

SKILL	USE	PROCEDURE	EXAMPLE
Attending The perceptual process of selecting specific stimuli that we have heard.	To focus your listening.	1. Analyze and, if possible, eliminate physical impediments. 2. Get ready to listen. 3. Make the shift from speaker to listener a complete one. 4. Hear a person out before you react. 5. Adjust your attention to the listening goals of the situation.	As Amanda perceives that she needs to pay attention to what Yvonne is saying, she turns down the radio and focuses her entire attention on Yvonne's words.
Understanding (Active Listening) The ability to decode a message by assigning a meaning to it.	To gain complete meaning from another person's communication.	1. Separate the governing idea (or purpose), key points, and details to help you understand a complex message. 2. Fully concentrate on words and nonverbal cues. 3. Ask yourself questions to help you anticipate material. 4. Silently paraphrase to help you understand.	As Hannah explains the baby's schedule, Tanya, the babysitter, concentrates on the message, silently paraphrases, and mentally sorts key points and details.

vocabulary, we are likely to behave foolishly if we do not ask what the word means. Politely saying, "I'm not sure I understand the word *nadir*; could you define it for me?" does not brand you as deficient. On the contrary, it indicates that you are serious about trying to understand the message.

At other times our failure to understand goes beyond vocabulary. When someone's explanation is too vague or incomplete, slurred, unorganized, or unintelligible, you need to ask for clarification. Suppose the department secretary says, "Just take the papers you want to run and put them in the tray, and the machine will run them, collate them, and staple them," you may have the general idea, but you still may not know how to set the papers up so that they will be stapled in the right place. The only way you will understand is to ask. You might say, "I can see that the papers need to be in order and face down, but should the top of the page be toward me or away from me?"

In Chapter 8, we will consider in detail how to ask for information in interpersonally appropriate ways.

SILENTLY PARAPHRASE

Active listeners are adept at paraphrasing. A *paraphrase* is a statement in your own words of your understanding of what someone else said. Paraphrasing can be done silently or aloud. For example, after a friend has spent a few minutes explaining how to prepare a certain dish, you can say silently to yourself, "In other words, how the mixture is put together may be more important than the ingredients used." Keep in mind that the accuracy of your paraphrase—especially with messages involving feelings—is likely to depend on how well you have attended to the nonverbal cues as well as to the words. If you cannot paraphrase a message, the message may not have been well encoded, there may have been contradictions between the verbal and nonverbal messages, or you may not have been listening carefully enough. In Chapter 8, you will have an opportunity to study and practice verbal paraphrases as a means of ensuring shared meaning and for purposes of making appropriate responses.

PRACTICE IN

Understanding

IN GROUPS

Have group members take turns talking for one to two minutes on a topic with which they are familiar and on which they have an opinion. The other members try to listen actively. When each speaker is finished, have the listeners quickly outline what they have understood to be the purpose and the key points. Afterward, share, compare, and discuss your outlines to determine both similarities in and differences between the intended meaning and the received meaning.

Remembering—Retaining Information

The third phase of the listening process, and a natural follow-up to understanding, is *remembering*—retaining information in memory. All our skill in understanding may go to waste if we cannot remember what we learned. As we observe our behavior, we sometimes have difficulty determining any pattern to what we remember and what we forget. On the one hand, we may find ourselves forgetting items that we want to remember almost immediately. How many times have you been unable to recall the name of a person to whom you were introduced just thirty seconds earlier? On the other hand,

some ideas and feelings seem to imprint themselves so deeply on our memories that a lifetime of trying to forget will not erase them. For instance, a song lyric may rattle around in your mind for days, or a cutting remark made by a loved one may haunt you for years. Nevertheless, we can take a great deal of control over what we remember. Effective listeners learn to apply three well-documented techniques: rehearsal, constructing mnemonics, and, when possible, note taking. We consider each of these techniques in turn.

● When you are trying to remember such specific information as the sales figures for the month, saying it to yourself several times increases your chances of remembering it.

REHEARSAL

The act of remembering involves moving information from short-term or working memory to long-term memory.[6] The simplest procedure for accomplishing this goal is rehearsal—the act of mentally repeating material immediately on receiving it. Rehearsing information two, three, or even four times makes it far more likely that we will remember the material at a later date. Rehearsal provides necessary reinforcement for the information, for if it is not reinforced, the information will be held in short-term memory for as little as twenty seconds and then forgotten. So, when you are introduced to a stranger named Jack McNeil, if you mentally say, "Jack McNeil, Jack McNeil, Jack McNeil, Jack McNeil," you increase the chances that you will remember his name. Likewise, when a person gives you the directions "Go two blocks east, turn left, turn right at the next light, and it's in the next block," you should immediately repeat to yourself, "Two blocks east, turn left, turn right at light, next block—that's two blocks east, turn left, turn right at light, next block."

CONSTRUCTING MNEMONICS

Constructing mnemonics helps listeners to put information in forms that are more easily recalled. A *mnemonic device* is any artificial technique used as a memory aid. One of the most common ways of forming a mnemonic is to take the first letters of a list of items you are trying to remember and forming a word. For example, an easy mnemonic for remembering the five Great Lakes is HOMES (*Huron, Ontario, Michigan, Erie, Superior*).

When you want to remember items in a sequence, try to form a sentence with the words themselves or assign words using the first letters of the words in sequence and form an easy-to-remember statement. For example, when you first studied music, you may have learned the notes on the lines of the treble staff (EGBDF) with the saying "*every good boy does fine.*" (And for the notes on the treble staff spaces (FACE), you may have remembered the word *face.*)

NOTE TAKING

Although note taking would be inappropriate in most casual interpersonal encounters, it represents a powerful tool for increasing our recall of information when we are involved in telephone conversations, briefing sessions, interviews, and business meetings. Note taking provides us a written record that we can go back to. Moreover, the literature suggests that the act of note taking may be more important than the notes themselves. That is, by engaging in taking notes, we take a more active role in the listening process.[7] Thus, when you are studying for an exam, taking the time to write out ideas you want to remember serves as a reinforcing agent.

What constitutes good notes varies depending on the situation. Useful notes may consist of a brief list of main points or key ideas plus a few of the most significant details. Or they may be a short summary of the entire concept (a type of paraphrase) after the message is completed. For lengthy and rather detailed information, however, good notes likely will consist of a brief outline of what the speaker has said, including the overall idea, the main points of the message, and key developmental material. Good notes are not necessarily long. In fact, many classroom lectures can be reduced to a short outline of notes.

Suppose that you are listening to a supervisor instruct her staff about the importance of clear writing in their reports. In the instructions, the supervisor discusses the need to test the readability of the report by computing a fog index. Anticipating the likelihood of receiving detailed information, the active listener will take notes. The supervisor might say:

> The boss is very concerned about the quality of the report writing that is coming from the major divisions. The word is that reports just aren't as readable as they should be. In the future, every report will be required to include its fog index, including a summary of the figures used for the computation.
>
> A fog index is one of the most common tests of readability. It's an easy one to use and generally reliable. Like most readability tests, it is based on computations of sentence length and word length. The theory is that the shorter the sentences and the words, the easier the reading.
>
> Computing a fog index for a report involves six easy steps.
>
> First, select five random sections of at least 100 words each. In a five-page report, this would be one passage per page. Begin at the start of a paragraph and count off 100 words, and then continue to count until the end of that sentence. So your passage will have 100 words or more.
>
> Second, compute the average sentence length of each passage. If a 116-word passage has five sentences, the average sentence length of that passage would be 23.2 words.
>
> Third, compute the number of difficult words per hundred. The beauty of this test is that "difficult" words are easily identified as any word of more than two syllables, except proper names and verbs that become three syllables by adding -es, -ed, or -ing. So, if that 116-word passage has 12 difficult words, you would divide 12 by 116. That passage then would have 10.3 difficult words per hundred. For both steps two and three, round off the figures to the nearest whole number.
>
> Fourth, add the average sentence length to the number of difficult words per hundred. In our example, you would add 23 and 10.
>
> Fifth, multiply the answer by .4. The result is the fog index. The resulting figure stands for the number of years of schooling required to read the passage easily.

Sixth, because you will have done five passages, you will then compute the average index for the five passages. Write that figure at the end of the report and include computations.

We have been instructed to rewrite reports until we achieve a fog index of between 10 and 13 for each.

This short passage includes a great deal of specific detail, much more than you will find in most oral instructions. Yet the 393 words of explanation can be outlined in just 134 words (see Figure 7.1). In good note taking, the number of words used may range from 10 percent of the original material to as high as 30 percent (the amount in our example). The point is not the number of words, however, but the accuracy of the notes in reflecting the sense of what the speaker said.

Remembering

PRACTICE IN

WITH A FRIEND

Have a friend assume the role of a fellow worker on your first day in an office job and read the following information to you once, at a normal rate of speech. As the friend reads the instructions, take notes. Then give yourself the test that follows, filling in the blanks but without referring to your notes. Then repeat the quiz, but use your notes this time. How much does your score improve? Although the temptation is great to read this item to yourself, try not to. You will miss both the enjoyment and the value of the exercise if you do.

Since you are new to the job, I'd like to fill you in on a few details. The boss probably told you that typing and distribution of mail were your most important duties. Well, they may be, but let me tell you, answering the phone is going to take most of your time. Now about the typing. Goodwin will give the most, but much of what he gives you may have nothing to do with the department—I'd be careful about spending all my time doing his private work. Mason doesn't give much, but you'd better get it right—she's really a stickler. I've always asked to have tests at least two days in advance. Bernstein is always dropping stuff on the desk at the last minute.

The mail situation sounds tricky, but you'll get used to it. Mail comes twice a day—at 10 A.M. and at 2 P.M. You've got to take the mail that's been left on the desk to Charles Hall for pickup. If you really have some rush stuff, take it right to the campus post office in Harper Hall. It's a

Figure 7.1

Example of effective note taking.

> *Notes*
>
> *Computing a Fog Index*
>
> I. *Include o fog Index on future reports.*
>   *Fog Index, a readability test based on sentence and word length.*
>   *Short sentences and words, easier reading.*
> II. *Computing involves six steps.*
>   1. *Select five random sections, at least 100 words each.*
>   2. *Compute the average sentence length of each.*
>   3. *Compute number of difficult words per hundred.*
>   *Count words three syllables or more.*
>   *Don't count proper names, verbs that become three syllables by adding es, ed, or ing.*
>   *Round off.*
>   4. *Add two figures.*
>   5. *Multiply answer by .4 to get a FI.,*
>   *Number of years of schooling required to read the passage easily.*
>   6. *Compute the average for the five passages.*
>   *Write figure at the end of the report with computations.*
> III. *Rewrite reports until FI is between 10 and 13.*

little longer walk, but for really rush stuff, it's better. When you pick up at McDaniel Hall, sort it. You'll have to make sure that only mail for the people up here gets delivered here. If there is any that doesn't belong here, bundle it back up and mark it for return to the campus post office.

Now, about your breaks. You get ten minutes in the morning, forty minutes at noon, and fifteen minutes in the afternoon. If you're smart, you'll leave before the 10:30 classes let out. That's usually a pretty crush time. Three of the teachers are supposed to have office hours then, and if they don't keep them, the students will be on your back. If you take your lunch at 11:45, you'll be back before the main crew goes.

Oh, one more thing. You are supposed to call Jeno at 8:15 every morning to wake him. If you forget, he gets very upset. Well, good luck.

With Notes	Without Notes	
_____	_____	1. Where should you take the mail that does not belong here?
_____	_____	2. How often does mail come?
_____	_____	3. When should you be back from lunch?
_____	_____	4. What is the problem with Bernstein's work?
_____	_____	5. Who gives the most work?
_____	_____	6. What is the problem with many of Goodwin's projects?
_____	_____	7. What are your main jobs, according to the boss?
_____	_____	8. Where should you take outgoing mail?
_____	_____	9. Where is the post office?
_____	_____	10. How many minutes do you get for your morning break?
_____	_____	11. What time do you prefer to take your lunch?
_____	_____	12. Who are you supposed to give a wake-up call to?

Answers: 1. Harper Hall; 2. Twice a day; 3. 12:30; 4. Last minute; 5. Goodwin; 6. Not work related; 7. Typing/Distributing mail; 8. Charles Hall; 9. Harper Hall, 10. 10; 11. 11:45; 12. Jeno.

IN GROUPS

Have each person in class select a newspaper or magazine article and prepare a two-minute reading of it. As each person reads, everyone in class takes notes. At the end of each reading, class members compare notes and discuss why they chose to write what they did.

Evaluating—Listening Critically

The fourth phase of the listening process is evaluating. In addition to using the active listening and remembering skills discussed in the last two sections, *evaluating* or *critical listening* consists of critically analyzing the message we have understood in order to determine how truthful, authentic, or believable we judge it to be. For instance, when someone tries to convince you to vote for a particular candidate for office or to support efforts to legalize RU 486 (the so-called abortion pill), you will want to listen critically to these messages so as to determine how much you agree with the speaker and how you wish to respond. If you fail to listen critically to the messages you receive,

● **Active listening skills help us understand.**

you risk inadvertently concurring in ideas or plans that may violate your own values, be counterproductive to achieving your goals, or be misleading to others (including the speakers) who value your judgment.

Critical listening includes (1) separating facts from inferences and (2) evaluating the inferences that have been made. Let's consider each of these in turn.

SEPARATING FACTS FROM INFERENCES

Critical listeners are able to separate facts from inferences. Facts are items of information, the accuracy of which can be verified or proven, often by direct observation. By contrast, inferences are conclusions or generalizations based on what has been observed. Separating fact from inference thus means being able to tell the difference between a verifiable observation and an opinion related to that observation.

Let's clarify this distinction with an example. Ellen tells a friend that she saw a Bob's TV Repair truck in her neighbor's driveway for the fifth time in the last two weeks. Ellen is reporting only what she saw; she is relating a fact. If, however, Ellen adds, "That new TV they bought is really a lemon," she would be making an inference. Ellen would be concluding—without actually knowing—that the truck was at her neighbor's house because someone was trying to repair the new television set. But think of how many other interpretations, or inferences, could be drawn from that fact. The driver of the truck may be a friend of Ellen's neighbor, or perhaps a special video system is being installed, or an old TV may have broken. The presence of the truck is fact; the explanation for the presence of the truck is inference.

The reason for distinguishing between facts and inferences is that an inference may be false, even if it is based on verifiable facts. Making sound judgments entails basing our opinions and responses to messages on facts or on inferences that we have evaluated for correctness. So, when we encounter statements such as "Better watch it; Steve is really in a bad mood today—did you see the way he was scowling?" or "I know you're hiding something from me; I can tell it in your voice," or "Olga and Kurt are seeing each other—I've seen them leave the office together nearly every night," we know that each of them is an inference. Each may be true, but none is necessarily true.

EVALUATING INFERENCES

Critical listeners not only recognize inferences but also know how to evaluate them to determine their validity. As we have said, inferences are conclusions or assertions drawn from or based on factual information. An inference is usually presented as part of an argument—that is, a person makes a claim (an inference) and then presents other statements in support of the claim. Here is an example of a simple argument. Joyce says, "Next year is going to be a lot easier than the past year. I got a $200-a-month raise, and my husband has been relieved of some of the extra work he had to do while they were looking for a replacement for Ed." Her claim "Next year is going to be a lot easier than the past year" is an inference—a statement that requires support to validate it. The statements "I got a $200-a-month raise, and my husband has been relieved of some of the extra work he had to do while they were looking for a replacement for Ed" are both facts that can be verified. Notice that Joyce's argument suggests that she infers a relationship between her claim and the facts she presents. Her argument is based on the assumption that more money per month and less work for her husband will make the year easier because it will relieve stress.

The critical listener asks at least three questions when evaluating any inference: (1) Is there factual information to support the inference? Perhaps there is no supporting information; perhaps there is not enough; or perhaps the supporting information is inaccurate. (2) Is the factual support relevant to the inference? Perhaps the actual or implied statement of relevance is logically weak. (3) Is there known information that would prevent the inference from logically following the factual statements? Perhaps there is information not accounted for that affects the likelihood of the inference. In the example, Joyce does have factual statements for support: She received a raise, and her husband has less work to do. Moreover, increased income is one kind of information that is relevant to "having an easier time." At this stage it would appear that Joyce does have the makings of a sound argument; however, if we learn that the $200-a-month raise involves extra duties for Joyce, we still might question whether the year is likely to be easier than the last one.

Let's consider one more example. Daniel says, "This is a great time to buy a car—interest rates are at the lowest point they've been in three years." The inference is that this is a great time to buy a car. First, does Daniel offer any support for the inference? Yes. Second, is the support relevant to the inference? Yes—interest rates are a factor in determining whether the time is right for car buying. Third, is there known information that would prevent the conclusion following from the data? If other indicators show that the economy is entering a period of recession, that information might be more important to the decision than is the stability of interest rates.

For many of us, the most difficult of the three questions to answer is the second one, "Is the support relevant to the inference?" This question is difficult to answer primarily because the listener must be able to verbalize a statement that shows the relevance. The listener must create the statement because in most informal reasoning the link is only implied by the person presenting the argument. Recall that in the first example, Joyce never said anything like "A raise and a reduction of work are two criteria for predicting that next year will be a lot easier." Because the relevance is more often implied than stated, we must learn to phrase it.

The key to phrasing the relationship between support and inference in order to judge its relevance is to ask yourself, "What can I say that would make sense for this inference to follow from this material?" For instance, suppose Hal says, "I see frost on the grass—I think our flowers are goners." What can we say that establishes the relevance of the supporting fact "frost on the grass" to the claim "our flowers are goners"? If I were Hal, I would likely be thinking, "The presence of frost means that the temperature is low enough to freeze the moisture on the grass—if it's cold enough to freeze the moisture on the grass, it's cold enough to kill my flowers." This seems to

Basic Communication Skills

SKILL	USE	PROCEDURE	EXAMPLE
Evaluating (Critical Listening)			
Analyzing what has been understood.	To determine how truthful, authentic, or believable we judge the meaning we have received to be.	1. Question whether the inference is supported with meaningful factual statements. 2. Question whether the stated or implied relevance between the support and the inference makes sense. 3. Question whether there is any other known information that lessens the quality of the inference.	When Julius says, "Fernando, you'll have to get more signs up if you are going to have any chance to get elected," Fernando evaluates the implied connection between the number of signs posted and his chances of getting elected.
Remembering			
The retention of information in memory.	To store information for recall.	1. Repeat information. 2. Create mnemonics. 3. Take notes when material seems complicated.	When Chris is introduced to Aileen Stewart, who is a candidate for Council, Chris says to himself, "Aileen Stewart—candidate for Council; Aileen Stewart—candidate for Council; Aileen Stewart—candidate for Council."

make sense because we can demonstrate a relationship between frost and the death of unprotected flowers. Let's try another one. Gina says, "I studied all night and got only a D on the first test. I'm not going to do any better on this one." This statement suggests that Gina sees relevance between the amount of study time before a test and the grade. We could phrase this implied relevance by saying, "Since the time of study before the test, which determines the grade, can be no greater, Gina can't improve her grade." In this case the relevance seems questionable. Her reasoning suggests that the only factor in determining a grade is the amount of study time before the test, but experience would suggest that many other factors, such as previous time studying and frame of mind, are of equal, if not greater, importance.

In short, you are listening critically when (1) you question whether the inference is supported with meaningful factual statements, (2) you question whether the stated or implied relevance between the support and the inference makes sense, and (3) you question whether there is any other known information that lessens the quality of the inference.

Figure 7.2 A summary of the four aspects of listening.

	GOOD LISTENERS	BAD LISTENERS
Attending	Attend to important information	May not hear what a person is saying
	Ready themselves physically and mentally	Fidget in their chairs, look out the window, and let their minds wander
	Listen objectively regardless of emotional involvement	Visibly react to emotional language
	Listen differently depending on situation	Listen the same way regardless of type of material
Understanding	Assign appropriate meaning to what is said	Hear what is said, but either cannot understand or assign different meaning to the words
	Seek out apparent purpose, main points, and supporting information	Ignore the way information is organized
	Ask mental questions to anticipate information	Fail to anticipate coming information
	Silently paraphrase to solidify understanding	Seldom or never mentally review information
	Seek out subtle meanings based on nonverbal cues	Ignore nonverbal cues
Remembering	Retain information	Interpret message accurately but forget it
	Repeat key information	Assume they will remember
	Mentally create mnemonics for lists of words and ideas	Seldom single out any information as especially important
	Take notes	Rely on memory alone
Evaluating	Listen critically	Hear and understand but are unable to weigh and consider information
	Separate facts from inferences	Don't differentiate between facts and inferences
	Evaluate inferences	Accept information at face value

Figure 7.2 summarizes how good listeners and poor listeners deal with the four aspects of listening—attending, understanding, remembering, and evaluating.

Figure 7.2

A summary of the four aspects of listening.

Evaluating

BY YOURSELF

1. Read the following story, and evaluate each witness's statement as either F (fact) or I (inference).

   Two people came hurrying out of a bank with several large bundles, hopped into a long black car, and sped away. Seconds later, a man rushed out of the bank, waving his arms and looking quite upset. You listen to two people discuss what they saw.

_____ a. "The bank's been robbed!"

_____ b. "Yes, indeed—I saw the robbers hurry out of the bank, hop into a car, and speed away."

_____ c. "It was a long black car."

_____ d. "The men were carrying several large bundles."

_____ e. "Seconds after they left, a man came out of the bank after them—but he was too late, they'd already escaped."

Answers: a. I; b. I; c. F; d. I (men?); e. I

2. For the following, ask and answer the following three questions: (1) Is the inference supported with meaningful factual statements? (2) Does the stated or implied relevance between the support and the inference make sense? (3) Is there any other known information that lessens the quality of the inference? Remember that to do this properly, you must phrase a reasoning link to tie the supporting information to the inference.

   a. "The chess club held a raffle, and they made a lot of money. I think we should hold a raffle, too."

   b. "Chad is aggressive, personable, and highly motivated—he ought to make a good salesman."

   c. "Three of my students last year got A's on this test, five the year before, and three the year before that. There certainly will be some A's this year."

   d. "I saw Kali in a maternity outfit—she must be pregnant."

   e. "Listen, I like the way Darren thinks, Solomon is an excellent mathematician, and Marco and Ethan are two of my best students. All four are Alpha Alphas. As far as I'm concerned, the Alphas are the group on campus with academic strength."

   f. "If Greg hadn't come barging in, I never would have spilled my iced tea."

   g. "Maybe that's the way you see it, but to me when high city officials are caught with their hands in the till and when police close their eyes to the actions of people with money, that's corruption."

   h. "Krista wears her hair that way and guys fall all over her—I'm getting myself a hairdo like that."

● ◆ ■ **Summary**

Listening is an active process that involves attending, understanding, remembering, evaluating, and responding. Effective listening is essential to competent communication.

Attending is the process of selecting the sound waves we consciously process. We can increase the effectiveness of our attention by (1) analyzing and, if possible, eliminating physical impediments to listening, (2) getting ready to listen, (3) making the shift from speaker to listener a complete one, (4) hearing a person out before we react, and (5) adjusting our attention to the listening goals of the situation.

Understanding is the process of decoding a message by assigning meaning to it. A key to understanding is to practice active listening: Look for or create an organization for the information, pay attention to nonverbal cues, ask for explanation, and silently paraphrase.

Remembering is the process of storing the meanings that have been received so that they may be recalled later. Remembering is increased by rehearsing or repeating information, constructing mnemonics through artificial language techniques, and when listening to instructions that are detailed, taking notes.

Evaluating, or critical listening, is the process of separating fact from inference and judging the validity of the inferences made. A fact is a verifiable statement; an inference is a conclusion drawn from facts. You are listening critically when (1) you question whether the inference is supported with meaningful factual statements, (2) you question whether the stated or implied relevance between the support and the inference makes sense, and (3) you question whether there is any other known information that lessens the quality of the inference.

● ◆ ■ Communication Improvement Goal Statement

Can you tell when you are really listening and when you are not? This evening, record five situations during the day in which you were cast as a "listener." Was your behavior the same or different in each of the instances? What, if anything, determined differences in your approach to your listening in each of these situations? In which of the situations were you the most effective listener? On what basis do you make this evaluation? What behaviors of yours differentiated "effective" listening from "ineffective"?

Which of the following items would you say were most typical of your listening?

1. I listened differently depending on whether I was listening for enjoyment, understanding, or evaluation.

2. I stopped listening when what the person was saying to me was no longer interesting.

3. I consciously recognized the speaker's purpose.

4. I pretended to listen to people when I was really thinking about other things.

5. When people talked, I differentiated between their main points and supporting details.

6. When the person's manner of speaking annoyed me (such as muttering, stammering, or talking in a monotone), I stopped listening carefully.

7. At various places in a conversation, I paraphrased what the speaker said in order to check my understanding.

8. When I perceived the subject matter as very difficult, I stopped listening carefully.

9. When a speaker presented detailed information, I took good notes of major points and supporting details.

10. When people used words that I found offensive, I stopped listening and started preparing responses.

In this list, the even-numbered items indicate negative listening behaviors, and the odd-numbered items indicate positive listening behaviors. Comment on whether your listening tended to reflect the positive or the negative listening behaviors. Discuss the outcome of your listening. In which situations did you feel most satisfied? least? Did your satisfaction have any correlation with the type of listening behaviors you exhibited during the episode? In the future, which of the guidelines mentioned in this chapter are you going to try to incorporate into your listening? Why?

Write a communication improvement goal statement focusing on the aspect of listening that you perceive to be your weakest. Write the contract following the guidelines presented on pages 31–33 of Chapter 1.

● ◆ ■ Featured Reading

Listening: The Forgotten Skill
Madelyn Burley-Allen
(New York: John Wiley & Sons, 1982)

Madelyn Burley-Allen, founder and president of Dynamics of Human Behavior, has taught listening seminars for the military as well as numerous other organizations. Her book *Listening: The Forgotten Skill* discusses the skills she teaches in her seminars. Although a portion of the book discusses the final stage of listening—response—she places a great deal of emphasis on attending, reception, and perception.

Burley-Allen discusses the importance of listening, how to become a good listener, barriers between listener and speaker, learning to listen to yourself, and making listening work for you. The book contains numerous checklists and exercises to help you put these ideas into practice.

Illustrative of the power of her work is the section on barriers between listener and speaker. She begins by pointing out that personal, competitive needs interfere with taking the time to listen. She then goes on to discuss such barriers as hearing only what you want to hear, biased listening, effects of emotions on listening, ineffective styles of listening, physical and semantic barriers, and failure to interpret nonverbal cues properly. In addition to a great number of real-life examples, she includes listening quizzes and awareness checks that allow you to apply what she is talking about.

Although we will cover response skills, the final stage of listening, in the next chapter, you'll find that much of her book focuses on skills such as describing behavior, paraphrasing, and perception checking. This book is useful for reviewing all phases of the listening process.

This short (150 pages), easy-to-read paperback is an excellent reinforcement for skills we discuss in our two chapters on listening.

●◆■ Notes

1. L. Barker, R. Edwards, C. Gains, K. Gladnes, and F. Holley, "An Investigation of Proportional Time Spent in Various Communication Activities by College Students," *Journal of Applied Communication Research* 8 (1980): 101–109.

2. Lyman K. Steil, Larry L. Barker, and Kittie W. Watson, *Effective Listening* (Reading, Mass.: Addison-Wesley, 1983), p. 38.

3. Andrew Wolvin and Carolyn Gwynn Coakley, *Listening,* 4th ed. (Dubuque, Iowa: Wm. C. Brown, 1992), pp. 70–71.

4. National Institutes of Health, *Hearing Loss* (Washington, D.C.: National Institutes of Health, 1982), p. 1.

5. Joan Gorham, "The Relationship Between Verbal Teacher Immediacy Behaviors and Student Learning," *Communication Education* 37 (1988): 51.

6. W. K. Estes, "Learning Theory," in Alan Lesgold and Robert Glaser, eds., *Foundations for a Psychology of Education* (Hillsdale, N.J.: Erlbaum, 1989), pp. 6–8.

7. Wolvin and Coakley, p. 251.

CHAPTER EIGHT

Empathic Response Skills

OBJECTIVES

After you have read this chapter, you should be able to define and/or explain:

Ways of determining emotional states of others

Questioning for information

Paraphrasing information

Supporting positive and negative feelings

Giving alternative interpretations

Praising

Giving and receiving constructive criticism

Eliminating inappropriate responses

"We need to take a phenomeno-logical approach to this issue. Once we understand that knowledge is not inferred from experience but is expressed in conscious experience itself, I think we can start to gain a necessary insight."

"For crying out loud—speak English."

"I'm not doing as well in his classes this quarter as I expected to. You know, I'm studying longer hours than I ever have, but something just isn't right."

"You can say that again—you're really screwing up."

"The last time we went out Beth seemed really cool to any show of intimacy. In fact, I've had the feeling that something's been troubling her, and I'm afraid it has to do with our relationship."

"Hm, I can see why you're concerned. Her behavior does seem a little different from what you've described in the past. Is there any chance that something else might be troubling her?"

Each of the preceding examples is a response, a reflection of how the receiver hears the message. But there are major differences in the examples. In neither of the first two do the receivers show sensitivity to the speaker's ideas or the speaker's feelings. The third example is different. In this one we get the sense that the speaker is sensitive to the situation. The first two are largely inappropriate; the third is helpful. As we go through this chapter, you will learn both what makes the difference and how to phrase appropriate responses.

As we discussed in Chapter 7, the final phase of listening is responding appropriately. Response is qualitatively different from the other phases of listening, for when we respond, we shift roles from receiver to sender. Nevertheless, responding is an integral part of listening because it is the response, or lack of it, that shows whether communication has really taken place, whether meaning is shared.

We begin the chapter with a discussion of empathy, a quality that lays the groundwork for effective response skills; then we continue with types of empathic responses. We conclude the chapter with a brief discussion of inappropriate responses that effective communicators should try to avoid.

Empathizing

Responding appropriately goes beyond using the skills of attending, understanding, remembering, and evaluating—it requires a degree of empathy with the speaker. Empathy relates to detecting and identifying another person's emotional state and responding appropriately.[1]

● Empathy relates to detecting and identifying another person's emotional state and responding appropriately.

DETECTING AND IDENTIFYING FEELINGS

The first aspect of this definition, detecting and identifying how a person is feeling, emphasizes that part of the skill of empathy is perceptual—noticing the person's verbal and nonverbal cues and then, based on these observations, identifying the person's emotional state. In Chapter 4, we noted that up to 65 percent of the meaning of a social message may be carried nonverbally. When Rico says, "Great catch, Jim," after Jim drops a lazy fly ball hit right to him, the sound of Rico's voice will signal that his message is just the opposite of what he said. Likewise, when Maren says, "Go on, I'll just finish my homework," we have to interpret cues such as tone of voice, body actions, and facial expression to tell whether Maren really wants to be left alone or whether she actually plans to do her homework. Thus being sensitive to the nonverbal behaviors that accompany the words is prerequisite to understanding the feeling that underlies a verbal message.

The ability to detect and identify feelings may be a result of (1) our own experience in a similar situation, (2) our fantasized reaction to that situation, or (3) our experiences in observing this person in similar situations. The key point is that in perceiving someone's emotional state, we see a situation through the other person's eyes. Our understanding is based not on what we think someone "should" feel in that situation but on what it is really like to be that person, having the feeling he or she is actually experiencing. Thus empathizing is "other" oriented rather than "I" oriented.

Let's look at an example of empathy. Troy says to Martha, "I worked a lot harder on this ad campaign and I really thought it was on the money, but the client said she wanted to see another plan." As Troy talks, Martha reads the look on Troy's face and notes the cues provided by his gestures, movements, and posture. As Martha hears the words Troy speaks, she perceives the changes in vocal quality and pitch as well as the presence or absence of vocal interferences. Then, based on both Troy's verbal and nonverbal cues, she can interpret Troy's feelings as expressed in the message. If, from her observation of Troy's words and nonverbal cues, Martha is able to identify with the disappointment Troy experienced, or if she can imagine the disappointment, she is empathizing.

RESPONDING APPROPRIATELY

The second aspect of the definition of empathy focuses on responding appropriately. When Troy says, "but the client said she wanted to see another plan," Martha could respond by saying, "That must have really jolted you," spoken in a way that suggests an understanding of Troy's pain and surprise. Such a response would show Troy that (1) Martha understands what happened,

(2) she shares in Troy's emotions in that she knows what it is like to suffer pain or surprise, and (3) she is willing to allow Troy to talk about his feelings and to offer what comfort she can.

People sometimes confuse empathy with sympathy. Although empathy and sympathy have similar meanings, sympathy usually denotes (1) a duplication of the feeling or (2) a feeling of pity or compassion for another person's trouble. For instance, Troy's description could cause Martha to feel so disappointed herself, or so sorry for Troy, that she begins to cry. But if she shares in his emotion to that extent, she is less likely to be able to help him through his feelings. Moreover, it is unnecessary for her to join in Troy's response in order to understand and empathize with it. Even if she thought his response was excessive, she could accept and understand his feelings. In general, empathy requires a more cognitive approach than merely participating in the other person's feelings.

In summary, empathy has two clearly definable elements—the recognition of another's feeling, which is a perception skill, and the response to it, which is a communication skill. Because both skills imply a genuine understanding of what the other person is experiencing, let's talk further about how to achieve an empathic state of mind.

INCREASING EMPATHY

Increasing our level of empathy involves caring and concentrating. How much we empathize is directly related to how much we really care about a person. This does not mean that we must have a deep, personal relationship with others to empathize with them. Caring can mean simply the ability to put ourselves in the other person's shoes. You are likely to feel better when the people you like or respect identify with your feelings of pain, fear, anger, joy, and amazement. Similarly, other people want and need the same expression of empathy from you that you want and need from them. By asking yourself how you would feel under the circumstances and acting accordingly, you are more likely to achieve an empathic state.

Sometimes we are reluctant to show that we care about others for fear of showing weakness or being vulnerable. For example, you may have learned that emotions should not be shared or acknowledged. Yet everybody has feelings, whether or not they display them, and the willingness to share feelings empathically is not unmanly or unwomanly or "un" anything. When you empathize with another person's joy or pain, your willingness to show it will usually be rewarding for both of you.

How much you can empathize is also related to how well you concentrate on observing behavior. When another person begins a conversation with you, develop the habit of silently posing at least two questions to yourself: "What state of mind do I believe the person is in right now?" and "What are the cues the person is giving that I am using to draw this conclusion?" Consciously raising these questions will help you to focus your attention on the nonverbal aspects of messages. Is this a realistic expectation? When people concentrate, they have been shown to be good at recognizing primary emotions such as happiness, sadness, surprise, anger, and fear (above 90 percent), and rather good at recognizing contempt, disgust, interest, determination, and bewilderment (80 to 90 percent).[2] And as researchers in the field have discovered, recognizing facial expressions is the key to perceiving emotion.[3] As you develop the habit of making these assessments, you will become more adept at sensing the moods, feelings, and attitudes of those with whom you are communicating.

In summary, when listening to what a person is saying, (1) concentrate on both the verbal and nonverbal messages, (2) adopt an attitude of caring for the person, (3) try to recall or imagine how you would feel in similar circumstances, (4) use the person's behavioral cues to speculate on his or her emotional state, and (5) respond in a way that indicates your sensitivity to the feelings you have perceived. We consider different types of appropriate and inappropriate responses in the remainder of this chapter.

Empathizing

BY YOURSELF

Consider the following three comments you might hear from a friend:

1. Tyrell sent me flowers for no apparent reason.

2. I got a C on the test.

3. I banged my head on the door frame.

In each of these cases, the speaker could have any of at least three states of mind: The speaker could look at the event as positive or humorous, as negative or troublesome, or as neither. List the nonverbal cues that you would expect to see to explain each of the possible frames of mind; then phrase statements that would show your recognition of each perceived state.

IN GROUPS

Have each person in the group relate a recent experience to which they had an emotional response without labeling the response. The response need not be a dramatic one. After the speaker has related an episode, have the group discuss what emotional states they perceive the speaker to have experienced as well as describe the verbal and nonverbal cues that led them to their conclusions. Then group members should indicate whether they were able to empathize based on experiences or based on fantasy. Finally, the group should solicit comments from the speaker concerning the accuracy of their perceptions.

JOURNAL ENTRY

Recall the last time you effectively empathized with another person. Write a short analysis of the episode. Be sure to cover the following: What type of relationship do you have with this person? How long have you known the person? What was the person's emotional state? How did you recognize it? What were the nonverbal cues? verbal cues? Did you identify with the person through remembering a similar situation you had experienced, or did you fantasize how you would feel? What did you do that showed you were empathizing? What was the outcome of this communication episode?

Clarifying Meaning

Perhaps the greatest barrier to effective communication is misunderstanding. Misunderstanding commonly results from erroneously assuming understanding of the meaning, from inattention to what is being communicated, and from the need to hurry. We misunderstand far more often than we realize. In Chapter 7, we focused on building internal listening skills; now we consider how you can test or increase your degree of understanding through appropriate responses. Two skills we can use to clarify meaning are questioning and paraphrasing.

QUESTIONING

When we don't have enough information to fully understand a person's message, we are likely to ask questions. Effective questioning is not always easy. When your questions don't elicit the information you want or irritate or fluster the other person, it may well be that they were poorly phrased. Here are guidelines for phrasing questions in a sensitive way that lessens the likelihood of arousing defensiveness.

1. *Be specific about the goal of the question.* Suppose Shana says to you, "I am really frustrated. Would you stop at the store on the way home and buy me some more paper?" At this point, you may need more information to understand what Shana is telling you. However, a response like "I don't get what you mean" is unlikely to elicit a helpful reply. The question you ask depends on the kind of information you need to make the communication complete.

You can ask questions to get important details. "What kind of paper would you like me to get, and how much will you need?"

You can ask questions to clarify the use of a term. "Could you tell me what you mean by 'frustrated'?"

You can ask questions to bring out a person's feelings. "What is it that seems to be frustrating you?"

Whether it is more details, how a word is used, or how the person feels, a well-phrased, specific question will help you obtain the information you want.

2. *Avoid one- or two-word questions that may be perceived as too curt or abrupt.* A person may often misinterpret the motivation behind a curt or abrupt question. For instance when Miles says "Molly just told me that I always behave in ways that are totally insensitive to her needs," instead of asking "What?" you might ask, "Did she give you specific behaviors she was concerned about?" Now instead of having to puzzle out the meaning of "What," Miles understands the kind of information you are seeking. Curt, abrupt questions often seem to challenge the speaker instead of focusing on the kind of information the respondent needs to understand the statement.

3. *Use positive nonverbal cues.* Ask questions with a tone of voice that is sincere—not a tone that could be interpreted as sarcastic, cutting, superior, dogmatic, or evaluative. We need to remind ourselves constantly that the way we speak can be even more important than the words we use.

4. *Put the burden of ignorance on your own shoulders.* People under tension may interpret any question as one that is critical of their ability to speak clearly. A useful strategy for avoiding defensive reactions is to put the burden of ignorance on your own shoulders. Try to preface your question with a short statement that suggests that any problem of misunderstanding is likely to be yours. For instance, when Drew says, "I've really had it with Malone jumping all over me all the time," you might say, "Drew, I'm sorry, I may have missed something you said—what kinds of things has Malone been doing?"

The following are examples that contrast appropriate empathic questions, with unhelpful or inappropriately phrased questions.

Tamara comes out of the committee room and says, "They turned down my proposal again!" Art asks:

Inappropriate: "Well, did you explain it the way you should have?" (This question is a veiled attack on Tamara in question form.)

Appropriate: "Did they tell you why?" (This question is a sincere request for additional information.)

Basic Communication Skills

SKILL	USE	PROCEDURE	EXAMPLE
Empathizing Being able to detect and identify the immediate affective state of another. Responding in an appropriate manner.	To create or to promote a supportive climate.	1. Consider both verbal and nonverbal messages. 2. Adopt an attitude of caring. 3. Try to recall or imagine what you would feel like under those same circumstances. 4. Speculate on the emotional state of the person. 5. Respond with words that indicate your sensitivity to those feelings.	When Jerry says, "I really feel embarrassed about wearing braces in college," Mary smiles ruefully and replies, "Yeah, it makes you feel like a little kid, doesn't it? I remember the things I had to put up with when I wore braces."
Questioning A sentence phrased to get additional information.	To help get a more complete picture before making other comments; to help a shy person open up; to clarify meaning.	1. Listen to the message. 2. Determine what kind of information you need to know. 3. Phrase the question(s) to achieve the goal. 4. Use appropriate nonverbal clues.	When Connie says, "Well, it would be better if she weren't so sedentary," Jeff replies, "I'm not sure I understand what you mean by 'sedentary'—would you explain?"

As Webster and Renee are driving home from a party, Renee says, "With all those executives there, I really felt strange." Webster asks:

Inappropriate: "When you're with our bosses, why do you always act so stupid around them?" (With this question, Webster is intentionally hurting Renee. He is making no effort to be sensitive to her feelings or to understand them.)

Appropriate: "What is it about our bosses' presence that makes you feel strange?" (Here the question is designed to elicit information that may help Renee.)

Note how the empathic questions elicit the necessary information but with less probability of a defensive reply. The inappropriate questions, however, seem deliberately designed to undermine or attack the person being questioned. Questioning represents a useful response when the information sought is relevant to the conversation and when the questions derive from a spirit of inquiry and support and not from a conscious or unconscious need to make the person look bad.

In summary, (1) listen carefully to the message, (2) determine the kind of information you need to increase your understanding of the message,

(3) phrase your questions so that they focus on getting that information, and (4) deliver them in a sincere tone of voice.

PARAPHRASING

Although it seems like common sense to ask a question to obtain additional information, most of us don't feel a need to say anything when we think we understand what a person means. Yet serious communication problems can occur even when we believe we are certain we understand the person. Why? Because what we think a person means may be far different from what the person really means.

Paraphrasing means putting *your* understanding of the message into words. Paraphrasing is not mere repetition. Suppose Scott, who blew the first test, says, "I'm really going to study this time." Replying "This time you're really going to study" is mere repetition. The reply shows that you have *heard* the statement but not that you have *understood* it. An effective paraphrase states the meaning received in the listener's own words. If you think Scott is talking about specific study skills, your paraphrase might be, "I take it that you're going to read and outline every chapter carefully." This statement is a paraphrase because it tells Scott the meaning that the words "really going to study" hold for you. If your interpretation is on the mark, Scott might say, "Right!" But if you have received a meaning different from what he intended, Scott has an opportunity to clarify the meaning with a statement such as "Well, I'm going to spend a lot more time reading chapters carefully, but I wasn't planning to outline them." And at this point, you have the chance to advance the communication by encouraging Scott to use additional study skills.

● ● **Types of Paraphrases** The meaning you get from any statement may focus on its content, the feelings represented, or both, depending on the situation. A *content paraphrase* summarizes the substantive or the denotative meaning of the message; a *feelings paraphrasing* expresses what you understand to be the emotions the person is experiencing as shown by his or her nonverbal cues.

To illustrate the difference, let's go back to Scott's statement, "I'm really going to study this time." The paraphrase "I take it that you're going to read and outline every chapter carefully" is a content paraphrase—it focuses on the denotative meaning of the message. Depending on how Scott sounded as he spoke, an appropriate feelings paraphrase might be, "So you were pretty upset with your grade on the last test." Which response is most appropriate for the situation depends on whether you perceive the emphasis of Scott's statement to be on *how* to study for a test or on *his feelings* about not doing as well as he should. Let's look at another example that contains a longer message.

> "Five weeks ago I gave the revised manuscript of my independent study to my project adviser. I felt really good about it because I felt the changes I had made really improved my explanations. You can imagine how I felt when I got the manuscript back yesterday and my adviser said she couldn't see that this draft was much different from the first."
> *Content paraphrase*: "If I have this correct, you're saying that your adviser saw little difference, yet you think your draft was both different and much improved."
> *Feelings paraphrase*: "You seem frustrated that your adviser didn't recognize the changes you had made."

Of course, in real-life settings, we often don't distinguish clearly between content and feelings paraphrases. Rather, we tend to use both together to give a more complete picture of the meanings we received. For instance, a combination content/feelings paraphrase of the manuscript message might well be, "If I have this right, you're saying that your adviser could see no real differences, yet you think your draft was not only different but much improved. I also get the feeling that your adviser's comments really irk you."

From the examples presented, we can see that several paraphrases can be appropriate for any given statement. As a final illustration, suppose you were talking with a friend about his or her summer. How would *you* respond to the following statement?

FRIEND: "I don't know how things went for you, but for me the summer really flew by. And I'm afraid I didn't get nearly as much done as I'd planned, but I guess I'm not surprised. I hardly ever accomplish as much as I plan. Anyway, I'm really looking forward to the new term. I look at it as getting a fresh start."

YOU: [Write a paraphrase here.]

Your paraphrase might resemble any one of the following:

> "I get the feeling that not accomplishing everything you intended isn't nearly as important to you as the excitement of starting a new term."

> "It sounds as if you enjoyed the summer but you're really excited about getting back to school."

"If I understand correctly what you're saying, you always expect to get more done during the summer than what you accomplish, but it doesn't bother you because you're always so excited about starting a new term."

You may be thinking that if people stated their ideas and feelings accurately in the first place, we would not have to paraphrase. Accurate wording might help us to understand better, but as our study of the communication process has shown, we can seldom be sure we accurately understand what others say. Both verbal and nonverbal messages can be misunderstood; internal or external noise can interfere with our understanding; and our beliefs, assumptions, and feelings may differ from those of the speaker. Perfecting our paraphrasing ability is a significant way to improve the effectiveness of our communication.

When to Paraphrase Common sense suggests that we wouldn't paraphrase every message we receive, nor would we paraphrase after every few sentences. Still, there are times when it is important to clarify meaning before stating your own ideas or feelings. Try paraphrasing the ideas or feelings of the other person when:

1. You need a better understanding of a message—in terms of content, feelings, or both—before you can respond appropriately.

2. You think you understand what a person has said or how the person feels, but you're not absolutely sure.

3. You perceive that what the person has said is controversial or was said under emotional strain and therefore may not really be what the person meant to say.

4. You have a strong reaction to what the person has said or how the person has said it that may have interfered with your interpretation of the message. Recall our earlier discussion of internal noise: such reactions may so interfere with accurate listening that you completely misunderstand the message the person is really trying to convey.

5. You are speaking in a language that is not your native language or talking with people in a language that is not their first. People speaking a foreign language may have difficulty choosing or understanding the expressions that native speakers use. Similarly, paraphrasing can be helpful when the other person speaks with an unfamiliar accent or uses verbal expressions that you aren't sure you understand.

In summary, to paraphrase effectively, (1) listen carefully to the message, (2) determine what the message means to you, and (3) if you believe a paraphrase is necessary, restate the message using your own words to indicate the meaning you have received.

Clarifying Meaning

BY YOURSELF

Try to clarify the following statements by providing an appropriate question or paraphrase. To get you started, the first conversation has been completed for you.

LUIS: "It's Dionne's birthday, and I've planned a big evening. Sometimes, I think Dionne wonders whether I take her for granted—well, I think after tonight she'll know I think she's something special!"

Question: "What are you planning to do?"
Content paraphrase: "I get the idea you've planned a night that's totally different from what Dionne expects on her birthday."
Feelings paraphrase: "From the way you're talking, I get the feeling you're really excited about your plans for the evening."

ANGIE: "Brother! Another nothing class. I keep thinking one of these days he'll get excited about something. Professor Romero is a real bore!"

Question:
Content paraphrase:
Feelings paraphrase:

GUY: "Everyone seems to be talking about that movie on Channel 5 last night, but I didn't see it. You know, I don't watch much on the 'idiot box.'"

Question:
Content paraphrase:
Feelings paraphrase:

KAELIN: "I don't know if it's something to do with me or with Mom, but lately she and I just aren't getting along."

Question:
Content paraphrase:
Feelings paraphrase:

PATTY: "I have a report due at work and a paper due in management class. On top of that, it's my sister's birthday, and so far I haven't even had time to get her anything. Tomorrow's going to be a disaster."

Question:
Content paraphrase:
Feelings paraphrase:

IN GROUPS

In this exercise for three people, A and B will hold a conversation on a topic such as "Why I like the type of work I'm doing," "The pros and cons of abortion," or "Dealing with drug or alcohol abuse," and C will observe the conversation. Speakers are not allowed to state their ideas until they paraphrase what the other person has just said. At the end of three to four minutes, C (the observer) discusses the paraphrasing of the two participants. Then B and C converse for three to four minutes while A observes; for the final three to four minutes, C and A converse while B observes. After completing the exercise, the participants should discuss how they felt about paraphrasing and how the paraphrasing affected the conversations.

Helping Responses

Helping responses, the second group of responses we consider, are statements that show approval of a person's feelings or acknowledgment of the person's right to have those feelings; at times they may reinforce people's behavior or show them how to do something better. In this section we consider supporting, interpreting, praise, and constructive criticism.[4]

SUPPORTING

People who express their feelings often look for or need some kind of supporting response. *Supporting responses* soothe, approve, reduce tension, or pacify. They show that the listener empathizes with a person's feelings, whether positive (joy, elation, pride, satisfaction) or negative (sadness, anger, sorrow, disappointment). Whatever the direction or intensity of the feeling, the supporting statement indicates that we care about the person and what happens to him or her.

Supporting Positive Feelings We all like to treasure our good feelings; when we share them we don't want them dashed by inappropriate or insensitive responses. When a person's feelings are positive, an effective supporting statement helps the person sustain the feelings. For example:

KENDRA (hangs up the telephone and turns to Selena): "That was my boss. He said that he'd put my name in for promotion. I didn't realize he had ever really considered me promotable."

SELENA: "Kendra, that's great. I'm so happy for you. You seem very excited."

Supporting positive feelings is generally easy; however, it does require a degree of empathy. Notice that first Selena must perceive that Kendra is happy about the news. For Selena to make an appropriate response, she need not share in Kendra's joy, but she must appreciate the feeling people get when they receive good news. Thus, when Selena says, "I'm so happy for you. You seem very excited," she is supporting Kendra's right to feel excited.

Statements like these are much needed. Think of times when you have experienced an event that made you feel happy, proud, pleased, soothed, or amused and needed to express it. Didn't it further your good feeling when others recognized and supported it?

Supporting Negative Feelings When someone's feelings are negative, an effective supporting statement acknowledges the person's right to the feelings and helps the person work through them without intensifying them or further upsetting the person.

Appropriate responses to negative feelings seem to be much more difficult for most of us to make. When something bad happens to someone, we may feel embarrassed by the other person's pain and, as a result, want to be somewhere else. But in these situations, people need supportive statements even more than they do when their feelings are positive. For example:

KENDRA (slams down the phone): "That was my boss—he called to tell me that they're letting me go at work, but he wouldn't even tell me why!"

SELENA: "Oh Kendra—that must hurt. Anything I can do to help?"

Effective supporting statements of negative feelings require the ability to empathize. Even those of us with the hardest of hearts know the pain that comes with being rejected, disappointed, disillusioned, or hurt. To support, we do not have to share in the feelings, but we do need to respond in a way that recognizes the person's right to them. Thus, in our example, Selena, empathizing with Kendra, perceives her shock and anger. The statement "Oh Kendra—that must hurt" verbalizes her recognition of the feeling; the statement "Anything I can do to help?" indicates that she cares about what is happening to Kendra and is ready to help her through this moment of pain and disbelief.

Because negative feelings and negative situations are the most difficult to handle, let's look at two more examples that deal with negative situations.

JIM (comes out of his boss's office clutching the report he had been so sure he would receive praise for): "Jacobs rejected my report. I worked my tail off, did everything she asked, and she rejected it."

AARON: "She rejected it? As hard as you worked, I can see why you're so upset. That's a real blow."

Aaron's response is primarily an empathizing statement that shows an understanding of why Jim is so upset. By saying "That's a real blow," Aaron also demonstrates that he is in tune with Jim's feelings. Perhaps you think Aaron should say, "Jim, I can see why you feel so bad. You deserved praise for what you did." Although such a statement would have supporting qualities, Aaron is in no position to judge whether the report did in fact deserve praise. The support comes with Aaron's showing an understanding of how hard Jim worked and, therefore, why Jim feels especially bad. Giving empathic support is not the same as making statements that aren't true or that only tell people what they want to hear. When supportive statements are out of touch with the facts, they can encourage behavior that is actually destructive.

Making an appropriate response may be most difficult in situations of high emotion and stress. A person whose feelings are highly negative may need a few seconds, a few minutes, or even a few hours to calm down and think rationally. Sometimes there is virtually nothing anyone can say that will be perceived as helpful. At these times perhaps the best way of showing support is with a purely nonverbal response. Consider this situation:

With a few seconds left in the basketball game and her team trailing by one point, Nancy steals the ball from her opponent, dribbles down the court for an uncontested lay-up, and misses. The gun sounds, ending the game. Nancy runs to her coach with tears in her eyes and cries, "I blew it! I lost us the game!"

A first reaction might be to say, "Don't feel bad, Nancy." But Nancy obviously does feel bad, and she has a right to that feeling. Another response might be, "It's OK, Nancy, you didn't lose us the game," but in fact Nancy's miss did affect the outcome, and she is unlikely to be helped by a response that she knows is inaccurate. Perhaps the best thing the coach can do at that moment is to put her arm around Nancy to show that she understands. At that time, or later, she could say, "Nancy, I know you feel bad—but without

● Sometimes, there is virtually nothing anyone can say that will be perceived as helpful. At these times perhaps the best way to show support is with a purely nonverbal response.

your steal, we wouldn't even have had a chance to win." Still, for the moment, Nancy will be difficult to console.

Making supporting statements is not always easy, and a frequent temptation is to give advice instead. But since your goal is to soothe or to reduce tension, giving advice may well be counterproductive and result in further irritation or increased tension.

In summary, to make effective supporting statements, (1) listen closely to what the person is saying, (2) try to empathize with the dominant feelings, (3) phrase a reply that is in harmony with the feeling you have identified,

Basic Communication Skills

SKILL	USE	PROCEDURE	EXAMPLE
Paraphrasing Putting into words your understanding of the meaning you get from another's statement.	To increase listening efficiency; to avoid message confusion; to discover the speaker's motivation.	1. Listen carefully. 2. Determine what the message means to you. 3. Restate the message using your own words to show the meaning you received from the message.	Grace says, "At two minutes to five, the boss gave me three letters that had to be in the mail that evening!" Bonita replies, "If I understand you correctly, you were really resentful that the boss would dump important work on you right before closing time."
Supporting Saying something that soothes, reduces tension, or pacifies.	To help people feel better about themselves or what they have said or done.	1. Listen to what the person is saying. 2. Try to empathize with the person's feelings. 3. Phrase a reply that is in harmony with these feelings. 4. Supplement your verbal response with appropriate nonverbal responses. 5. Indicate your willingness to be of help if possible.	In response to Tony's statement, "I'm really frosted that I didn't get the promotion," Alex replies, "I can understand your disappointment; you've really worked hard for it."

(4) supplement your verbal response with appropriate nonverbal responses, and (5) if it seems appropriate, indicate your willingness to help.

INTERPRETING

When a person sees only one possible explanation for a given event, the most helpful response may provide an interpretation. *Interpreting* consists of attempting to point out an alternative or hidden view of an event to help a person see things from a different perspective.

Many times, especially when people are depressed, they say things that show a very limited view. Consider the following situation:

After returning from his first date with Nola, a woman he believes he might become very fond of, Sam is very upset. He had an excellent time, yet the end of the evening was very disappointing.

SAM: "I take her to dinner and a great show, and when I get to her door, she gives me a quick little kiss, says, 'Thanks a lot,' and rushes into the house. We didn't even have much time to talk about the play. I guess she didn't like me."

Sam is interpreting Nola's behavior negatively—he sees her action as a rejection of him as a person. Martin does not know what Nola thinks, but since he perceives that Sam is taking a very limited view of the events, he might respond as follows: "I wonder whether she might not have been afraid that if she said or did any more, she'd be leading you on?"

Whose interpretation is correct? We don't know. What we do know is that behavior can frequently be interpreted in more than one way. Too often, especially when people feel slighted, angry, or hurt, they interpret events negatively.

The following are two additional examples of appropriate interpreting:

KARLA: "I just don't understand Dion. I say we've got to start saving money, and he just gets angry with me."

SHELLEY: "I can understand why his behavior would concern you [a supportive statement prefacing an interpretation]. Perhaps he feels guilty about not being able to save money or feels resentful that you seem to be putting all the blame on him."

MICAH: "I just don't seem to understand Bradford. He says my work is top-notch, but I haven't received a pay raise in over a year."

KHALIF: "I can see why you'd be frustrated, but maybe the company just doesn't have the money."

In summary, to interpret effectively, (1) listen carefully to what a person is saying; (2) if there are other reasonable ways to look at the event, phrase an alternative to the person's own interpretation—one that is intended to help the person see that other interpretations are available; and (3) when appropriate, preface the interpretive statement with a supportive one.

Remember, you are not a mind reader—you cannot know for sure why something was done or said. Your primary goal when interpreting is to help someone look at an event from a different point of view. As with supporting statements, it is important to offer interpretation only when it seems plausible and worth considering. The point is not merely to soothe the person's feelings but to help the person see a possibility he or she has overlooked.

PRAISE

Too often the positive things people say and do are passed over with little comment. Yet, from our earlier discussion of self-concept, you'll remember that our view of who we are, as well as our behavior, is often shaped by how others respond to us. Praise reinforces positive behavior as well as recognizes accomplishments. When people have done something you appreciate, take the time to tell them.

● **When people have done something you appreciate, take the time to tell them.**

For praise to achieve its goal and not be perceived merely as flattery, we need to focus the praise on the specific action and make sure that the wording is in keeping with the value of the accomplishment or behavior. If a child who tends to be forgetful remembers to return the scissors he borrowed, that's an event that needs to be praised. In this case, saying, "Thanks for returning the scissors—I appreciate that," praises the behavior and describes the specific feeling the behavior has caused in a credible way. In contrast, saying, "You remembered to return the scissors—that's wonderful—I want to tell everyone about this," is likely to be perceived as overkill or even sarcasm. Likewise, saying, "You're so wonderful, you're on top of everything" is general flattery—it doesn't reinforce a particular behavior.

Consider the following examples of appropriate praise:

When Sonya helps you to select a gift for a co-worker for the office party, you might say, "Sonya, thank you for helping me with this one. Your idea was just right for the occasion."

Basic Communication Skills

SKILL	USE	PROCEDURE	EXAMPLE
Interpreting			
Attempting to point out an alternative or hidden meaning to an event.	To help a person see the possible meanings of words, actions, and events.	1. Listen carefully to what the person is saying. 2. Phrase an alternative to the person's interpretation—one that is intended to help the person see that other interpretations are possible. 3. When appropriate, preface the interpretation with a supportive statement.	Pam says, "Sue must really be angry with me. Yesterday she walked right by me at the market and didn't even say 'Hi.'" Paul replies, "Maybe she's not angry at all—maybe she just didn't see you."
Praising			
Giving people a verbal reward for what they have said or done.	To help people see themselves positively.	1. Make sure the context allows for praise. 2. Describe the behavior. 3. Focus on one behavior. 4. Be specific. 5. Identify the positive feeling you experience.	"Marge, that was an excellent writing job on the Miller story. Your descriptions were particularly vivid."

When Cole offers to share his lunch with a student who forgot his lunch money that day, you might say, "Cole, that was nice of you to share your lunch with Tim. You're a very considerate person."

When your mother prepares an excellent dessert, you might say, "Mom, after working all day you still had energy to make a pie. Thanks."

Praising effectively doesn't take much time, and it is almost always appreciated. In summary, (1) make sure the context allows for praise, (2) describe the behavior you are praising, (3) focus on that specific behavior, (4) be specific, and, if possible, (5) identify the positive feeling you experience as a result of the praiseworthy behavior.

CONSTRUCTIVE CRITICISM

At times we seek information from others to identify and correct our mistakes. At other times we feel a need to identify and correct the mistakes of others. Both receiving and giving criticism can make us uncomfortable and even harm the relationship, however, especially if we haven't used the appropriate skills. In this section we first look at guidelines for asking for criticism and then consider guidelines for giving constructive criticism.

Asking for Criticism Although asking for constructive criticism is the most direct way to find out whether our behavior is effective, people are often reluctant to do so because they feel threatened by criticism. Instead people rely entirely on others' nonverbal cues. Yet even when we interpret nonverbal cues accurately, they fail to help us understand why our behavior missed the mark. Nor will such cues help us decide what changes are needed for us to improve. By employing the verbal skill of asking for criticism, we accomplish these two objectives.

The following guidelines can help you ask for constructive criticism.

Ask for criticism so that you will avoid surprises. Taking initiative in asking for criticism prepares you psychologically to deal with the criticism.

Think of criticism as being in your best interest. No one likes to be criticized, but through valid criticism we often learn and grow. When you receive a negative appraisal—even when you expected a positive one—try to look on it not as critical of you personally but as a statement that reveals something about your behavior that you did not know. Whether you will do anything about the criticism is up to you, but you cannot make such a decision if you do not know that the behavior exists or how it affects others.

Specify the kind of criticism you are seeking. Rather than asking very general questions about ideas, feelings, or behavior, ask specific questions. If you say, "Colleen, is there anything you don't like about my ideas?" Colleen is likely to consider this a loaded question. But if you say, "Colleen, do you think I've given enough emphasis to the marketing possibilities?" you will encourage Colleen to speak openly to the specific issue.

Ask for criticism only when you really want an honest response. If you ask a friend, "How do you like this coat?" but actually want the friend to agree that the coat is attractive on you, you are not being honest. Once others realize that when you request an appraisal you are actually fishing for a compliment, valuable appraisals will not be forthcoming.

Try to avoid contradiction between your verbal and nonverbal cues. If you say, "How do you like my paper?" but your tone of voice indicates that you do not really want to know, the other person may be reluctant to be honest with you.

Give reinforcement to those who take your requests for criticism as honest requests. Imagine that you ask your colleagues how they like your ideas for the ad campaign, and you get the response "The ideas seem a little under-stated." If you then get annoyed and say, "Well, if you can do any better you can take over," your colleagues will learn not to give you criticism even when you ask for it. Instead, reward people for their constructive criticism. Perhaps you could say, "Thanks for the opinion—I'd like to hear what led you to that conclusion." In this way you encourage honest appraisal.

• *Be sure you understand the criticism.* Before you react to what you've heard, paraphrase your understanding to make sure it is what the person meant.

Asking for criticism does not require that you always act on every comment. You may decide against making a change in what you've said or done for other good reasons. But asking for criticism does enable you to make a conscious, rational choice about whether you will change your behavior.

Giving Constructive Criticism Even though some people learn faster and better through praise, there are still times when criticism is useful—especially when a person requests it. Even when people don't ask, we are sometimes in the best position to offer critical comments to help others perform better. Unfortunately, most of us are far too free in giving criticism—we often feel a need to help others "become better people" even if they aren't interested in hearing from us at the moment. Moreover, even when the time is right for criticism, we may not do the best job of giving it. The following guidelines should help you compose criticism that is both constructive and beneficial.

• *Make sure that the person is interested in hearing criticism.* The safest rule to follow is to withhold any criticism until it is asked for. Criticism will seldom help if a person is not interested in hearing it. If you believe that criticism is called for, ask whether the person is interested in hearing it. For instance, you might ask a group chairperson, "Are you interested in hearing my comments about the way you handled the meeting?" Remember, however, that even if the answer is "yes," you must proceed carefully.

• *Describe the person's behavior carefully and accurately. Describing behavior* means accurately recounting behavior without labeling the behavior good or bad, right or wrong. By describing behavior you lay an informative base for the criticism and increase the chances that the person will listen receptively. Criticism that is preceded with detailed description is less likely to be met defensively. Your description shows that you are criticizing the behavior rather than attacking the person, and it points the way to a solution. For example, if DeShawn asks, "What do you think of the delivery of my report?" instead of saying "It wasn't very effective," you might better say something like "You tended to look down at the report as if you were reading it verbatim—this detracted from your relating with your clients." This criticism does not attack DeShawn's self-concept, and it tells him what he needs to do to be more effective.

• *Preface a negative statement with a positive one whenever possible.* When you are planning to criticize, it is a good idea to start with some praise. Of course, common sense suggests that superficial praise followed by crushing criticism will be seen for what it is. Thus, saying, "Leah, that's a pretty blouse

● By describing be-
havior you lay an in-
formative base for the
criticism and increase
the chances that the
person will listen
receptively.

you have on, but you did a perfectly miserable job of running the meeting,"
will be rightly perceived as patronizing. A better approach would be, "Leah,
you did a good job of drawing Jarrell into the discussion. He usually sits
through an entire meeting without saying a word. But you seem hesitant to
use the same power to keep the meeting on track. By not taking charge more,
you let people talk about things that were unrelated to the agenda." Here the
praise is relevant and significant. If you cannot preface a criticism with significant praise, don't try. Empty praise will not help the person to accept the
criticism that follows.

● *Be as specific as possible.* The more specific the criticism, the more effectively a person will be able to deal with the information. In the situation just
discussed, it would not have been helpful to say, "You had some leadership
problems." This comment is so general that Leah would have little idea of
what she did wrong. Moreover, she may infer that she is, in your eyes, inca-
pable of leadership. If the point was that Leah wasn't in control, say so; if
Leah failed to obtain agreement on one item before moving on to another,
say so.

● *Restrict criticism to recent behavior.* People are not helped much by hearing
about something they did last week or last month. With the passage of time,
memories fade and even change, and it may be difficult to reach an agree-

Basic Communication Skills

SKILL	USE	PROCEDURE	EXAMPLE
Asking for Criticism Asking others for their reaction to you or your behavior.	To get information that will help you understand yourself and your effect on others.	1. Ask to avoid surprises. 2. Think of criticism as in your best interest. 3. Outline the kind of criticism you are seeking. 4. Ask only when you want an honest response. 5. Avoid verbal/nonverbal contradictions. 6. Give reinforcement to those who take requests seriously. 7. Paraphrase what you hear.	Lucy asks, "Tim, when I talk with the boss, do I sound defensive?" Tim replies, "I think so—your voice gets sharp and you really look nervous." "Thanks for verifying that for me, Tim."
Giving Constructive Criticism Evaluation of behavior given to help a person identify or correct a fault.	To help people see themselves as others see them.	1. Make sure the person is interested in hearing criticism. 2. Describe the person's behavior accurately. 3. Precede negative statements with positive ones if possible. 4. Be specific. 5. Consider recent behavior. 6. Consider behavior that can be changed. 7. Include guidelines for improvement.	Carol says, "Bob, I've noticed something about your behavior with Jenny. Would you like to hear it?" After Bob assures her that he would, she continues. "Well, the last few times we've all been together, whenever Jenny starts to relate an experience, you interrupt her and finish telling the story."

ment about the behavior being criticized. If you have to spend time recreating a situation and refreshing someone's memory, the criticism probably will be ineffective.

Direct criticism at behavior the person can change. It is pointless to remind someone of a shortcoming over which the person has no control. It may be true that George would find it easier to prepare arguments if he had taken a course in logic, but pointing this out to him will not improve his reasoning. Telling him that he needs to work on stating main points clearly and backing them up with good evidence is helpful because he can change these behaviors.

If possible, include a statement that shows how the person could correct the problem. Don't limit your comments to what someone has done wrong. Tell the person how what was done could have been done better. If Gail, the chairperson of a committee, cannot get her members to agree on anything, you might suggest that she try phrasing her remarks to the committee differently; for example, "Gail, when you think discussion is ended, say something like, 'It sounds as if we agree that our donation should be made to a single agency. Is that correct?'" By including a positive suggestion, not only do you help the person to improve—which is the purpose of constructive criticism—you also show that your intentions are positive.

Helping Responses

BY YOURSELF

1. For each of the following situations, supply two responses, one supportive and one interpretive.

"The pie is all gone! I know there were at least two pieces left just a while ago. Kids! They can be so inconsiderate."
Supportive response:
Interpretive response:

"My boss was really on me today. I worked hard all day, but things just didn't gel for me. I don't know—maybe I've been spending too much time on some of the accounts."
Supportive response:
Interpretive response:

"I just got a call from my folks. My sister was in a car accident. They say she's OK, but the car was totaled. Apparently she had her seat belt fastened when it happened. But I don't know whether she's really all right or whether they just don't want me to worry."
Supportive response:
Interpretive response:

2. Write down one to three specific communication-related behaviors that you would like to have criticized. For instance: "Does the way I dress make me look younger than I am?" "Do you think I talk too much at meetings?" "Did the way I presented my analysis of Carlo's plan help the discussion?"

3. Ask a close friend for criticism on one or more of the communication behaviors you have listed. Note how you react to the criticism.

Consider the following two situations. Work out an appropriate phrasing of constructive criticism for each. Then, with others in your group, share your phrasings of the criticism. Which of the wordings best meets the guidelines for constructive criticism?

You have been driving to school with a fellow student whose name you obtained from the transportation office at school. You have known him for only three weeks. Everything about the situation is great except that he drives too fast for you.

A good friend says "you know" more than once every sentence. You like her very much, but you see that others are beginning to avoid her. She is very sensitive and does not usually take criticism well.

Write out exactly what you said the last time you criticized someone's behavior. Which, if any, of the guidelines for constructive criticism did you follow or violate? If you were to do it again, what would you say differently?

Problem Responses

Sometimes even the best communicators respond in ways that create problems. Good communicators are aware of when they have made mistakes and try to repair them immediately and avoid them in the future. Responses create problems when they cause people to feel defensive or question their self-worth, and when they fail to achieve their goal.

We have already considered evaluation as a problem response. Four others are irrelevant, tangential, incongruous, and interrupting responses. You will see that most of these problem or inappropriate responses also violate the rules of conversational coherence and turn taking discussed in Chapter 6.

IRRELEVANT RESPONSES

An *irrelevant response* (violating Grice's relevancy maxim) is one that bears no relation to what has been said. In effect, it ignores the speaker's message entirely.

JOSH: "I'm concerned about the way Jamie is handling arrangements for the benefit."

ZACH: "Umm. Hey, Guns & Roses are coming to town—I've got to get tickets for that."

When people's statements are ignored, they not only question whether they were heard but also wonder about the worth of what they were thinking or saying. In this example, Zach's irrelevant response causes Josh to wonder about the importance to Zach of what he was saying.

TANGENTIAL RESPONSES

A *tangential response* is really an irrelevant response phrased in tactful language. Although the tangential response at least suggests acknowledgment of what a person was saying, the net result—changing the subject—is the same as with an irrelevant response.

JOSH: "I'm concerned about the way Jamie is handling arrangements for the benefit."

ZACH: "Well, you know Jamie. I remember once when I was in charge of arrangements and forgot who I was supposed to contact."

Even though Zach has acknowledged Josh's statement, by shifting emphasis to his own experience Zach appears to be saying that the issue bothering Josh is not important enough to discuss. Again, such responses chip away at a person's feelings of self-worth. Josh thought that he was raising a significant issue. Either Zach fails to see the importance of Josh's statement or Josh places too much emphasis on Jamie's behavior. The real problem is that Zach's response addresses neither possibility, and the subject of Jamie's behavior is left unresolved. Zach's apparent withdrawal from discussing Jamie's behavior thus creates a problem between Josh and Zach.

INCONGRUOUS RESPONSES

In our discussion of nonverbal communication, we indicated that problems occur when nonverbal messages appear to conflict with verbal messages. An *incongruous response* is an example of this problem.

JOSH: "Well, we got some things done today."

ZACH (in a sarcastic tone): "Yeah, that was a great meeting."

On the surface, Zach seems to be acknowledging and verifying Josh's statement, but his sarcastic tone causes Josh to wonder whether he is confirming Josh's ideas or making fun of them. Because nonverbal reactions are likely to override verbal meaning with most people, Josh will probably take Zach's words as sarcasm. If they are in fact sarcastic, Zach's insensitivity to Josh's honest statement of feelings will contribute to the creation of a barrier between them. And if Zach's words are sincere, Josh's confusion about Zach's meaning likewise will lead to a barrier between them.

INTERRUPTING RESPONSES

An *interrupting response* (violating turn-taking rules) occurs when a person breaks in before the other person has finished a statement.

JOSH: "I'm concerned about the way Jamie . . ."

ZACH: "I know—that Jamie is something else, but I don't think there's any real problem."

People interrupt inappropriately when they believe what they have to say is more important than what the other person is saying, when they believe they know what the other person is going to say and they want that person to know that they already know, or when they are not paying close attention. All these factors leading to interrupting responses communicate either a lack of sensitivity, a superior attitude, or both. People need to be able to verbalize their ideas and feelings fully; inappropriate interruptions are bound to damage their self-concepts or make them hostile—and possibly both. Whatever you have to say is seldom so important that it requires you to interrupt someone. When you do interrupt, you should realize that you may be perceived as putting the person down and are increasing the chance of a defensive reaction. The more frequent the interruptions, the greater the potential harm.

Are you an interrupter? This behavior is so common that many of us don't even realize how often we do it. To check on your own interrupting behavior, for the rest of the day try to be conscious of any time you interrupt—whatever the reason. Then ask whether the interruption was necessary or whether you could have waited for the other person to finish. Although interrupting behavior has been attributed to men more than women, in their recent study of sex-related behavior, Tammy Marche and Carole Peterson report that total acceptance of sex differences in interruption behavior is not warranted.[5] They go on to say that interruption is most likely influenced by personality and social variables that are likely to change depending on contexts and situations.

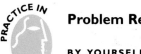

Problem Responses

BY YOURSELF

Think back over conversations with your friends and acquaintances in the last day or two. Which kinds of problem responses (irrelevant, tangential, incongruous, and interrupting) did you use most frequently? Under what circumstances did they occur? What do you need to do to limit your use of these responses?

● ◆ ■ Summary

Responding appropriately is the final phase of listening. Responding well involves a complete set of skills.

Appropriate responses show a person's empathy. Empathy relates to determining the emotional state of another person and responding in an appropriate manner. Empathic responses recognize the person's right to his or her feelings and show that we can share in those feelings.

Clarifying responses help to ensure that people are sharing the same meanings. Questioning and paraphrasing are two skills that you can use to ensure understanding. Well-phrased questions are specific and sensitive. Paraphrases can check understanding of message content, feelings, or both.

Helping responses give people information about themselves or their behavior. These responses include supporting, interpreting, praising, and giving constructive criticism. Both praise and criticism should be specific and timely. In addition, several guidelines can ensure that criticism is beneficial: Make sure the person is interested in hearing criticism, describe the behavior on which the criticism is based, precede negative statements with positive ones if possible, be specific, criticize only recent behavior, direct criticism at behavior the person can do something about, and show what a person can do to correct a problem.

Problem responses hinder communication by planting the seeds of discontent within people about themselves or about the relationship. Furthermore, inappropriate responses can scuttle efforts at understanding meaning. Irrelevant, tangential, incongruous, and interrupting responses are some of the most common types of problem responses.

● ◆ ■ Communication Improvement Goal Statement

Select one of the response skills that you would most like to improve: empathy, questioning, paraphrasing, supporting, interpreting, praising, asking for criticism, or giving criticism. Write a communication improvement goal statement following the guidelines on page 33 of Chapter 1.

● ◆ ■ Featured Reading

"I Don't Know What to Say . . .": How to Help and Support Someone Who Is Dying
Robert Buckman
(Boston: Little, Brown and Company, 1989)

Undoubtedly one of the most difficult challenges for a person is learning how to respond to those who are seriously ill and who are dying. Dr. Robert

Buckman, a British oncologist living in Toronto, has seen the process from both sides. Not only is he a doctor who has treated dying patients, but he has also recovered from dermatomyositis, a rare autoimmune disease that brought him to the brink of death.

Although a large section of the book is about the process of dying, much more of it is about communication, and in particular how to empathize with those who are dying. The first section of the book deals with empathic listening and focuses on response skills. The remaining chapters in the book discuss the importance of responsive listening at all stages of the dying process. Among his guidelines for empathic listening, he suggests encouraging a patient to talk, using silence and nonverbal communication, describing feelings, paraphrasing, and perception checking.

His advice is specific; he offers sound techniques for dealing with the emotions of depression, anger, denial, and fear that patients experience. Moreover, nearly everything he discusses can be applied to other real-life situations in which we find ourselves dealing with people who are experiencing serious problems. In several places he provides a comparison of responses, making the point that when a patient makes a statement like "I'm going to die—and I'm not ready," you have two choices. One is to pass it off with comments like "Don't talk like that" or "There is a season for all things." The other is to engage the person with such comments as "It's not easy for you, is it?" or "What's the most scary part?"

Written with clarity, compassion, and a comforting sense of humor, Dr. Buckman's book is both reassuring and informative. No one can read it without gaining a much greater understanding of empathy and how to show it in our communication. This book will be important to all of us at some time in our lives.

● ◆ ■ Notes

1. Robert J. Campbell, Norman Kagan, and David R. Krathwohl, "The Development and Validation of a Scale to Measure Affective Sensitivity (Empathy)," *Journal of Counseling Psychology* 18 (1971): 407.

2. See Dale G. Leathers, *Successful Nonverbal Communication: Principles and Applications*, 2nd ed. (New York: Macmillan, 1992), p. 42.

3. Ibid., p. 26.

4. George Gazda et al., *Human Relations Development: A Manual for Educators*, 3rd ed. (Needham Heights, Mass.: Allyn & Bacon, 1984).

5. Tammy A. Marche and Carole Peterson, "The Development and Sex-Related Use of Interruption Behavior," *Human Communication Research* 19 (March 1993): 405.

CHAPTER NINE

Interpersonal Influence

O B J E C T I V E S

After you have read this chapter, you should be able to define or explain:

Influence

Compliance gaining

Persuasion

Reasoning

Sources of credibility

Emotional language

Assertiveness

Cultural considerations concerning assertiveness

Power and its sources

As Stanley and Nora watch their newborn baby asleep in the crib, Stanley says, "You know, when you really think about it, being a parent is an awesome responsibility. I hope that we can always be a good influence on her."

"Ward, would you talk to Mark?" Ward's mother asks. "He's a good kid, but he's just not studying the way he should. I'm asking you because he really seems to respect you, and I think he'll pay attention to what you say."

"We've got to do something to change Hill's methods," Andrea says. "Maybe we can convince him that the way he's acting is causing the women who work here to resent his leadership."

Each of these three examples represents an interpersonal situation in which one person is in a position to influence others. The study of influence and how to achieve it is fundamental to effective interpersonal communication.

Influence consists of the ability to bring about changes in the attitudes and/or actions of others. Knowing that something you said or stood for has influenced (or seemed to influence) people to alter their thinking or behavior satisfies basic interpersonal needs.

Influence can be unintentional or intentional. We often are able to influence others without being aware of it. For example, if you have a new hairstyle or are wearing a new outfit or have purchased a flashy new car, you may well influence someone else to try your hairstyle or to buy a similar outfit or car. Likewise, professors frequently exert unintentional influence on their students. For instance, students may observe their professor's style in answering difficult questions and adopt that style in their own interpersonal communication without even realizing that their style is patterned after their professor's. Parents and older brothers and sisters influence young children in a similar manner.

In this chapter, however, we will focus on intentional influence. Traditionally, intentional influence has been called *persuasion*. Recently, intentional influence has been discussed in interpersonal literature as *compliance gaining*. In this chapter we will consider the means or bases of compliance gaining through persuasion and the importance of assertiveness. Throughout the chapter we will address the importance of ethical means of accomplishing intentional influence.

Compliance Gaining Through Persuasion

Much of the research in interpersonal influence has been directed to the kinds of specific strategies that people use to gain compliance. In their review of compliance-gaining methods, Lawrence Wheeless, Robert Barraclough, and Robert Stewart have listed more than fifty different techniques that various researchers have identified.[1] In a more recent article, Dan O'Hair and Michael J. Cody have grouped most strategies into the following seven categories of messages:[2]

1. Direct requests, in which a person asks another to comply, such as "May I borrow your curling iron?"

2. Exchange, in which a person seeks compliance by offering trade-offs, such as "I'll help you carry out the trash if you'll let me use your curling iron."

3. Distributive, in which a person attempts to coerce someone or make someone feel guilty, such as "For crying out loud, I'm asking to borrow your curling iron for only a minute, not for the rest of your life."

4. Face maintenance, in which a person uses indirect, emotion-eliciting statements, such as "Gee, I really want to look my best tonight, but I just can't seem to get my hair to work right—I wish I had a curling iron."

● Much of our inter-
personal communica-
tion involves attempts
to influence the be-
havior of others.

5. Supporting evidence, in which a person presents reasons and evidence for compliance, such as "I really would like to have some curl in my hair tonight and I'll need the curling iron for only a few minutes."

6. Other-benefit, in which a person presents reasons that benefit the other person, such as "If my hair looks good, I'm more likely to get a higher paying job that will allow me to buy what I need so I won't be asking to borrow so many things of yours."

7. Referent influence or empathic understanding, in which a person appeals to another's love or affection, such as "Come on, we're used to sharing with each other because we respect the other person's needs."

Although all seven of these are common, they are not all equally desirable. For instance, although distributive strategies of coercing, threatening, and manipulating may gain compliance, they are often seen as unethical.

In this text we consider ethical compliance-gaining efforts as persuasion. *Persuasion* is the intentional verbal attempt to influence the attitudes or behaviors of others. Researchers have verified that persuasion is central to interpersonal communication.[3] Persuasion is an appropriate means of influencing people primarily because it allows freedom of choice. Persuasion relies on argumentation rather than coercion through threat or guilt and allows the individual freedom of choice.[4] Thus knowledge of means of persuasion is vital in maintaining what Paul Keller and Charles Brown describe as the *interpersonal ethic*, which requires that your influence attempts allow others freedom of choice in accepting them.[5] In keeping with their guideline, we focus on *ethical behavior*, behavior that is in keeping with the standards of moral conduct.

In this section we discuss the traditional approach that considers persuasion as a product of reasoning with people, relying on source credibility, and motivating by appealing to emotional needs.[6] We show how the compliance-gaining strategies that O'Hair and Cody have identified function from a base of reasoning, credibility, and kindling of emotions.

REASONING

Because human beings pride themselves on being "rational"—that is, they seldom do anything without some real or imagined reason—you increase the likelihood of persuading them if you can give them good reasons. Sometimes the reasons for behavior are not clearly stated; sometimes they are neither real nor very good; and sometimes the reasons are offered *after* people do something rather than before. Nevertheless, whether the reasons are good, bad, before, or after the fact, people seek reasons for their actions and beliefs.

Reasons are statements that answer the question "Why?" As you think about something you did during the past couple of days, you probably can identify reasons that affected or justified what you did. Suppose you took some time to watch a television program last night. If you asked yourself "Why?" you could probably think of several reasons. Perhaps you watched because (1) you needed a little relaxation, (2) the program is a favorite of yours, or (3) you were bored and had nothing else to do. Each of these is a reason.

When we want to influence other people's beliefs or actions, we are likely to give them reasons. To determine what we will say to them, we may think of a number of possible reasons and then choose the ones that we think they will accept. Suppose that you want to influence a fellow student to run for Student Senate. With a few moments of thought, you might decide to tell her that the work of the senate is in the best interests of all students, that she might obtain valuable experience, and that as a result of the kind of work done, she might develop good contacts with members of the faculty and administration.

There are times when you need to explore other sources to ensure that you offer the best reasons. Suppose that you believe students should publish a department newsletter each term, prior to preregistration, that lists and discusses course offerings but you need the support of the department chairperson for this project. In such a situation, you would want to supplement reasons gained from your own thinking with reasons you obtain from reading, polling, or interviewing. For instance, after talking with other students from other departments and other colleges, you might come up with the following list of reasons:

1. Students would like to have brief sketches of courses offered the next quarter.

2. Students are capable of publishing such a newsletter.

3. Students who prepare such newsletters in other departments and colleges experience high levels of satisfaction.

4. Students get valuable practical writing experience.

5. Student newsletters don't cost a lot of money to publish.

Once you have a list of reasons, you can use the following criteria to determine which are good reasons, ones you will use.

1. *Select reasons that give the best support for your proposal.* In any list you'll find that some reasons are better than others. For the reasons offered in support of starting a newsletter, "Students get valuable practical writing experience" is true, but it's not a particularly strong reason. It suggests an additional benefit, but it doesn't really give direct support for starting a department newsletter.

2. *Select reasons you can support with specific information.* Some reasons sound good, but if they cannot be supported with facts, they shouldn't be

used. You cannot be sure that you can support a reason until you have done the appropriate research. For instance, "Students who prepare such newsletters in other departments and colleges experience high levels of satisfaction" is a good reason to establish a newsletter—if you have facts to support it. If, in your discussion with students from other departments or colleges, you cannot find any real support for the reason, you shouldn't use it.

3. *Select reasons that will have an impact on the person you are trying to persuade.* A reason will have impact on a person if that person is likely to accept it. Although you cannot always be sure about the potential impact of a reason, you can make a reasonably good estimate of possible impact if you know the person you are trying to persuade.[7] So if you are planning to say that "students would like to have brief sketches of courses offered the next quarter," this would be especially good if the department chairperson cared about student frustration concerning accurate information about courses.

Now let's return to the compliance-gaining strategies based on O'Hair and Cody's list. Two of their categories, "supporting evidence" and "exchange," owe their foundation to reasoning. Let's look at specific applications of these two:

1. *Giving supporting evidence.* You'll recall that strategies in this category are those in which a person presents reasons and evidence for compliance. When using this strategy, you will make statements such as "Let me give you what I think are the three best reasons for holding on to the job you have" or "Here are the bills and canceled checks that show that I have kept up to date on the account."

2. *Making exchanges.* You'll recall that strategies in this category are those in which a person seeks compliance by offering trade-offs. Although an exchange strategy is not directly giving reasons, it does imply the presentation of a reason. To use this strategy a person might say, "I'll help you with calculus if you help me with history," or "I'll agree to the price if you'll throw in free delivery." In short, it uses the negotiated element as a type of a reason: "Why will I help you with calculus? Because you'll help me with history."

CREDIBILITY

You increase the likelihood of persuading people when they perceive you as *credible*; that is, they like, trust, and/or have confidence in you. Research studies confirm a significant association of credibility with message acceptance.[8]

Why are people willing to determine their behavior based on the word of someone else? Many times people look for shortcuts in their decision making—they rely on the judgment of others. Their thinking often goes something like this: "Because I don't want to spend the time to learn about the tax proposal, when someone I trust tells me it's a good idea, I'll vote for it." Or "Because I don't have the money to try every restaurant in town, when someone I trust tells me that The Haven is the best, I go there."

Characteristics of Credibility How do we determine who we will rely on? Is it blind faith? No, when a person appears to have characteristics we value, the person is perceived as a high-credibility source. Although the specific number of distinguishing characteristics of credibility differs somewhat in various analyses, most lists include knowledge/expertise, trustworthiness, and personality.

1. *Knowledge/expertise.* We perceive as competent a person who has knowledge and expertise. Knowledge and expertise include having good information, being sure of the facts and figures, having a history of giving good advice, and being clear thinkers. If Alan sees his friend Shanda as a competent mathematician who understands mathematical principles and is able to apply them, Alan may be willing to rely on her to do his income taxes, to help him with calculus, or to manage the budget.

2. *Trustworthiness.* Persuasive messages are likely to be stronger when we perceive the source as trustworthy. Trustworthiness includes a person's mental and ethical traits. People are more likely to trust and believe in a person whom they perceive as honest, industrious, dependable, strong, and steadfast. As a result, people often overlook what are otherwise regarded as shortcomings if a person shows character. Just as a presence of traits that people identify with trustworthiness will increase our persuasiveness, a lack of those qualities will decrease our persuasiveness. If, for instance, we are perceived as dishonest, people will put much less stock in what we say.

In addition to these character traits, we also consider people trustworthy when we perceive them as having good intentions. People's intentions or motives are particularly important in determining whether another person will like them, trust them, have respect for them, or believe them. For instance, you know that clothing salespeople are attempting to sell you the garments they help you try on, so when they say to you, "This is perfect for you," you may well question their intentions. However, if a bystander looks over at you and exclaims, "Wow, you really look good in that!" you are likely to accept the statement at face value. The bystander has no reason to say anything, so you have no reason to doubt his or her intentions. The more positively you view the intentions of people, the more credible their words will seem to you.

3. *Personality.* A third major criterion of credibility is perceived personality—the total of your behavioral and emotional tendencies. Sometimes people have a strong emotional reaction to a speaker based solely on a first impression created by the person's physical attractiveness. Certain people may strike us as friendly, warm, enthusiastic, and positive. Because they have ready smiles and really seem to care, we cannot help liking them.

Building Your Credibility Over time, you can build your credibility. To achieve credibility, you must first demonstrate expertise. Competent people show that they know what they are doing and why they are doing it. By contrast, some people are perceived as incompetent because they are careless, because they try to do too many tasks at one time, or because they do not double-check details.

Second, you can show that you care about the effects on others of what you say and do. Some people develop reputations as manipulators because, although their intentions are good, they fail to state why they behave as they do. Remember, people are not mind readers. When you don't explain your behavior, others may assume they know your intentions or may misread your behavior. Although you can't change your character or personality on the spur of the moment, you can make your actions reflect your character and personality. For instance, if you perceive yourself as hardworking, you can give yourself totally to the jobs at hand. Likewise, if you are friendly or likable, you can smile when you meet strangers or offer to help people with their jobs. If people do not see you as a credible person, you may be able to change your image by improving your competence and sharing your intentions.

Third, and perhaps most important, you can build your credibility by behaving in ways that are ethical—that is, in keeping with the standards of moral conduct that determine behavior. When you believe strongly in the rightness of your cause, you may well be tempted to say or do anything, ethical or not, to achieve your goals. Before you succumb to such temptation, think of all the people in the world who have ridden roughshod over any moral or ethical principles operating within society to achieve their goals. If your credibility is important to you, you will not want to adopt the philosophy that the end justifies the means. Even if you achieve your short-term goal, it will be at the cost of satisfying relationships with others.

How you handle ethical questions says a great deal about you as a person. What is your code of ethics? The following behaviors are widely accepted for providing a base for ethical persuasion.

1. *Tell the truth.* Of all the attitudes about trustworthiness, this may be the most important. If people believe you are lying to them, they will reject you and your ideas. If they think you are telling the truth but later learn that you lied, they will look for ways to get back at you. If you are not sure whether information is true, don't use it until you have verified it. Ignorance is seldom accepted as an excuse. Credible communicators do not twist facts. When facts are well documented, they make the most of them; when the facts are weak, they acknowledge potential weakness. Many times an honest "I really don't know, but I'll find out," is far more positive than trying to deflect a comment or use somewhat irrelevant information to try to make points.

2. *Keep your information in perspective.* Many people get so excited about their information that they exaggerate its importance. Although some people seem willing to accept a little exaggeration as a normal product of human nature, when the exaggeration is defined as "distortion" most people consider the exaggeration the same as lying. Because the line between some exaggeration and gross exaggeration or distortion is often difficult to distinguish, most people see any exaggeration as unethical.

3. *Resist personal attacks against those who oppose your ideas.* There seems to be an almost universal agreement that name calling is detrimental to your trustworthiness. Even though many people name-call in their interpersonal communication, it is still unethical.

4. *Disclose the complete picture.* If you don't disclose all the information, you are likely to be accused of misrepresenting—giving an impression that is not supported by the facts. People can make something sound good or bad, better or worse, by the phrasing they select, and if they purposely put a favorable spin on unfavorable information, it is unethical. For instance, Hector's mother asks, "Why were you out until 3:00 A.M. this morning?" Hector replies indignantly, "I wasn't out anywhere near 3:00 A.M." (He got home at 2:20!) Marjorie says to Allison, "I want you to know that I was not the one who told your mother that you were smoking. I'd never do that." What Marjorie fails to say is that she did tell Brenda and suggested to Brenda that perhaps she could tell Allison's mother! Such people often say to themselves, "I did not tell a lie," and then feel rather good about their characters. Yet the behavior is still unethical.

In interpersonal interactions involving only two persons, some people do not judge speaker responsibility in quite the same way as they do in, say, public speeches. We believe, however, that any message source has the same responsibility, regardless of the setting in which statements are made, to ethical conduct. Thus any attempt to influence others should follow some ethical guidelines. Justifying unethical behavior on the ground of informal setting is itself unethical and reprehensible.

Now let's return to the compliance-gaining strategies based on O'Hair and Cody's list. Two of their categories, "direct requests" and "referent influence/empathic understanding," owe their foundation to credibility.

1. *Making direct requests.* You'll recall that strategies in this category are those in which a person seeks compliance by asking another to behave in a particular way. For instance, when people ask, "Can I borrow your pencil?" or "Will you lend me five dollars?" they are making direct requests. Their effectiveness depends on perceived credibility—they are saying, "You know me, you know I'm trustworthy and cooperative, and I will return what I have asked for."

2. *Making referent influence or empathic understanding statements.* You'll recall that strategies in this category are those in which a person seeks compliance by appealing to another's love or affection. Sometimes people word the persuasive statements in ways that seek to show the importance of how others feel about them. For example, when someone says, "If you really loved me and respected my feelings, you wouldn't try to drive when you have been drinking," or "You know we can't get along without you, and if you don't go in for treatment we fear we may lose you." These statements suggest that the person should behave a certain way because of ties based on expertise, trustworthiness, or personality.

Other examples are based on showing similarity of values. A person says, "Since we're in this together, why don't we join forces," or "You and I have always looked at things the same way, so it's only logical that we do this together," or "If you want to get your supervisor to pay attention to you as a person, you will have to dress more the way I do." These statements are saying, "Because we have so much in common or think of each other so highly, we should behave in similar ways."

KINDLING EMOTIONS

You increase the likelihood of persuading people when you use language that affects their emotions.[9] Although you may induce people to act on the basis of good reasons alone, people frequently believe they should do something but don't act on that belief. For instance, Jonas may believe that he should give money to his church, but he may not do so. What motivates you to move from simply believing in something to acting on the belief often is the degree of your emotional involvement. Emotions are the driving force behind action, the instrument that prods or nudges you from passive to active.

The effectiveness of emotional elements seems to depend a great deal on factors such as the mood and attitude of the person you are persuading and the language itself. Our experience has been that emotion is best used to supplement or to highlight good reasons. Because effective persuasion is likely to be logical-emotional, reasoning and emotion ought to be inseparable elements of a persuasive message.

Suppose that you are talking to your friend about the need for more sympathetic treatment of the elderly in our society. Saying "Our present means of dealing with the elderly are ineffective" provides little motivation for your listener to respond, let alone act, however true the statement may be. By making the statement more specific, however, you add some emotional power: "Our present means alienate the elderly from the society they worked so many years to support." "Alienate" and "worked so many years to support" are phrasings that may arouse guilt, sadness, or some other sympathetic feeling.

In informal interpersonal communication, what can you do to create a mental state for yourself in which you can phrase statements that will have greater emotional impact—that will motivate?

1. *Identify your own feelings about the situation.* Are your feelings inspired by sadness? happiness? guilt? anger? caring? grief? If you don't really have any strong feelings, you probably will not be able to say anything that will trigger feelings on the part of the person you are talking with.

2. *Select information that will stimulate those emotions.* If you want your listeners to feel sad about elderly people's lack of positive goals, seek out information that will show that lack. Perhaps you have had specific talks with older relatives and their friends and you've seen that their only talk of the future is the inevitability of death. Or perhaps you have visited nursing homes and seen that they give their residents little to look forward to. These are examples of information that is likely to arouse sadness in a listener.

3. *Describe your feelings to the other person.* The more you practice the skill of describing feelings, the better you will become at it in spontaneous settings. Your major means of motivating is through language that is adapted to the needs of the person you are talking with.

Now let's return to the compliance-gaining strategies based on O'Hair and Cody's list. Two of their categories, "face maintenance" and "other-benefit," owe their foundation to kindling emotions.

1. *Making face-maintenance statements.* You'll recall that strategies in this category are those in which a person seeks compliance by using indirect statements that kindle positive emotions. For instance, in an effort to put a friend in a good mood, a person says, "Is there something I can get for you now?" Or to make a friend more receptive to comments, someone might say, "You know I find you really attractive—and I think we share many of the same feelings."

2. *Making other-benefit statements.* You'll recall that strategies in this category are those in which a person seeks compliance by presenting reasons that benefit the other person. For instance, a person may say, "I think this car is just right for the kind of driving you do" or "Georgia, I believe that going away to college would be in your best interest." In these cases the kindling of emotion is tied to the meeting of interpersonal needs.

We have considered reasoning, credibility, and kindling of emotions as means of persuading. Moreover, we have shown how many of the most common compliance-gaining strategies gain their power from these means. When you wish to influence another person directly, which of these means should you focus on or which strategy should you select? As Cody and Mc-Laughlin point out, situational perceptions are highly important in making these decisions.[10] In short, then, your choice depends a great deal on how effective you believe a given method will be in a particular situation. The better you are at making assessments of a situation, the more likely you are to succeed. The more you believe people are likely to react to reasoning, the more you should rely on reasoning; the more you believe people are likely to respect your credibility, the more you can rely on personal strategies; and the more you believe people are likely to see the importance of meeting their needs, the more you can rely on kindling their emotions. But, please understand, these are not mutually exclusive. A good reason can come from a credible source and appeal to a person's emotion.

Persuading

BY YOURSELF

1. Try to frame a series of reasons for supporting each of the following: (a) sending your child to a parochial school, (b) not smoking in the classroom, (c) registering to vote, (d) not doing drugs.

2. Develop emotional appeals for each of the issues above.

3. List ways that you could show your credibility for each issue.

IN GROUPS

1. Your instructor will give you goal cards. One member of each group will pick a goal and then try to influence another member of the group to support that goal. The other group members should observe the power bases the persuader works from and the means of persuasion that were used.

2. Try to define some of the main tenets of your ethical code. You might start by making a series of statements that begin, "It is wrong to _____; if someone does this, I am likely to react by _____." When you are finished, divide into groups of six and share as much as you feel comfortable in sharing. Notice the similarities in and differences between your code and others' codes.

JOURNAL ENTRY

Consider the last time someone was effective in influencing you to believe something or to do something. Write down, as nearly as you can remember, the nature of the language that they used to appeal to you. Now analyze that language. Were they giving you reasons? Appealing to your perception of their credibility? Kindling your emotions?

Now consider the last time someone failed in influencing you to believe something or to do something. Again, write down, as nearly as you can remember, the nature of the language that they used to appeal to you. Now analyze that language. Were they giving you reasons? Appealing to your perception of their credibility? Kindling your emotions? Why did they fail?

Now contrast the two efforts. What conclusions about persuasion can you draw from the two experiences?

Assertiveness

Related to persuasion or compliance gaining is the skill of assertiveness. Many people who understand the means of persuasion nevertheless are ineffective at exerting influence in their relationships because they are not assertive. *Assertiveness* means standing up for ourselves in interpersonally effective ways that exercise our personal rights while respecting the rights of others. It entails describing our feelings honestly, verbalizing our position on an issue for purposes of achieving a specific goal. Assertiveness may focus on describing feelings, giving good reasons for a belief, or suggesting a behavior or attitude we think is fair, without exaggerating for dramatic effect or attacking

the other individual. We can understand the specific qualities of assertive behavior best if we contrast it with other ways of responding to adversity.

Suppose that you have been unable to pin your professor down in arranging a specific time to discuss the mistakes you made on your first paper, yet you need to talk with him before you turn in the second paper, which is due at the end of the week. In this case your goal is to get an appointment before the end of the week. One way of being assertive would be to say to your professor, "I'm really feeling anxious about not getting to talk with you about my paper—I'm afraid that if we don't talk I'm likely to make the same kinds of mistakes again. Could we please meet to talk about my writing before Thursday?" This wording builds from a description of feelings. Another way of being assertive would be to stop your professor after class and say, "I really need to talk to you before I turn in my next paper—I don't want to make the same mistakes I made last time. Can we please get together before Thursday?" This wording focuses on the reason for requesting the meeting. Note, too, that both this approach and the previous one represent reasonable behavior that neither exaggerates for dramatic effect nor represents an attack on the other individual.

● **Assertiveness means standing up for ourselves in interpersonally effective ways that exercise our personal rights while respecting the rights of others.**

CONTRASTING METHODS OF COPING WITH ADVERSITY

When we believe we have been wronged, we are likely to behave in one of three ways: passively, aggressively, or assertively.

● ● **Passive Behavior** People behave passively when they are reluctant to state their opinions, share feelings, or assume responsibility for their actions. Thus, instead of attempting to influence others' behavior, they often submit to other people's demands, even when doing so is inconvenient or against their best interests. For example, when Udi uncrates the new color television set he purchased at a local department store, he notices a large, deep scratch on the left side of the cabinet. If Udi is angry about the scratch but nevertheless keeps the set without trying to influence the store clerk to replace it, he is behaving passively.

● ● **Aggressive Behavior** People who behave aggressively lash out at the source of their discontent with little regard for the situation or for the feelings of those they are attacking. Unfortunately, too many people confuse aggressiveness with assertiveness. Unlike assertive behavior, aggressive behavior is judgmental, dogmatic, fault-finding, and coercive.

Suppose, for example, that after discovering the scratch on the cabinet of his new television set, Udi storms back to the store, loudly demands his money back, and accuses the clerk of intentionally or carelessly selling him damaged merchandise. During his tirade, he might threaten the store with a lawsuit. Such aggressive behavior might or might not get Udi a new television set; it would certainly damage his interpersonal relationships with the store personnel.

● ● **Assertive Behavior** As we have noted, behaving assertively means standing up for ourselves in an interpersonally effective way. The difference between assertive behavior and passive or aggressive behavior is not the original feeling behind the response but the way in which we choose to react as a result of the feeling. If Udi behaves assertively, he will still be angry about bringing home a damaged set. But instead of either doing nothing or verbally assaulting the clerk, Udi calls the store and asks to speak to the clerk from whom he purchased the set. When the clerk answers, Udi describes his feelings on discovering a large scratch on the cabinet when he uncrated the set. He then goes on to say that he is calling to find out how to return the damaged set and get a new one. Aggressive behavior might also achieve Udi's purpose of getting a new television set, but assertive behavior achieves the same result at lower emotional costs to everyone involved.

EXAMPLES OF PASSIVE, AGGRESSIVE, AND ASSERTIVE RESPONSES

That our interpersonal exchanges will often involve the need to assert ourselves is inevitable. For this reason, and because so much difficulty in relationships stems from ineffective responses to adversity, learning to distinguish among passive, aggressive, and assertive responses is a key interpersonal skill. To highlight the contrast among the response styles, let's examine situations in which the issue is the quality of interpersonal relations.

● ● **At Work** Tanisha works in an office that employs both men and women. Whenever the boss has an especially interesting and challenging job to be done, he assigns it to a male co-worker, Ben, whose desk is next to Tanisha's. The boss has never said anything to Tanisha or to Ben that would indicate he thinks less of Tanisha or her ability. Nevertheless, Tanisha is hurt by the boss's behavior.

> *Passive*: Tanisha says nothing to the boss. She is very hurt by what she feels is a slight but swallows her pride.
> *Aggressive*: Tanisha marches into her boss's office and says, "Why the hell do you always give Ben the plums and leave me the garbage? I'm every bit as good a worker, and I'd like a little recognition!"
> *Assertive*: Tanisha arranges a meeting with her boss. At the meeting, she says, "I don't know whether you are aware of it, but during the last three weeks, every time you had a really interesting job to be done, you gave the job to Ben. To the best of my knowledge, you believe that Ben and I are equally competent—you've never given me any evidence to suggest that you thought less of my work. But when you reward Ben with jobs that I perceive as plums and continue to offer me routine jobs, it hurts my feelings. Do you understand my feelings about this?" In this statement she has described both her perception of the boss's behavior and her feelings about that behavior.

If you were Tanisha's boss, which of her responses would most likely achieve her goal of receiving better assignments? Probably the assertive behavior. Which of her responses would most likely get her fired? Probably the aggressive behavior. And which of her responses would be least likely to "rock the boat"? Undoubtedly the passive behavior—but then she would continue to get the boring job assignments.

With a Friend Don is a doctor doing his residency at City Hospital. He lives with two other residents in an apartment they have rented. Owen, one of the other residents, is the social butterfly of the group. It seems whenever he has time off, he has a date. But like the others, he is a bit short of cash. He doesn't feel bashful about borrowing clothes, money, or jewelry from his roommates. One evening, Owen asks Don if he can borrow the new, expensive watch that Don received as a present from his father only a few days before. Don is aware that Owen does not always take the best care of what he borrows, and he is very concerned about the possibility of Owen's damaging or losing the watch.

> *Passive*: "Sure."
> *Aggressive*: "Forget it! You've got a lot of nerve asking to borrow a brand-new watch. You know I'd be damned lucky to get it back in one piece."
> *Assertive*: "Owen, I know I've lent you several items without much ado, but this watch is special. I've had it only a few days, and I just don't feel comfortable lending it. I hope you can understand how I feel."

What are likely to be the consequences of each of these behaviors? If he behaves passively, Don is likely to worry the entire evening and harbor some resentment toward Owen even if he gets the watch back undamaged. Moreover, Owen will continue to think his roommates feel comfortable in lending him anything he wants. If Don behaves aggressively, Owen is likely to be completely taken aback by his explosive behavior. No one has ever said anything to Owen before, so he has no reason to believe that he can't borrow whatever he'd like. Moreover, the relationship between Don and Owen might become strained. But if Don behaves assertively, he puts the focus on his own feelings and on this particular object—the watch. His response isn't a denial of Owen's right to borrow items, nor is it an attack on Owen. It is an explanation of why Don does not want to lend this item at this time.

In a Social Situation Mui has invited two of her girlfriends and their dates to drop by her dormitory room before the dance. Shortly after the group arrives, Nick, who has come with Ramona, Mui's best friend, reaches into his pocket for a flask of whiskey, takes a large sip, and passes it to Mui. Mui knows that alcohol is strictly off-limits in the dorm and, moreover, is concerned about anyone in the group drinking before driving.

> *Passive*: Muttering, "Uh, well," Mui pretends to take a sip and passes the flask on.
> *Aggressive*: "Nick, that's really stupid, bringing whiskey into my dorm room. Can't anybody here have a good time without drinking, or are you

all lushes? Now get out of here before somebody notices, and take the bottle with you."

Assertive: "Nick, Ramona probably didn't tell you that drinking isn't allowed in the dorm. Besides, I'd feel a lot more at ease if we all stayed sober in order to drive to the dance. So I'd appreciate it if you would take the whiskey out to the car. We can have a great time without getting into trouble or risking an accident."

Again, let's contrast the three behaviors. In this case the passive behavior is not at all in Mui's interests. Mui knows the dormitory rules, and even if no one finds out, she'll feel uncomfortable because she did nothing to protect her friends from needlessly risking their safety. But the aggressive behavior is hardly better. She knows nothing about Nick, but her outburst assumes bad intentions not only from Nick but also from her friends. If Nick is at all inclined to be belligerent, her method is only going to incite him and perhaps damage her relationship with Ramona. The assertive behavior firmly represents the issue—the dorm rules must not be violated, especially since it is her room, and her feelings about the group's safety are described firmly but pleasantly. She also follows up with her original reason for getting together—to have a good time.

Now let's consider some of the characteristics of behaving assertively that are illustrated or implied in the examples.

1. *Owning feelings*. In all cases, the assertive statement acknowledged that the thoughts and feelings were those of the person making the statement.

2. *Avoiding confrontational language*. In none of the cases did the speaker act aggressively by using threats, evaluations, or dogmatic language.

3. *Using specific statements directed to the behaviors at hand*. In each case, potential issues could have been raised. For instance, Don could have brought up Owen's untrustworthiness, but in the particular situation he chose to focus on the issue that was most relevant—his feelings about a special possession.

4. *Maintaining eye contact and firm body position*. People will not be perceived as firm if they shift gaze, look at the floor, sway back and forth, hunch over, and use other signs that may be perceived as indecision or lack of conviction.

5. *Maintaining a firm but pleasant tone of voice*. Whereas aggressiveness is signaled with yelling or harsh tones, assertiveness is shown through steady, firm speech at a normal pitch, volume, and rate.

6. *Avoiding hemming and hawing.* Recall the passive example where Mui says, "Uh, well." Vocalized pauses and other nonfluencies are other signs of indecisiveness.

7. *Speaking clearly.* Sometimes when people have something uncomfortable to say, they mutter so that what they say is almost unintelligible. Again, lack of clarity will be seen as indecision.

It is important to recognize that assertiveness will not always achieve your goals. The skills discussed in this book are designed to increase the probability of achieving interpersonal effectiveness. Just as with self-disclosure and describing feelings, however, there are risks involved in being assertive. For instance, some people will label any assertive behavior as "aggressive." But people who have difficulty asserting themselves often do not appreciate the fact that the potential benefits far outweigh the risks. Remember, our behavior teaches people how to treat us. When we are passive and thus teach people that they can ignore our feelings, they will. When we are aggressive, we teach people to respond in kind. By contrast, when we are assertive, we can influence others to treat us as we would prefer to be treated.

Cultural Considerations

Although assertiveness can be thought of as a basic human need, assertive behavior is primarily practiced in Western cultures. In Asian and Hispanic cultures assertiveness is less valued. In Asian cultures, how one is seen is often felt to be more important than asserting one's beliefs or rights, and a premium is often placed on maintaining a formally correct standard of social interaction. For people from these cultures, maintaining "face" and politeness may be more important than achieving personal satisfaction. In Latin and Hispanic societies, however, men especially are frequently taught to exercise a form of self-expression that goes far beyond the guidelines presented here for assertive behavior. In these societies the concept of "machismo" guides male behavior. Thus the standard of assertiveness appropriate to a white European American can seem inappropriate to people whose cultural frame of reference leads them to perceive it as aggressive or weak.

For this reason, with assertiveness—just as with any other skill—we need to be aware that no single standard of behavior ensures we will achieve our goals. Although what is labeled appropriate behavior varies across cultures, the results of passive and aggressive behavior seem universal. Passive behavior

Basic Communication Skills

SKILL	USE	PROCEDURE	EXAMPLE
Assertiveness Standing up for yourself and doing so in interpersonally effective ways that describe your feelings honestly and exercise your personal rights while respecting the rights of others.	To show clearly what you think or feel.	1. Identify what you are thinking or feeling. 2. Analyze the cause of these feelings. 3. Choose the appropriate skills necessary to communicate these feelings, as well as any outcome you desire. 4. Communicate these feelings to the appropriate person. Remember to own your feelings.	When Gavin believes that he is being unjustly charged, he says, "I have never been charged for a refill on iced tea before—has there been a change in policy?"

can cause resentment and aggressive behavior can lead to fear and misunderstanding. When talking with people whose culture, background, or life-style differs from your own, you may need to observe their behavior and their responses to your statements before you can be sure of the kinds of behavior that are likely to communicate your intentions effectively.

PRACTICE IN

Being Assertive

BY YOURSELF

1. Identify five situations in the past in which you were nonassertive or aggressive. Try to write the dialogue for each situation. Then substitute an assertive response for the nonassertive or aggressive reactions you expressed in each case.

2. For each of the following situations write a passive or aggressive response and then contrast it with a more appropriate assertive response.

   You come back to your dorm, apartment, or house to type a paper that is due tomorrow, only to find that someone else is using your typewriter.
   Passive or aggressive response:
   Assertive response:

   You're working at a store part-time. Just as your hours are up and you are ready to leave (you want to rush home because you have a nice dinner planned with someone special), your boss says to you, "I'd like you

to work overtime if you would—Martin was supposed to replace you, but he just called and can't get here for at least an hour."
Passive or aggressive response:
Assertive response:

During a phone conversation with your parents, who live in another state, your mother says, "We're expecting you to go with us when we visit your uncle on Saturday." You were planning to spend Saturday working on your résumé for an interview next week.
Passive or aggressive response:
Assertive response:

You and your friend made a date to go dancing, an activity you really enjoy. When you meet, your friend says, "If it's all the same to you, I thought we'd go to a movie instead."
Passive or aggressive response:
Assertive response:

JOURNAL ENTRY

For the next day or two, observe people and their behavior. Make notes of situations in which you believe people behaved in passive, aggressive, and assertive ways. Which of the ways seemed to help the people achieve what they wanted? Which of the ways seemed to maintain or even improve their interpersonal relationship with the other person or other people?

Assertiveness and Social Power

Why are some people less likely to assert themselves? For many the answer is that they do not believe they have the social power necessary to affect the outcome positively. *Social power* is a potential for changing attitudes, beliefs, and behaviors of others. The presence of power does not ensure change, but the absence of power makes it nearly impossible for people to be willing to assert themselves. This sense of power refers to our personal capacity to be effective in the world, and it is perfectly consistent with treating other people with respect—as centers of power in their own right.

Even though everyone has some power at some times and under some circumstances, most people, as a result of many interpersonal and environmental factors, occasionally regard themselves as powerless. They may feel that, for one reason or another, they have no control over their own destinies, no power to influence any aspect of their own lives. It is frustrating to know that change must occur but that one lacks the power to bring it about. For instance, suppose that you believe you have some excellent ideas for how the accounting office where you work could be run. But, despite your efforts, no one in the organization listens to you. You have trouble getting your ideas heard, and the few times that they are heard they are dismissed out of hand. At the same time you see that a co-worker's ideas not only are heard but also are implemented. When this happens, you may feel powerless, and as a result you stop offering ideas for improvement.

TYPES OF POWER

In the 1950s John French and Bertram Raven pioneered our understanding of power by identifying five sources of power: coercive, reward, legitimate, expert, and referent.[11] In 1989, T. R. Hinken and C. A. Schriesheim published a study that sharpened our understanding of these sources.[12] As we discuss power, we will focus on how the power balance in a relationship can increase or decrease the likelihood of the participants acting assertively.

Coercive Power Coercive power is derived from the perception that someone can harm you either physically, psychologically, or both. Perceptions of physical coercion are influenced by relative size, strength, and armament. The elements that lead to perceptions of psychological coercion are threats, fear that affection will be withdrawn, and tone of voice.

Whether a person behaves in any of these ways is not important. What is important is our belief that someone is *likely* to act in these ways, and our desire to avoid the consequences of their actions if they do in fact materialize. Thus if we *expect* that someone may harm us, we can say that the person has power over us.

Many people are unassertive because they feel intimidated by someone. You may be familiar with the old vaudeville routine: "Where does a gorilla sit when he comes into a room?" "Anywhere he wants to!" But many people feel so intimidated by aggressive people that they grant coercive power to others even when the others are not trying to be coercive.

Some people do not assert themselves because they are afraid of the consequences. They fear that if they assert themselves, the person they are dealing with will punish them or withhold some reward. Is this fear real? Certainly, there will be times when you are penalized for being assertive—some people with power are very defensive and will react this way if they think you are threatening their security.

Reward Power The giving of money, other tangible goods, or affection constitutes reward power. Reward power works when the person being rewarded sees the reward as large enough or important enough to compensate for the pain of the action called for. For instance, you may know you will be rewarded with a good grade if you write a good paper. If a good grade is important to you or if you regard a B or an A as sufficient reward for the time and effort you have to put in, the reward might motivate you. For reward power to work, a person must believe that one who promises rewards has the power to give them. If your boss promises you consideration for promotion if you do a particular job well, you may not do it well because you doubt your boss really has the power to grant you a promotion at this time.

Some people are unassertive because they fear that what they say may get in the way of their receiving a reward. For instance, if Jud's boss is giving him more to do than Jud thinks is fair, Jud may be reluctant to assert his position because his boss may decide not to reward him in the future. Many people let others take advantage of them because they think that giving in will help them get a reward they seek.

Legitimate Power Influence that comes from being elected, being selected, or holding a position is legitimate power. The rationale for bestowing legitimate power is the belief that people in certain positions have the responsibility of attempting to exert influence. Thus people give power to presidents, senators, and members of Congress because they were elected; to teachers, cabinet members, and committee chairpersons because they were appointed; and to oldest children, parents, or older members of a family because of tradition or cultural norms.

Legitimate power is highly valued in our society, yet some people are excessively intimidated by position. That a person is a senator, a teacher, or a parent does not mean that person is infallible. Some people bestow more power on such an individual than the person deserves or wants. We have all heard of people accepting unfair actions of officials or currying favor from those who have legitimate power. Both of these behaviors are thought to be negative because they ask people to reduce their own self-worth.

However, recognizing our legitimate power can be very important in building our potential to influence. One way to be empowered, then, is to identify the circumstances in which people grant you legitimate power. Think about other people's perception of your potential legitimate influence. Perhaps you are a chairperson of an organization, a coach of a team, or a parent or guardian. In these cases the members of the organization, the members of the team, or your children are likely not only to accept your attempts at influence but even to look to you to influence them because they recognize your position of authority.

Expert Power Expert power derives from having knowledge in a specific field. Expert power is influential when you admit that another person holds information that you need. Your instructors have the potential for expert power in your classes because they have knowledge and expertise you need; coaches have the potential for expert power because they have knowledge that players seek.

Some people are unassertive because they downplay their own expertise in whatever subject is being considered. A student is unlikely to challenge a professor on a matter in which the professor is far more knowledgeable than the student; but to grant the professor expert power on any subject just because the person is a professor would be foolhardy. We are far too often blinded by the perception of expert power. For instance, when buying clothing, people are often intimidated by a salesperson just because that person is selling a particular line of clothes. Salespeople are not usually hired because they are masters of information; they are hired because they are persuasive. As salespeople work with a certain line of goods, they may develop true

● **Expert power derives from having knowledge in a specific field.**

expert power. But no one should be intimidated by the fear of being shown up by another person's knowledge. Whether buying a coat, having the car repaired, or having the furnace fixed, a customer must have the right to ask questions about what is happening and why.

However, as discussed in the previous section on credibility, you have a potential for increasing your social power by gaining expertise in areas where other people need information. When you really have more information, and when people recognize that your information is indeed extensive and accurate, they will be inclined to listen to what you say. Building expertise may be the easiest and perhaps the best way of increasing your empowerment.

Referent Power The potential to influence others through image, charisma, or personality is known as referent power. Many of us will listen to someone for no reason other than that we like the person or have a certain respect for the person's judgment. Many times it is convenient for us to grant others this kind of power. We seldom have the time and energy to solve every issue that comes before us. If your best friend recommends a movie he saw or a restaurant she went to, you may well decide to attend that movie or eat at that restaurant because the person is a friend.

But on many important issues our reliance on the power of personality is misplaced. Too often we vote for someone only because "there's something about her" that we like; too often we do things that may not be in our best interest because someone said we should. We are often unassertive because we do not think highly enough of our own judgment to trust it—we rely too much on the word of others.

Some people do not assert themselves because they feel inferior. Perhaps because of problems in childhood or because of persistent failures as adults, they don't have confidence in their own thoughts and feelings. Let's consider two typical examples in which people don't assert themselves because they question their self-worth. First, suppose that both Simon and Bonnie have something they want to say and they begin talking at the same time. Simon stops talking and lets Bonnie talk. Is this a matter of politeness? Perhaps, but it is also possible that Simon defers to Bonnie because she is attractive, intelligent, and poised, qualities Simon feels he lacks. Second, suppose that Tran receives a C on a term paper. As he reads his paper over, he's sure that what he said was worth more than a C. He thinks about going to talk to his professor but says to himself, "He's not going to listen to me—I'm just a student." Is this a realistic appraisal? Maybe. It is also possible that Tran doubts his ability to argue for the worth of his paper even though he really believes it deserved a better grade than the professor gave it.

Whether it is because of coercive power, reward power, legitimate power, expert power, referent power, or some combination of these, we sometimes give up our right to be heard, and that is a mistake.

Just as with expertise, we have great potential for expanding our persuasive efforts by building our own referent power. Again, as we discussed in the section on credibility, you can show yourself to be trustworthy, and you can show yourself to be a pleasant, energetic personality. As you build these sources of credibility, you will see that others become more likely to pay attention to you and to your ideas.

There are two additional reasons why people fail to assert themselves:

1. *They believe it's not worth the time or effort.* Some people are not assertive because they believe it takes too much work to be assertive. Sometimes it does. If, however, you find yourself thinking or saying it's not worth the time or effort in most situations, then you are offering an excuse, not a reason, for your behavior.

Occasionally, you may find a champion, someone who will look out for your interests. Usually, however, you are the only one in a position to represent your interests.

2. *They accept others' expectations.* A number of American women exhibit passive behavior because they accept the stereotype that society has taught them: Women are expected to be accepting, warm, loving, and deferential to men. Any signs of assertiveness thus are considered unfeminine. Fortunately, the stereotype that guides such passive behavior is no longer as influential as it once was, and many women who have spent the better portion of their lives being passive now recognize the value of learning to be assertive. However, we should make the point that this behavior is not restricted to women. We may be socialized to be unassertive regardless of whether we are male or female.

Identifying Types of Power

BY YOURSELF

1. The following statements represent attempts to influence based on some type of power. Mark each statement as an example of C (coercive power), R (reward power), L (legitimate power), E (expert power), or Rf (referent power).

   _____ a. You will wear your hair the way I tell you to wear your hair because I'm your mother.

_____ b. After studying the effects of radiation for eight years, I have concluded that . . .

_____ c. As long as you do what I say, no one will get hurt.

_____ d. Sara, I'll be so proud of you if you make the dean's list.

_____ e. If you'll drop my books at the library, I'll clean the room.

_____ f. Trust me—I can do it.

Answers: a. L; b. E; c. C; d. R; e. R; f. Rf

2. Consider a relationship (with a parent, a brother or sister, a roommate, a boyfriend or girlfriend) in which you are dominant. What is the principal source of your power?

3. Consider a relationship in which you are in a position of dependency. What is the dominant person's primary source of power over you? What, if anything, are you doing to try to balance the power in the relationship?

JOURNAL ENTRY

As you observe people who failed to behave assertively, what kind of power were they granting to other people? What kind of power might they have really had but didn't seem to recognize?

Summary

Influence is the ability to affect people's attitudes and behaviors. Conscious efforts to influence others are made through persuasion.

The discourse we use to get people to behave in certain ways is known as compliance-gaining discourse. Compliance-gaining messages are classified according to the kinds of power employed by communicators in efforts to gain compliance. One's choice of strategy may depend on a communicator's perception of the situation in which compliance is being sought. Many of the strategies used may be grouped under the broad heading of persuasion.

Persuasion is the verbal effort to influence. Persuasion is the product of several elements that may be used alone or in concert. Persuasion can be a product of logical reasoning, of motivation through emotional language, and/or of speaker credibility. Effective interpersonal persuasion is always ethical persuasion—it does not depend on lying, distortion of fact, or acting in the interests of the persuader at the expense of the one being persuaded.

Assertiveness is the skill of stating our ideas and feelings openly in interpersonally effective ways. Some of the characteristics of behaving assertively are owning feelings, avoiding confrontational language, using specific statements directed to the behaviors at hand, maintaining eye contact and firm body position, maintaining a firm but pleasant tone of voice, avoiding hemming and hawing, and speaking clearly.

Assertiveness is possible when people believe that they have power over their fate. Social power is the potential ability to influence another person's attitude or behavior. The sources of people's social power may be coercive, reward, legitimate, expert, or referent. People lacking in assertiveness often feel intimidated by people to whom they grant various kinds of social power. Passive people are often unhappy as a result of not stating what they think and feel; aggressive people get their ideas and feelings heard but may create more problems for themselves because of their aggressiveness.

Communication Improvement Goal Statement

If you would like to improve your skill in being assertive, write a communication improvement goal statement following the guidelines on page 33 of Chapter 1.

Featured Reading

Your Perfect Right: A Guide to Assertive Living, 6th ed.
Robert E. Alberti and Michael L. Emmons
(San Luis Obispo, Calif.: Impact Publishers, 1990)

Alberti and Emmons's book has long been regarded as the assertiveness-training bible. Their discussion of assertiveness is in keeping with the information in this chapter, but the material goes far beyond what we have covered. They begin with the assumption that "assertive behavior promotes equality in human relationships, enabling us to act in our own best interests, to stand up for ourselves without undue anxiety, to express feelings honestly and comfortably, to exercise personal rights without denying the rights of others." After discussing important differences between assertive behavior and both nonassertive and aggressive behavior, they detail a complete program of assertiveness training.

They suggest that, first, you must understand the basic principles of assertion; second, you must decide whether you are ready to begin trying self-assertive behavior on your own; third, you should choose initial attempts that have a high potential for success. The authors discuss a process for observing your own behavior to monitor change. This includes keeping track of assertiveness, setting realistic goals, concentrating on a particular situation, reviewing responses, observing an effective model, considering alternative responses, imagining yourself handling the situation, practicing positive thoughts, getting help if you need it, trying it out, getting feedback, shaping behavior, testing your ability in a real situation, getting further training, and looking for social reinforcement.

Your Perfect Right is written for the general reader and is filled with realistic and provocative examples on how to cope with everyday situations. The authors offer no quick fix. They acknowledge that changing to a more assertive self is hard work. But by using the process they outline, change is possible.

● ◆ ■ **Notes**

1. Lawrence R. Wheeless, Robert Barraclough, and Robert Stewart, "Compliance-Gaining and Power in Persuasion," in Robert N. Bostrom, ed., *Communication Yearbook* 7 (Beverly Hills, Calif.: Sage, 1983), pp. 115–116.

2. Dan O'Hair and Michael J. Cody, "Machiavellian Beliefs and Social Influence," *Western Journal of Speech Communication* 51 (Summer 1987): 286–287.

3. Gerald R. Miller, Franklin J. Boster, Michael E. Roloff, and David R. Seibold, "MBRS Rekindled: Some Thoughts on Compliance Gaining in Interpersonal Settings," in Michael E. Roloff and Gerald R. Miller, eds., *Interpersonal Processes: New Directions in Communication Research* (Beverly Hills, Calif.: Sage, 1987), p. 89.

4. Sarah Trenholm, *Persuasion and Social Influence* (Englewood Cliffs, N.J.: Prentice Hall, 1989), p. 5.

5. Paul W. Keller and Charles T. Brown, "An Interpersonal Ethic for Communication," *Journal of Communication* 18 (1968): 79.

6. More than two thousand years ago Aristotle, in *The Rhetoric*, identified these means of persuasion.

7. For a more complete analysis of reasoning, you may want to look at Howard Kahane, *Logic and Contemporary Rhetoric*, 6th ed. (Belmont, Calif.: Wadsworth, 1992), pp. 3–17; Kahane provides an excellent analysis of forms of reasoning, with emphasis on detection of fallacies. Chapter 15 of Rudolph F. Verderber, *The Challenge of Effective Speaking*, 9th ed. (Belmont, Calif.: Wadsworth, 1994), provides a more detailed analysis of the reasoning process than is given in this book.

8. Jean-Charles Chebat, Pierre Filiatrault, and Jean Perrien, "Limits of Credibility: The Case of Political Persuasion," *Journal of Social Psychology* 130 (April 1990): 165.

9. Steven J. Breckler, "Emotion and Attitude Change," in Michael Lewis and Jeannette M. Haviland, eds., *Handbook of Emotions* (New York: Guilford Press, 1993), p. 461.

10. Michael J. Cody and Margaret L. McLaughlin, "Situation Perception and Message Strategy Selection," in Margaret L. McLaughlin, ed., *Communication Yearbook* 9 (Beverly Hills, Calif.: Sage, 1986), pp. 390–422. See also Michael J. Cody and Margaret L. McLaughlin, "The Situation as a Construct in Interpersonal Communication Re-

search," in Mark L. Knapp and Gerald R. Miller, eds., *Handbook of Interpersonal Communication* (Beverly Hills, Calif.: Sage, 1985), pp. 263–312.

11. John R. P. French, Jr., and Bertram Raven, "The Bases of Social Power," in Dorwin Cartwright and Alvin Zander, eds., *Group Dynamics*, 3rd ed. (New York: Harper & Row, 1968), pp. 259–270.

12. T. R. Hinken and C. A. Schriesheim, "Development and Application of New Scales to Measure the French and Raven (1959) Bases of Social Power," *Journal of Applied Psychology* 74 (1989): 561–567.

CHAPTER TEN

Managing Conflict

O B J E C T I V E S

After you have read this chapter, you should be able to define and/or explain:

Conflict

Inappropriateness of withdrawal, surrender, and aggression

Role of persuasion in managing conflict

Role of discussion in managing conflict

Guidelines for managing conflict

Kinds of conflict

Competitive versus cooperative approaches to conflict

Negotiation

Arbitration

"Come on, the movie starts at 7:30."

"Movie? I thought we were going dancing after dinner."

"Well, I saw that *Jurassic Park* was still playing, and since we haven't seen it yet . . ."

"But the other day we settled that we were going dancing. There you go, changing our plans without asking me. Just when I think we've got it settled that we'll make joint decisions on things like this, you go and pull another one of these power plays."

"I was just trying to surprise you."

"Well, you know I don't like that kind of a surprise."

"I just found out the Anderson party is tomorrow night, not next week as you told me."

"Hmm, I guess I made a mistake. It's OK, isn't it?"

"No, it's not OK."

"But we're free tomorrow night anyway, so what's the problem?"

"You're missing the point. I don't see you messing up a date for something you really want to do. But if we get asked to be involved in something I want to do, I can never trust you to keep things straight."

In each of these two episodes, we see examples of people's communication leading them into serious conflict.

Perhaps the ultimate test of your communication competence is how you react to conflict. In this chapter we look at the nature of conflict, patterns of managing conflict, and application of interpersonal communication skills in a constructive program of managing conflict.

The Nature of Conflict

In his research review, Dudley Cahn defines *interpersonal conflict* as "interaction between persons expressing opposing interests, views, or opinions."[1] Many people view conflict as bad because conflict is likely to make us extremely uncomfortable. However, it is not necessarily the conflict itself that is destructive to interpersonal relationships, but the unhealthy methods of managing conflict that we use. Conflict occurs because each of us has unique ideas, feelings, motives, and ways of behaving. This chapter, therefore, does not discuss avoiding or suppressing conflict but instead focuses on managing conflict within interpersonal relationships.

Patterns of Managing Conflict

Left to their own devices, people engage in many behaviors, both negative and positive, to cope with or manage their conflicts. The various methods of dealing with conflict can be grouped into five major patterns: withdrawal, surrender, aggression, persuasion, and problem-solving discussion. Let's consider each.

WITHDRAWAL

One of the most common, and certainly one of the easiest, ways to deal with conflict is to withdraw. When people withdraw, they physically or psychologically remove themselves from the situation. Withdrawal is a form of the passive behavior that we discussed in Chapter 9.

Physical withdrawal is, of course, easiest to identify. Suppose that Eduardo and Justina get into a conversation about Eduardo's smoking. Justina says, "Eduardo, I thought you told me that whether you stopped smoking completely or not, you weren't going to smoke around the house. Now here you are lighting up!" Eduardo may withdraw physically by saying "I don't want to talk about it" and going to the basement to finish a project he was working on.

Psychological withdrawal may be less noticeable but is every bit as common. Using the same example, as Justina talks about Eduardo's smoking in the house, Eduardo may sit quietly in his chair, looking at Justina but all the while thinking about the poker game he will play tomorrow evening.

Besides being quite common, both kinds of withdrawal are basically negative. Why? Because they neither eliminate nor attempt to manage the nature

● **Withdrawal usually leaves the conflict unresolved and is likely to produce resentments that will surface later on.**

of the conflict. As Michael Roloff and Denise Cloven say, "Relational partners who avoid conflicts have more difficulty resolving their disputes."[2] In the case of physical withdrawal, Justina may follow Eduardo to the basement, where the conflict will be resumed; if not, the conflict will undoubtedly surface later—and will probably intensify—when Justina and Eduardo try to resolve another, unrelated issue. In the case of psychological withdrawal, Justina may force Eduardo to address the smoking issue, or she may go along with Eduardo's ignoring it but harbor a resentment that may negatively affect their relationship.

Another reason withdrawal is negative is that it results in what Cloven and Roloff call "mulling behavior." By *mulling* they mean thinking about or stewing over an actual or perceived problem until they perceive the conflict as more severe and begin to engage in blaming behavior.[3] Thus in many cases not confronting the problem when it occurs only makes it more difficult to deal with in the long run.

Nevertheless, conflicts do occasionally go away if left alone.[4] There appear to be two sets of circumstances in which withdrawal may work. First, when the withdrawal represents temporary disengagement for the purpose of letting the heat of the conflict subside, it can be an effective technique for managing conflict. Consider this example: Bill and Margaret begin to argue over inviting Bill's mother for Thanksgiving dinner. During the conversation, Margaret begins to get angry about her mother-in-law's recent criticism of the way she and Bill are raising their daughter. Margaret says, "Hold it a minute; let me make a pot of coffee. We can both relax a bit, and then we'll talk about this some more." A few minutes later, having calmed down, she returns, ready to approach the conflict more objectively. Margaret's action is not true withdrawal; it's not meant as a means of avoiding confrontation. Rather, it provides a cooling-off period that will probably benefit them both.

The second set of circumstances in which withdrawal may work is when a conflict occurs between people who communicate infrequently. Consider Roger and Mario, who work in the same office. At two office gatherings they have gotten into arguments about whether the company really cares about its employees. At the next office gathering, Mario avoids sitting near Roger. Again, this form of withdrawal serves as a means of avoiding conflict rather than contributing to it. In this case Mario judges that it simply isn't that important to resolve the disagreement. It is fair to say that not every conflict needs to be resolved. Withdrawal is a negative pattern only when it is a person's major way of managing conflict.

SURRENDER

A second method of managing conflict is to surrender. As you might suspect, to *surrender* means to give in immediately to avoid conflict. Although altering a personal position in order to accommodate another can be positive when it's done in the spirit of cooperation, using surrender as a primary coping strategy is unhealthy.

Some people are so upset by the prospect of conflict that they will do anything to avoid it. For instance, Juan and Mariana are discussing their vacation plans. Juan would like just the two of them to go, but Mariana has talked with two of their friends who will be vacationing the same week about going together. After Juan mentions that he'd like the two of them to go alone, Mariana replies, "But I think it would be fun to go with another couple, don't you?" Juan replies, "OK, whatever you want." Even though Juan really wants the two of them to go alone, he gives in to avoid conflict rather than describe his feelings or give reasons for his position.

Habitual surrender is a negative way to deal with conflict for at least two reasons. First, decisions should be made on merits, not to avoid conflict. If one person gives in, there is no testing of the decision—no one knows what would really be best. Second, surrender can be infuriating to the other person. When Mariana tells Juan what she thinks, she probably wants Juan to see her way as the best. But if Juan simply surrenders, Mariana might still believe that Juan dislikes her plan but that Juan is playing the martyr. And his unwillingness to present his reasons could lead to even more conflict.

The contention that surrender is a negative way to deal with conflict should be qualified to the extent that it reflects the perspective of largely Western culture. In some cultures, surrendering is a perfectly legitimate way of dealing with conflict. In Japanese culture, for instance, it is thought to be more humble and face-saving to surrender than to risk losing respect through conflict.[5]

AGGRESSION

A third method of dealing with conflict is through aggression. *Aggression* entails the use of physical or psychological coercion to get one's way. Through aggression, people attempt to force others to accept their ideas or wishes, thereby emerging as "victors" in conflicts.

Aggression seldom improves a relationship, however. Rather, aggression is an emotional reaction to conflict—thought is short-circuited, and the person lashes out physically or verbally. People who use aggression are not concerned with the merits of an issue but only with who is bigger, who can talk louder, who can act nastier, or who can force the other to give in. With either physical or verbal aggression, conflict is escalated or obscured but not managed.

PERSUASION

A fourth method of managing conflict is by persuasion. *Persuasion* is the attempt to change either the attitude or the behavior of another person in order to seek accommodation. At times during the discussion of an issue, one party might try to persuade the other that a particular action is the right one. Suppose that at one point in their discussion about buying a car, Sheila says, "Don't we need a lot of room?" Kevin might reply, "Enough to get us into the car together, but I don't see why we need more than that." Sheila and Kevin are now approaching a conflict situation. At this point Sheila might say, "Kevin, we are constantly complaining about the lack of room in our present car. Remember last month when you were upset because we couldn't even get our two suitcases in the trunk and we had to put one of them in the backseat? And how many times have we been embarrassed when we couldn't drive our car with friends because the backseat is too small for even two normal-sized people?" Statements like these represent an attempt to resolve the conflict through persuasion.

When persuasion is open and reasonable, it can be a positive means of resolving conflict; however, persuasion can also degenerate into manipulation, such as when a person says, "You know, if you back me on this, I could see to it that you get a few more of the good accounts, and if you don't, well. . . ." Although persuasive efforts may fuel a conflict, if that persuasion has a solid logical base, it is at least possible that the persuasion will resolve the conflict.

DISCUSSION

A fifth method of dealing with conflict is through *problem-solving discussion*, the verbal weighing and considering of the pros and cons of the issues in conflict. Discussion is the most desirable means of dealing with conflict in a relationship because it provides for open consideration of issues and because it preserves equality. Resolving conflict through discussion is often difficult to accomplish, however, because it requires all parties involved to cooperate: the participants must be objective in their presentation of issues, honest in stating their feelings and beliefs, and open to the solution that proves to be most satisfactory and in the best interests of those involved.

Problem-solving discussion includes defining and analyzing the problem, suggesting possible solutions, selecting the solution that best fits the analysis, and working to implement the decision. We discuss these stages of problem solving in Chapter 12, "Interpersonal Communication in Groups." Not all five steps are always considered completely in everyday situations, nor are they necessarily considered in the order given. But when two people perceive a conflict emerging, they need to be willing to step back from the conflict and proceed systematically toward a solution.

Does this process sound too idealized? Or impracticable? Discussion is difficult, but when two people commit themselves to trying, chances are they will discover that through discussion, they can arrive at solutions that meet the needs of them both and do so in a way that maintains their relationship.

PRACTICE IN — Identifying Conflict

JOURNAL ENTRY

In your journal describe a conflict situation that arose between you and a friend. Did you and your friend cope with the conflict through withdrawal, surrender, aggression, persuasion, or discussion? What was the outcome of the conflict? If the outcome was negative, sketch a method of coping with the conflict that would have been more productive for you.

Guidelines for a Constructive Program of Managing Conflict

Now that we have seen that discussion offers the best means of managing conflict, let's consider guidelines you can follow in developing a constructive program of conflict management. Although some conflicts may not be resolvable, guidelines that increase the probability of satisfactory management include having a mutual desire to manage the conflict, recognizing types of conflict, cooperating rather than competing, reading nonverbal signs, using humor, communicating directly, trying to negotiate the conflict, seeking help from a facilitator or arbitrator when needed, and learning from failures of conflict management.

USE MUTUAL DESIRE FOR SUCCESSFUL MANAGEMENT

Conflicts are extremely difficult to manage unless there is a mutual desire to reach an accommodation. If one of the people involved really doesn't care about preserving the relationship, management will be difficult at best; if neither cares about the relationship, they are unlikely even to try to manage conflict successfully. Thus when people are more interested in putting down the other person, forgetting everything except getting what they want, and bringing up past transgressions just to be disruptive, there is little chance of a positive outcome.

But even if people aren't bent on short-circuiting conflict management, they still can drift into deep waters if they are not alert. Many of the difficulties of conflict management arise because people get caught in negative conflict management patterns before they even recognize what they are doing. If we are inclined to react before we think, the conflict may escalate too quickly and too much to manage it constructively.

Mutual desire for successful management means being alert to the signs of conflict. A person who perceives a conflict brewing needs to verbalize that recognition. A simple statement such as, "I think we're going to be in conflict over this" may be enough to alert participants to try to engage in positive patterns of management.

People who are committed to maintaining a relationship approach conflict with agreement on statements such as "We value our relationship, so it is important that we work out our differences" or "We recognize problems in our relationship, and we know we need to work them out." C. E. Rusbult argues that satisfaction with the relationship depends a great deal on whether partners use positive management skills or withdrawal, aggression, or neglect.[6]

Keep in mind that you need not fear conflict. In fact, fear of conflict is likely to bring about withdrawal or surrender. Conflicts are going to occur, but when they are approached constructively, the relationship is likely to grow rather than deteriorate.

RECOGNIZE THE TYPES OF CONFLICT

People who are committed to attempts to manage conflicts need to recognize what their conflicts are really about. By recognizing the type of conflict that seems to be brewing, people can sometimes resolve it satisfactorily before it escalates into a type that is likely to get out of hand. As C. H. Coombs says, conflict is not a static entity but a process that can move to a stage where the nature of the relationship can be seriously affected.[7] The goals of interpersonal communication skills in conflict management are to keep conflict from escalating to an irresolvable stage. Ordinarily, conflicts will fall into one of the following four broad categories that represent stages of escalation.

Pseudoconflict A *pseudoconflict* is a conflict that is not real but can become real—it is a conflict waiting to happen. A common type of pseudoconflict is what we can call gaming. Some people in relationships enjoy badgering each other—and if light badgering is a recognized part of a pair's normal interaction, it is not always bad. However, such badgering can be destructive when the real goal is to draw a person into a conflict not about the issue at hand but about some unresolved long-term issue. The goal of the "game" is to get the other person hooked so that a real conflict with deeper implications comes about. For instance, as Derek and Amberly are talking about the party they're going to that evening, Amberly says, "Why don't you wear your new sportscoat?" to which Derek replies, "There you go, telling me what to wear again." Derek's badgering reply may be an invitation to fight, not really about what he is going to wear but about a power struggle that the two tend to engage in. If Amberly accepts the invitation by saying something like "I have to—if I don't help you, you'll look as if you dressed in the dark!" the real conflict may ensue. If, however, Amberly replies, "No, Derek, I'm not telling you what to wear; I'm only making a suggestion. Which jacket would you like to wear?" either Derek will accept her explanation as a "Let's not go to war over this" or he'll say something else that says, "Let's fight." The answer to managing this kind of pseudoconflict is to recognize it for what it is—false conflict—and not letting yourself get drawn in.

A second common type of pseudoconflict occurs when two people argue over goals that they believe cannot be achieved simultaneously. For instance, Alberto says, "Hey the Bengals–49ers game is on television—I've got to see this," to which Consuela replies, "But you promised that you'd take me to see *The Fugitive*!" A real conflict ensues when the people put the choice between the actions in an either/or framework—in this case either Alberto and Consuela stay home or they go to the movie. This is a real conflict if it is truly impossible to do both within the prescribed time period. More often than not, however, the conflict is avoidable, because with some creative adaptation, it may be possible to do both. If Consuela is willing to delay going to the movie for a few hours, Alberto can watch the game; or if Alberto can tape the game to watch later, he and Consuela can go to the movie. In this case the answer to management is whether the conflict can be resolved by meeting the goals of both people.

Content Conflict A conflict concerning message accuracy is known as *content conflict*. So-called content conflicts tend to be over issues for which the correct answer can be discovered, such as "Julian said that he would come and pick us up." "No he didn't."

Many conflicts start on just such a factual level, and if we can keep the focus of the discussion of the conflict on this lower level, the chances of the conflict growing out of proportion are lessened. For example, Jay says to Nina, "Mike asked if I could go with him to the basketball game next Wednesday," to which Nina replies, "You can't do that; that's parents' night at school." "No," says Jay, "parents' night is the following Wednesday." At this point Nina and Jay have two choices: (1) They can stop for a minute and say, "Let's double-check the date." (2) They can begin to escalate the argument into a conflict about Jay's insensitivity, or Jay's not paying attention, or Nina's shooting from the hip, or why Jay always puts trivia before the family's welfare, and so forth.

If you find yourself in a conflict over a fact, try to disengage until a source for verifying the fact can be found or until some guidelines for selecting from among competing sources can be determined. Likewise, when the conflict centers on an interpretation of a fact, an inference drawn, or a definition, collect supporting material that is related closely to the issue. In short, confine the conflict to the issue at hand.

Some authorities refer to such conflicts as "simple" conflicts because they can be easily resolved by verifying the facts. In many relationships, however, there is no such thing as a simple conflict. Arguments that appear to be over insignificant issues such as who gets the front page of the newspaper first or whose responsibility it is to let the dog out often turn out to be much deeper than even the participants realize. Still, when the goal is successful management, both participants need to paraphrase, check perceptions, and describe feelings skillfully, for through these methods we can gain an understanding of what the apparent conflict is really about. Nevertheless, many conflicts will reveal competing value systems, which will confound conflict management.

● ● **Value Conflict** Conflicts build and become more difficult to resolve as competing value systems are brought to bear on the issues. *Values* are the attitudes or beliefs—economic, aesthetic, social, political, and religious—a person holds that serve as guidelines for measuring the worth of various aspects of life. For instance, if you value a trim, solid, healthy body, you may have strong beliefs about not smoking, getting exercise, and generally taking care of your body. If you value spiritual development, you may have strong beliefs about attending church. A *value conflict*, then, represents a difference in views of life in general (or of an aspect of life) that is brought into focus on a particular issue.

We generally order our values hierarchically and use them to guide our behavior at certain moments. This means that we have certain values that we view as more important than others. Thus we make "trade-offs" in our lives according to our individual hierarchy of values. For example, if you value spiritual development more than intellectual development, you are likely to attend worship services rather than spend that time studying. When we do not have to consider the wants and needs of another, we are likely to make value based choices automatically.

Value conflicts occur in a relationship when an issue arises that puts our hierarchy of values in opposition to the hierarchy of values of the other person. For instance, George and Lawanda are a married couple who make only a modest income and sometimes have trouble making ends meet. George's employer offers him the opportunity to work a twelve-hour shift on Christmas day, and earn double time. He knows that this would enable the family to have a little extra to spend on Christmas presents. Since he sees providing financial security as the most important responsibility that he has toward his family, he believes that he should accept the offer. When he approaches Lawanda with this opportunity, she is unenthusiastic. While she understands the importance of financial security, she values spending time with family on important religious holidays more highly. In her value hierarchy, spending time with family and religious observations are more important than economic security.

Conflicts over values can be impossible to resolve. Many times, we must simply be content to "agree to disagree." But if any resolution is possible, we must recognize that the issue is a value conflict. In the George and Lawanda scenario, it is important that they both realize that the other person is not "just being stubborn" or "spoiled" or "just wanting his or her own way." Instead they must draw on the trust and mutual respect that they have established to recognize that the issue before them is one on which they have competing values. Then, recognizing these differences, they may be able to discuss their emotional attachment to the issue. This might result in a compromise or may result in one person accomodating the wishes of the other in order to maintain the relationship. So once George and Lawanda acknowledge that each of them are interested in doing what is "right" for the family, they can move to a respectful discussion of what to do in this specific case. Lawanda may propose a way that the family can keep Christmas expenses down so that George won't need to work overtime. George may see if Lawanda would be open to his working only part of the day providing his boss agrees. Or either George or Lawanda may come to understand that the other is more emotionally attached to the issue and then "give in" or accommodate the other out of affection and respect.

As you can see, the less congruence there is between the value hierarchies of two people, the more likely they are to experience value conflicts. Since these conflicts are difficult to resolve, mutually satisfying, long-term intimate relationships are unlikely between individuals whose value hierarchies are dissimilar.

Ego Conflict Ego conflict occurs when the people in conflict view "winning" or "losing" the conflict as a measure of who they are, what they are, how competent they are, whom they have power over, and how much they know. Thus "winning" becomes more important than what is just or right. Ego conflict is the most difficult kind of conflict to manage.

Ego conflicts develop when discussion of content or values is undermined by personal or judgmental statements. The more competent you see yourself on a certain issue, the more likely you are to become ego-involved when your word on that issue is questioned. Once your ego becomes involved, your ability to remain rational often is lost. Before you realize it, emotions become involved in the conflict, words are said that cannot be taken back, and the conflict is blown out of proportion. For example, a simple disagreement over whether the youngest daughter should be allowed to stay out until midnight may escalate into a value conflict and eventually into an ego conflict when one or both parties views the real question to be who is rightly responsible for being the keeper of family morals.

The best way to resolve ego conflicts is to keep the conflict from reaching the ego level. If it does reach that level, the participants must try to move the conflict back to a content level. For instance, when Grant says, "I really resent your doubting the validity of my comment—we're talking about my family. I ought to know a lot more about how it functions than you," Darlene may reply, "Grant, I'm not doubting your understanding of the motives of members of your family. The point I'm making is whether you or I have a more accurate recollection of what your mother said."

Now let's consider specific ways to manage conflict positively.

COOPERATE RATHER THAN COMPETE

When a conflict arises, whether it will be managed successfully depends on the participants' level of competitive or cooperative behavior. If the participants are competitive, they are likely to introduce negative strategies in order to "win" the conflict. Furthermore, framing the conflict in terms of winning and losing means that their egos are more likely to be involved, and thus the conflict is immediately raised to an ego-conflict level. Conversely, if the participants are cooperative, they are willing to follow the steps of the problem-solving method to reach a solution that satisfies both parties—a "win-win" outcome.

In some conflicts, one person initially looks at the outcome competitively, whereas the other has a cooperative outlook. In this situation the nature of the conflict will depend on whether the person looking at the conflict competitively draws the other person into the competition or whether the person looking at the outcome cooperatively influences the other person to cooperate.

How do you go about bringing the other person into a cooperative state so that the conflict can be considered rationally? First, do not talk about the issue at hand until you demonstrate to the other person that you wish to resolve the conflict in a mutually satisfactory way. Second, avoid any statements that would escalate the potential conflict or result in defensive behavior. The following examples illustrate language of cooperation, language that is likely to prevent the conflict from escalating:

"I know you feel very strongly about what you believe is right. Before we consider whether your plan is the best one, perhaps we could consider what we want to accomplish."

"I know I sometimes get a little hotheaded when you disagree with me. I'm going to try to look at this problem as objectively as I can, but I may need your help."

"You have good reasons for your belief, and I believe I have, too. Perhaps if we share our reasons and then consider the consequences of each of them, we can make a decision that we'll both find satisfying."

Remember, both our language and our nonverbal cues indicate our feelings not only about the conflict but also about the people with whom we are in conflict. If we approach others openly and respectfully, we should at least get a hearing; however, if we demean people's ideas or the people themselves by our words or actions, we will probably create defensiveness, cause hard feelings, and escalate the conflict.

Developing a cooperative atmosphere takes practice. You can, however, learn to recognize when you start to become ego-involved, at which time you can mentally step back, take a deep breath, and reapply yourself to seeking a workable solution. When you see people becoming competitive, you can paraphrase their feelings as well as the content of their message, perhaps with a statement such as "From the way you're making your point, I get the feeling that this particular approach is very important to you personally." The skills of describing feelings, listening, paraphrasing, and maintaining a climate of positive communication are especially relevant to creating a cooperative atmosphere.

Let's look at the specifics of positive rather than negative behaviors. In conflict management, positive behaviors help people to integrate their resources toward a common task; negative behaviors foster a win-lose strategy between people—that is, if one person wins, it must be at the other person's expense. Conflicts that develop from these behaviors are difficult to resolve. The difference between positive and negative win-lose behaviors may be illustrated by comparing the behavior of people completing a jigsaw puzzle to that of people playing poker. In solving a jigsaw puzzle each person works with the other—the result is a win-win situation; in a poker game each individual works at the expense of the others—the result is a win-lose situation. Let's look at five contrasting sets of positive and negative behaviors:

Behaviors that will reduce conflict or result in positive or useful conflict	*Behaviors that will result in negative conflict*
1. Purposefully pursuing goals held in common	**1.** Purposefully pursuing your own goals
2. Maintaining openness	**2.** Maintaining secrecy
3. Accurately representing your own needs, plans, and goals	**3.** Disguising or misrepresenting your own needs, plans, and goals
4. Being predictable—using behavior consistent with past experience	**4.** Being unpredictable—using the elements of surprise
5. Avoiding threats or bluffing	**5.** Threatening and bluffing

Suppose that Jesse has a luncheon meeting with two of his colleagues to talk about a marketing strategy. Although these luncheon meetings usually last until 2 P.M., Jesse wants to make sure that this one ends by 1 P.M. so that he can keep another appointment. If he doesn't reveal his intention of trying to finish the meeting by 1 P.M., he is likely to engage in behaviors that will result in negative conflict. For instance, because he is being secretive instead of open, his colleagues might get upset at his efforts to "rush" business. In his deliberate pursuit of the goal of hurrying the meeting, he might interrupt people and short-circuit discussion that would lead to additional conflict. His need to get the meeting over with may be so overpowering that it alters his ordinary behavior—he may threaten or bluff to get his way. If, however, at the beginning of the meeting Jesse says, "I've got a meeting at 1 P.M. today— let's try to finish by then. If we can't, either you can continue without me or we can meet at another time," he is establishing a base for a cooperative approach. People will understand why he might be appearing to rush the process, and his efforts will be less likely to create conflict. Moreover, if his behavior does create conflict, members will have a better idea of how to respond to his behavior.

Cooperation is also furthered by keeping an open mind. As you'll recall from our discussion in Chapter 5, *open-mindedness* refers to flexibility in the way we process information. Rather than seeing concepts in absolute terms, an open-minded person is willing to tolerate other views and examine other information. Dogmatism is just the opposite: A *dogmatic* person clutches tenaciously to his or her value system and judges every event on the basis of how it fits into that value system. Highly dogmatic people have a narrow perspective on the way the world operates, are rigid in their thinking, and believe only those people who are in positions of strong authority. By contrast, open-minded people may be committed to certain beliefs or attitudes that develop from their value systems, but they are aware of the common ground that exists between what they believe in and what they reject.

For example, suppose a Baptist and a Catholic are talking about baptism, a topic of conversation with religious ramifications. If both people involved are open-minded, they can discuss rationally and intelligently the issues of immersion versus sprinkling and baptism by choice versus baptizing as a baby. In discussion they may come to understand why their denominations have different practices. Participants who are dogmatic, however, focus on their differences. They view the controversy in terms of black and white and never see the gray areas that lie between their two positions. As a result, management is nearly impossible and conflict escalates.

In managing conflicts, try to look for the common ground on which some agreement can be built. Several of the skills we considered previously for creating a good communication climate—being descriptive, provisional, and open, and treating others as equals—can be used to help you keep an open mind.

READ THE NONVERBAL SIGNS

Just as with every other kind of interpersonal communication, the ability to read nonverbal behavior is an important factor. As Berger argues, failure to account for the nonverbal communication is to "doom oneself to study the tip of a very large iceberg."[8]

What information can nonverbal communication provide partners in a conflict situation? Deborah Newton and Judee Burgoon argue that nonverbal communication serves many functions that are relevant to conflict between intimate partners.[9] Primarily by analyzing nonverbal behaviors you can tell how a person is feeling, his or her degree of intimacy, whether a person is

● **Reading nonverbal signs is especially important in conflict resolution because they express emotions, and foster and manage impressions, as well as exert control.**

intentionally sending mixed messages, and when a person is attempting to exert control.

For instance, suppose that Risa asks, "Where did you put my dress that you got from the cleaners?" and Lonnie replies, "Oh no, I forgot all about it." If Risa then says, "Sure, I could have predicted that," the real meaning of her comment is likely to be revealed more by her nonverbal communication than by her words. If she has a gleam in her eye and a chuckle in her voice, Lonnie might infer that he is forgiven for being a forgetful lout. If, however, the statement is made in a deep brooding tone, Risa may well be commenting on how she perceives their relationship—that she is very unimportant in the scheme of things. In this case Lonnie might want to check out his perceptions, apologize for his forgetfulness, and clear up the misunderstanding.

Successful use and reading of nonverbal communication, then, can defuse or fuel a conflict. To put it another way, none of the suggested wordings mentioned thus far can help if the nonverbal cues contradict them; likewise, even poorly worded efforts to manage conflict can be successful if both parties read the others' nonverbal cues as positive signs that they really are trying to manage the conflict.

USE HUMOR

As suggested by the Risa and Lonnie example, humor can be an important part of your conflict-management repertoire. Janet Alberts reminds us that humor "can serve to promote solidarity, establish intimacy, and excuse a slight."[10] Yet she also tells us that the success of humor depends a great deal on the perceived success of the relationship.[11] That is, if two people believe that they have a good relationship, they are likely to perceive ribbing, teasing, and joking in a positive way rather than taking offense. For instance, Graham goes to the refrigerator for an egg for breakfast only to find that all the eggs are gone. He looks at Greg, his roommate, and says, "Damn it, Greg, can't you remember to replace something when you've used the last one? For crying out loud!" Greg replies, "Oh woe is me! What a colossal blunder! Oh, I have sinned—stone me, take me to the stocks." At this point Graham may be disarmed and reply, "OK, it's not a big deal, but I do wish you'd be a little more considerate." Notice, though, that Greg's histrionics will work only if Greg and Graham usually get along. If their relationship has been severely strained, Greg's attempt at humor in a conflict setting may be taken as sarcastic or as a sign that he really doesn't care about Graham's feelings. In that case using humor is likely to exacerbate rather than defuse the conflict. To be helpful in a conflict, humor must be both well intended and likely to be well received.

COMMUNICATE DIRECTLY

Communication is likely to be most effective, and result in the least conflict, when it goes directly to the person who wants or needs the information. Often, however, we are content to deliver information serially through intermediaries instead of going directly to the target person. If Marvin tells Kate to tell Henry that his failure to keep their appointment hurt his feelings, Marvin is engaging in serial communication. Such serial communication often results in communication breakdown that leads to conflict. You've probably played the game called "Gossip" (or "Telephone"), in which one person whispers a statement to another, who in turn whispers what he thinks he heard to another, who whispers what she thinks she heard to the next person, and so on through five, six, seven, or more people. By the time it reaches the last person, the message may be so garbled that it is unintelligible.

Unscrupulous people have used the technique of serial communication purposely to spread rumors. *Rumors* are statements that are passed from person to person and that are usually embellished along the way. Furthermore, messages containing many facts are not only distorted in serial communication but also shortened, which means important information is likely to be lost. By contrast, messages that are storylike, with a plot and maybe even dialogue, usually are expanded—certainly they are distorted.

To avoid serial communication, be sure, whenever possible, to give information directly to those who need it. If you are caught in the middle of serial communication, make a deliberate effort to check the accuracy of your understanding. Refrain from passing a message until you are sure you have it right.

NEGOTIATE THE CONFLICT

Negotiation means managing conflicts through trade-offs. Conflict often results when two actions are proposed but only one can be taken. You cannot go to a baseball game and a concert at the same time; you cannot eat at a Chinese and an Italian restaurant at the same time; if you can afford only one housing payment, you can't buy a house and rent a house at the same time. Even after people have considered every aspect of a conflict rationally, they may each still truly believe that their own way is the best; perhaps then they should negotiate.

For some simple problems, it is relatively easy to negotiate a solution. For example, in trying to resolve whether to go to the ball game or the concert, a statement such as "I'll tell you what, Tammy, I'll go to the concert with you tonight if you'll go to the ball game with me this weekend," will probably achieve the desired results. Since both activities can be undertaken at different

● **Basic Communication Skills**

SKILL	USE	PROCEDURE	EXAMPLE
Negotiating Managing conflict through trade-offs.	To help both parties achieve a positive outcome.	1. Determine whether activities in conflict cannot both be accomplished. 2. Determine whether negotiable elements are of fairly equal importance. 3. Suggest a compromise position, or suggest that if one person's idea is followed now, the other person's will be followed next.	"You've got to get to the store, and I've got to get this paper done. I'll drive you to the store tonight and help you with the shopping if you'll help me by typing my paper tomorrow morning."

times, this is not an either/or situation, unless both parties insist on making it so. Thus one question to ask is whether a small concession can actually satisfy both parties.

For negotiation to work, the activities, goals, or ideas being negotiated must be of fairly equal importance. Thus, in a dispute over whether to eat Chinese or Italian food, the conflict may be resolved if one of the participants says, "Joe, if you'll let me make the decision on where to eat tonight, I'll go along with you on whatever movie you want to see." But a statement such as "Alice, if you'll let me decide on the kind of car to buy, I'll let you decide where to go on our next weekend trip," does not stand a chance unless Alice is an unusually passive person. Obviously, selecting a car is a far more important decision. A person negotiating in this manner is not acting in good faith.

In negotiation, as in all kinds of conflict management, a climate of equality is essential. Finding trade-offs that are indeed parallel in importance may be difficult, but when they can be found, they make an excellent base for negotiation.

SEEK OUTSIDE HELP

If an issue is truly not negotiable—such as a conflict about whether to rent a house or buy one—and you and the other person cannot work out a decision cooperatively by yourselves, you are not necessarily defeated. When negotiation fails, you may wish to seek outside help from a facilitator or arbitrator.

A *facilitator* is an impartial third person who can help you to discuss the conflict cooperatively. This person will not make the decision for you but will

● **Sometimes a facilitator, an impartial third person, may be able to help two people resolve their conflict.**

help the two of you apply the problem-solving method to your conflict. Psychologists, psychiatrists, marriage counselors, and other clinicians are skilled in facilitating decision making. A good facilitator not only sees to it that you are following the steps of problem solving but also helps you weigh and evaluate the variables.

An *arbitrator* is an impartial third person who, after hearing both sides, weighs and evaluates the alternatives and makes a binding decision for you. Labor unions and management sometimes use arbitration. It may work for you.

For interpersonal conflicts, arbitration will work if you can agree on an arbitrator who, in turn, will agree to make the decision for you. The arbitrator must be a person whose judgment you both trust. The arbitrator also should be competent in some way to make a decision on the issue. Referees in domestic court act as arbitrators in many divorce actions when parents cannot agree about child custody arrangements. Likewise, your financial counselor may arbitrate a conflict over whether to invest in a high-risk stock or a high-dividend stock but not a conflict over whether to live in the city or the country.

Too often people seek to pull in a close friend or a relative to arbitrate. Not only may these bystanders not have the expertise needed for the particular issue, but, more important, they are not independent, impartial agents. They may well be close to both parties or may have a vested interest in the outcome. Calling on such people puts them in a no-win situation (someone may be upset by their decision) or, at best, makes them feel very uncomfortable in the role.

If you do agree to arbitration, the verbal contract between you and the other person should include a clause stating that whatever decision is made, you will both willingly and happily comply. Remember, you will have gone to a third person because the two of you were unable to come to an agreement; if you are unwilling to abide by the decision, whichever way it goes, you should not agree to arbitration in the first place.

LEARN FROM CONFLICT-MANAGEMENT FAILURES

Ideally, you want to resolve every conflict as it comes up. As the Biblical saying goes, "Never let the sun set on your anger" (Ephesians 4:26). There will be times, however, when no matter how hard both persons try, they will not be able to resolve the conflict, for as Sillars and Weisberg point out, conflict can be an extremely complex process, and some conflicts may not be resolvable even through improved communication.[12]

Especially when the relationship is important to you, take time to analyze the failure of the conflict resolution. Ask yourself questions such as "Where did things go wrong?" "Did one or more of us become competitive or defensive?" "Did we fail to implement the problem-solving method adequately?" "Were the vested interests in the outcome too great?" You may find that attempts failed because you need more work on basic communication skills such as paraphrasing, describing feelings, and perception checking. By learning why conflict resolution failed, you put yourself in a better position to manage the next conflict more successfully.

Identifying Methods of Dealing with Conflict

BY YOURSELF

1. Label the following as P (pseudoconflict), C (content conflict), V (value conflict), or E (ego conflict).

        _____ a. Joe wants to live with Mary, but Mary wants the two of them to get married.

316

_____ b. Stan believes that because he is an insurance salesman, Jerry should not dispute his position on annuities.

_____ c. Ira defends his failure to present an anniversary gift to Agnes by asserting that their anniversary is not today (May 8) but May 18.

_____ d. Martin calls to announce that he is bringing the boss home for dinner. His wife replies, "That will be impossible. The house is a mess and I need to go shopping."

_____ e. Jane says, "Harry, pick up your clothes—I'm not your maid!" Harry replies, "I thought we agreed that it's your job to take care of the house. I take care of the yard."

Answers: a. V; b. E; c. C; d. P; e. C

2. Suppose that you and a close friend (or fiancé or spouse) were involved in the conflicts above. Select two of them and prepare a procedure that you believe would be most likely to manage the conflicts.

WITH A GROUP

Discuss your conflict management plans to determine the likelihood of success of each.

JOURNAL ENTRY

Recount in your journal a recent conflict situation in which you believe you "won" or "lost." What contributed to the outcome? Did you have any control? What skills mentioned in this chapter might have improved the means of resolving the conflict? Reflect on a time when you won a battle but lost the war; that is, you appeared to come out ahead at the moment but the long-term quality of the relationship was damaged. What behaviors were responsible for the damage? What might you have done to salvage the relationship?

● ◆ ■ **Summary**

Conflict is often defined as interaction between persons expressing opposing interests, views, or opinions. We cope with conflicts in a variety of ways. Negative behaviors include withdrawal, surrender, and aggression. Positive behaviors include discussion and persuasion.

Conflict management begins with a mutual desire to manage conflict successfully. Those in conflict may begin by trying to identify the true subject of the conflict. Although pseudoconflicts are not really conflicts at all, there are many sources of genuine conflict. They may be content conflicts over facts, interpretations of facts, definitions, or choices; they may be value conflicts over competing value systems that are brought to bear on the issues; or they may be ego conflicts that personalize the nature of the conflict. Conflicts become more complicated as they escalate to involve values and egos.

Successful conflict management incorporates a number of options. By cooperating rather than competing, partners may be able to prevent the conflict from escalating to a win-lose situation. By being aware of nonverbal reactions, partners may be able to understand each other's feelings, motivations, and methods. By using humor, partners may be able to defuse conflict. By communicating directly people can avoid misunderstanding. By negotiating, partners may be able to resolve choices equitably, and by seeking arbitration, partners may be able get necessary help in resolving conflicts that they cannot resolve on their own.

● ◆ ■ Communication Improvement Goal Statement

If you would like to improve your skill at negotiating, write a communication improvement goal statement following the guidelines on page 33 of Chapter 1.

● ◆ ■ Featured Reading

Getting Together: Building a Relationship That Gets to Yes
Roger Fisher and Scott Brown
(Boston: Houghton Mifflin Company, 1988)

In this book, Fisher and Brown, who are director and associate director of the Harvard Negotiation Project, apply much of the information from Fisher and Ury's 1981 best-seller *Getting to Yes: Negotiating Agreement Without Giving In* to the context of a "working" relationship. The result is a book that not only stresses elements of conflict management but also helps us to see how these elements work in our interpersonal relationships.

The authors define a "healthy" relationship as one that is able to deal well with differences. They argue that when people are unclear about what they want and need in their relationships, it is easy for conflicts to arise that are difficult to cope with. How should people deal with differences? Fisher and Brown cover six fundamental qualities of healthy relationships: balancing reason and emotion, understanding, effective communication, being reliable, relying on persuasion rather than on coercion, and mutual acceptance.

At the heart of their recommendations is the necessity for a person to adopt the strategy of being unconditionally constructive. This means that "I do only those things that are both good for the relationship and good for me, whether or not you follow the same guidelines" (p. 37).

In their final section the authors assert that to develop an effective working relationship, one must choose actions that are congruent: specifically, our actions must be congruent with the particular relationship and situation, congruent with each other, and congruent with our own beliefs. As a way to ensure that relationships stay on target, Fisher and Brown provide a checklist that enables us to see how well the relationship is going.

Much of what is said in this easy-to-read book seems like common sense. The fact that so many relationships are troubled, however, indicates the usefulness of the material. The authors skillfully illustrate every suggestion with realistic examples that make it easy to apply their recommendations.

● ◆ ■ **Notes**

1. Dudley D. Cahn, "Intimates in Conflict: A Research Review," in Dudley D. Cahn, ed., *Intimates in Conflict: A Communication Perspective* (Hillsdale, N.J.: Lawrence Erlbaum, 1990), p. 1.

2. Michael E. Roloff and Denise H. Cloven, "The Chilling Effect in Interpersonal Relationships: The Reluctance to Speak One's Mind," in Dudley D. Cahn, ed., *Intimates in Conflict: A Communication Perspective* (Hillsdale, N.J.: Lawrence Erlbaum, 1990), p. 49.

3. Denise H. Cloven and Michael E. Roloff, "Sense-Making Activities and Interpersonal Conflict: Communicative Cures for the Mulling Blues," *Western Journal of Speech Communication* 55 (Spring 1991): 136.

4. Alan L. Sillars and Judith Weisberg, "Conflict as a Social Skill," in Michael E. Roloff and Gerald R. Miller, eds., *Interpersonal Processes: New Directions in Communication Research* (Beverly Hills, Calif.: Sage, 1987), p. 146.

5. Michael Argyle, "Intercultural Communication," in Larry A. Samovar and Richard E. Porter, *Intercultural Communication: A Reader*, 6th ed. (Belmont, Calif.: Wadsworth, 1991), p. 40.

6. Jonathan G. Healey and Robert A. Bell, "Assessing Alternative Responses to Conflicts in Friendship," in Dudley D. Cahn, ed., *Intimates in Conflict: A Communication Perspective* (Hillsdale, N.J.: Lawrence Erlbaum, 1990), p. 29. In their article, Healey and Bell discuss findings from C. E. Rusbult, "A Longitudinal Test of the Investment Model: The Development (and Deterioration) of Satisfaction and Commitment in Heterosexual Involvements," *Journal of Personality and Social Psychology* 45 (1983): 101–117.

7. C. H. Coombs, "The Structure of Conflict," *American Psychologist* 42 (1987): 355–363.

8. C. R. Berger, "Social Power in Interpersonal Communication," in M. L. Knapp and G. R. Miller, eds., *Handbook of Interpersonal Communication* (Beverly Hills, Calif.: Sage, 1985), p. 483.

9. Deborah A. Newton and Judee K. Burgoon, "Nonverbal Conflict Behaviors: Functions, Strategies, and Tactics," in Dudley D. Cahn, ed., *Intimates in Conflict: A Communication Perspective* (Hillsdale, N.J.: Lawrence Erlbaum, 1990), p. 77.

10. Janet K. Alberts, "The Use of Humor in Managing Couples' Conflict Interactions," in Dudley D. Cahn, ed., *Intimates in Conflict: A Communication Perspective* (Hillsdale, N.J.: Lawrence Erlbaum, 1990), p. 109.

11. Ibid., p. 117.

12. Sillars and Weisberg, p. 143.

PART

III

Communication in Professional Relationships

Much of our interpersonal communication occurs in professional relationships. In this part we begin with a discussion of communicating in work relationships. We develop the part with chapters on communication in groups, leadership, and job interviewing.

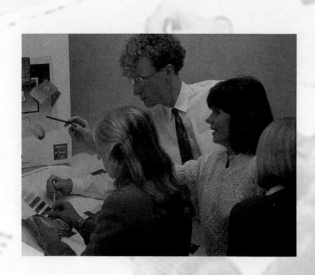

CHAPTER ELEVEN

Communication in Work Relationships

O B J E C T I V E S

After you have read this chapter, you should be able to define and/or explain:

Characteristics of the organizational context

Supervisor-subordinate relationships

The vertical dyadic linkages model

Co-worker relationships

Relationships with customers and clients

Boundary spanning

"So," Phyllis asked, "how was your first day at work?"

"Exciting," Tony replied, "but rather confusing. The first person I met with was my boss. She showed me around and gave me an idea of where things were and what I need to do to get started—I thought she was really pleasant, and I figured things would go pretty well. Well, about an hour later I met Damien Coyle, who has the cubicle next to mine. The first thing he said was 'So what do you think of the Dragon Lady?' Well, I didn't know how to react. As I said, I kind of liked her, but here's a guy who is a veteran and he's kind of telling me that she's a problem and expecting me to share his views. Well, I got by by being sort of noncommittal. Then this afternoon I called Parson Plastics, one of the accounts I'm suppose to handle, and did I get an earful! It really makes me question how ethical my predecessor was in handling this account in the past. So by the end of the day I was pretty confused—not about my job responsibilities, I know that I'll be a good service representative—but about the people I'm going to be working with. Ironing out some of these relationships may be pretty tricky, and I wasn't counting on that."

Organizations are ubiquitous. Thus most of the relationships that we negotiate and maintain occur within organizations. Most of us were born in hospitals, were cared for at day care centers, attended schools and colleges, participate in religious organizations, donate our time to service organizations, derive our income from business or government organizations, are married and divorced by religious and government organizations—and, when we die, will be processed by a funeral home, yet another organization. So it is important for us to understand how the organizational context affects our interactions and communications.

Good communication skills are universally recognized as essential for successful interactions in organizations, for these skills are critical in determining employability and promotability.[1] Most successful executives recognize the importance that their communication skills have played in their career. For example, Lee Iacocca, the recently retired chairman of Chrysler Corporation, and Mary Kay Ash, founder of Mary Kay Cosmetics, in their respective books both repeatedly emphasize the importance of many of the skills presented earlier in this book.[2]

In this chapter we begin by discussing several of the important characteristics of work organizations that depend on effective communication. These characteristics affect the way we experience our relationships at work. Then we will focus most of our discussion on the three types of communication relationships that dominate organizational life. These are the ones that Tony was confronted with on his first day of work: his relationship with his boss, his co-worker relationships, and the relationships he will have with his clients. For each type of relationship we will explain the key dynamics in the relationship, discuss how and why these relationships are changing over time, and finally discuss the communication skills that are useful in developing and maintaining each type of relationship.

Characteristics of Work Organizations

Organizations are composed of individuals and groups of individuals who come together to achieve certain goals and objectives that are beyond the ability of one individual. Some organizational members are volunteers who receive no monetary compensation for their efforts on behalf of the organization's goals. Other organizational members are employees, who receive monetary compensation for the work that they do. We will focus on employees of an organization and the relationships they experience, but much of what we discuss can be applied to volunteers as well.

A number of characteristics of organizations influence the way that relationships develop and are maintained. These include the following.

1. *Organizations exist to achieve specific purposes.* Organizational purposes or goals are frequently expressed as vision statements or as formal mission statements. Vision statements articulate the corporate philosophy and indicate the central values that should guide behavior. For example, the "Statement of Corporate Purpose" of Merck, a large U.S. health care group, reads "We are in the business of preserving and improving human life. All of our actions must be measured by our success in achieving this." Disney's vision is simply stated: "To make people happy."[3] As you can see, visions are quite nebulous and difficult to assess, so many organizations create mission statements that are more concrete expressions of their goals: they define the organization's practical objectives and set specific time limits for their accomplishment.

Understanding Visions, Missions, and Goals

To underscore the difference between visions and missions and lesser goal statements, examine the following statements from a hypothetical organization called ROTO (Reaching Out To Others), which runs a food pantry.

VISION: We are dedicated to eliminating hunger by working cooperatively with others.

MISSION: We will strive to be recognized as the leading organization in the collection and distribution of nonperishable foodstuffs free of charge to those with certifiable needs.

GOAL: Operating as a 100 percent volunteer organization, during the next five years we will seek to increase the number of clients we serve from 200 households per month to 2,000 households per month.

The specific goals that organizations pursue are important because, to a large extent, they determine what behaviors will be valued and how individual contributors will be rewarded. Today many companies publish their vision and mission statements so that employees and customers will understand what purposes the organization exists to serve.

To return an acceptable profit to its owners is a primary goal of some organizations. For example, your local McDonald's operates as a franchise and has as one of its goals making money for the franchisee. Organizations that operate "for profit" are generically referred to as "businesses."

Other organizations do not have the primary goal of making a profit. Instead they seek to reach their goals within a specific budget. These "nonprofit organizations" include government and quasi-government organizations; benevolent and religious organizations; some hospitals; social service agencies; and environmental, consumer, and other special-interest advocacy groups. For example, the NAACP, which seeks to advance the cause of racial equality, establishes a yearly budget based on funds it has raised and operates its programs within that budget.

Whether or not organizations pursue profit goals is an important determinant of other processes within the organization and can affect the emphasis and character of the relationships that are encouraged.

2. *Organizations develop distinct cultures.* Just as countries and ethnic groups can be viewed as having different cultures, organizations develop what are referred to as organizational cultures. These cultures reflect core values that are shared to some extent by all members of the organization. Organizational cultures differ from one another. In part, these differences are a result of the environment or external situation that the organization faces. Even so, all organizational cultures can be described by their orientation toward action, degree of individualism, mode of decision making, and type of performance feedback.[4]

First, organizations differ on the extent to which activity versus action is valued. In activity-oriented cultures what is important is doing *something,* whether or not what is done actually contributes to the reaching of organizational goals. So, for example, in some work settings employees know that it is important to "look busy" even if there is little to do or even if what they are doing is counterproductive. Some organizations value the number of products produced, whether or not those products are needed to meet demand or whether they meet the quality standards of the customers. In other organizations it is action, not just activity, that is valued. When action is valued, organization members engage in creative work in which the outcomes of activity are what is important, not the activity of the work itself. In these organizations, for example, members of the organization would be valued for producing the amount of product that met customer requirements and could be sold profitably.

Second, organizational cultures can be described by the degree of individualism that they encourage. Some cultures value individual effort, whereas others emphasize cooperative team effort. When individual effort is emphasized, competition between co-workers is likely to be keenly felt and individuals are generally rewarded for their specific job performance, whether or not the organization meets its goals. In these cultures individuals are often promoted based on their individual accomplishments, with little regard for the job requirement in the new position (which may in fact require greater cooperative skills). When the organization values cooperative effort, emphasis is placed on using all available talents to solve the problem. In these cultures co-workers are seen as allies and resources. Rewards are distributed based on team performance, and promotions are earned by those who are adept at managing the technical and relational aspects of work.

A third characteristic of culture on which organizations can be differentiated is the mode by which they make decisions. In some organizations members are encouraged to decide quickly, even if all the information is not available. These organizations believe that it is better to respond quickly to perceived opportunities than to proceed cautiously and perhaps miss out. Other firms are not so daring, and thus are more likely to value careful decision making. They will engage in well-thought-out and thoroughly documented decision-making processes that minimize the chance that the organization will be wrong and suffer harm. Obviously, the persuasive skills that one needs to succeed in these types of organizations will differ.

Finally, organizational cultures differ on the type of performance feedback that they provide to their members. Members of some organizations receive little feedback about how well they are performing their jobs. And when they do receive it, it is likely to be ambiguous or based on how well the person complies with various established procedures and rules, regardless of whether this actually affects goal accomplishment. In other organizations frequent, specific, goal-related feedback is valued and encouraged. In these organizations members understand how well they are doing at helping the organization reach its goals. Obviously, when this type of performance feedback is valued, the communication skills associated with giving feedback become critical.

Although organizational cultures may evolve over time, they are difficult to change because they are rooted in shared values. Yet it is within this cultural context that interaction and work-related relationships must be managed, so it is important for new members of an organization to understand its culture. Rather than distill the culture of an organization in a simple statement published for all to read, organizations communicate their cultures through the following means: (1) the stories that members continually retell ("Remember the day Jones got canned for reading a book at his desk because he didn't have any work to do?"); (2) the myths that develop around certain people or events of the past; (3) rituals (such as recognizing top sales associates at pep-rally-like sales meetings, or holding annual twenty-year service award luncheons); (4) heroes (the exceptional human successes who become role models for the culture's values); and (5) informal organizational communication with other members.[5]

3. *Individuals assume specific work tasks for the organization.* The goals of an organization are so broad that each member is responsible for only part of the overall task. Because of this, in an organization, a member has specific roles. As we discussed in Chapter 2, a *role* is a set of behaviors or tasks the individual is expected to perform. These behaviors or tasks may be accurately noted in a job description or formal employment contract such as a union might negotiate, or they may evolve over time depending on the skills and the interests of the individual and the needs and culture of the organization. Individuals may play more than one role during the same time period. For example, Ayanna may have three different roles. She may be a production facilitator for one product group, she may serve on the Diversity Education Task Force, and she may be a member of the plantwide Continuous Improvement Committee.

Even in situations where there is no formal job description, the individual must become aware of his or her responsibilities. Responsibility awareness is usually accomplished through some type of job training process. During this process the individual is exposed to messages from a variety of sources about what type of work behavior is expected. If the system the organization uses to communicate these expectations is effective, individuals are likely to understand and perform their roles effectively. Clear communication of role expectations is important both when individuals take on a new role, and when, because of important organizational needs, an existing role evolves to require different behaviors.

When the organization does an inadequate job of communicating role expectations, individuals do not know what behaviors are expected of them and become confused. This confusion, called "role ambiguity," can lead to poor performance and individual dissatisfaction with the job. For example, many organizations are now moving away from the old style of management in which supervisors do the thinking and problem solving while workers are simply "paid to work, not to think." Instead of "Boss as Authority and Problem Solver," they are moving to the new paradigm of management in which supervisors are being supplanted by "self-managed work teams." These well-trained teams of six to eighteen workers, acknowledged as valuable resources, assume full responsibility for turning out a well-defined segment of finished work. In doing this they are empowered to take on many behaviors, such as problem solving and decision making, that traditionally have been part of the manager's role. Although studies have shown that, overall, organizations reap substantial benefits from such teams,[6] unless organizations carefully prepare, communicate, and train existing managers for their new role responsibilities as coach and facilitator, these managers are likely to experience role ambiguity and become disillusioned with their role in the new work group.

If members are to understand and perform their roles effectively so that organizations can meet goals, both members and those responsible for training members in new roles must be competent communicators. Organizations also must carefully plan how members are to be educated about appropriate role behaviors. Finally, organizations must work toward eliminating role conflicts and provide supportive communication environments where members experiencing such conflicts will feel safe in discussing and resolving them.

4. *Individual roles are grouped in various ways to help organizations accomplish their goals.* In organizations, roles are grouped together into work units to facilitate coordination and fix responsibility. Some roles to which individuals are assigned are grouped and become part of the formal structure of the organization. These groups, which are referred to by various names such as department, group, and division, are often displayed graphically on organizational charts and usually consist of a task group and the manager to whom the task group is responsible.

Other roles necessary to organizational goal attainment are not part of the formal organizational structure but are grouped. These groups are generally "cross-functional," drawing members from relevant departments or divisions or groups in the formal structure. Some cross-functional groups are standing committees whose members rotate according to a schedule. For example, many organizations have a safety committee responsible for developing and implementing programs that make the work environment less hazardous. Other groups are designed to solve a particular problem and thus are generally temporary. These groups, called task forces or project teams, are usually planned so that individuals with different but relevant expertise and points of view are chosen. In each case the group dissolves once it has accomplished its specific goal.

5. *Organizational goal attainment depends on effective coordination processes.* Because organizations assign specialized roles to individual members in order to accomplish goals, and because no one person is capable of doing all of the work, the tasks must be synchronized. This is the process of *coordination*, and it depends on effective communication between people. The coordination needs of organizations are a mixed blessing to individual workers. On the one hand, effective coordination enables people to achieve results that would be impossible for each alone. Yet, on the other hand, coordination efforts limit the flexibility that workers might otherwise have to choose when, how, and with whom they will work. Several mechanisms are used in organizations to coordinate work.

The first mechanism, known as mutual adjustment, is usually the preferred coordination strategy for very small businesses. *Mutual adjustment* involves individuals working in close proximity to one another to discuss and to decide how to coordinate their work efforts. For example, Fredrico owns a small appliance repair business that has three retail locations. At each location he may employ a worker who handles routine repairs but sends difficult repairs to a central location, where Fredrico, who is a highly skilled mechanical and electrical service technician, handles the tough orders. To determine when to promise a customer that he or she can expect to pick up a difficult repair, the store clerk might simply call Fredrico and ask him to set a date based on his current workload. Then the clerk could tell the customer when to expect to pick up the appliance, based on when Fredrico could finish the repair. Here the primary coordination is done through interpersonal communication.

When an organization becomes too large or the work becomes too complicated to coordinate through mutual adjustment processes, it begins to develop rules and procedures to coordinate routine repetitive work. For example, on an assembly line, workers often take their breaks at the same time or in a rotation at predetermined times, which allows the assembly process to continue to operate. An example from a different context that is familiar to many of us is the return policy that many retail establishments have. To ensure that customers wishing to make new purchases are not inconvenienced by the lengthier process of returning merchandise, most stores prohibit checkout clerks from accepting returned merchandise and direct them to send customers with returns to a Customer Service Department or to a manager.

How effectively rules and procedures achieve coordination is often a direct result of how well they are understood by workers. Thus when rules and procedures are established, it is important that the reason for each rule be communicated as well as the rule itself. When workers do not understand the reasons for a rule, they often fail to comply with it, causing coordination problems. Both workers and those who formulate rules and procedures need to work to ensure accuracy and understanding.

For routine matters, organizations also use reports and forms to coordinate effort. For example, in a restaurant, the server prepares a written work order for the chef, who then prepares the meals. This form allows the server and the cook to coordinate their work. Orders attached to the order wheel signal to the chef that there are orders to be filled; plates with orders attached signal the servers that orders are awaiting delivery. Budget reports provide an overview of how a division is progressing; the oral budget meeting is a routine reporting procedure that permits two-way communication about expenditures. Although forms and reports are usually written communications, decisions to use them and evaluations of their usefulness are accomplished using interpersonal communication.

Sometimes the work that needs to be coordinated is not routine, so rules, procedures, forms, and reports are not appropriate, but the organization is too large and complex to rely on mutual adjustment. When this occurs organizations will appoint a *liaison*—a person charged with the responsibility of coordinating the work between two different organizational groups.

6. *Organizations are composed of differing levels of authority and responsibility.* As organizations become larger and begin to differentiate the work of members, some members take on roles that require them to assume responsibility to plan, organize, coordinate, and monitor the work of others. In traditional organizations such authority and responsibility are given to a person who is part of the management group of the organization. In more modern organizations this responsibility and authority may be shared by the members of a self-managed work team. Nonetheless, we can think of organizational groups as being arranged in a hierarchical fashion depending on the level of authority and responsibility given to the individual or group.

Most people and groups in the organization are at the *operating* level. They may control their own work, but they have no authority to control the work of others. Assembly-line workers, order clerks at a fast-food chain, nursing teams, teachers, and accountants are examples of roles at the operating level. A second level of the hierarchy comprises those roles that are traditionally seen as *lower management* positions. Traditionally, individuals in these roles see that operating-level employees' work is planned, assigned, and monitored. With the advent of self-managed work teams, however, this role is evolving into that of a coach (teaching operating employees how to cooperatively plan, assign, and monitor their own work) and a liaison to other groups to handle disturbances. Examples of lower managerial positions include head nurses, office managers, and shift supervisors at fast-food restaurants.

The third level in the hierarchy of authority is the *middle management* level. This level traditionally was responsible for developing information that enabled the organization to set strategic goals and for implementing the strategic decisions about goals that had been made by the executive-level managers. In addition, some middle management was responsible for coordinating the work of lower-level managers. As you might anticipate, with the widespread use of computer technology making information processing less labor intensive, and with the increasing recognition that operating-level employees are capable of managing and coordinating their own work, the number of middle managers needed to run an organization has decreased substantially in recent years. Thus many organizations have downsized, that is, cut their work force and significantly reduced the number of members who occupy middle management positions.

The final level of the hierarchy is the *executive* level. Executive-level or top managers are concerned with studying long-term trends in the environment of the organization that suggest new challenges and opportunities. Based on their understanding of these, executives formulate long-term plans and objectives and make decisions about how scarce resources in the organization are to be used. They are also responsible to key constituencies for the overall goal performance of the organization.

Because of the hierarchical nature of organizations, the potential for communication problems is great. When messages are passed down this "chain of command," the serial nature of the process invites distortions. Thus the messages from executive managers that are received by operating-level employees are often poor reflections of the original intentions.

The preceding discussion introduced the basic characteristics of organizations that form the context in which work relationships are developed and maintained. In the next sections we turn our attention to the three types of work relationships that are most critical to organizational goal attainment.

Supervisor-Subordinate Relationships

Of all relationships at work, the supervisor-subordinate relationship has been studied most exhaustively. This type of relationship is characterized by one person, the boss or supervisor, having formal authority and responsibility for the work performance of the other person, the subordinate.

Supervisors are responsible for seeing that the people who report to them perform their job duties. Three tasks of central concern to supervisors in modern organizations are (1) developing their subordinates' skills and abilities to meet the changing requirements of the group, (2) giving feedback to subordinates to indicate whether they are performing their jobs well, and (3) influencing subordinates to meet personal and work goals.

To accomplish these tasks effectively, supervisors must be competent communicators.[7] Instruction of subordinates requires not only that a supervisor be knowledgeable about the tasks that subordinates perform but also that the supervisor be able to transmit this knowledge to the subordinates. Thus effective supervisors are adept in describing behavior, using clear and vivid language, and offering constructive criticism. To provide effective feedback to subordinates, supervisors must know both how to praise and how to criticize. If supervisors are to be successful at influencing their subordinates, they must become aware of subordinates' needs. Thus they must be effective listeners who are skilled at paraphrasing and perception checking. With this information they can then use influence skills to communicate their willingness to meet employees' needs if performance goals are reached.

Of course, everyone in an organization—from the chief executive officer (CEO) or president to the operating-level employee—is in the subordinate role in a supervisor-subordinate relationship. The organization's CEO is sub-

● Instructing subordinates requires not only that the supervisor be knowledgeable, but also that the supervisor be able to transmit this knowledge to the subordinate.

ordinate to the board of directors, the vice president of marketing is subordinate to the CEO, the branch manager is subordinate to the vice president of marketing, and so on down the hierarchy of authority.

Individuals in the subordinate roles of relationships must also communicate skillfully if the relationship is to be effective. Subordinates can increase the likelihood that conversations with their bosses will be effective by knowing how to listen, question, paraphrase, ask for feedback, and assert themselves. When both persons in a supervisor-subordinate relationship recognize the importance of communication and jointly assume responsibility for sharing meaning, communication breakdowns are less likely to occur and the needs of both relationship members are likely to be met.

As with any other relationship, the one between a supervisor and a subordinate develops over time. Yet not all individuals who have the same supervisor establish the same type or level of relationship with that person. Why do the relationships between a given supervisor and his or her subordinates vary? Is it a matter of interpersonal attraction, luck, or something else? One widely studied explanation for how traditional supervisor-subordinate relationships develop was proposed by George Graen.[8]

VERTICAL DYADIC LINKAGES THEORY

Graen called his theory the vertical dyadic linkages (VDL) model. The word *dyadic* acknowledges that a relationship exists between two people. The *vertical* label is used because the two people are at different levels of the organization's hierarchy—one person is subordinate to the other. The word *linkage* in the model's title reminds us that the supervisor-subordinate relationship joins or links levels in the hierarchy in order to reach the organization's goal.

The theory begins with the assumption that supervisors are given responsibility for more work than can be accomplished by their work unit if everyone performs only the specific duties that his or her formal job description calls for. Therefore, supervisors must find subordinates who are willing to perform more than their normal responsibilities. These subordinates take on special assignments to help out the boss. Over a period of time these individuals become more and more valuable to the boss, and as a result they establish a greater power base from which to negotiate. Obviously, individuals who perform more than their assigned role tasks would not continue to do so if rewards were not in line with their contributions to the work unit.

To maintain a fair exchange with these individuals, the supervisor must begin to negotiate special rewards, thus initiating an exchange-centered relationship that differs from the usual formal one. An exchange-centered relationship is one in which the subordinate performs duties beyond those formally expected of a person in the job. As a result, the supervisor gives or "exchanges" special rewards. These rewards can take many forms; they may be financial bonuses, for example. But they are more likely to be subtle things such as choice task assignments, better office space, public praise for special assignments, access to information not usually shared with employees at that level, and a closer interpersonal relationship with the boss. Individuals who have attained this close working relationship with their boss often describe it as a mentoring relationship, indicating that what they have gained has helped them to develop skills and expertise beyond the learning that would normally take place on the job. These skills make them more valuable to the organization and will help them to advance in their careers.

● ● **Outcome of the Model** What, then, becomes of individuals who perform their role assignments well but do not do anything extra to help out the boss? According to the VDL model, these individuals maintain role-centered relationships with their bosses. A role-centered relationship is one in which subordinates perform only the duties formally ascribed to the job and so receive only the rewards normally accorded by the organization. They may receive good work evaluations, adequate raises, and fair treatment, but they will find it difficult to be promoted or to develop a close working relationship with their bosses.

Thus, if you observe your boss with his or her subordinates over a period of time, you will notice that certain subordinates seem to be close to the boss, whereas other, equally competent people appear to be relating to the boss only on a formal business level. Those subordinates who are close to their supervisors form what can be called an "in-group." This group is composed of individuals who the boss has learned can be trusted to go beyond what is expected and to help in areas not formally prescribed as part of their job. Subordinates who do not have this exchange relationship with the boss can be thought of as forming an "out-group." This group is composed of individuals who may or may not perform their jobs competently but who, regardless of their performance, are usually not asked to perform extra assignments because in the past they either have been unwilling to do so or have failed to perform well.

Linking Pin Effect Now imagine the total organizational consequence of this process. You can be "in" or "out" with your boss, who may be "in" or "out" with his or her boss, who may be "in" or "out" with his or her boss, and so on. When you consider this *linking pin effect,* you can begin to appreciate how individual perceptions of the same organization can differ.

Let's suppose that James, a computer programmer working in one programming group, has developed an effective exchange relationship with his boss, Janet. Katherine, another programmer in a different group, has also developed an effective exchange relationship with her boss, Lamar, who reports to the same boss that Janet does. Whereas Lamar has established an in-group relationship with this boss, Janet never volunteers her group for extra-tough assignments and thus has only a role relationship with the boss. If this boss has an opening for another group leader and both James and Katherine are recommended by their bosses, the linking pin effect suggests that the promotion is most likely to go to Katherine, because her boss, Lamar, has a closer relationship with the boss who will make the decision. Similarly, if the boss is faced with making budget cuts, it is less likely that he will cut the budget of Lamar's group because this group, through Lamar, is perceived as more productive or helpful. This linking pin effect suggests that the rewards a person receives depend not only on the type of relationship (exchange or role) that she has with her boss but also on the types of relationships that all of her hierarchical superiors have with their bosses.

If the vertical dyadic linkages model accurately describes supervisory relationships, an important question arises: "How can you develop an effective working relationship with your boss?"

Three steps are required. First, you must begin by assessing the skills and expertise you possess that may help your boss to accomplish work that falls outside of the formal role prescriptions of your job. These skills may be those that are in short supply in your work unit or those that your boss lacks. If you think you have no special skills or expertise, see whether you can develop some. If a company is considering a new computer application that the boss is unfamiliar with, a subordinate might do some research, take a course at the local college, or volunteer for the company training program in order to become a valuable asset. For example, Marian noticed that her boss seemed to labor over what were, to her, simple reports. Because she knew that this task took her boss an inordinate amount of time, she volunteered to write the report for a project with which she was familiar even though it wasn't part of her normal duties. Her boss took note of the speed and ease with which she completed that report, and soon he was relying on her to edit and advise him on writing more complex reports and memos.

Once you are aware of the skills you can bring to an exchange relationship, the second step is to communicate your willingness to perform extra assignments that require these skills. Supervisors often feel embarrassed about asking for help, and so a request for assistance many times is hidden in a vague statement such as "I'm just swamped with work and now Personnel says they have to have these affirmative action forms filled out and returned by Monday." This statement is a subtle cry for help. Some employees might respond, "Yeah, Personnel is so unreasonable. Well, I've got to get back to my desk." But the individual seeking to establish an exchange relationship with the boss might respond with a feelings paraphrase: "Gee, Barb, I get the feeling you don't really think you'll have time to do it. How can I help?"

The essential bond in a close supervisor-subordinate relationship is mutual trust. Thus being willing to take on additional assignments will further your relationship only if you successfully complete the third step: Additional assignments must be performed well and on time. To do this often means working more, although you may be able to negotiate with your boss to be removed from other mundane assignments. Thus, had Marian's additional editing assignments overburdened her with work, her volunteering would ultimately create some type of performance failure. Either the individual's own work will suffer, the additional work will be poorly done, or the individual will experience great stress.

You may be thinking that these recommendations sound like a prescription for "buttering up" the boss. To a certain extent they are. But the reality of traditional relationships between supervisors and subordinates is that power in the relationship is unequally distributed. The boss has more power than most of the subordinates. By increasing the boss's dependence, however, a subordinate can develop a more evenly balanced relationship. Notice that this is not the same as getting the boss to like you. People need not like their bosses or their subordinates in a special sense to have mutually satisfying work relationships. They simply must understand that at work, more than in other contexts, reciprocity is the essential outcome. If a boss and subordinate become friends, they have begun a different relationship. Although it may influence their work relationship and may in fact be a benefit of an effective work relationship, other mutually acceptable exchanges must continue to take place if the work relationship is to remain close.

Communication is the process through which supervisor-subordinate relationships are established, negotiated, and maintained. Thus, although the majority of examples in this book focus on personal applications of communication skills, communication competence is critical in work-based relationships as well. By skillful use of listening, perception checking, describing, questioning, and paraphrasing, you can control the manner in which your vertical dyadic relationships develop. Without careful and attentive use of these skills, you are likely to have a distant and ineffective work relationship with your boss and, in time, with your subordinates.

It is important to note that diversity can affect the supervisor-subordinate relationship. Most of us are well aware of the "glass ceiling" that exists in many organizations for women and minorities. Although Graen's theory suggests that managers base their relationships only on work-related criteria, other evidence would suggest that managers who have not received diversity training and who work in organizational cultures that do not value diversity are likely to favor subordinates who are most like them. This similarity bias may well result in diverse people's work being undervalued and in their being excluded from opportunities to perform more challenging assignments that would prepare them for promotions.

Giving Feedback in Work Sessions

BY YOURSELF

Think of your last job. How would you characterize your relationship with your boss? Did that boss seem to depend on certain individuals more than on others? If so, what effect did it have on the work group?

IN GROUPS

Working in groups of three, two people role-play a supervisor-subordinate feedback session. Decide who will be the supervisor and who will be the subordinate. Use the following scenarios. Be sure to use praise and effective criticism skills. Develop and enact first a praise session and then a criticism session. The third person observes the use or abuse of the essential communication skills. Switch roles until all three people have had an opportunity to serve in each role.

In each case, "you" refers to the supervisor.

Vivian (Vincent), an African-American, recently undertook a special project. It resulted in a report that summarized the current customer service practices in two of your branch banks. The report is very well written and offers several suggestions for improvement that you are pleased with. Unfortunately, some of the conclusions are based on financial analyses that are wrong. You are not sure why the numbers are wrong, but you suspect that Vivian (Vincent) does not understand how to use the management information system database correctly.

Mark (Myra) has been working for you for three years. In that time he/she has always done an excellent job with the duties that are normally required of one in that position but has not volunteered to take on any extra projects. You have recently been asked to nominate someone for a promotion and chose Dwight, whose work has been good but who has also completed several additional projects for you. Mark (Myra) has asked to speak to you about why he/she was not nominated.

Miguel (Marla) is supervisor of the night-shift crew at the local burger franchise and reports to you as the manager. During the last six months—since this person took over—the restaurant has been much cleaner than before. It appears that Miguel (Marla) is doing an excellent job of making sure that standards for cleaning are maintained. You have also noticed, however, that turnover of the night-shift crew has increased 40 percent during this period.

Co-Worker Relationships

Your co-workers are the other members of your work group, team, or department who are at the same job level you are. It has been shown that co-workers, among other things, influence both the quality of our performance levels and our satisfaction with our jobs.[9] Because people need people, the threat of social isolation is a very powerful influence on what we do at work. Organization members form relationships with their co-workers not only to satisfy social needs and complete interdependent work tasks but also to obtain information about the organization. Organizational activities are so complex that people rarely can rely on their own senses and experiences to obtain

● Co-workers influ-
ence both the quality
of our performance
levels and our satisfac-
tion with our jobs.

a complete or accurate picture of what is happening in the organization. Co-workers thus are a major source of organizational information.[10]

When co-workers have the same general perceptions of and experiences in the organization, they are unlikely to disagree with one another. Even when these perceptions differ, most individuals, especially in a work situation, wish to avoid disagreement. Many times, therefore, real differences that exist in the ways co-workers view the organization are glossed over. This pressure to conform reduces the interpersonal discomfort caused by conflict and is especially strong during times of high work stress (such as when layoffs are threatened, when a new boss has suddenly taken over, or when a new co-worker enters an established work group). Unfortunately, when organization members do not communicate differing viewpoints, the organization may miss important information and alternative perspectives useful for solving problems. Thus it is important for co-workers to use assertive communication skills in order to express divergent opinions and avoid problems associated with overconformity.

Like other relationships, your relationships with your co-workers are developed through your communication experiences with them. But just as you will not choose your boss, you also will not be in charge of selecting those with whom you work. Thus, as in supervisor-subordinate relationships, how well you get along with your co-workers depends to a great extent on your communication competence. For example, if you choose to be insensitive to the needs and feelings of your co-workers by not listening attentively, or by being unaware of cultural differences, you are likely to find these relationships unsatisfying.

In the past many U.S. businesses encouraged co-workers to view one another as competitors for promotions and other rewards. This led to many bright and ambitious people having their careers short-circuited because they were insensitive to their co-workers' feelings and needs. It was also partially to blame for the end of U.S. domination in many businesses. Today U.S. managers realize that cooperation between co-workers is essential for organizational success. Moreover, today most successful business people attribute part of their success to effective working relationships with their co-workers.

Co-worker cooperation does not depend on co-workers being close friends or always agreeing on everything. Indeed, as the work force becomes more diverse, it is likely that disagreements between co-workers will become more frequent. Most managers recognize this as a potential strength on which they can draw. They reason that, if managed, the disagreements may lead to more creative and productive solutions to organizational problems. If this is to happen, co-workers must develop and maintain healthy working relationships. Maintaining them depends on effective interpersonal communication. Skills such as turn taking, listening, collaborative problem-solving approaches to conflict resolution, empathy, and effective group communication skills will be critical to workers in the 1990s and beyond.

As mentioned earlier in this chapter, the use of self-managed teams or self-managing work groups is increasing in organizations today. In these organizations it is the responsibility of co-workers to decide on and institute work assignments as well as to problem-solve and to monitor work quality. The trend toward self-managed teams is expected to spread and may become a dominant fact of organizational life. This will result in co-workers' relationships becoming more important and supervisor-subordinate relationships less important.

Self-managed teams succeed in part because people support things that they helped to create. When the team sets high standards for work and these standards are communicated to and accepted by most group members, the team generates the pressure that will keep the work group productive. Recently, a self-managed work team had a constructive confrontation with a co-worker who had fallen behind on his assigned tasks. When asked to explain why his part of the project was late, the person replied that he had been working fifty hours a week and just couldn't get it done. The team's unanimous response was indignation. The rest of the team members had been working eighty-plus hours a week each to finish their parts of this critical project. They informed their co-worker that they were not sure they wanted him to remain on the team if that level of effort was to continue. A second reason self-managed teams succeed is that individual co-workers can share a wealth of job-related information that will help new members develop the skills they need to be productive in the organization. A third benefit of self-managed teams is that individuals who have good working relationships with co-workers generally like their jobs and thus are less likely to leave the organization. Because it is expensive to train new employees, most organizations prefer to keep turnover rates low.

People working in self-managed teams find that group process is facilitated by the skills of paraphrasing, describing behavior, and using precise and specific language, as well as by steps for conflict management and effective listening.

Analyzing Work Relationships

BY YOURSELF

1. Consider your last job. How would you characterize your co-workers? Were they close-knit? If so, why? If not, why not? What communication skills were used most often to create a positive climate? Which were missing?

2. Have you ever quit a job or felt like quitting simply because of the other individuals you had to work with? Try to describe what made you feel that way.

Relationships with Customers and Clients

Customers and clients are the people who use the results of one's work. Traditionally, we think of customers and clients as individuals or other organizations who are not members of our organization. In every organization some individuals occupy roles whose central tasks are to deal with people outside the organization. These boundary-spanning roles require their occupants to form work-related relationships with individuals who are not

members of the organization. Examples of typical boundary-spanning roles include sales representatives, customer service technicians, delivery persons, social workers, buyers, purchasing agents, dispatchers, real estate agents, public relations personnel, marketing research interviewers, and caregivers such as nurses. People who communicate about business-related matters with individuals who are not members of their organization, or their part of the organization, must use communication skills to overcome four potential pitfalls that otherwise might hinder their effectiveness.

● In every organization some individuals occupy roles whose central tasks are to deal with people outside the organization.

FAILURE TO RECOGNIZE THE DEPENDENCE IN THE RELATIONSHIP

Boundary-spanning or internal customer relationships exist because members of organizations must relate to outsiders in order to conduct business. Individuals who occupy boundary-spanning roles are responsible for developing good relationships with the publics they serve, even though they are often asked to take adversarial positions and may have little control over organizational policies and deadlines. Thus, even though the customer or client may not always be right, it is imperative for the boundary spanner to communicate effectively to the client or customer the organization's needs and concerns.

A problem often found in boundary-spanning relationships in U.S. organizations today is the failure of boundary spanners to recognize their dependence on other individuals. Because most boundary-spanning roles involve some type of customer-client relationship, failure on the part of the boundary spanner to recognize and acknowledge a client's needs can cause many problems. More than one high-fashion store or expensive restaurant has failed in business because the salesclerks or servers conveyed an attitude of superiority in their communication styles when dealing with customers. A friend recently related a story that dramatically illustrates this point. After playing tennis, she stopped to shop in a very exclusive and expensive store. She asked a salesclerk to show her some merchandise. The salesclerk, noting that the customer was dressed in an old sweat suit, wrinkled her nose and said loudly, "I don't really think you could afford these. Perhaps you should look at . . . ," and named a different store. Our friend, who has a preferred credit line at the store, was of course very hurt by what she felt was a particularly rude comment based on confusion of fact and inference. Such behavior causes stores to lose customers.

By contrast, most of us can cite at least one salesperson whose behavior is so gracious that we prefer to buy from that salesperson whenever we can. For instance, a woman might buy her cosmetics from only one salesclerk at one department store when she finds that this clerk goes out of her way to explain how to use the products, to recommend colors, and to send cards to the customer when special offers are available. This special attention and extra communication effort on the part of the salesclerk are likely to ensure the loyalty of that customer. This translates directly into profits for the company. Unfortunately, many people who are supposed to deal with the public on behalf of the organization have not been trained to use the communication skills that would lead to effective performance of their jobs. Customer service providers need to have refined communication skills such as empathizing, listening, responding effectively to conflict, and using equality-oriented language.

FORMATION OF ADVERSARIAL RELATIONSHIPS

Individuals in boundary-spanning roles often find themselves placed in adversarial relationships. For instance, purchasing agents for firms are charged with the responsibility of obtaining the best deal on the supplies needed by their companies. Of course, the vendors with whom the purchasing agents must deal are also trying to make financially advantageous sales for their companies. In the past, when agents and sales representatives met, each was primarily concerned with securing the deal that was in the best interest of the company they represented, regardless of the outcome for the other company. Today the most profitable firms know that by establishing long-term "partnership relationships," both companies can benefit.

Thus, in today's business environment, effective boundary spanners spend time listening to, sharing information with, and learning from those with whom they do business. Relationships are viewed as primary, and deals are often negotiated to be in both companies' best interest. Obviously, it is critical that those who work at these boundaries be adept in using problem-oriented communication strategies. They must also be able to negotiate and use collaborative conflict-resolution skills.

LACK OF CONTROL

Boundary-spanning roles are also fraught with tension because individuals occupying these positions may have little control over the company policies that they must follow and communicate to those with whom they deal. For example, the extent to which a customer service representative is free to accept any returned merchandise varies. The retail-store policies that guide and direct what such individuals can say or do usually were established much higher in the company. Similarly, sales agents can promise delivery to their clients on a certain date, but they are dependent on other members of the organization to actually deliver the goods on time. In both of these cases the boundary spanner has little control of the situation. Yet the customer who is not satisfied will hold the boundary spanner responsible.

Boundary spanners can, however, maintain good communication climates with their customers by explaining not only the policy they are following but the reason for it. Many discount stores have a no-return policy. This policy can be communicated to customers not only on in-store signs but also by the cashier at the time of purchase with a simple explanation: "We cannot accept returns and keep our prices low, so be sure to check the merchandise before you leave." This practice may reduce the number of customer complaints. Similarly, instead of promising delivery in days, a sales representative should explain to the client that the company policy is to ship 90 percent of all orders in three days but there is no guarantee that this order might not take longer. A representative who explains delivery in these terms should be able to maintain a good working relationship with a client even if the merchandise is late.

A boundary spanner's lack of control should be clearly and specifically communicated to clients. In this way effective relationships can be established even in the face of business uncertainty. These language skills, when used to honestly communicate the nature of a situation, help to establish the boundary spanner as ethical.

USE OF TECHNICAL JARGON

In most cases individuals working for the same organization have been socialized to use a common job-related language. This technical jargon may be idiosyncratic to a particular organization and thus may create decoding difficulties for people who are not part of that organization. People who must deal with government employees, for example, often find it impossible to understand the "alphabet soup" of agency abbreviations that are commonplace symbols within the bureaucracy. Imagine the recently hired government clerk who tries to help an inexperienced company representative complete several government forms by saying, "All you have to do is get your CEO to assign ASOP the compilation of the K-10 to the V.P. of R&D. This form should be attached to your FTC-LOB forms and mailed to us annually." Although such a sentence makes perfect sense to the government clerk, it probably lost the company representative at the first string of letters.

The fact that individuals in boundary-spanning roles may not speak the same language can be a source of relational difficulty. Because your organization's terminology is second nature to you, you may be unaware of its effect on others. Boundary spanners therefore need to be sensitive to nonverbal cues that indicate a client may be confused by a term. When confusion is sensed, the boundary spanner should quickly try to reexplain the message in more common language. For explaining very technical information to nontechnical specialists, analogies that refer to things with which the other is familiar are useful.

Many organizations recently have realized that it is useful to acknowledge and manage relationships with internal customers and clients as well as with external customers and customer groups. An internal customer is a co-worker or group of co-workers who will use the results of your work. For example, in a hospital, the Medical Records Department is the internal customer for the Admitting Department, since Medical Records will take the information that was obtained from the patient and, based on it, will prepare the medical record. Similarly, the Accounting Department is the internal customer of the Medical Records Department, since it will use the information on the medical record to prepare the statement of charges. Although some of the issues may be slightly different, many issues that exist between boundary spanners and external clients also are relevant for spanning internal boundaries with internal clients.

Analyzing Boundary-Spanning Roles

JOURNAL ENTRIES

1. Make a list of the individual boundary spanners you encounter in a typical week. Note the ones with whom you have a continuing relationship. (Don't forget your professors!) To what extent are each of the four pitfalls discussed above part of your relationship? Which communication skills might help you to be more effective in avoiding each pitfall?

2. Think of one satisfying and one unsatisfying episode you have had with a boundary spanner. Write a short essay in which you compare and contrast the communication processes in each encounter.

●◆■ Summary

Adults spend approximately half their waking hours at work. Thus many of the relationships that adults maintain occur within the organizational context. These relationships are different from friendships and family relationships—for the most part they serve different purposes and are not voluntary. The majority of work relationships occur between supervisors and subordinates, co-workers, and organizational representatives and clients.

Of all the relationships at work, the supervisor-subordinate relationship has been studied the most. Nearly everyone in an organization is involved in a relationship of this type. The vertical dyadic linkages model helps to explain how these relationships evolve over time. The VDL model states that in order to accomplish all of the work, supervisors establish exchange relationships with individuals who are willing to do extra work and maintain more traditional role relationships with those who are not. Subordinates in exchange relationships may not be paid more but will receive other intangible rewards for successfully completing additional assignments. To engage in exchange relationships, subordinates must know what skills they possess, communicate their willingness to take on extra work, and perform both it and regular assignments well.

A second type of relationship at work is with co-workers. Organization members form relationships with co-workers to satisfy social and informational needs. Co-worker relationships are powerful forces in determining individual work standards and levels of satisfaction. As organizations move to self-managed work teams, co-worker relationships will become more important.

Some people in organizations occupy boundary-spanning roles in which they must form relationships with people outside the organization. Differences in organizational policies can create potential problems for these relationships. Problems also result if the boundary spanner fails to recognize dependencies in the relationship, views the other as an adversary, has insufficient decision control, and uses technical jargon. Many effective boundary-spanning relationships are based on individual trust that develops over time.

● ◆ ■ Featured Reading

Doing Business with Japanese Men: A Woman's Handbook
Christalyn Brannen and Tracey Wilen
(Berkeley, Calif.: Stone Bridge Press, 1993)

Each year those who communicate in work relationships become increasingly involved in international settings, and no setting has proven to be more difficult and more important than communicating with Japanese professionals. Christalyn Brannen and Tracey Wilen, two businesswomen with a wealth of experience in working with Japanese, have written a book that is must reading for any international businessperson. Although it focuses on work relationships with Japanese, it covers many of the issues we have considered throughout this text.

In Part One, the book considers a dozen important issues including establishing authority, traveling in a group or alone, and socializing. In Parts Two and Three, it gives insights into both Japanese men and women and gives tips about traveling to and from Japan.

Each chapter contains actual experiences that illustrate positive or negative behaviors. In the chapter on establishing authority, a situation is cited where the female executive laid the groundwork by asking her team members to enter the room first, introduce themselves, and be seated. The team was told not to start the meeting until the female executive arrived and to leave the center seat at the negotiating table open for her. Better than any verbal introduction, these visible actions clearly established her position and authority. In the chapter on what to wear, examples are given to show the importance of staying away from any low-cut or tight-fitting clothes, trendy outfits, and elaborate jewelry. The authors recommend conservative suits or dresses with jackets for most business dealings.

In short, this book provides a collection of insights that are designed to give women a competitive edge in international markets in general and Japanese markets in particular.

●◆■ Notes

1. D. A. Whetten and K. S. Cameron, *Developing Management Skills*, 2nd ed. (New York: HarperCollins, 1991).

2. M. K. Ash, *Mary Kay on People Management* (New York: Warner Books, 1984); L. Iacocca with W. Novak, *Iacocca: An Autobiography* (New York: Bantam Books, 1984).

3. T. D. Jick, "The Vision Thing (B)," in T. D. Jick, *Managing Change: Cases and Concepts* (Homewood, Ill.: Irwin, 1993).

4. T. Deal and A. Kennedy, *Corporate Cultures* (Reading, Mass.: Addison-Wesley, 1982).

5. Ibid.

6. Peter Lazes and Marty Falkenberg, "Workgroups in America Today," *Journal for Quality and Participation* 14(3) (June 1991): 58–69.

7. W. C. Redding, *Communication Within the Organization: An Interpretive Review of Theory and Research* (New York: Industrial Communication Council, 1972).

8. George Graen, "Role Making Processes Within Complex Organizations," in M. D. Dunette, ed., *Handbook of Industrial and Organizational Psychology* (Chicago: Rand McNally, 1976), Chapter 28.

9. Frederick M. Jablin, "Task/Work Relationships: A Life-Span Perspective," in Mark L. Knapp and Gerald R. Miller, eds., *Handbook of Interpersonal Communication* (Beverly Hills, Calif.: Sage, 1985), p. 637.

10. D. C. Feldman, "The Multiple Socialization of Organization Members," *Academy of Management Review* 6 (1981): 309–318.

Interpersonal Communication in Groups

After you have read this chapter, you should be able to define and/or explain:

Key variables of effective group communication

Task roles and maintenance roles

Negative roles

Questions of fact, value, and policy

Analysis of questions of policy

Brainstorming for possible solutions

Several of the sales division's leading members were gathered to determine how to proceed with the new advertising program. At the beginning of the first committee meeting, Hope Levine, head of the sales division, began, "You know why I called you together—to determine how to proceed with the new sales program idea. Well, what do you say?" After a few seconds of silence, Hope said, "Les, what have you been thinking?"

"Well, I don't know," Les replied, "I haven't really given it much thought. What are we supposed to be doing?"

"I wanted to get your ideas on how we should proceed with this new program."

"Whatever you think is OK with me, Hope," said Barry Miller.

"Right, what do you want to do, Hope?" Les asked.

"I thought maybe you folks would like to make some suggestions," Hope replied.

"I'd sure like to talk about it," Sue Maxley said. "If you'd give us some of the background, I know I'd be glad to comment."

"But I sent around preliminary data earlier this week," Hope explained.

"Oh, is that what that was?" Marcus Jones asked. "I read the part about the meeting, but I guess I didn't pay much attention to the material."

"I'd really like to start using some of the new sales ideas," Hope said.

"Sure, go ahead—we'll back you," Anna Hernandez replied.

"Well, I'll think it through and make some suggestions next time," Hope announced. "Meeting's adjourned."

As people filed out, Hope overheard Anna commenting to Les: "These meetings sure are a waste of time, aren't they?"

Is this the way your group works? Maybe the problem was Hope's. As leader she could have shown more direction. But for the most part, the problem with the group falls directly on the membership—the participants. Because almost all of us spend some of our communication time in groups, we need to know how to participate in groups. Whether your groups work well depends on each and every group member.

A work group is a small, cohesive unit whose members interact face-to-face while solving a problem or making a decision. The specific type of goal for which a group strives may vary: A family meets to plan a vacation; a student committee meets to handle details for a campus concert series; a board of directors meets to set policy for a major corporation. Yet for each of these groups to succeed, its members must work together effectively.

In this chapter we consider criteria for assessing effective work groups, preparation for discussion, the problem-solving method, and specific role functions. In the next chapter we will consider one of the most important role functions: leadership.

Characteristics of Effective Work Groups

Group research shows that effective groups generally have a good work environment, have an optimum number of members, show cohesiveness, have a commitment to the task, respect norms, find ways to achieve consensus, and meet key role requirements.[1]

A GOOD WORK ENVIRONMENT

The best work environment is one that promotes group interaction. The ideal arrangement is the circle, where everyone can see everyone else. At least in terms of seating position, everyone has equal status. If the meeting place does not have a round table, you may be better off without a table or with an arrangement of tables that makes a square, which approximates the circle arrangement. The advantages of the circle are that sight lines are better and motivation to speak is higher. At an oblong table, for example, those at the ends will be perceived as having higher status—they will be treated as leaders. Those sitting on the corners will tend to speak less than those on the ends or in the middle.

AN OPTIMUM NUMBER OF MEMBERS

Effective groups contain a sufficient number of members to ensure good interaction but not so many members that discussion is stifled. Most research finds that although optimum size depends on the nature of the task, groups consisting of five members are most desirable.[2] Why five? Groups with fewer than five members almost universally complain that they are too small and that there are not enough people for specialization. To be effective, a group needs certain skills. When the group contains only three or four members, chances are that not all these skills will be present. Moreover, if one member of a group of three does not feel like contributing, you no longer have much of a group. By the same token, for small tasks the three-person group often works well. It's easier to get three people together than five or more. And if the task is relatively simple or within the expertise of the individuals, the three-person group may be a good choice.

When a group numbers more than seven or eight people, reticent members are even less likely to contribute. As the group grows larger, two, three, or four people may become the central spokespersons, with others playing more passive roles.[3]

COHESIVENESS

You'll recall that cohesiveness means sticking together, pulling for one another, and being caught up in the task. Remember the Three Musketeers, who were all for one and one for all? They are the prototype of a cohesive group.

● **The best working environment for a work group is the circle where everyone can see everyone else and where everyone has equal status.**

At least three qualities seem particularly important in developing group cohesiveness: (1) attractiveness of the group's purpose (fraternal groups, for example, build cohesiveness out of devotion to service or brotherhood); (2) similarity of the needs and interests of members; and (3) reinforcement of interpersonal needs such as affection (showing affection to and receiving affection from others), inclusion (including others in activities and being included by others in their activities), and control (having a role in determining what will happen).[4]

Cohesiveness is difficult to develop in a one-meeting group, but it is and should be characteristic of ongoing groups. Cohesiveness is usually generated after initial meetings and should be well established during or before the group reaches its most productive stages.

COMMITMENT TO THE TASK

Whether the group is assigned a task or the group determines its task, members must be sufficiently committed to the group for it to succeed. When the task is deemed important and when the group believes that what it is doing will matter, members are much more inclined to devote their full energies to the task.

DEVELOPMENT OF AND ADHERENCE TO GROUP NORMS

Norms are the guidelines for behavior that are established or are perceived to be established for conducting group business. They are the most powerful determinants of behavior in groups. Norms begin to be established at the onset of a group's deliberations, and they grow, change, and solidify as people get to know one another better.

Norms for a group may be formally spelled out in a group's operating guidelines (such as in parliamentary procedures for organizational meetings); they may be adapted from proven social guidelines (such as "Don't talk about yourself in a decision-making group meeting"); or they may simply develop within a particular context. For instance, without a conscious decision, group members may avoid using common four-letter words during the meeting. When business has ended, conversation may become more earthy.

Norms help a group to develop cohesiveness. As members conform to stated or implied guidelines of behavior, they find themselves relating to one another more effectively. If you believe that certain norms are detrimental or destructive, you will need to make your position and the reasons for that position known. If norms become established, they are difficult to change.

CONSENSUS

If a decision is not a product of group thought and group interaction, the advantages of group decision making are lost. Group members often feel more pleased about the process and more committed to the group decisions when such decisions are reached through group interaction. The ideal is to reach decisions by consensus, or total group agreement. After the group has discussed a point for a while, one member might pose a question that is phrased to capture the essence of the group's position. For example, after a group has been discussing departmental problems, someone might ask, "Are we in agreement that lack of direction is frustrating the efforts of department members?" If everyone agrees, the decision is reached by consensus.

If the group does not agree, the group continues to discuss the point until a statement can be made that incorporates differing viewpoints without compromising the principles behind the viewpoints. But it takes the participation of most group members to arrive at a statement that represents the group position.

A role is a pattern of behavior that characterizes an individual's place in a group. Group members fill task and maintenance roles. Task roles reflect the work that a group must do to accomplish its goal; maintenance roles reflect the group behaviors that keep the group working together smoothly. As we proceed, you will notice that many of the roles correlate with interpersonal skills that we discussed earlier in the text. Of course, not all roles played in a group are positive. By accident or, occasionally, by design, people say and do things that hurt the group's ability to work together. Because leadership is so important to any group, the next chapter is devoted to a discussion of this vital role.

Group Characteristics

Select a committee or problem-solving group in which you participated.

1. How large was the group?

2. Was the group a cohesive unit? How can you tell?

3. What sense of commitment did you have to the task? What about the commitment of other members?

4. What norms, if any, seemed to be operating? What effect, if any, did size, cohesiveness, commitment, and norms have on the productivity of the group?

Roles of Group Members

As we have said, in productive groups individual members serve in both task and maintenance roles.

TASK ROLES

The major work in groups is carried out by people playing roles of information or opinion giver, information seeker, expediter, and analyzer. Let's examine the function of each.

● ● **Information or Opinion Giver** The information or opinion giver provides content for the discussion. Giving information actually constitutes about 50 percent of what is done in a group, because without information (and well-considered opinions) the group will not have the necessary material from which to draw its conclusions. Chances are that everyone in the group will fill this role during the discussion.

Playing the information-giving role well requires solid preparation and objective presentation. The more material you have studied, the more valuable your contributions will be. As information giver you will want to draw material from several different sources, and you will usually bring your sources with you to the discussion.

Regardless of the nature of the problem you are considering, the better the quality of the information shared, the better the quality of the group decisions. To be well prepared you will want to read circulated information carefully before the meeting, think about relevant personal experience, survey library sources, and interview for information.

Effective information givers present information clearly without getting emotionally involved. For instance, in answer to the question of whether dormitory theft is increasing, you might say, "According to statistics gathered by the campus police, theft has increased by at least 10 percent each of the last three years." Because you always want to be sure that any related information is presented, you might then add, "I wonder whether anyone else has found any other data that indicate the levels of theft?" Raising such a question tells the group that you want discussion of the data and that, whether it is substantiated or disproven, you have no personal relationship with it.

Information givers introduce their material with statements such as "When the Chang Corporation considered this problem, they found . . ." "The other day I ran across these figures that relate to your point." "According to the Controller's analysis, it doesn't necessarily work that way. He presented material that shows . . ."

● ● **Information Seeker** The information seeker asks for more information when it is needed. Frequently, groups try to draw conclusions before they have enough information. The information seeker asks the kinds of questions that stimulate members to share more of their information on the topic. Again, in most groups more than one person assumes the role of information seeker during the discussion, and one or more members often are especially perceptive in noticing when more information is needed.

Information seekers ask such questions as "What did we say the base numbers were?" "Have we decided how many people this really affects?"

"Well, what functions does this person serve?" "Have we got anything to give us some background on this subject?"

Expediter The expediter keeps the group on track. Whether the group is meeting once or is an ongoing group, almost invariably some remarks will tend to sidetrack the group from the central point or issue. Apparent digressions sometimes are necessary to establish the background of the problem, enlarge its scope, or give people an opportunity to air their feelings. Yet in a group these momentary digressions may lead the group off on tangents that have little to do with the assignment. Expediters are the people who help the group stick to its agenda.

When the group has strayed, expediters lead it back on track with statements such as "This is an interesting point, but I can't see that it is related to finding out the causes of the drop in sales over the quarter." "Let's see, aren't we still trying to find out whether these are the only criteria that we should be considering?" "I've got the feeling that this is important to the point we're on now, but I can't quite get hold of the relationship—am I off base?" "Say, time is getting away from us and we've considered only two possible solutions. Aren't there some more?"

Analyzer The analyzer probes both the content and the reasoning involved in the discussion. Analyzers know the steps that a group must go through to solve a problem. They know when the group has skipped a point, has passed over a point too lightly, or has not considered relevant material. Analyzers go beyond expediting and help the group penetrate to the core of the problem it is working on.

First, the analyzer probes the contributions of group members to determine whether information is accurate, typical, consistent, and otherwise valid. Suppose a group member reports that according to Paul Stewart, who oversees subscriptions to cable television, the number of new subscriptions dropped last month. As an analyzer you should ask questions such as "How many new subscriptions has the company been averaging each month over the last year? In how many months were the new subscriptions below the average for the year? for last year? Has this drop been consistent?" The purpose of such questions is to test the data. If data are partly true, questionable, or relevant only to certain aspects of the issue, a different conclusion or set of conclusions would be appropriate.

Second, analyzers examine the reasoning of various participants. The analyzer makes statements such as "Tom, you're generalizing from only one instance. Can you give us some others?" "Wait a minute; after symptoms, we have to take a look at causes." "I think we're passing this possible solution too lightly. There are still questions about it that we haven't answered."

MAINTENANCE ROLES

Group interpersonal relations are preserved by people playing roles of supporter, harmonizer, and gatekeeper. Let's consider the functions of each.

Supporter The supporter helps members of the group to feel good about their participation by recognizing their contributions. Although we expect that nearly everyone will be supportive, people sometimes get so wrapped up in their own ideas that they may neglect to acknowledge others' positive comments.

The supporter responds verbally, or at least nonverbally, whenever a good point is made. Supporters give nonverbal cues such as a smile, a nod, or a vigorous head shake and make statements such as "Good point, Mel." "I really like that idea, Susan." "It's obvious you've really done your homework, Peg." "That's one of the best ideas we've had today, Bernie."

● Supporters help members of the group feel good about their participation with such nonverbal cues as a smile, a nod, or a vigorous headshake.

● ● **Harmonizer** The harmonizer brings the group together. It is a rare group that can expect to accomplish its task without some minor, if not major, conflict. Even when people get along well, they are likely to become angry over some inconsequential point in a heated discussion. Most groups experience some classic interpersonal conflicts caused by different personality types and by polarization. Norbert Kerr shows that when an issue is especially important, group members are likely to experience greater polarization and thus greater conflict.[5]

Harmonizers are responsible for reducing tensions and for straightening out misunderstandings, disagreements, and conflicts. They soothe ruffled feathers, encourage objectivity, and mediate between hostile or aggressively competing sides. A group cannot avoid some conflict, but if there is no one present to harmonize, participation can become an uncomfortable experience.

Harmonizers put into practice the skills covered in the section Guidelines for a Constructive Program of Managing Conflict, in Chapter 10. Harmonizers are likely to make statements such as "Brandon, I don't think you're giving Jana a chance to make her point"; "Ernie, Jack, hold it a second. I know you're on opposite sides of this, but let's see where you might have some agreement"; "Lynne, I get the feeling that something Todd said really bugged you. Is that right?"; or "Hold it, everybody, we're really coming up with some good stuff; let's not lose our momentum by getting into name calling."

● ● **Gatekeeper** Gatekeepers help to keep communication channels open. In an effective group, all the members should have something to contribute. To ensure balanced participation, those who tend to dominate need to be held in check, and those who tend to be shy need to be encouraged. The gatekeeper is the one who sees that Juanita is on the edge of her chair, eager to speak but unable to break in, or that Don is rambling a bit and needs to be directed, or that Larry's need to talk so frequently is making Ramon withdraw from the conversation, or that Betty has just lost the thread of the discussion. Gatekeepers assume responsibility for helping interaction by making statements such as "Joan, I see you've got something to say here," or "You've made a really good point, Woody; I wonder whether we could get some reaction on it," or "Amir and Kristen, it sounds as if you're getting into a dialogue here; let's see what other ideas we have."

Gatekeepers can also be sensitive to social and cultural factors that may affect group members' participation. For example, even within the same culture, group members may bring very different backgrounds, vocabularies, and stores of information to the discussion. Thus some members may not understand some of the terms, historical allusions, or other information that other speakers take for granted—and they may be too embarrassed to ask for clarification. The same point applies, only more so, when a group consists of people from different cultures.[6] Furthermore, some members may appear more hesitant to get involved because they are used to a different set of "unwritten rules" for group interaction. For instance, Deborah Tannen in discussing differences in male and female styles in groups, points out that men have been socialized to exhibit knowledge and skill and hold center stage even in settings made up of people they know less well, whereas women are more comfortable talking when they feel safe and close among friends and equals.[7] These differences can lead to conflict and hurt feelings. By carefully attending to nonverbal cues, gatekeepers can notice when some members are being inhibited by the group process and help bring them into the discussion.

NEGATIVE ROLES

Group members will need to be on the lookout for people playing the roles of aggressor, joker, withdrawer, and monopolizer—negative roles that can have an adverse effect on the group problem-solving process. Let's consider each role.

- **Aggressors** Aggressors are the people who seek to enhance their own status by criticizing almost everything or blaming others when things get rough. Aggressors' main purpose seems to be to deflate the ego or status of others. One way to deal with aggressors is to confront them by asking them whether they are aware of what they are doing and of the effect it is having on the group.

- **Jokers** Jokers' behavior is characterized by clowning, mimicking, or generally disrupting by making a joke of everything. Jokers also are usually trying to call attention to themselves—they must be the center of attention. However, a little bit of joking goes a long way. If the group cannot get the jokers to consider the problem seriously, their antics will be a constant irritant to other members. One way to deal with jokers is to encourage them when tensions need to be reduced but to ignore them when there is serious work to be done.

- **Withdrawers** Withdrawers refuse to be a part of the group. Simply stated, withdrawers are mental dropouts. Sometimes they are withdrawing from something that was said; sometimes they are just showing their indifference. There are several ways to deal with withdrawers. One is to try to draw them out with questions; another is to find out what they are specifically good at and rely on them when their skill is required. Sometimes compliments will draw them out of their shell.

● ● **Monopolizers** Monopolizers need to talk all the time. Usually they are trying to impress the group with how well read and knowledgeable they are and with how valuable they are to the group. They should, of course, be encouraged when their comments are helpful. When they are talking too much or when their comments are not helpful, however, the leader needs to interrupt them or draw others into the discussion.

PRACTICE IN

Identifying Roles

BY YOURSELF
In each of the following, identify the statements as A (giving information), B (seeking information), C (expediting), D (analyzing), E (supporting), F (harmonizing), or G (gatekeeping).

_____ **1.** Janet, it looks as if you wanted to comment on the last point.

_____ **2.** We had been talking about whether students have access to department requirements. Shouldn't we finish that before we get into faculty availability?

_____ **3.** The questionnaire that we distributed indicated that more than 40 percent of majors didn't believe they were getting adequate advising.

_____ **4.** I don't know how meaningful that statistic is. Could you give me some of the background on the survey? Like, how many majors responded?

_____ **5.** Good point, Jenna. You've really put the problem in perspective.

_____ **6.** May, you've given us some good statistics—can we determine whether or not this is really an upward trend or just a seasonal factor?

_____ **7.** Fritz and Gwen, I know you see this issue from totally different positions. I wonder whether we might not profit by seeing whether there are any points of agreement; then we can consider differences.

JOURNAL ENTRY

Think of the last time you worked with a work group to try to solve a problem or make a decision. What was your primary role or roles in the group? Discuss your level of success. In light of what you have learned in this chapter, what would you do differently if you were to play that role or those roles in the future?

Problem Solving in Groups

Groups are likely to follow two distinct approaches to problem solving, approaches that have been called *descriptive* and *prescriptive*. A descriptive approach allows for a group to proceed much as they would if they are left to their own devices. Those who subscribe to this approach suggest that a normal process of problem solving will occur unless some external force intrudes. A prescriptive approach involves the conscious attempt to follow a set procedure. Those who subscribe to this approach suggest that groups will behave more efficiently if they follow suggestions for the development of a group agenda. The following section explains the essentials of the prescribed, or traditional, approach.

The traditional approach to problem solving is patterned after John Dewey's steps of reflective thinking and involves identifying, defining, and analyzing problems and suggesting, selecting, testing, and implementing solutions.[8] In this section we consider those aspects of the problem-solving method that relate directly to the topic of group communication—namely, defining and analyzing the problem, determining possible solutions, and selecting the best one.

DEFINING THE PROBLEM

Much of the wheel-spinning that takes place during the early stages of group discussion results from members not understanding what they are trying to accomplish. The person, agency, or parent group that forms a particular work group usually gives them a charge, such as "determine the nature of the curriculum" or "prepare guidelines for hiring at a new plant." Then, for purposes of group discussion, the charge is phrased in question form. A group begins from the assumption that answers are not yet known. Although some decision-making groups serve merely as rubber-stamping agencies, the group ideally has freedom of choice. Phrasing the group's purpose as a question furthers the spirit of inquiry. Once a group has the question down on paper, it considers the following:

1. *Does the question contain only one central idea?* The question "Should the college abolish its foreign language and social studies requirements?" is poorly phrased because it contains two distinct problems. Either one would make a good topic for discussion, but they cannot both be discussed at once.

2. *Is the wording of the question clear to all group members?* Sometimes a topic question contains a word so ambiguous that the group may waste time quibbling over its meaning. For instance, a group that is examining a department's curriculum might suggest the following question: "What should the department do about courses that aren't getting the job done?"

Although the question is well intentioned and participants may have at least some idea about their goal, such vague wording as "getting the job done" can lead to trouble in the discussion. Instead of waiting until trouble arises, reword questions in specific terms before the group begins discussion. Notice how this revision of the preceding question makes its intent much clearer: "What should the department do about courses that receive low scores on student evaluations?"

3. *Does the question encourage objective discussion?* The phrasing of a question may drastically affect a group's decisions. Consider the following: "Should our ridiculous set of college requirements be revised?" What kind of objective discussion is likely to occur when, right from the start, the group has agreed that the requirements are ridiculous? With such wording the scales are tilted before the group even gets into the issues involved. The phrasing of the question should not indicate which direction the group will go in even before discussion commences.

4. *Can the question be identified easily as one of fact, value, or policy?* How you organize your discussion will depend on the kind of question. Later we will discuss organization; for now, let's consider the three types of questions.

Questions of fact concern the truth or falsity of an assertion. Implied in such questions is the possibility of determining the facts by way of direct observed, spoken, or recorded evidence. For instance, "Is Smith guilty of robbing the warehouse?" is a question of fact. Smith either committed the crime or he did not.

Questions of value consider whether a certain belief or value is justified. They are often characterized by the inclusion of some evaluative word such as *good, reliable, effective,* or *worthy.* For instance, advertisers may discuss "Is the proposed series of ads too sexually provocative?" In this case the words "too sexually provocative" stand as the evaluative phrase. Another group may discuss the question "Is the sales force meeting the goals effectively?" Although we can set up criteria for "too sexually provocative" and "effectively" and measure material against those criteria, there is no way to verify our findings. The answer is still a matter of judgment, not fact.

Questions of policy judge whether a future action should be taken. The question is phrased to invite a solution or to test a tentative solution to a problem or a felt need. For instance, a student group might address the question "What should we do to lower the instances of theft in dorm rooms?" Such a question seeks a solution that would best address the problem of the increase in theft. "Should the university give equal amounts of money to men's and women's athletics?" seeks a tentative solution to the problem of how to achieve equity in the financial support of athletics. The inclusion of the word *should* in all questions of policy makes them the easiest to recognize and the easiest to phrase of all discussion questions. Most issues facing work groups are questions of policy.

If you are discussing either a question of fact or a question of value, the remaining steps of problem solving (analyzing the problem, determining possible solutions, and selecting the best solution) are not relevant to your discussions. What kind of a structure, then, is appropriate for discussions of questions of fact and value?

Discussions of questions of fact focus primarily on finding the facts and drawing conclusions from them. For instance, in the discussion of the question "Is Smith guilty of stealing equipment from the warehouse?" the group would decide (1) whether facts can be assembled to show that Smith did take equipment from the warehouse and (2) whether his taking the equipment constituted stealing (as opposed to, say, borrowing or filling an order for equipment).

Discussions of questions of value follow a similar format. The difference is that with questions of value the conclusions drawn from the facts depend on the criteria or measures used to weigh the facts. For instance, in the discussion of the question "Is the proposed series of ads too sexually provocative?" the group would decide (1) what the criteria are for determining "too sexually provocative" and (2) whether the ad program meets those criteria.

ANALYZING THE PROBLEM

Once the group agrees about the exact nature of the problem, it should move on to the next step—analyzing the problem. To analyze means to determine the nature of the problem: its size, its causes, the forces that create or sustain it, and the criteria for evaluating solutions. Sometimes analysis takes only a few minutes; at other times it takes longer. Both in preparation for problem solving and in the discussion itself, however, analysis is too often ignored because most groups want to move directly to possible solutions. For instance, if your group is charged with determining what should be done to reduce the instances of theft in dormitories, you may be inclined to start by listing possible solutions. A solution or a plan, however, can work only if it solves the problem at hand. Before you can shape a plan, you must determine what obstacles the solution must overcome and what obstacles the solution must eliminate, as well as whom your plan has to satisfy.

Analysis of a problem entails finding out as much as possible about the problem and determining the criteria that must be met to find an acceptable solution. If you were discussing the question "What should be done to equalize athletic opportunities for women on campus?" these two aspects of your analysis might be outlined like this:

1. What has happened on campus that signifies the presence of a problem for women? (*nature of the problem*)

    a. Have significant numbers of women been affected?
    b. Do women have less opportunity to compete in athletics than men?
    c. Has the university behaved in ways that have adversely affected women's opportunities?

2. By what means should we test whether a proposed solution solves the problem? (*criteria*)

    a. Does the proposed solution cope with each of the problems uncovered?
    b. Can the proposed solution be implemented without creating new and perhaps worse problems?

DETERMINING POSSIBLE SOLUTIONS

For any problem an infinite number of possible solutions exists. At this stage of discussion the goal is not to worry about whether a solution is a good one but to come up with a list of potential answers.

One way to identify potential solutions is to brainstorm for ideas. Brainstorming is a free-association procedure—that is, it involves stating ideas as they come to mind, in random order, until you have compiled a long list. In a good ten- or fifteen-minute brainstorming session you may think of several solutions by yourself. Depending on the nature of the topic, a group may

● **One way to identify potential solutions to a problem is to brainstorm for ideas. Brainstorming is a free-association procedure that involves stating ideas as they come to mind, in random order, until the group has compiled a long list.**

come up with a list of ten, twenty, or more possible solutions in a relatively short time.

Brainstorming works best when the group doesn't evaluate each solution as it is mentioned. If people feel free to make suggestions—however bizarre they may sound—they will be much more inclined to think creatively than if they fear that each idea will be evaluated on the spot. Later, each solution will be measured against the criteria. The solution that meets the most criteria or the one that meets several criteria best should be selected. For determining possible solutions to the problem of equalizing athletic opportunities for women, your problem-solving outline might continue as follows:

3. What can be done to equalize opportunities? (*possible solutions*)

   a. Can more scholarships be allocated to women?
   b. Can time allocated to women's use of university facilities be increased to a level comparable with men's use?

SELECTING THE BEST SOLUTION OR COMBINATION OF SOLUTIONS

At this stage in the discussion the group evaluates each prospective solution on the basis of how well it meets the criteria agreed on earlier. For selecting the best way to equalize athletic opportunities for women, you could continue with the following item in your outline for discussing the problem:

4. Which proposal (or combination) would work the best? (*best solution*)

   a. Will increasing women's scholarships solve the problems without creating worse problems?
   b. Can women's time for use of facilities be increased without creating worse problems?

Group Process

BY YOURSELF

1. Label the following questions F (fact), V (value), or P (policy).

   _____ a. Is Ohio State the largest single-campus university in the United States?
   _____ b. Should United Cable raise its fee for the Basic Service Package?
   _____ c. Which microcomputer costs the least to own and operate?
   _____ d. Is Compton Electronics' drug abuse education program effective in lowering instances of abuse?
   _____ e. Should tuition be increased at Miller University next year?

   Answers: a. F; b. P; c. F; d. V; e. P

2. Select a question of policy (perhaps one of the type listed above) and outline the problem-solving steps you would follow in a discussion of this question.

IN GROUPS

1. Divide into groups of about four to six. Each group has ten to fifteen minutes to arrive at a solution to the following dilemma: Five people are boating: the father, a fifty-five-year-old heart specialist reputed to be the best in the state; the mother, a thirty-six-year-old dermatologist; their eight-year-old child; and a couple who live next door, a forty-three-year-old industrial salesman for a major corporation and a thirty-five-year-old

Figure 12.1

Decision analysis form

Decision Analysis

---

1. Did the group arrive at a decision?

---

2. What action is taken as a result of the discussion?

---

3. Was the group consensus a good one?

---

4. Comments?

former model who appears in television commercials. If the boat started to sink and only one of the five could be saved, who should it be? One observer will be appointed for each group. The observer should use the decision analysis in Figure 12.1.

2. After discussion each group should determine (a) what roles were operating in the group during the discussion, (b) who was filling those roles, and (c) what factors helped or hurt the problem-solving process.

Select one of the most recent work groups in which you have participated. Which of the following had the greatest effect on group interaction or quality of the group decision: environment, group size, presence or lack of cohesiveness, commitment to task, adherence to norms, methods of decision making, or group preparation? In your journal discuss the rationale for your decision.

●◆■ Summary

Effective groups are identified by several criteria: They work in a physical and psychological setting that facilitates good interactions; they are of an optimum size; they work as a cohesive unit; they show a commitment to the task; they develop norms that help the group work; members interact freely to reach consensus; and they contain people who have enough expertise and aggregate skills to meet key role requirements.

In your group you may perform one or more of the task roles of giving or seeking information, expediting, and analyzing. You may also perform one or more of the maintenance roles of supporting, harmonizing, and gatekeeping. You will want to try to avoid the negative roles of aggressor, joker, withdrawer, and monopolizer.

Effective work groups discussing questions of policy define the problem, analyze the problem, select possible solutions, and then determine the best solution.

●◆■ Featured Reading

Teamworks!
Barbara Sher and Annie Gottlieb
(New York: Warner Books, 1989)

Teamworks! is based on the premise that a group of people working together can provide a system of support that will enable each person to accomplish more than they could on their own. Sher and Gottlieb discuss the building of informal support systems as well as structured support systems that they call "success teams," groups of people whose only goal is to help every member get what he or she wants.

What stands in the way of getting things that we want but that we perceive are out of our reach? Uncertainty, money, time, lack of information, and—the single most important factor—negativity. What can teams do for us? Teams can help us work through and overcome the common problems that prevent us from reaching our goals, including the problem of negativity. The authors observe that people have better ideas for each other than they have for themselves, and they also have more courage for others than for themselves. Thus teams are a powerful source of support for goal attainment.

In this highly practical book, Sher and Gottlieb explain how to form success teams in a variety of contexts, such as home teams, job clubs, create-an-event teams, kick-the-habit teams, guilds, and mentor/apprentice teams. Not only are issues of team formation addressed, but also the authors provide blueprints for running successful team meetings, including guidelines for team building, brainstorming, setting goals, and managing interaction. Finally, the authors discuss and recommend solutions to common problems that affect voluntary leaderless teams.

Sher and Gottlieb write in an easy-to-read style that is illustrated with numerous experiences of real people. Although the book at times seems to be designed to sell readers on attending the authors' seminars, everything you need to start your own group or run a seminar yourself is provided in this book, and the authors encourage you to do just that.

●◆■ Notes

1. A great deal of relevant research is summarized in Marvin E. Shaw, *Group Dynamics: The Psychology of Small Group Behavior,* 3rd ed. (New York: McGraw-Hill, 1981). Cragan and Wright point out that very little research on these issues has been done in the 1980s; see John F. Cragan and David W. Wright, "Small Group Communication Research of the 1980s: A Synthesis and Critique," *Communication Studies* 41 (Fall 1990): 216.

2. Paul Hare, *Handbook of Small Group Research,* 2nd ed. (New York: The Free Press, 1976), p. 214.

3. Shaw, p. 202.

4. William Schutz, *The Interpersonal Underworld* (Palo Alto, Calif.: Science and Behavior Books, 1966), pp. 18–20.

5. For a review of research, see Norbert L. Kerr, "Issue Importance and Group Decision Making," in Stephen Worchel, Wendy Wood, and Jeffry A. Simpson, eds., *Group Process and Productivity* (Newbury Park, Calif.: Sage, 1992), pp. 69–74.

6. Arthur D. Jensen and Joseph C. Chilberg, *Small Group Communication: Theory and Application* (Belmont, Calif.: Wadsworth, 1991), pp. 367–371.

7. Deborah Tannen, *You Just Don't Understand: Women and Men in Conversation* (New York: Ballantine, 1990), pp. 76–77.

8. See John Dewey, *Logic: The Theory of Inquiry* (New York: Henry Holt & Company, 1938), pp. 105–117.

CHAPTER THIRTEEN

Leadership in Group Communication

O B J E C T I V E S

After you have read this chapter, you should be able to define and/or explain:

Characteristics of leadership

Differences between task and maintenance leadership

Preparation for leadership

Seven leadership responsibilities

Allen Weiss was tossing and turning through the night—he knew that tomorrow was the day when a decision was expected. And he was the leader of the organization.

Allen paused as he walked through the huge set of doors. "The Summit," he said to himself. "I never dreamed I'd ever go through these doors." All he had ever heard or read came rushing through his mind. The Leader's Summit. Here was where the decisions were made. Here was where the policies of corporate America were made. The all-knowing Leader sat daily on his throne at the Summit—and today Allen would have an audience. He had grappled with his problem for months. Whether to start the project could affect the lives of everyone in the organization. He had taken the question to leaders of the various divisions of the company, but everyone said the decision needed the special wisdom of the Leader. And so here he was.

He made his way into the foyer and was led at last to the Throne. The Leader sat in regal splendor with a Gold Scepter in his hand.

"You have come a long way for guidance," the Leader said quietly. "State the situation."

Slowly Allen itemized the complexities underlying the decision that had to be made.

"Well stated," the Leader said. And now came the moment Allen had been waiting for. The Leader gazed at him intently. Slowly he reached into his gold lamé tunic and drew out what appeared to be a tiny metal disc with the seal of the Leader stamped on the surface. And with a sweep of his hand, he propelled the disc into the air. The Leader whispered, "Heads you start the project—tails you don't."

Leadership means many things to many people. To some it is an inherent, almost divine complex of traits that sets one person apart from his or her peers. To others it is the luck of being in the right place at the right time. Yet within most of us is some deep feeling that whatever leadership is, we have what it takes. Although we may say publicly that we wouldn't take the job of leader "for all the tea in China," in private we may see ourselves as the only logical candidates for the job.

Absolutely nothing is wrong with thinking you are the best person for the job. However, leadership is not something that should be taken lightly. Our goal in this chapter is to show what it means to be the leader of a work group, how to proceed if you want to try for leadership, and what you are responsible for doing in the group after you get the job. Although much of this discussion is applicable to all leadership situations, we will focus on the question of leadership in the decision-making or work group context.

What Is Leadership?

The definition of leadership varies from source to source, yet common to most definitions are the ideas of influence and accomplishment. *Leadership* means being in charge—exerting influence—and leadership means reaching a goal.[1] Let's explore these two ideas.

1. *Leadership means exerting influence.* Influence is the ability to bring about changes in the attitudes and actions of others. Influence can be indirect (unconscious) or direct (purposeful). As we discussed in Chapter 9, we often exert influence without being aware of it. In this section, however, we focus on the potential for direct purposeful influence by examining what leaders can do consciously to help guide their group through the decision-making process.

We should also mention that the exercise of influence is different from the exercise of raw power. When you exercise raw power, you force a person or a group to submit, perhaps against its will; when you influence others, you show them why an idea, a decision, or a means of achieving a goal is superior in such a way that members of the group will seek to follow those ideas of their own free will. Members will continue to be influenced as long as they are convinced that what they have agreed to is right or is in their individual best interest or in the best interest of the group.

2. *Leadership results in reaching a goal.* In the context of task or problem-solving discussions this means accomplishing the task or arriving at the best solution available at that time.

In an organizational setting a leader is usually appointed or elected. In a decision-making group setting, however, the struggle for leadership often proceeds without benefit of election or appointment. In fact, those involved may not perceive that a struggle takes place. In settings in which one individual has strong urges to control and the others have equally strong urges to be controlled, leadership will be established with no struggle at all. In most decision-making group settings, however, leadership is shared, switches back and forth, or develops into power struggles in which people exercise their need to lead.

Leadership Traits

What kind of person is most likely to be the leader of a group? Are there such things as leadership traits that, if discovered within a person, will predict his or her success as a leader? Studies conducted over the years seem to substantiate portions of the trait perspective of leadership.[2]

Marvin Shaw believes that enough consistency among individual traits and leadership measures exists to conclude that leaders exemplify traits related to ability, sociability, motivation, and communication skills to a greater degree than do nonleaders.[3] In group studies, with regard to ability, leaders exceed average group members in intelligence, scholarship, insight, and verbal facility. Leaders exceed group members in aspects of sociability such as dependability, activeness, cooperativeness, and popularity. In the area of motivation, leaders exceed group members in initiative, persistence, and enthusiasm. And leaders exceed average group members in various communication skills we focus on in this text. This does not mean that people with superior intelligence, those who are most liked, those with the greatest enthusiasm, or those who communicate best will necessarily be the leaders. However, we believe it does mean that people are unlikely to be leaders if they do not exhibit at least some of these traits to a greater degree than do those they are attempting to lead.

Do you perceive yourself as having any or many of these traits? If you see these traits in yourself, you are a potential leader. Because several individuals in almost any group of people have the potential for leadership, which one ends up actually leading others depends on many factors other than possession of these traits. These factors are discussed in the following sections.

● Leaders exceed average group members in successful use of communication skills.

Leadership Styles

There is no one "right" way to lead. A casual examination of groups in operation will reveal a variety of leadership styles. Some leaders give orders directly; others look to the group to decide what to do. Some leaders appear to play no part in what happens in the group; others seem to be in control of every move. Some leaders constantly seek the opinions of group members; other leaders do not seem to care what members think. Each person tends to lead a group with a style that reflects his or her own personality, needs, and inclinations. Nevertheless, it is possible to identify the most common styles of leadership and how they affect the way groups work in various circumstances.

What are the major leadership styles? Most recent studies look at leadership styles as either task oriented (sometimes called authoritarian) or person oriented (sometimes called democratic). As you read about these two major styles, notice that they correspond to the task and maintenance functions of groups described in the last chapter.

The *task-oriented leader* exercises more direct control over the group. Task leaders will determine the statement of the question. They will make the analysis of procedure and state how the group will proceed to arrive at the decision. They are likely to outline specific tasks for each group member and suggest the roles they desire members to play.

The *person-oriented* or *democratic* leader may suggest phrasings of the question, suggest procedure, and suggest tasks or roles for individuals. Yet in every facet of the discussion, the person-oriented leader encourages group participation to determine what actually will be done. Everyone feels free to offer suggestions to modify the leader's suggestions. What the group eventually does is determined by the group itself. Person-oriented leaders listen, encourage, facilitate, clarify, and support. In the final analysis, however, it is the group that decides.

Pioneering work by Ralph White and Ronald Lippitt suggests the following advantages and disadvantages of each style: (1) More work is done under a task-oriented leader than under a person-oriented leader, (2) the least amount of work is done when no leadership exists, (3) motivation and originality are greater under a person-oriented leader, (4) task-oriented leadership may create discontent or result in less individual creativity, and (5) more friendliness is shown in person-oriented groups.[4]

So which style is to be preferred? Research by Fred Fiedler suggests that whether a particular leadership style is successful depends on the situation: (1) how good the leader's interpersonal relations are with the group, (2) how clearly defined are the goals and tasks of the group, and (3) to what degree the group accepts the leader as having legitimate authority to lead.[5]

The favorability of leadership situations varies. Some situations are favorable to the leader on all dimensions. In these, the leader has good interpersonal relations with the group, the goal is clear, and the group accepts the leader's authority. Some situations are unfavorable to the leader on all dimensions. In these, the leader has poor interpersonal relations with the group, the goal is unclear, and the group fails to accept the leader's authority. Then, of course, there are situations that are partly favorable or partly unfavorable to the leader on the various dimensions. Fiedler proposes that task leaders are most effective in favorable or extremely unfavorable situations.

In positive situations where the leader has good interpersonal relations, a clear goal, and group acceptance, the leader can focus entirely on the task. Likewise, in very negative situations, the leader can do little to improve member perceptions, so the leader may as well storm forward on the task. People-oriented leadership is likely to be most effective in moderately good or bad situations where the leader has the most to gain by improving interpersonal relations, clarifying the goal, and building credibility with the group.

Let's consider two specific examples, one of a mostly favorable situation and one of a moderately unfavorable situation. Suppose you are leading a group of employees who are meeting to determine the recipient of a merit award. If you have good interpersonal relations with the group, if the criteria for determining the award are clearly spelled out, and if the group accepts your authority, you are likely to be highly effective by adopting a task-oriented style of leadership. The group will understand what it is supposed to do and will accept your directions in proceeding to accomplish the task. If, however, your interpersonal relations with two of the group's other four members has been shaky, the group is not sure how it is supposed to go about making the decision, and at least two members of the group are undecided about your ability to lead, a person-oriented style of leadership is necessary. Before the group can really begin to function with the task, you will need to build your interpersonal relations with at least two members of the group, work with them to clarify the goal, and engage in behaviors that will help build your credibility. So it isn't a matter of which style is always best; it is a matter of what kinds of circumstances are present.

PRACTICE IN

Assessing Your Leadership Style

JOURNAL ENTRY

Identify your leadership style. On what basis did you make this determination? Under what circumstances is your natural style most likely to be effective? Under what circumstances will you need to rely on someone else in the group to share in accomplishing leadership roles?

Preparing for Leadership

As you begin work in a group, you will find yourself in one of three situations in which you may wish to provide leadership: (1) You have been appointed or selected leader, (2) no one has been appointed or selected leader, or (3) another person has been appointed or selected leader but is not doing much leading. Regardless of the situation, the group will need leadership, and you may be in a position to provide it. As we have seen from our discussion of leadership styles, you may not be able to provide effective leadership if the group won't accept you. What can you do to earn group support for your leadership?

1. *Be knowledgeable about the particular group tasks.* Although the leader is not the primary information giver in a group, group members are more willing to follow when the leader appears to be well informed. The more knowledgeable you are, the better you will be able to analyze individual contributions.

2. *Work harder than anyone else in the group.* Leadership is often a question of setting an example. When a group sees a person who is willing to do more than his or her fair share for the good of the group, they are likely to support the person. Of course, such effort often requires a lot of personal sacrifice, but the person seeking to lead must be willing to pay the price.

3. *Be personally committed to the group goals and needs.* To gain and maintain leadership takes great commitment to the particular task. When you lose that sense of commitment, your leadership may wane and be transferred to others whose enthusiasm is more attuned to a new set of conditions.

4. *Be willing to be decisive at key moments in the discussion.* When leaders are unsure of themselves, their groups may ramble aimlessly. When leaders are unskilled at making decisions, their groups can become frustrated and short-tempered. Sometimes leaders must make decisions that will be resented; sometimes they must decide between competing ideas about courses of action. Any decisions that leaders make may cause conflict. Nevertheless, people who are unwilling or unable to be decisive are not going to maintain leadership for long.

5. *Interact freely with others in the group.* One way to show potential for leadership is to participate fully in group discussions. This does not mean that you should always dominate the discussion—but no one can know what you think, how you feel, or what insights you have unless you are willing to share your ideas in discussion. Too often people sit back silently, thinking, "If only they would call on me for leadership, I would do a really good job." Groups do not want unknown quantities. Perhaps by talking you run the risk of showing your lack of qualifications for leadership, but it is better to find out during the early stages of group work, before you try to gain leadership, whether you can talk sensibly and influence others.

6. *Develop skill in maintenance functions as well as in task functions.* Effective leaders make others in their groups feel good, contribute to group cohesiveness, and give credit where it is due. Although a group often has both a task leader and a maintenance leader, the overall leader is equally as likely as, if not more likely than, others to be the one who shows maintenance skills.

Analyzing Leadership

BY YOURSELF

1. What leadership traits do you believe you have?

2. What is your leadership style? Are you more of a task-oriented leader or a person-oriented leader? What are the strengths and weaknesses of your style?

3. Under which leadership style do you work best? Why?

Functions of Group Leadership

Becoming a leader and carrying out leadership are two different processes. Many people reach the top of the leadership pole only to slide slowly to oblivion. The effective leader prepares the meeting place, plans the agenda, orients group members, ensures that all group members have a chance to contribute, asks appropriate questions, and summarizes the discussion as needed.

PREPARING THE MEETING PLACE

We have already talked about the importance of a good work environment. If the environment is not good, you need to take responsibility for improving it. As leader, you are in charge of physical matters such as heat, light, and seating. Make sure the temperature of the room is comfortable. Make sure that lighting is adequate, and, most important, make sure the seating arrangements will promote spirited interaction.

PLANNING THE AGENDA

An *agenda* is an outline of the topics that need to be covered at a meeting. You may prepare the agenda yourself or in consultation with the group. When possible, the agenda should be in the hands of the group several days before the meeting. How much preparation any individual member will do is based on many factors, but unless an agenda is established beforehand, group members will not have an opportunity for careful preparation. Too often, when no agenda is planned, the group discussion is a haphazard affair, often frustrating and usually unsatisfying.

Figure 13.1

Agenda for discussion
group meeting

March 1, 1994

To: Campus commuter discussion group

From: Janelle Smith

Re: Agenda for discussion group meeting

Date: March 8, 1994

Place: Student Union, Conference Room A

Time: 3:00 P.M. (Please be prompt)

Please come prepared to discuss the following questions. Be sure to bring specific information you can contribute to the discussion of questions 1 through 5. We will consider question 6 on the basis of our resolution of the other questions.

Agenda for Group Discussion

Question: What should be done to integrate the campus commuter into the social, political, and extracurricular aspects of student life?

1. What percentage of the student body commute?
2. Why aren't commuters involved in social, political, and extracurricular activities?
3. What specific factors hinder their involvement?
4. What criteria should be used to test possible solutions to the problem?
5. What are some of the possible solutions to the problem?
6. What one solution or combination of solutions will work best to solve the problem?

What goes into the agenda? Usually included is a sketch of some of the things that need to be accomplished. In a problem-solving discussion the agenda should include a suggested procedure for handling the problem. In essence, the agenda comprises an outline form of the steps of problem solving discussed earlier in this chapter. Suppose that you are leading a group concerned with integrating the campus commuter into the social, political, and extracurricular aspects of student life. Figure 13.1 shows a satisfactory agenda for a group discussing the question "What should be done to integrate the campus commuter into the social, political, and extracurricular aspects of student life?"

Although the meeting is unlikely to follow the exact sequence of the agenda, group members understand that the agenda questions will need to be answered before the group has finished its work.

ORIENTING GROUP MEMBERS

At the beginning of the group's first meeting, you need to introduce the topic and establish procedures. In a newly formed group, commitment may be low for some members, expectations may be minimal, and the general attitude may be skeptical. People may be thinking, "We know that many group sessions are a waste of time, so we'll take a wait-and-see attitude." A good leader will start the group process by drawing a verbal contract and motivating members to live up to it. The leader will answer questions such as "Why are we here?" "Who got us together?" "What is our mission?" "To whom are we responsible?" "What kinds of responsibilities will each group member have?" "What rules or guidelines for behavior will the group follow?" and "How much will each member be expected to do?" Some of these questions will already have been discussed with individuals, but the first meeting gives the leader a chance to put everything together.

GIVING EVERYONE AN EQUAL OPPORTUNITY TO SPEAK

For the group process to work, group members need to be encouraged to express their ideas and feelings. Yet, without leader intervention, some people are likely to dominate and some people are likely to feel that they haven't been heard. For instance, in an eight-person group, left to its own devices, two or three people may tend to speak as much as the other five or six together; furthermore, one or two members may contribute little, if anything. At the beginning of a discussion, you must assume that every member of the group has something to contribute. You may have to hold in check those who tend to dominate, and you may have to work to draw reluctant members into the discussion.

Accomplishing this ideal balance is a real test of the gatekeeping skill of a leader. If ordinarily reluctant talkers are intimidated by a member of the group, they may become even more reluctant to participate. Thus you may have to clear the road for shy speakers. For example, when Dominique gives visual or verbal clues of her desire to speak, say something like, "Just a second, Lenny, I think Dominique has something she wants to say here." Then instead of "Dominique, do you have anything to say here?" you may be able to phrase a question that requires more than a "yes" or "no" answer, such as "Dominique, what do you think of the validity of this approach to combating crime?" When people contribute a few times, it builds up their confidence, which in turn makes it easier for them to respond later when they have more to say.

Similar tact is called for with overzealous speakers. If garrulous yet valuable members are constantly restrained, their value to the group may diminish. For example, Lenny, the most talkative member, may be talkative because he has done his homework—if you turn him off, the group's work will suffer.

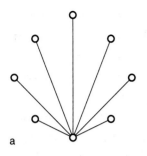

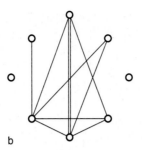

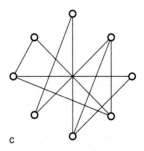

a   b   c

Figure 13.2

Three common patterns of group communication.

After he has finished talking, try statements such as "Lenny, that's a very valuable bit of material; let's see whether we can get some reactions from other members of the group on this issue." Notice that a statement of this kind does not stop him; it suggests that he should hold off for a while.

There are three common patterns of group communication, as depicted in Figure 13.2, in which the lines represent the flow of discussion among eight participants. Figure 13.2a shows a leader-dominated group. The lack of interaction often leads to a rigid, formal, and usually poor discussion. Figure 13.2b shows a more spontaneous group. Because three people dominate and two are not heard from, however, conclusions will not represent group thinking. Figure 13.2c shows something close to the ideal pattern. It illustrates a great deal of spontaneity, a total group representation, and—theoretically, at least—the greatest possibility for reliable conclusions.

ASKING APPROPRIATE QUESTIONS

Although the members of any group bring a variety of skills, information, and degrees of motivation to the group, they do not always operate at peak efficiency without help from the leader. Perhaps one of the most effective tools of leadership is the ability to question appropriately. This skill requires knowing when to ask questions and what kinds of questions to ask.

By and large, the leader should refrain from asking questions that can be answered "yes" or "no." To ask group members whether they are satisfied with a point that was just made will not lead very far, for after the "yes" or "no" answer you must either ask another question to draw people out or change the subject. The two most effective types of questions are those that call for supporting information and those that are completely open ended and give members complete freedom of response. For instance, rather than ask Bjorn whether he has had any professors who were particularly good lecturers, you could inquire, "Bjorn, what are some of the characteristics that made your favorite lecturers especially effective?"

● Perhaps one of the most effective tools of leadership is the ability to question appropriately—knowing when to ask questions and what kind of questions to ask.

Knowing when to ask questions is particularly important. Although we could list fifteen to twenty circumstances, let's focus on four essential purposes of questioning:

1. *To focus discussion.* Individual statements usually have a point; the point of each statement relates to a larger point being made; and the general discussion relates to an issue or to an agenda item. You can use questions to determine speakers' points or to determine the relationship of the points to the issue or agenda item. For instance, to relate a statement to the larger topic in a discussion of marijuana use, you might ask, "Are you saying that the instances of marijuana leading to hard-drug use don't indicate a direct causal relationship?" Or, in response to what has just been said, "How does that information relate to the point that Eva just made?" Or, to ask about an issue or an agenda item, "In what way does this information relate to whether or not marijuana is a health hazard?"

2. *To probe for information.* Many statements need to be developed, supported, or in some way dealt with. Yet often members of a group apparently ignore or accept a point without probing it. When the point seems important, the leader should do something with it. For example, to test the support for an assertion, you can say, "Where did you get that information, Miles?" or "That seems pretty important; what do we have that corroborates the point?" To test the strength of a point, you might ask, "Does that statement represent the thinking of the group?"

3. *To initiate discussion.* During a discussion there are times when lines of development are apparently ignored, when the group seems ready to agree before sufficient scrutiny of a point. At these times it is up to the leader to suggest a question for further discussion. For instance, "OK, we seem to have a pretty good grasp of the nature of the problem, but we haven't looked at any causes yet. What are some of the causes?"

4. *To deal with interpersonal problems that develop.* Sometimes the leader can use questions to help members ventilate personal feelings. For example, "Juan, I've heard you make some strong statements on this point. Would you care to share them with us?" At times a group may attack a person instead of the information that is being presented. Here you can say, "Ted isn't the issue here. Let's look at the merits of the information presented. Do we have any information that runs counter to this point?"

Questions by themselves are not going to make a discussion. In fact, too frequent use of questions can hurt discussion. The effective leader therefore uses questions sparingly but incisively.

SUMMARIZING WHEN NECESSARY

Often a group talks for a considerable time, then takes a vote on how the members feel about the subject. A consensus is more likely to develop if the group moves in an orderly manner toward intermediate conclusions represented by summary statements that express the group's agreement. For instance, on the question "What should be done to lower the amount of employee theft?" the group should reach agreement on each of the following questions:

1. What is the problem?

2. What are the symptoms of the problem? (Draw intermediate conclusions; ask whether the group agrees.)

3. What are the causes? (Draw an intermediate conclusion on each cause separately or after all causes have been considered; ask whether the group agrees.)

4. What criteria should be used to test the solutions?

5. What is one criterion? (Draw conclusions about each criterion.)

6. What are some of the possible solutions? (Determine whether all worthwhile solutions have been brought up.)

7. How does each of the solutions meet the criteria? (Discuss each and draw conclusions about each; ask whether the group agrees.)

8. Which solution best meets the criteria? (The answer to this final question concludes the discussion; ask whether all agree.)

During the discussion, the group might draw six, eight, ten, or even fifteen conclusions before it is able to arrive at the answer to the topic question. The point is that the group is far more likely to agree on the final conclusion if each of the subordinate questions has been answered to the satisfaction of the entire group.

It is up to the leader to point out intermediate conclusions by summarizing what has been said and seeking consensus. Everyone in the group should realize when the group has arrived at some decision. If left to its own devices, a group may discuss a point for a while and then move on to another point before a conclusion is drawn. The leader must sense when enough has been said to reach a consensus. Then the leader must phrase the conclusion, subject it to testing, and move on to another area. Here are examples of phrases that can be used during the discussion:

"I think most of us are stating the same points. Are we really in agreement that . . ." (State the conclusion.)

"We've been discussing this for a while, and I think I sense an agreement. Let me state it, and then we'll see whether it does summarize the group's feeling." (State the conclusion.)

"Now we're getting into another area. Let's make sure that we are really agreed on the point we've just finished." (State the conclusion.)

"Are we ready to summarize our feelings on this point?" (State the conclusion.)

Figure 13.3

Leadership analysis form

Leadership Analysis					
For each of the following questions, rate the leadership on a 1 to 5 basis: 1, high; 2, good; 3, average; 4, fair; 5, poor.					
Leadership Traits:	1	2	3	4	5
Has sufficient understanding?					
Stimulates group?					
Has the respect of the group?					
Leadership Methods:	1	2	3	4	5
Establishes good working climate?					
Has an agenda?					
Promotes systematic problem solving?					
Directs the flow of discussion?					
Encourages balanced participation?					
Asks good questions?					
Clarifies and crystallizes ideas?					
Summarizes frequently?					
Maintains necessary control?					
Brings the discussion to a satisfactory close?					

Analysis: Write a short profile of this person's leadership based on the above checklist. Consider the person's relative effectiveness in helping the group achieve its goal.

PRACTICE IN

Analyzing Leadership

IN GROUPS

Each group is given or selects a task that requires some research. In class each group discusses their topic for approximately thirty to forty minutes. While group A holds its discussion, members of group B observe and, after the discussion, analyze the proceedings. Leadership can be analyzed by using Figure 13.3. In the next class period group B discusses and group A observes and critiques. Some sample questions for discussion are "What should be done to improve parking (advising, registration) on campus?" "What should be done to increase the participation of minorities in college or university teaching (governance, administration)?"

●◆■ Summary

Leadership means exerting influence to accomplish a goal. Although leaders may show greater degrees of ability, sociability, motivation, and communication skills than others in the group, the presence of such traits does not guarantee that you will lead effectively.

How well you lead may depend on your style and how you put it into operation. Some leaders adopt the task-oriented style, focusing on what needs to be done and how to do it; others adopt the person-oriented style, focusing on interpersonal relationships of group members. As Fiedler's work has shown, how a leader performs depends on the interaction of task structure, leader-member relations, and position power. If you hope to earn the support of group members for leadership, you will want to be knowledgeable about the task, work harder than others in the group, be personally committed to group goals and needs, be willing to be decisive, interact freely with others in the group, and develop skill in maintenance and task functions.

Leaders have several specific functions. To lead a group well, you must prepare the meeting place, plan an agenda, introduce the topic and establish procedures, ensure everyone has an equal opportunity to speak, ask appropriate questions, and summarize as needed.

●◆■ Featured Reading

Principle-Centered Leadership
Stephen R. Covey
(New York: Simon & Schuster, 1992)

In this book Stephen Covey adapts his seven habits of highly effective people to leadership. He believes that highly effective leadership is the result of inner discipline. He argues that a leader's success comes from being neither dependent on others nor completely independent, but rather from being physically, emotionally, and intellectually interdependent. Principle-centered leadership is a long-term, inside-out approach to developing people and organizations. His insights and guidelines can help you apply these principles both at work and at home. His insights and guidelines can help you apply these principles both at work and at home. He focuses on how to increase quality and productivity, and moreover on how to appreciate the importance of building personal and professional relationships in order to enjoy a more balanced, more rewarding, and more effective life.

He begins by identifying key characteristics of principle-centered leaders; those who are continual learners, are service oriented, radiate positive energy, believe in other people, lead balanced lives, see life as an adventure, are synergistic, and exercise for self-renewal.

He focuses on resolving a number of dilemmas including: how to unleash the creativity, talent, and energy of a work force whose jobs neither require nor reward such resources; how to create team spirit and harmony among people and departments that have been attacking and criticizing each other; how to have a culture characterized by change, flexibility, and continuous improvement and still maintain a sense of stability and security; and how to maintain control yet give people the freedom and autonomy they need to be effective and fulfilled in their work.

Covey's books have deservedly achieved tremendous popularity. They are easy to read and motivating.

●◆■ **Notes**

1. See Bernard M. Bass, *Bass and Stogdill's Handbook of Leadership: Theory, Research, and Managerial Applications,* 3rd ed. (New York: The Free Press, 1990), pp. 19–20. He focuses on the idea that leaders are agents of change.

2. Ibid. See Chapter 5 for a review of studies up to 1970 and subsequent chapters for analysis of studies through the 1980s.

3. Marvin E. Shaw, *Group Dynamics: The Psychology of Small Group Behavior,* 3rd ed. (New York: McGraw-Hill, 1981), p. 325.

4. Ralph White and Ronald Lippitt, "Leader Behavior and Member Reaction in Three 'Social Climates,'" in Dorwin Cartwright and Alvin Zander, eds., *Group Dynamics,* 3rd ed. (New York: Harper & Row, 1968), p. 334. The point that groups are largely unproductive under laissez-faire leadership is reinforced by Bass, *Handbook of Leadership,* p. 559.

5. Fred E. Fiedler, *A Theory of Leadership Effectiveness* (New York: McGraw-Hill, 1967).

CHAPTER FOURTEEN

Job Interviewing

OBJECTIVES

After you have read this chapter, you should be able to define and/or explain:

Methods of interviewing

Open and closed, neutral and leading, and primary and secondary questions

Procedures for conducting an informative interview

Procedures used by job interviewers

Writing a résumé

How to participate in a job interview

"Morgan Hoffman, how are you? I'm Penny Sanchez, assistant personnel director here at Powell's. I have already looked at your résumé, but to get us started, tell me a little about yourself—you know, those kinds of things that one can't really understand simply by reading a résumé."

So begins Morgan's interview for a position in the Marketing Division of Powell Enterprises. Applicants for nearly every job in nearly any field will go through an interview, and it is often traumatic, especially for those who are experiencing it for the very first time. At its worst an interview can be a waste of time for everyone; at its best an interview can reveal vital information about an applicant, as well as allow the applicant to judge the suitability of the position, the company, and the tasks that will be performed. A skillfully conducted interview can help interviewers determine the applicants' specific abilities, ambitions, energy, ability to communicate, knowledge and intelligence, and integrity. Moreover, it can help the interviewees show their strengths in these same areas.

The job interview is a special type of interpersonal situation with specific demands. Let's first discuss the types of questions used in an interview and then consider some of the procedures and methods that an interviewer uses in conducting an interview and that an interviewee uses in taking part in one.

Questions in Interviewing

An interview differs from other forms of interpersonal communication in its reliance on the asking and answering of questions. Although we deal here specifically with questions in the interview situation, a knowledge of good question construction can be applied to any interpersonal encounter. Questions may be phrased as open or closed, neutral or leading, primary or secondary.

OPEN VERSUS CLOSED QUESTIONS

Open questions are broad-based questions that ask the interviewee to provide whatever information he or she wishes to answer the questions. Open questions range from those with virtually no restrictions, such as "What can you tell me about yourself?" to those that give some direction, such as "What do you believe has prepared you for this job?" Interviewers ask open questions to encourage the person to talk, allowing the interviewer an opportunity to listen and to observe. Through the open question the interviewer finds out about the person's perspectives, values, and goals. Keep in mind, however, that open questions take time to answer, which means interviewers can lose sight of their original purpose if they are not careful.[1]

By contrast, *closed questions* are narrow-focus questions that require very brief answers. Closed questions range from those that can be answered "yes" or "no," such as "Have you had a course in marketing?" to those that require only a short answer, such as "How many restaurants have you worked in?" By asking closed questions, interviewers can control the interview; moreover, they can obtain large amounts of information in a short time. However, the closed question seldom enables the interviewer to know why a person gave a certain response, nor is the closed question likely to yield much voluntary information.

Which type of question should you use? The answer depends on what kinds of material you are seeking and how much time you have for the interview. Both kinds of questions are used in most information and employment interviews.[2]

NEUTRAL VERSUS LEADING QUESTIONS

Neutral questions are questions to which the person is free to give an answer without direction from the interviewer. An example of a neutral question would be "How do you like your new job?" Nothing about the wording of the question gives the respondent any indication of how the question should be answered.

By contrast, *leading questions* are questions phrased in a way that suggests the interviewer has a preferred answer. For instance, "You don't like the new job, do you?" is a leading question. In the majority of interviewing situations, leading questions are inappropriate because they try to force the person in one direction and tend to make the person defensive.

PRIMARY VERSUS FOLLOW-UP QUESTIONS

Primary questions are questions the interviewer plans ahead of time. Primary questions serve as the main points for the interview outline, a plan of the major questions and subquestions prepared for an interview. Primary questions may be open or closed, depending on the kind of information you want; in addition, they may be neutral or leading. As you plan an interview, be sure to include enough primary questions that you will obtain all the information you want.

Follow-up questions are designed to pursue the answers given to primary questions. Follow-up questions may be planned ahead if you can anticipate possible interviewee answers. More often than not, however, follow-up questions are composed as the interview goes along. To come up with well-worded follow-up questions that stimulate the interviewee to provide the information you want, you need to pay close attention to what the interviewee is saying. Some follow-up questions encourage the person to continue ("And then?" "Is there more?"); some probe into what the person has said ("What does 'frequently' mean?" "What were you thinking at the time?"); and some plumb the feelings of the person ("How did it feel to get the prize?" "Were you worried when you didn't find her?").

The major purpose of follow-up questions is to motivate a person to enlarge on an answer. Such follow-up questions are often necessary because interviewees' answers may be incomplete or vague, because they may not really understand how much detail you are looking for, or occasionally because they may purposely be trying to be evasive.

Your effectiveness with follow-up questions may well depend on your interpersonal skill in asking them. Because probing questions can alienate the interviewee (especially when the questions are perceived as threatening), such in-depth probes work best after you have gained the confidence of the interviewee and when the questions are asked within the atmosphere of a positive interpersonal climate. We discuss these aspects of interviewing in the next section.

Identifying and Phrasing Questions

BY YOURSELF

1. Indicate which of the following are O (open questions) and which are C (closed questions). If the question is open, write a closed question seeking similar information; if the question is closed, write an open question (make sure that all your write-in questions are neutral rather than leading).

_____ a. What makes you think that Conti will be appointed?
_____ b. How many steps are there in getting a book into print?
_____ c. Will you try out for cheerleading?
_____ d. What is your opinion about guidelines for promotion?
_____ e. How do you think the school should make its budgetary decisions?

Answers: a. O; b. C; c. C; d. O; e. O

2. Change the following leading questions to neutral questions:

a. Doesn't it depress you to see so many patients who never get well?
b. After what Angeline did, I bet you are really out to get her, aren't you?
c. Wouldn't you be upset about going to Toronto if you were traded?
d. Aren't you really excited about your promotion?
e. After the way he acted, I'll bet you're going to chew him out the next time you see him, aren't you?

3. You are interviewing your professor for an article for the school paper. To the question "What motivated you to choose college teaching as a career?" the professor answers, "It seemed to me like a really good job." Write three well-phrased follow-up questions you would be likely to ask.

a.
b.
c.

Responsibilities of the Interviewer

As an interviewer you represent the link between a job applicant and the company. Much of the applicant's impression of the company will depend on his or her impression of you, so you will want to be able to provide answers to questions that applicants may have about your company. In addition to the obvious desire for salary information, applicants may also seek information about opportunities for advancement, influences of personal ideas on company policy, company attitudes toward personal life and life-style, working conditions, and so forth. Moreover, you are primarily responsible for determining whether this person will be considered for the position available and whether this person will be kept in the running for possible future company employment.

DETERMINING THE PROCEDURE

The most satisfactory employment interview is probably a highly to moderately structured one. In the unstructured interview the interviewer tends to talk more and to make decisions based on less valid data than in the structured interview.[3] Especially if you are screening a large number of applicants, you want to make sure that all applicants have been asked the same questions and that the questions cover subjects that will most reveal the kind of information you will need to make a reasonable decision.

Before the time scheduled for the interview, become familiar with all available data about the applicant: application form, résumé, letters of recommendation, and test scores if available. Such written data will help determine some of the questions you will want to ask.

CONDUCTING THE INTERVIEW

A well-planned interview has an opening, a body, and a closing.

● ● **The Opening** Open the interview by greeting the applicant warmly by name, by shaking his or her hand, and by introducing yourself so that he or she can use your name. Be open with applicants. If you plan either to take notes or to record the interview, let the applicants know why you are doing so.

A major concern of many interviewers is whether to begin with warm-up questions to help establish rapport or whether to move right into the question schedule. A good interviewer senses the nature of the situation and tries to use a method that is most likely to encourage applicants to talk and provide adequate answers. Although warm-up questions may be helpful, most applicants are ready to get down to business immediately, in which case warm-up questions may be misinterpreted.[4] Applicants may wonder about the motivation for such questions, and the questions may make them even more nervous. Unless you have good reason for proceeding differently, it

● Open the interview by greeting the applicant warmly by name, by shaking his or her hand, and by introducing yourself so he or she can use your name.

seems advisable to move into the question schedule right away in as warm and friendly a manner as possible.

The Body The body of the interview consists of the questions you are planning to ask. Let's begin with some guidelines for presenting yourself and your questions.

1. *Be careful of your own presentation.* Talk loudly enough to be heard. Try to be spontaneous. Interviewees do not respond well to obviously memorized questions fired in machine-gun fashion. Be sensitive to your own nonverbal communication. Interviewees look for signs of disapproval—any inadvertent looks or unusual changes in quality or rhythm of your speech may give a false impression. Remember, too, that you can load a question by expressing it in a particular tone of voice.

2. *Do not waste time.* You have available a wide variety of information about the candidates from their résumés, application forms, and so on. Ask questions about things you already know only if you have some special reason for doing so. For instance, if an applicant indicates employment with a particular organization but does not give any detailed account of responsibilities, questions relating to that employment period would be appropriate.

3. *Avoid trick or loaded questions.* Applicants are always leery of questions that may be designed to make them look bad. Moreover, if candidates believe that you are trying to trick them, the suspicion may provoke a competitive rather than a positive atmosphere. Anything that serves to limit the applicant's responsiveness will harm the interview by limiting the information needed to get a fair impression.

4. *Avoid questions that violate fair employment practice legislation.* In 1964 Congress created the Equal Employment Opportunity Commission (EEOC). In subsequent years EEOC has written detailed guidelines that spell out the kinds of questions that are lawful and those that are unlawful. For example, questions directed to a woman about her plans for marriage or, if she is married, about her plans to have children are not only irrelevant but illegal. Actually, any questions about marital status, family, physical characteristics, age, education, arrests, or social security are illegal unless this information is deemed to be a bona fide occupational qualification. By and large, the interview should focus on questions that are relevant to the person's capabilities in fulfilling the job requirements.

5. *Give the applicant an opportunity to ask questions.* Usually, near the end of the interview, you should take the time to ask whether the applicant has any questions.

Now let's look at some of the specific questions that interviewers usually ask. The following list was compiled from a variety of sources and is only representative, not exhaustive. It sets no limitations on your own creativity but is intended to suggest the kinds of questions you may wish to ask. Notice that it focuses questions on personal interests, educational background, and job-related attitudes, goals, and skills—three areas of information that are relevant to making a decision on a candidate. You might use this as a starter list or as a checklist for your own wording of questions. Notice that some questions are open-ended and some are closed, but none is a "yes" or "no" question.

School:

How did you select the school you attended?

How did you determine your major?

What extracurricular activities did you engage in at school?

In what ways does your transcript reflect your ability?

How were you able to help with your college expenses?

Personal:

What are your hobbies?

How do you work under pressure?

At what age did you begin supporting yourself?

What causes you to lose your temper?

What are your major strengths? weaknesses?

What do you do to stay in good physical condition?

What kind of reading do you like to do?

Who has had the greatest influence on your life?

What have you done that shows your creativity?

Position:

What kind of position are you looking for?

What do you know about the company?

Under what conditions will you be willing to relocate?

Why do you think you would like to work for us?

What do you hope to accomplish?

What qualifications do you have that make you feel you would be beneficial to us?

How do you feel about traveling?

What part of the country would you like to settle in?

With what kind of people do you enjoy interacting?

What do you regard as an equitable salary for a person with your qualifications?

What new skills would you like to learn?

What are your professional goals?

How would you proceed if you were in charge of hiring?

What are your most important criteria for determining whether you will accept a position?

● ●   **The Closing**   Always, toward the end of the interview, tell the applicant what will happen next. Explain the procedures for making the decision. Answer any questions about who has the authority for the hiring decision, when the decision will be made, and how applicants will be notified. Then close the interview in a courteous, neutral manner. Avoid building up false hopes or seeming to discourage any given applicant.

Responsibilities of the Job Applicant

Interviews are an important part of the process of seeking employment. Even for part-time and temporary jobs you will benefit if you approach the interviewing process seriously and systematically. There is no point in applying for positions that you have no intention of taking or that are obviously outside your area of expertise; it may seem a good idea to get interviewing experience, but you are wasting your time and the interviewer's.

When you are granted an employment interview, remember that all you have to sell is yourself and your qualifications. You will recall from our discussion of self-presentation how much your nonverbal behavior contributes to the impression you make. You want to show yourself in the best possible light. Take care with your appearance; if you want a particular job, dress in a way that is acceptable to the person or organization that may—or may not—hire you.

PREPARING FOR THE INTERVIEW

Of course, you'll want to be fully prepared for the interview. Two important tasks you must complete before the interview itself are writing the cover letter and writing the résumé, for although they do not get you jobs, "they advertise you for interviews."[5]

● ●   **Cover Letter**   The cover letter is a short, well-written letter expressing your interest in a particular position. Always address the letter to the person with the authority to hire you (and not, for example, to the personnel department). If you do not already have the appropriate person's name, you can probably obtain it by telephoning the company. Because you are trying to stimulate the reader's interest in you, the applicant, take care that your cover letter does not read like a form letter. The cover letter should include the following elements: where you found out about the position, your reason for being interested in this company, your main qualifications (summary of a few key points), how you fit the requirements for the job, items of special interest about you that would relate to your potential for the job, and a request for an interview. Keep the letter to one page if possible, and include a résumé with the letter.

● ● **Résumé** Although there is no universal format for résumé writing, there is some agreement on what should be included and excluded.[6] In writing your résumé you should consider including the following information cast in a form that increases the likelihood of your being asked to interview:

1. *Contact information:* Your name, address, and telephone numbers at which you can be reached.

2. *Job objective:* A one-sentence objective focusing on your specific area(s) of expertise.

3. *Employment history:* Paid and nonpaid experiences, beginning with the most recent.

4. *Education:* Degrees, schools, and years, with focus on courses that are most directly related to the job.

5. *Military experience:* Include rank and service, and achievements, skills, and abilities.

6. *Professional affiliations:* Memberships, offices held.

7. *Community involvement:* Offices, organizations, dates.

8. *Special skills:* Foreign languages, computers.

9. *Interests and activities:* Only those that are related to your objective.

10. *References:* Include only a statement that references are available on request.

Notice that the list does not include personal information such as height, weight, age, sex, marital status, health, race, religion, or political affiliation, nor does it include any reference to salary. Also notice that although you need not include references, you should already have the permission of people whom you will use as references.

In addition, you should consider what format your résumé will follow— how wide your margins will be, how elements will be spaced and indented, and so on. The résumé should be no more than three pages, preferably one or two, because your goal is to make an immediate impact. Moreover, you want to make the résumé neat, proofread it carefully, and reproduce it on decent quality paper. Try to determine what to include from the employer's point of view. What you have to present is something that can help an employer solve his or her problems. Think in terms of what the company needs, not personal characteristics of your own that are irrelevant to the job. Think creatively, but foremost, write your résumé from an ethical position. You want to emphasize your strengths, but you want to avoid exaggerating facts, a procedure that is both deceptive and unethical. Figure 14.1 shows a sample résumé of a person who has just graduated from college.

Rehearsing the Interview For most of us, job interviews are at least somewhat stressful. To help prepare yourself so that you can perform at your best, it is a good idea to give yourself a practice interview session. Try to anticipate some of the questions you will be asked and think carefully about your answers. You need not write out or say answers aloud; before the actual interview, however, you can anticipate key questions and give careful thought to subjects such as your salary expectations, your possible contributions to the company, and your special skills.

THE INTERVIEW

You are likely to make a favorable impression in your interview if you follow these guidelines.

1. *Do your homework.* Know about the company's services, products, ownership, and financial health. Knowing about a company shows your interest in that company and usually impresses the interviewer. Moreover, you'll be in a better position to address how you can contribute to the company's mission.

2. *Be prompt.* The interview is the company's only clue to your work behavior. If you are late for such an important event, the interviewer may well conclude that you are likely to be late for work. Give yourself plenty of time in travel to cover any possible traffic problems.

3. *Be alert and look at the interviewer.* Remember that your nonverbal communication tells a lot about you. Company representatives are likely to consider eye contact and posture as clues to your self-confidence.

4. *Give yourself time to think.* If the interviewer asks you a question that you had not anticipated, give yourself time to think before you answer. It is better to pause and think than to give a hasty answer that may cost you the job. If you do not understand the question, paraphrase it before you attempt to answer.

Figure 14.1

Sample résumé

JOYCE M. TURNER

Temporary Address: Permanent Address:

2326 Tower Avenue   914 Market Street
Cincinnati, Ohio 45220   Columbus, Ohio 43217
513-861-2497   614-662-5931

PROFESSIONAL   A challenging position in sales
OBJECTIVE   or public relations with a
                  medium-sized corporation. Geo-
                  graphical preference for the
                  Midwest.

EXPERIENCE

1994   Internship WLW-TV. Received 3
                  credit hours for working 10
                  hours per week spring quarter.
                  Worked with sales force selling
                  commercial time.

1993   Sales. Lazarus Department Store.
                  Full-time summer and Christmas
                  vacation; part-time during
                  school year. Experience in
                  clothing, appliances, and
                  jewelry.

EDUCATION

1990-1994   University of Cincinnati, Cin-
                  cinnati, Ohio. Candidate for
                  B.A. degree in June 1994. Major
                  in Communication with minor in
                  Business (Marketing). Overall
                  grade point average of 3.3.

ACTIVITIES   Forensics. Represented the Uni-
                  versity of Cincinnati at five
                  individual events tournaments
                  over a two-year period. Won
                  first place in extemporaneous
                  speaking at Ohio Forensic Cham-
                  pionships in 1993.
                  President, Women in Communica-
                  tion, an organization for women
                  who aspire toward careers in
                  communication.

INTERESTS   Sports (tennis and racquetball);
                  travel.

REFERENCES   On request

● Show enthusiasm for the job. The interviewer is likely to reason that if you are not enthusiastic during an interview, then you may not be the person for the job.

5. *Ask questions about the type of work you will be doing.* The interview is your chance to find out if you would enjoy working for this company. You might ask the interviewer to describe a typical workday for the person who will get the job. If the interview is conducted at the company offices, you might ask to see where you would be working.

6. *Show enthusiasm for the job.* The interviewer is likely to reason that if you are not enthusiastic during an interview, you may not be the person for the job. Employers look for and expect applicants look and sound interested.

7. *Do not engage in long discussions on salary.* If the company representative tries to pin you down, ask, "What do you normally pay someone with my experience and education for this level position?" Such a question allows you to get an idea of what the salary will be without committing yourself to a figure first.

8. *Do not harp on benefits.* Detailed questions about benefits are more appropriate after the company has made you an offer.

Employment Interviewing

BY YOURSELF

Prepare a cover letter and a résumé for a position you might seek in the foreseeable future.

IN PAIRS

Select a partner in class and interview each other for a particular job for which the résumé was prepared. Try to follow the guidelines suggested for employment interviewing discussed in this section.

JOURNAL ENTRY

Think of a job interview that you have had. What parts of the interview were most difficult for you? Why? If you were to engage in that same interview again, what would you do differently?

If you have never had a job interview, talk with someone who has. Find out what parts of the interview were most difficult for him or her, and why.

In light of this information, where are you likely to put your greatest emphasis in preparation for your next job interview?

● ◆ ■ Summary

Interviewing can be a productive way to obtain information from an expert for a paper, an article, or a speech.

The key skill of interviewing is using questions effectively. Open questions allow for flexible responses; closed questions require very brief answers. Primary questions stimulate response; follow-up questions stimulate additional information. Neutral questions allow the respondent free choice; leading questions require the person to answer in a particular way.

Job interviews are a specific type of communication setting with particular demands on both interviewer and interviewee.

When you interview a prospective applicant for a job, structure your interview carefully to elicit maximal information about the candidate. Before the interview starts, become familiar with the data contained in the interviewee's application form, résumé, letters of recommendation, and test scores if available. Be careful how you present yourself, do not waste time, avoid loaded questions, do not ask questions that violate fair employment practice legislation, and give the applicant an opportunity to ask questions. At the end of the interview explain to the applicant what will happen next in the process.

Before being interviewed for a job, take the time to learn about the company and prepare an appropriate cover letter and résumé that are designed to motivate an employer to interview you. For the interview itself you should be prompt, be alert and look directly at the interviewer, give yourself time to think before answering difficult questions, ask intelligent questions about the company and the job, and show enthusiasm for the position.

●◆■ **Featured Reading**

What Color Is Your Parachute? A Practical Manual for Job-Hunters and Career-Changers
Richard Nelson Bolles
(Berkeley, Calif.: Ten Speed Press, 1994)

What Color Is Your Parachute? is a book that addresses the reality of job hunting and career planning. Hunting for jobs or trying to change careers is not fun. Based on a summary of the research that has been done on successful versus unsuccessful job hunters, the book dispels several myths and reveals that most jobs, and the best jobs, are not gained through answering classified ads or by sending out random résumés. Richard Bolles explains that successful job hunters take advantage of the contacts they have that can help them get an interview with the person in charge of hiring.

Bolles explains that unsuccessful job hunters or career changers are often crushed when they discover how much power is in the hands of others, whereas successful job hunters or career changers see this reality but then ask "What is within my power?" The book emphasizes what you can do about the parts of the job search that are within your power.

Bolles also emphasizes the importance of enthusiasm in people making a job search. Effective job hunting is based on having a clear goal. People who know what they want are more likely to succeed than those who are merely going through the motions of looking for a job.

Once you know what you want to do and where you'd like to do it, you must get to the right person in the organization—the person who has the power to hire you. Bolles identifies strategies for locating this person and explains the value of networking. Because so much is at stake in the interview, a section of the book is devoted to preparing for the interview and how to act during the interview. Although interviewers may have a long list of questions to ask, Bolles argues, they are really looking for answers to just four questions: (1) Why are you here? (2) What can you do for the company? (3) What kind of person are you? (4) Can we afford you?

This highly practical and realistic book has become the standard in the field. First published in 1970, it has been updated every year since 1975. It has rightfully earned a reputation as a must-read classic for job seekers.

●◆■ Notes

1. Craig D. Tengler and Frederic M. Jablin, "Effects of Question Type, Orientation, and Sequencing in the Employment Screening Interview," *Communication Monographs* 50 (September 1983): 261.

2. For more information on asking questions, see Charles J. Stewart and William B. Cash, *Interviewing: Principles and Practices,* 6th ed. (Dubuque, Iowa: Wm. C. Brown, 1991).

3. Richard D. Arvey and James E. Campion, "The Employment Interview: A Summary and Review of Recent Research," *Personnel Psychology* 35 (1982): 281–321.

4. John W. Cogger, "Are You a Skilled Interviewer?" *Personnel Journal* 61 (1982): 842–843.

5. Ronald L. Krannich and William J. Banis, *High Impact Résumés and Letters,* 4th ed. (Woodbridge, Va.: Impact Publications, 1990), p. 21.

6. In addition to the sources already mentioned, you can find up-to-date copies of many books on résumés and letters at most bookstores, including Adele Lewis and Gary Joseph Grappo, *Better Résumés,* 4th ed. (New York: Barrons Educational Series, Inc., 1993).

Appendix A Glossary of Basic Communication Skills

SKILL	USE	PROCEDURE	EXAMPLE
Appropriateness (pp. 91–96) Using language that adapts to a specific person or persons and the context of the conversation.	To increase interaction effectiveness.	1. Assess whether the word or phrase used is less appropriate than it should be. 2. Pause to mentally brainstorm alternatives. 3. Select a more appropriate word.	When talking to a minister, Jamie thinks, "I just feel so bummed out," but says, "I just feel so depressed lately."
Asking for Criticism (Feedback) (pp. 252–253, 255) Asking others for their reaction to you or your behavior.	To get information that will help you understand yourself and your effect on others.	1. Ask to avoid surprises. 2. Think of criticism as in your best interest. 3. Outline the kind of criticism you are seeking. 4. Ask only when you want an honest response. 5. Avoid verbal/nonverbal contradictions. 6. Give reinforcement to those who take requests seriously. 7. Paraphrase what you hear.	Lucy asks, "Tim, when I talk with the boss, do I sound defensive?" Tim replies, "I think so—your voice gets sharp and you really look nervous." "Thanks for verifying that for me, Tim."

SKILL	USE	PROCEDURE	EXAMPLE
Assertiveness (pp. 276–282, 283) Standing up for ourselves and doing so in interpersonally effective ways that describe our feelings honestly and exercise our personal rights while respecting the rights of others.	To show clearly what you think or feel.	1. Identify what you are thinking or feeling. 2. Analyze the cause of these feelings. 3. Choose the appropriate skills necessary to communicate these feelings, as well as any outcome you desire. 4. Communicate these feelings to the appropriate person. Remember to own your feelings.	When Gavin believes that he is being unjustly charged, he says, "I have never been charged for a refill on iced tea before—has there been a change in policy?"
Attending (pp. 206–210, 213) The perceptual process of selecting specific stimuli that we have heard.	To focus your listening.	1. Get ready to listen. 2. Analyze and, if possible, eliminate physical impediments. 3. Make the shift from speaker to listener a complete one. 4. Hear a person out before you react. 5. Adjust your attention to the listening goals of the situation.	As Amanda perceives that she needs to pay attention to what Yvonne is saying, she turns down the radio and focuses her entire attention on Yvonne's words.
Crediting Others (pp. 179–180, 182) Verbally identifying the source of ideas you are using.	To give credit to others in order to confirm them, avoid possible hard feelings, and clarify the source.	Include the names of sources of ideas.	"We've got to make some changes in our course offerings. Laura suggested that we offer a course in attitude change, and I agree."
Dating Generalizations (pp. 85–86, 87) Including a specific time referent that indicates when a fact was true.	To avoid the pitfalls of language that allow you to speak of a dynamic world in static terms.	1. Before you make a statement, consider when the observation was true. 2. If not based on present information, include when it was true.	When Jake says, "How good a hitter is Steve?" Mark replies by dating his evaluation: "When I worked with him two years ago, he couldn't hit the curve."
Describing Feelings (pp. 191–196, 198) Putting emotional state into words.	For self-disclosure; to teach people how to treat you.	1. Identify the feeling you are having specifically, for example, hate, anger, joy. 2. Put the feeling into words. 3. Indicate what has triggered the feeling. 4. Own your feeling.	"I'm depressed and discouraged because I didn't get the job" or "I'm feeling very warm and loving toward you right now because of the way you stood up for me when I was being put down by Leah."

SKILL	USE	PROCEDURE	EXAMPLE
Descriptive Speaking (pp. 158–159) Stating what you see or hear in objective language.	To create or promote a supportive climate.	1. Consider what you are about to say. 2. Consider whether it contains words or phrases that indicate or imply evaluation. 3. Recast the sentence to eliminate evaluation.	Instead of saying "That was a dumb thing you said to Marge," say "You told Marge that she could move in with us. Had you thought of how we would set up sleeping arrangements if she agreed to do it?"
Empathizing (pp. 233–236, 239) Being able to detect and identify the immediate affective state of another. Responding in an appropriate manner.	To create or to promote a supportive climate.	1. Consider both verbal and nonverbal messages. 2. Adopt an attitude of caring. 3. Try to recall or imagine what you would feel like under those same circumstances. 4. Speculate on the emotional state of the person. 5. Respond with words that indicate your sensitivity to those feelings.	When Jerry says, "I really feel embarrassed about wearing braces in college," Mary smiles ruefully and replies, "Yeah, it makes you feel like a little kid, doesn't it? I remember the things I had to put up with when I wore braces."
Equality (pp. 159–160) Seeing others as worthwhile as oneself.	To create or promote a supportive climate.	1. Consider what you are about to say. 2. Consider whether it contains words or phrases that indicate or imply that you are in some way superior to the receiver. 3. If so, recast the sentence to alter the tone.	Instead of saying, "As you gain maturity, you'll learn to cope with these situations," say, "That was a difficult one. But handling difficult ones helps you gain experience—and we all need experience to help us with special cases."
Evaluating (Critical Listening) (pp. 220–225) Analyzing what has been understood.	To determine how truthful, authentic, or believable we judge the meaning we have received to be.	1. Question whether the inference is supported with meaningful factual statements. 2. Question whether the stated or implied relevance between the support and the inference makes sense. 3. Question whether there is any other known information that lessens the quality of the inference.	When Julius says, "Fernando, you'll have to get more signs up if you are going to have any chance to get elected," Fernando evaluates the implied connection between the number of signs posted and his chances of getting elected.

SKILL	USE	PROCEDURE	EXAMPLE
Eye Contact (pp. 105–106, 107) Looking directly at people while you are talking with them.	To strengthen the sense of interaction.	1. Consciously look at the face of another while you are talking. 2. If your eyes drift away, try to bring them back.	[Not applicable]
Giving Constructive Criticism (pp. 253–256) Evaluation of behavior given to help a person identify or correct a fault.	To help people see themselves as others see them.	1. Make sure the person is interested in hearing criticism. 2. Describe the person's behavior accurately. 3. Precede negative statements with positive ones if possible. 4. Be specific. 5. Consider recent behavior. 6. Consider behavior that can be changed. 7. Include guidelines for improvement.	Carol says, "Bob, I've noticed something about your behavior with Jenny. Would you like to hear it?" After Bob assures her that he would, she continues. "Well, the last few times we've all been together, whenever Jenny starts to relate an experience, you interrupt her and finish telling the story."
Indexing Generalizations (pp. 86–88) Mentally or verbally accounting for individual differences.	To avoid "allness" in speaking.	1. Before you make a statement, consider whether it pertains to a specific object, person, or place. 2. If you use a generalization, inform the listener that it is not necessarily accurate.	"He's a politician and I don't trust him, although he may be different from most politicians I know."
Interpreting (pp. 248–249, 251) Attempting to point out an alternative or hidden meaning to an event.	To help a person see the possible meanings of words, actions, and events.	1. Listen carefully to what the person is saying. 2. Phrase an alternative to the person's interpretation—one that is intended to help the person see that other interpretations are possible. 3. When appropriate, preface the interpretation with a supportive statement.	Pam says, "Sue must really be angry with me. Yesterday she walked right by me at the market and didn't even say 'Hi.'" Paula replies, "Maybe she's not angry at all—maybe she just didn't see you."
Listening (pp. 204–229) An active five-step process of attending, understanding, evaluating, remembering, and responding.	To receive oral communication.	See **Attending, Understanding, Evaluating, Remembering.**	[Not applicable]

SKILL	USE	PROCEDURE	EXAMPLE
Negotiating (pp. 312–313) Managing conflict through trade-offs.	To help both parties have a positive outcome.	1. Determine whether activities in conflict cannot both be accomplished. 2. Determine whether negotiable elements are of fairly equal importance. 3. Suggest a compromise position, or suggest that if one person's idea is followed now, the other person's will be followed next.	"You've got to get to the store, and I've got to get this paper done. I'll drive you to the store tonight and help you with the shopping if you'll help me by typing my paper tomorrow morning."
Openness (pp. 160–161, 162) Feeling comfortable sharing true thoughts and feelings without resorting to manipulation and hidden agendas.	Helps create or maintain a positive communication climate.	1. Consider what you are about to say. 2. Determine whether the phrasing will cloud the issue or give misinformation about the goal of the conversation. 3. If it does, formulate a message that is clearer and more honest.	Instead of saying "Tom, I'm thinking of moving you to marketing for a while to give you broader experience" (a statement that is not open), say "Tom you're not doing as well in the finance department as I had hoped, so I'm going to move you to marketing where you will be able to use your talents more directly."
Owning Feelings (pp. 197–199) Making an "I" statement to identify yourself as the source of an idea or feeling.	To help the listener understand that the thought or feeling is yours.	When an idea, opinion, or feeling is yours, say so.	Instead of saying, "Maury's is the best restaurant in town," say, "I believe Maury's is the best restaurant in town."
Paraphrasing (pp. 240–243, 248) Putting into words your understanding of the meaning you get from another's statement.	To increase listening efficiency; to avoid message confusion; to discover the speaker's motivation.	1. Listen carefully. 2. Determine what the message means to you. 3. Restate the message using your own words to show the meaning you received from the message.	Grace says, "At two minutes to five, the boss gave me three letters that had to be in the mail that evening!" Bonita replies, "If I understand you correctly, you were really resentful that the boss would dump important work on you right before closing time."

SKILL	USE	PROCEDURE	EXAMPLE
Perception Checking (pp. 63–65) A verbal statement that reflects your understanding of the meaning of another person's nonverbal cues.	To clarify the meaning of non-verbal behavior.	1. Watch the behavior of another. Describe the behavior to yourself or aloud. 2. Ask yourself: What does that behavior mean to me? 3. Put your interpretation of the nonverbal behavior into words to verify your perception.	As Dale frowns while reading Paul's first draft of a memo, Paul says, "From the way you're frowning, I take it that you're not too pleased with the way I phrased the memo."
Praising (pp. 249–251) Giving people a verbal reward for what they have said or done.	To help people see themselves positively.	1. Make sure the context allows for praise. 2. Describe the behavior. 3. Focus on one behavior. 4. Be specific. 5. Identify the positive feeling you experience.	"Marge, that was an excellent writing job on the Miller story. Your descriptions were particularly vivid."
Precision (pp. 80, 82) Choosing words that are recognized by others in our culture as symbolizing those thoughts and feelings.	To increase the probability of the receiver's decoding the message accurately.	1. Assess whether the word or phrase used is less precise than it should be. 2. Pause to mentally brainstorm alternatives. 3. Select a more precise word.	"Bill, would you go get my watch off the [thinks hutch, mentally corrects] buffet?"
Provisional Statements (pp. 161–163) Wordings that suggest that an idea is an opinion or may not be entirely true.	Allows you to express your opinion but recognizes that others may have different ideas; helps create or maintain a positive communication climate.	1. Consider what you are about to say. 2. Determine whether it contains a wording that shows an attitude of finality or certainty. 3. If it does, add a qualifying statement that recognizes (a) that the statement is your opinion or (b) that the statement may not be entirely true or is true only under these circumstances.	Instead of saying, "That was the wrong way to sell the consumer on the product," say, "I don't think that was the best way to sell the consumer the product" or "It seems to me that in this situation there were better ways of focusing on the strengths of the product."

SKILL	USE	PROCEDURE	EXAMPLE
Questioning (pp. 237–240) A sentence phrased to get additional information.	To help get a more complete picture before making other comments; to help a shy person open up; to clarify meaning.	1. Listen to the message. 2. Determine what kind of information you need to know. 3. Phrase the question(s) to achieve the goal. 4. Use appropriate nonverbal clues.	When Connie says, "Well, it would be better if she weren't so sedentary," Jeff replies, "I'm not sure I understand what you mean by 'sedentary'— would you explain?"
Remembering (pp. 214–220, 224) The retention of information in memory.	To store information for recall.	1. Repeat information. 2. Create mnemonics. 3. Take notes when material seems complicated.	When Chris is introduced to Aileen Stewart, who is a candidate for Council, Chris says to himself, "Aileen Stewart—candidate for Council; Aileen Stewart—candidate for Council; Aileen Stewart—candidate for Council."
Self-disclosure (pp. 183–187) Sharing biographical data, personal ideas, and feelings that are unknown to another person.	Necessary to the initiation and development of a relationship.	1. Begin with information you want others to disclose. 2. Determine risk. Remember that people's attitudes about disclosure vary. 3. Move gradually to deeper levels. 4. Restrict intimate disclosures to long-term relationships. 5. Continue disclosure only if it is reciprocated.	May tells her current boyfriend, "I've been engaged three times before."
Specific, Concrete Words (pp. 80, 82) Using words that indicate a single item within a category or a single representation of an abstract concept or value.	To help the listener picture thoughts analogous to the speaker.	1. Assess whether the word or phrase used is less specific than it should be. 2. Pause to mentally brainstorm alternative choices. 3. Select a more specific word.	Instead of saying, "Bring the stuff for the audit," say, "Bring the records and receipts from the last year for the audit."

SKILL	USE	PROCEDURE	EXAMPLE
Supporting (pp. 244–248) Saying something that soothes, reduces tension, or pacifies.	To help people feel better about themselves or what they have said or done.	1. Listen to what the person is saying. 2. Try to empathize with the person's feelings. 3. Phrase a reply that is in harmony with these feelings. 4. Supplement your verbal response with appropriate nonverbal responses. 5. Indicate your willingness to be of help if possible.	In response to Tony's statement, "I'm really frosted that I didn't get the promotion," Alex replies, "I can understand your disappointment; you've really worked hard for it."
Turn Taking (pp. 180–182) Engaging in appropriate conversational sequencing.	Determining when a speaker is at a place where a person could talk if he or she wanted to.	1. Avoid speaking too often. 2. Avoid turns that are too long. 3. Listen and watch for turn-taking and turn-exchanging cues. 4. Be careful of giving inadvertent turn-taking cues. 5. Listen for conversation-directing behavior. 6. Keep interruptions to situations that are appropriate. 7. Be sensitive to people's nonverbal reactions to your conversational method.	When John lowers his voice at the end of the statement "I really thought they were going to go ahead during those last few seconds," Melissa says, "I did, too."
Understanding (Active Listening) (pp. 210–214) The ability to decode a message by assigning a meaning to it.	To gain complete meaning from another person's communication.	1. Separate the governing idea (or purpose), key points, and details to help you understand a complex message. 2. Fully concentrate on words and nonverbal cues. 3. Ask yourself questions to help you anticipate material. 4. Silently paraphrase to help you understand.	As Hannah explains the baby's schedule, Tanya, the babysitter, concentrates on the message, silently paraphrases, and mentally sorts key points and details.

Appendix B Glossary of Communication Problems

PROBLEM	DEFINITION	COST	SUGGESTIONS
Aggression (pp. 278, 300)	Attempting to force another to accept your ideas through physical or psychological threats or actions.	Conflicts are created or escalated.	1. Resist the urge to threaten. 2. Describe your feelings.
Competitive Attitude (pp. 307–310)	Viewing conflict as a win-lose situation.	Creates or escalates conflict. Heightens competitive feelings in others.	1. Approach the situation cooperatively. 2. Demonstrate your desire to resolve the perceived conflict in a mutually beneficial way.
Defensiveness (p. 158)	A negative feeling and/or behavior that results when a person feels threatened.	Interferes with open communication.	1. Be descriptive rather than evaluative. 2. Be problem solving rather than control oriented. 3. Be spontaneous rather than strategic. 4. Be empathic rather than neutral. 5. Be equal rather than superior. 6. Be tentative rather than dogmatic.
Evaluative Response (p. 158)	Statements that judge a person's ideas, feelings, or behaviors.	Creates defensiveness.	Be descriptive rather than evaluative.

PROBLEM	DEFINITION	COST	SUGGESTIONS
External Noise (p. 15)	External factors clogging the channels of communication.	Overrides or interferes with message reception.	1. Listener can eliminate the noise or turn up powers of concentration. 2. Speaker can compensate for the noise.
Hidden Agenda (pp. 160–161)	A reason or motive for behavior that is undisclosed to others.	May destroy trust between individuals; causes defensiveness; is manipulative.	1. Speaker should disclose motives. 2. Listener should describe behavior and check perceptions.
Incongruous Response (p. 258)	Message whose verbal cues conflict with nonverbal cues.	Causes defensiveness.	1. Speaker should be honest and describe true feelings. 2. Listener should check perceptions.
Internal Noise (p. 15)	When thoughts and feelings of the listener interfere with meaning.	Overrides or interferes with message reception.	Turn up power of concentration.
Interrupting Response (pp. 181–182, 259)	Breaking in before the speaker has finished.	Creates climate of superiority.	Allow person to finish sentence or complete thought.
Irrelevant Response (pp. 257–258)	Response that bears no relation to what has been said.	Tends to disconfirm, to make people question their own value.	Listen to what people have to say; at least acknowledge that you heard.
Problem Response (pp. 257–260)	Response that does not meet the expectation of the other person or that disconfirms the other person.	Causes defensiveness.	Substitute paraphrasing, questioning, interpreting, or supporting.
Semantic Noise (p. 15)	Decoding with a different meaning from what the speaker intends.	Distortion of meaning.	1. As speaker, determine meanings, encode with care, analyze receivers to determine whether they are likely to understand language you have selected. 2. As listener, listen actively and paraphrase if possible.
Surrender (pp. 299–300)	Giving in to another for sole purpose of avoiding conflict.	Can become a martyr; can infuriate others.	1. Describe your feelings. 2. Credit your feelings.
Tangential Response (p. 258)	Statement that changes the subject without appropriate response.	Implies that speaker's statements are not important enough to deal with.	Consider what people were saying; then, before you change the subject, deal with the implications of their statements.
Vocal Interference (pp. 112–114)	Speaking with such fillers as "you know," "um," and "well, uh."	Tends to antagonize others; increases noise; hurts message reception.	1. Become aware of usage. 2. Practice to see how long you can go without an interference. 3. In conversation note usage.
Withdrawal (pp. 297–299)	Removing oneself physically or psychologically from setting.	Conflicts are not resolved, only put off.	Resist urge to withdraw; describe feelings.

Index

A

Abelson, R. P., 24, 35n
Abstraction levels, 81
Accuracy. *See* Precision
Acquaintances, 143
Active listening, 210–214
Adaptability, 146
Adaptors, 110
Affect displays, 109
Affection, 137, 143
Agendas, 160, 383–384
    hidden, 160–161, 422
Aggression, 278, 279, 280–281, 300, 421
Aggressor, role of, 362
Alberti, Robert E., 291
Alberts, Janet K., 311, 319n
Alienation, 184
Altman, Irwin, 151, 152, 171n, 201n
American Heritage Dictionary, The, 76, 99n
Analyzer, role of, 359–360
    leadership, 390
    problems for discussion, 366
Andersen, J. F., 170n
Andersen, Peter, 11, 35n
Appropriateness, 91–96, 413
Arbitration, 314–315
Ardner, Edwin, 89
Ardner, Shirley, 89
Argyle, Michael, 171n, 318n
Aries, E. J., 170n
Aristotle, 292n
Arvey, Richard D., 411n
Ash, Mary Kay, 325, 349n
Assertiveness, 276–282, 283, 414
Association, 95
Attending, 206–210, 213, 414

Attraction, 152–155
Attributions, 59–60
Authority, levels, 332–333
Avoidance, 165
Axtell, Roger E., 130n

B

Bach, K., 179, 210n
Baesler, E. James, 130n
Banis, William J., 411n
Barker, Larry, 229n
Barraclough, Robert, 265, 292n
Barriers to communication
    aggression, 278, 279, 280–281, 300, 421
    competitive attitude, 307–310, 421
    defensiveness, 158, 421
    hidden agendas, 160–161, 422
    noise, 15, 208, 422
    problem responses, 158, 257–260, 422
    surrender, 299–300, 422
    vocal interferences, 112–114, 282, 422
    withdrawal, 165, 297–299, 422
Bass, Bernard M., 392n
Baxter, Leslie, 165, 171n
Beaven, Janet H., 35n
Bell, Robert R., 170n, 318n
Berg, John H., 201n
Berger, Charles R., 53, 68n, 152, 171n, 310, 318n
Berscheid, Ellen, 149, 170n
Bettini, Lorraine, 170n
Bloch, J. D., 170n
Bochner, Arthur P., 184, 201n
Body motions, 105–111
    types, 105–107
    uses, 108–111

Bolles, Richard Nelson, 410

Boster, Franklin J., 292*n*

Boundary spanning, 343–346

Bower, Gordon H., 69*n*

Brada, James J., 68*n*, 53, 152, 171*n*

Brainstorming, 83–85, 367–368

Brannen, Christalyn, 348

Breckler, Steven J., 292*n*

Brown, Charles T., 267, 292*n*

Brown, Jonathon D., 68*n*

Brown, Scott, 317–318

Buckman, Robert, 260

Buller, David B., 129*n*

Burgoon, Judee K., 116, 129*n*, 130*n*, 310, 319*n*

Burley-Allen, Madelyn, 228

C

Cahn, Dudley, 297, 318*n*

Camden, C. T., 201*n*

Cameron, K. S., 349*n*

Campbell, Jennifer D., 68*n*

Campbell, Robert J., 261*n*

Campion, James E., 411*n*

Canary, Daniel J., 157, 171*n*

Cash, William B., 411*n*

Centi, Paul J., 68*n*

Channels, 14–15

Cegala, Donald J., 130*n*

Character, 270

Chebat, Jean Charles, 292*n*

Chilberg, Joseph C., 372*n*

Chronemics, 116–117

Clarity, 79–91

Client relationships, 342–347

Closed questions, 397

Clothing, 114–116

Cloven, Denise, 298, 318*n*

Coakley, Carolyn Gwynn, 205, 229*n*

Cody, Michael J., 265, 267, 269, 273, 274, 275, 292*n*

Coercing, 265, 300
  power, 285

Cogger, John W., 411*n*

Cohesiveness, 145, 354–355

Colors, 122

Communication. *See* Interpersonal communication

Communication barriers. *See* Barriers to communication

Communication improvement goal statement, 30–33

Communication model, 16–18

Communication skills
  active listening, 210–214, 420
  appropriateness, 91–96, 413
  asking for criticism, 252–253, 255, 413
  assertiveness, 276–282, 283, 414
  attending, 206–210, 213, 414
  crediting others, 179–180, 182, 414
  critical listening, 220–225, 415
  dating generalizations, 85–86, 87, 414
  describing feelings, 191–196, 198, 274, 414
  descriptive speaking, 158–159, 415
  empathizing, 233–236, 239, 245, 415
  equality, 159–160, 415
  evaluating, 220–225, 415
  eye contact, 105–106, 107, 124–125, 126, 281, 416
  giving constructive criticism, 253–256, 416
  indexing generalizations, 86–88, 416
  interpreting, 248–249, 251, 416
  listening, 204–229, 416
  negotiating, 312–313, 417
  openness, 160–161, 162, 417
  owning feelings, 197–199, 281, 417
  paraphrasing, 214, 240–243, 248, 417
  perception checking, 63–65, 418
  praise, 249–251, 418
  precision, 80, 82, 418
  provisional statements, 161–163, 418
  questioning, 177, 212–213, 237–240, 364–365, 419
  remembering, 214–220, 224, 419
  self-disclosure, 183–187, 419
  specific and concrete, 80–82, 419
  supporting, 244–248, 360, 420
  turn taking, 180–182, 420

understanding, 210–214, 420
Competence, 27–28
Competitive attitude, 307–310, 421
Complementary relationships, 25
Compliance gaining, 265–267
Concrete words, 80–82, 419
Conflict, 296–317
   defined, 297
   guidelines for managing, 302–315
   patterns for managing, 297–301
   types, 303–307
Confrontation, 166
Connotation, 77–79
Consensus, 356–357
Constructive criticism, 251–256
Content conflict, 304–305
Context, 8–11
Control, 138
Conversation, 154–156
   characteristics, 175–177
   coherence, 178–179
   crediting others, 179–180, 414
   turn taking, 180–182, 420
Coombs, C. H., 303, 318*n*
Cooperation, 307–310
Cooperative principle of conversation,
   178–179
Cost-reward theory, 139–142
Cover letter, 404
Covey, Stephen R., 391–392
Co-workers, 339–342
Cragan, John F., 372*n*
Creativity, 76
Credibility, 269–273
Crediting
   others, 179–180, 182, 414
   self, 197–199, 281, 417
Critical listening, 220–225, 415
Criticism
   asking for, 252–253, 255, 413
   giving, 253–256, 416
Cultural considerations, 10–11, 29
   assertiveness, 282
   conflict, 300
   culture *defined*, 10

describing feelings, 193
determining meaning, 89
eye contact, 124, 125
facial expression, 125
gesture, 125
language use, 88–89
nonverbal meaning, 105
in organizations, 327–328
perception, 60
prejudice, 56–57
racism, 57–58
self-concept, 52
self-disclosure, 185
space, 126
stereotyping, 55–58
time, 125–126
touching, 125
Cupach, William R., 35*n*, 165, 171*n*
Customer relationships, 342–347
Custrini, Robert J., 123, 130*n*

 D

Dane, Francis C., 68*n*
Dating generalizations, 85–86, 87, 414
Davidson, L. R., 170*n*
Davitz, J. R., 130*n*
Deal, T., 349*n*
Deaux, Kay, 68*n*
Decision making, 20–21
Decoding, 13–14, 124
Defensiveness, 158, 421
Demo, D. H., 68*n*
Denotation, 77
Derlaga, Valerian J., 201*n*
Describing, 158–159
   behavior, 253
   feelings, 191–196, 198, 274, 414
Descriptive speaking, 158–159, 415
Dewey, John, 364, 372*n*
Discussion, 301. *See also* Group
   communication
Displaying feelings, 189–190
Dissatisfaction, 163–164
Dogmatism, 161–162, 309
Drifting apart, 164–165

Duberman, L., 170*n*

Duck, Steve, 151, 169*n*, 171*n*

Duncan, S. Jr., 180, 201*n*

E

Ego conflict, 306–307

Ekman, Paul, 105, 106, 129*n*

Emblems, 108–109

Emmons, Michael L., 291

Emotions, 58–60, 273–275. *See also* Feelings

Empathy, 233–236, 239, 245, 415

Encoding, 13–14, 23–24, 124

Ending relationships, 165–166

Environment, 118–122, 354, 383

Equal Employment Opportunity Commission, 402

Equality, 159–160, 415

Estes, W. K., 229*n*

Ethics, 267, 270, 271–273

Evaluating, 158, 421

  critical listening, 220–225, 415

  group communication, 370

Evans, D. A., 200*n*

Evidence, 266, 270

Exaggerating, 272

Exchanges, 265, 269, 335

  theory, 139–142

Expediter, 359

Expertise, 270

Expert power, 287

Expressing feelings, 189–190

External noise, 15, 422

Eye contact, 105–106, 124–125, 126, 281, 416

F

Face maintenance, 265, 274–275

Facial expression, 106, 125, 126

Facilitator, 313–314

Fact, questions of, 365

Fact-inference, separating, 221–222

Falkenberg, Marty, 349*n*

Family relationships, 46–47, 145–146, 305–306

Fazio, Russell H., 68*n*

Feedback, 15–16

  asking for, 252–253, 255, 413

  giving, 253–256, 416

  organizational, 328

Feelings, 240–241

  describing, 191–196, 198, 414

  displaying, 188–189

  owning, 197–199, 417

  sharing, 156

  withholding, 189

Feldman, Robert S., 123, 130*n*

Female relationships, 148

Feldman, D. C., 349*n*

Fiedler, Fred, 380, 392*n*

Filiatrault, Pierre, 292*n*

Fischer, J. L., 148, 170*n*

Fisher, Roger, 317–318

Fiske, D. W., 180, 201*n*

Fitzpatrick, Mary Anne, 170*n*, 171*n*

Follow-up questions, 398

Forgas, Joseph P., 58, 69*n*

French, John R. P., Jr., 285, 293*n*

Friends, 143–145

Friesen, W. V., 106, 129*n*

Functions of communication, 19–21

Furnham, A., 171*n*

G

Gains, C., 229*n*

Games, 161, 303

Gatekeeper, 361–362, 385–386

Gazda, George, 261*n*

Gaze, 105

Gender considerations

  assertiveness, 289

  eye contact, 126

  facial expression, 126

  female relationships, 148

  first impressions, 55

  gesture, 126

  group communication, 362

  job interviews, 402

  language use, 73, 89–90

  male-female relationships, 148–151

  male relationships, 146–148

in organizations, 338

self-disclosure, 185–186

sexism, 57–58, 92

social perception, 60

touch, 126

Generalization, 86

dating generalizations, 85–86, 87, 414

indexing generalizations, 86–88, 416

Generic language, 93–94

Gestures, 106, 125, 126

Gibb, Jack R., 171*n*

Gilmour, Robin, 169*n*

Gladnes, K., 229*n*

Goals, organizational, 326

Gorham, Joan, 229*n*

Gossip, 155

Gottlieb, Annie, 371–372

Graen, George, 334, 349*n*

Gray, John, 67–68

Grice, H. Paul, 178, 201*n*

Group communication, 352–372

characteristics, 353–357

defined, 353

evaluating, 370

leadership, 376–391

problem solving, 364–369

roles of members, 357–363

Grove, Theodore G., 58, 69*n*

Gudykunst, William B., 99*n*, 125, 130*n*, 171*n*, 185, 201*n*

H

Hall, Edward T., 99*n*, 116, 120, 130*n*

Hall, Judith A., 129*n*, 130*n*

Halo effect, 55

Haptics (touch), 116

Hare, Paul, 372*n*

Harmonizer, 361

Harnish, R. M., 179, 201*n*

Hatfield, John D., 169

Hattie, John, 68*n*

Healey, Jonathan G., 318*n*

Hearing, 206–210

Helping, 244

Herr, Paul M., 68*n*

Hidden agenda, 160–161, 422

Hill, Charles T., 201*n*

Hinken, T. R., 285, 293*n*

Hobbs, J. R., 200*n*

Hodgson, J. W., 148, 170*n*

Holley, F., 229*n*

Hollman, T. D., 55, 69*n*

Humor, 311

Huseman, Richard C., 169

I

Iacocca, Lee, 325, 349*n*

Idea-exchange communication, 155, 175–182

Illustrators, 109

Implicit personality theories, 55

Inclusion, 137–138

Incongruence, 48

Incongruous response, 258, 422

Indexing generalizations, 86–88, 416

Inferences, 221–224

Influence, 21, 264–291. *See also* Persuasion

defined, 264

Information

exchange, 21

giver, 358

seeker, 358–359

In-group, 336

Inman, Christopher C., 146, 170*n*

Insensitivity, 96

Intention, as a component of credibility, 270

Internal noise, 15, 422

Interpersonal communication. *See also* Communication skills

appropriateness, 27

competence, 27–28

defined, 7

effectiveness, 27

functions, 19–21

goal statements, 32–33

learning model, 29–31

model, 16–18

principles, 21–26

Interpersonal communication (*continued*)
  process, 8–16
  relationships, 136–169
  skill development, 28–29
  theories, 137–142
  as transaction, 7
Interpersonal needs, 137–139
Interpreting, 248–249, 251, 416
Interrupting, 181–182, 259, 422
Intimate relationships, 145–151
Irrelevant response, 257–258, 422
"I" statements, 197–199, 282

J

Jablin, Frederick, M., 349*n*, 411*n*
Jackson, Don D., 35*n*
Jargon, 346
Jensen, Arthur D., 372*n*
Jick, T. D., 349*n*
Job interview, 396–410
  defined, 397
  questions in, 397–398
  responsibilities of applicant, 404–408
  responsibilities of interviewer, 399–
    404
Johnson, F. L., 170*n*
Joker, role of, 362
Jones, Edward E., 69*n*
Jordan, Judith V., 68*n*

K

Kagan, Norman, 261*n*
Kahane, Howard, 292*n*
Keller, Paul W., 267, 292*n*
Kellerman, Kathy, 22, 35*n*, 171*n*
Kelley, Harold H., 139, 169*n*
Kelly, Lynne, 68*n*
Kennedy, A., 349*n*
Kennedy, C. W., 201*n*
Kerr, Norbert L., 372*n*
Kim, Young Yun, 99*n*, 126, 130*n*, 171*n*,
    185, 201*n*
Kinesics, 105
Kitayama, Shinobu, 68*n*
Knapp, Mark L., 129*n*, 130*n*, 151, 152,
    171*n*

Knowledge, 270
Koester, Jolene, 34*n*, 69*n*
Kotlowitz, Alex, 12, 35*n*
Krannich, Ronald L., 411*n*
Krathwohl, David R., 261*n*

L

Language, 71–99
  appropriateness, 91–96
  clarity, 79–91
  connotation, 77–79
  and culture, 88–89
  defined, 73
  denotation, 77
  emotional, 273–275
  and gender, 89–90
  and meaning, 75–76
  and perception, 76
  sexism in, 93–95
  uses, 73–74
Lazes, Peter, 349*n*
Leadership, 376–391
  defined, 377
  evaluating, 390
  preparing for, 381–383
  responsibilities, 383–389
  styles, 379–381
  traits, 378
Leading questions, 398
Learning model, 29–31
Leathers, Dale, 130*n*, 261*n*
Lee, J. A., 149, 170*n*
Legitimate power, 286
Levine, D., 99*n*
Lewis, R. A., 170*n*
Liaison, 331
Lighting, in environment, 122
Linking pin effect, 336–338
Lippitt, Ronald, 380, 392*n*
Listening, 204–229, 416
  attending (hearing), 206–210, 213,
    414
  critical, 220–225, 415
  defined, 205
  remembering, 214–220, 419

responding, 232–259
understanding, 210–214, 420
Littlejohn, Steven W., 99n, 178, 201n
Loewen, Karen R., 69n
Loudness, 111
Love, 149–150
Lustig, Myron W., 34n, 69n
Lying, 272

M

Maintenance roles, 360–362, 380
Male-female communication. *See*
    Gender considerations
Male-female relationships, 148–151
Male relationships, 146–148
Manipulation, 165
Marche, Tamma A., 259, 261n
Markers, 121
Marking, 94–95
Markus, Hazel R., 68n
Marriage, 150–151
Maxims of conversation, 178–179
McCroskey, James C., 129n
McGill, Michael E., 147, 170n
McLaughlin, Margaret L., 200n, 292n
Meaning, 13, 75–76
Mentoring, 335
Messages, 13–14
Metts, Sandra, 165, 171n
Michael, William B., 35n
Miller, Gerald R., 183, 292n
Misrepresenting, 272
Mission, organizational, 326
Misunderstanding, 237
Mnemonics, 216
Molloy, John T., 130n
Monochronic view of time, 125
Monopolizer, role of, 363
Moylan, Stephanie J., 69n
Mulling, 298

N

Narus, L. R., 170n
Nation, I. S. P., 99n
National Institutes of Health, 229n
Needs theory, 137–139

Negative roles, 362–363
Negotiation, 312–313, 417
Neutral questions, 397–398
Newman, Edwin, 98
Newton, Deborah, 310, 319n
Nofsinger, Robert E., 180, 200, 201n
Noise, 15, 208
Noller, Patricia, 127, 130n, 170n, 171n
Nonverbal communication, 22–23,
    101–129
  assertiveness, 281
  body motions, 105–111
  chronemics (time), 116–117
  clothing, 114–116
  color, 122
  conflict management, 301–311
  contrasts with verbal, 103–105
  and culture, 124–126
  defined, 103
  empathy, 234, 235–236
  and gender, 126–127
  lighting, 122
  listening, 211
  and meaning, 13
  nature of, 103–105
  paralanguage, 111–114
  perception checking, 63–65
  and questioning, 238
  self-presentation, 114–117
  space, 118–122
  temperature, 122
  touch (haptics), 116
  in turn taking, 180
Nonparallel language, 94–95
Norms, 356
Note taking, 216–218
Nurius, P., 68n
Nussbaum, Jon F., 170n

O

Ogden, C. K., 78, 99n
O'Hair, Dan, 265, 267, 269, 273, 274,
    292n
Olson, D. H., 170n
Openness, 160–161, 162, 309, 417

Open questions, 397
Organization, 41, 211
Organizational culture, 327–328
Oster, H., 105, 129*n*
Out-group, 336
Owning feelings, 197–199, 281, 417

P

Paralanguage, 111–114
Paraphrasing, 214, 240–243, 248, 417
Passive behavior, 278, 279, 280
Patterson, Brian R., 170*n*
Pearson, Judy Cornelia, 89, 99*n*, 127,
    130*n*, 185, 201*n*
People, in transactions, 11–13
Perception, 38–68
    and communication, 42
    defined, 39
    improving, 51–52, 62–65
    interpretation, 42
    organization, 41
    of others, 50–51, 53–65
    selection, 39–41
    and self-concept, 43–53
Perception checking, 63–65, 418
Perrien, Jean, 292*n*
Personality, 271
Persuasion, 267–275
    in conflict resolution, 300–301
    defined, 267
Peterson, Carole, 259, 261*n*
Philippot, Pierre, 123, 130*n*
Pitch (vocal), 111
Pleck, J. H., 146, 170*n*
Pogrebin, Letty Cottin, 170*n*
Poise, 107
Policy, questions of, 366
Polychronic view of time, 125–126
Porter, Richard E., 130*n*
Posture, 106
Power, 57, 284–298
Praise, 249–251, 253–254, 418
Precision, 80, 82, 418
Prejudice, 56–57
Primary questions, 398

Prisbell, M., 170*n*
Problem responses, 257–260
    defined, 257
    evaluative, 158, 421
    incongruous, 258, 422
    interrupting, 181–182, 259, 422
    irrelevant, 257–258, 422
    tangential, 258, 422
Problem-solving method, 301, 364–369
Provisional statements, 161–163, 418
Proxemics, 120
Pseudoconflict, 303–304
Punctuality, 117
Purpose, 22

Q

Quality of voice, 111
Questioning, 177, 213, 237–240, 364,
    419
    in interviewing, 397–398
    as a leader's responsibility, 386–388
Questions for group discussion, 364–366

R

Racism, 57–58, 92
Rapport-talk, 185–186
Rate of speech, 111
Raven, Bertram, 285, 293*n*
Reardon, Kathleen K., 35*n*
Reasoning, 267–269
Redding, W. C., 349*n*
Referent power, 267, 273, 288–289
Regulators, 110
Rehearsal, 215–216
Relationships, 136–169
    attraction, 152–154
    building, 152–156
    defined, 136
    disintegration, 163–166
    family, 145–146
    intimate, 145–151
    life cycles, 151–166
    stabilizing, 156–163
    theoretical explanations, 137–142
    types, 142–157

work, 333–347
Remembering, 214–220, 224, 419
Repetition, 215–216
Report-talk, 185–186
Requests, 265, 273
Responses, types of
   constructive criticism, 251–256, 416
   empathizing, 233–236, 239, 415
   interpretive, 248–249, 251, 416
   paraphrases, 240–243, 248, 417
   praise, 249–251, 253–254, 418
   problem, 257–259, 422
   questions, 177, 213, 237–240, 364,
      397–398, 419
   supportive, 244–248, 360, 420
Resumes, 405–406, 407
Reward power, 285–286
Reynolds, Rodney, 171n
Richards, I. A., 78, 99n
Richmond, Virginia P., 129n
Risk, 143, 186
Robick, Mildred C., 35n
Robinson, Adam, 83, 99n
Roles
   defined, 43
   maintenance, 360–362
   negative, 362–363
   in organizations, 329–330
   and self-concept, 43–44
   task, 357–360
Roloff, Michael E., 292n, 298, 318n
Rules, 11, 331
Rumors, 312
Rusbult, C. E., 302, 318n
Russell, C., 170n

S

Samovar, Larry, 130n
Satran, Pamela, 130n
Schriesheim, C. A., 285, 293n
Schutz, William C., 137, 169n, 372n
Scripts, 24
Seibold, David R., 292n
Self-concept, 43–53
   accuracy, 47–48

defined, 43
   formation of, 45–47
   roles, 43–44
Self-disclosure, 183–187, 419
   defined, 183
   guidelines for, 186–187
   in intimate relationships, 156
Self-esteem, 49–52
   improving, 51–52
   role in communication, 49–51
Self-fulfilling prophecies, 48
Self-image, 44–49
   accuracy of, 47–48
   formation of, 45–47
   role in communication, 48–49
Self-reflexive, 75
Semantic noise, 15, 208, 422
Sensitivity. *See* Empathy
Serial communication, 312
Setting, 8–11
Sex, 149
Sexism, 57–58, 92
Sexual harassment, 121
Shaw, Marvin E., 169n, 372n, 378, 392n
Sher, Barbara, 371–372
Sherman, Steven J., 68n
Silence, 208
Sillars, Alan L., 130n, 315, 318n, 319n
Skills. *See* Communication skills
Small talk, 155
Smart, S. April, 68n
Social penetration theory, 183–184
Social perception, 50–51, 53–60
Social power, 284–289
Space, management of, 118–122, 126
Specific words, 80–82, 419
Spitzberg, Brian, 35n
Sprenkle, D., 170n
Stabilization, 156
Stafford, Laura, 157, 171n
Steil, Lyman K., 229n
Stereotyping, 55–58
Sternberg, R. J., 149, 170n
Stewart, Charles J., 411n
Stewart, Robert, 265, 292n

Stull, Donald E., 201*n*

Styles of leadership, 379–381

Summarizing, 388–389

Superiority, 159–160

Supervisor-subordinate relations, 333–338

Supporting, 244–248, 249, 360, 420

Surrender, 299–300, 422

Symbols, 13

Symmetrical relationships, 25–26

Sympathy, 235

Tangential responses, 258, 422

Tannen, Deborah, 185, 201*n*, 362, 372*n*

Task commitment, 355–356

Task roles, 357–360, 380

Taylor, Dalman A., 151, 152, 171*n*, 201*n*

Temperature, and environment, 122

Temple, Linda E., 69*n*

Tengler, Craig D., 411*n*

Territoriality, 121

Thibaut, John W., 139, 169*n*

Time, 116–117, 125–126

Todd-Mancillas, William, 89, 99*n*, 127, 130*n*, 185, 201*n*

Tone of voice, 281

Touch, 116, 125, 126

Traits, 55, 378

Transaction, 7

Trenholm, Sarah, 169*n*, 170*n*, 292*n*

Trust, 143

Trustworthiness, 270

Truth, 272

Turn taking, 180–182, 420

Turner, Lynn H., 89, 99*n*, 127, 130*n*, 185, 201*n*

Uncertainty reduction, 53, 152

Understanding, 210–214, 420

Values, 305

conflict over, 305–306

questions of, 365–366

Verbal communication. *See* Language

Verderber, Rudolph F., 292*n*

Vertical dyadic linkages model, 335–338

Visions, organizational, 326

Vocabulary, 82–83, 192

Vocal characteristics, 111–112, 281

Vocal interference, 112–114, 282, 422

Vocal quality, 111

Vocalics, 111

Volume, 111

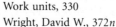

Walster, Elaine., 149, 170*n*

Walther, Joseph B., 130*n*

Warmth, 143

Watson, Kittie W., 229*n*

Watzlawick, Paul, 35*n*

Webbink, Patricia, 128

Weisberg, Judith, 315, 318*n*, 319*n*

Weiten, Wayne, 68*n*

Werkman, Doris L., 58, 69*n*

Wheeless, Lawrence R., 265, 292*n*

Whetten, D. A., 349*n*

White, Ralph, 380, 392*n*

Wilen, Tracey, 348

Wilson, John A. R., 35*n*

Withdrawal, 165, 297–299, 422

Withdrawer, role of, 362–363

Withholding feelings, 189

Wolvin, Andrew, 205, 229*n*

Wood, Julia T., 73, 89, 99*n*, 130*n*, 146, 170*n*

Woodall, W. Gill, 129*n*

Work relationships, 324–348

co-worker, 339–342

customer-client, 342–347

organizational characteristics, 325–333

supervisor-subordinate, 333–338

Work units, 330

Wright, David W., 372*n*

Wrightsman, Lawrence S., 68*n*

Zebrowitz, Leslie A., 55, 69*n*

Photo Credits

p. 9, Ben Barnhart/Offshoot; p. 2 left and p. 16, Polly Brown/Actuality Inc.; p. 20, Peter Menzel/Stock Boston; p. 4 and p. 23, Laura Lewis/Offshoot; p. 27, Owen Franken/Stock Boston; p. 44, Charles Harbutt/Actuality Inc.; p. 2 right and p. 45, Fredrik D. Bodin/Offshoot; p. 54, Michael McGovern/The Picture Cube; p. 36 and p. 59, Eric Breitenback/The Picture Cube; p. 74, Ruth Dixon/Stock Boston; p. 78, Susie Fitzhugh/Stock Boston; p. 90, Michael Newman/PhotoEdit; p. 70 and p. 93, Lisa Quinones/Black Star; p. 104, James Carroll/Stock Boston; p. 2 middle and p. 108, Jean-Claude LeJeune/Stock Boston; p. 115, Herb Snitzer/The Picture Cube; p. 100 and p. 119, Will & Deni McIntyre/AllStock; p. 138, Janice Fullman/The Picture Cube; p. 140, Ron Chapple/FPG International; p. 144, Polly Brown/Actuality Inc.; p. 147, Danny Lyon/Magnum Photos; p. 153, Christopher K. Walter/The Picture Cube; p. 132 left, p. 134, and p. 157, Charles Harbutt/Actuality Inc.; p. 172 and p. 176, Barbara Alper/Stock Boston; p. 181, Bart Batholomew/Black Star; p. 184, Gloria Karlson/The Picture Cube; p. 132 middle and p. 190, Bob Daemmrich/Stock Boston; p. 191, Emilio Mercado/The Picture Cube; p. 202 and p. 207, Charles Harbutt/Actuality, Inc.; p. 132 right and p. 212, Fredrik D. Bodin/Offshoot; p. 215, Beringer-Dratch/The Image Works; p. 221, Chester Higgins Jr./Photo Researchers, Inc.; p. 233, Addison Geary/Stock Boston; p. 247, Rhoda Sidney/PhotoEdit; p. 250, John Coletti/Stock Boston; p. 230 and p. 254, Nita Winter Photography; p. 266, Jill Fineberg/Photo Researchers, Inc.; p. 262 and p. 277, Tim Barnwell/Stock Boston; p. 287, Sue Klemens/Stock Boston; p. 298, Richard Hutchings/Photo Researchers, Inc.; p. 310, Chester Higgins/Photo Researchers, Inc.; p. 294 and p. 314, D. Witbeck/The Picture Cube; p. 320 left and p. 334, Gans/The Image Works; p. 322 and p. 340, Courtesy of Lotus Development Corporation; p. 343, Michael Weisbrot/Stock Boston; p. 355, Charles Gupton/Tony Stone Images; p. 320 right and p. 360, Ron Chapple/FPG International; p. 350 and p. 368, David Aronson/Stock Boston; p. 374 and p. 379, Ron Thomas/Bettmann; p. 387, Andy Sacks/Tony Stone Images; p. 320 middle and p. 401, Jim Pickerell/The Image Works; p. 394 and p. 408, Bob Daemmrich/Stock Boston.